P9-CRN-648

# Human Adaptive Strategies

# Human Adaptive Strategies

## Ecology, Culture, and Politics

### *Third Edition*

**DANIEL G. BATES**

HUNTER COLLEGE,
THE CITY UNIVERSITY OF NEW YORK

and

ISTANBUL BILGI UNIVERSITY

Boston ■ New York ■ San Francisco
Mexico City ■ Montreal ■ Toronto ■ London ■ Madrid ■ Munich ■ Paris
Hong Kong ■ Singapore ■ Tokyo ■ Cape Town ■ Sydney

Series Editor: Jennifer Jacobson
Series Editorial Assistant: Emma Christensen
Marketing Manager: Kris Ellis-Levy
Composition and Prepress Buyer: Linda Cox
Manufacturing Buyer: JoAnne Sweeney
Cover Coordinator: Kristina Mose-Libon
Editorial-Production Coodinator: Mary Beth Finch
Editorial-Production Service: The Book Company
Electronic Composition: Omegatype Typography, Inc.

For related titles and support materials, visit our online catalog at www.ablongman.com.

Copyright © 2005, 2001, 1998 Pearson Education

All rights reserved. No part of the material protected by this copyright notice may be reproduced or utilized in any form or by any means, electronic or mechanical, including photocopying, recording, or by any information storage and retrieval system, without the written permission of the copyright owner.

To obtain permission(s) to use material from this work, please submit a written request to Allyn and Bacon, Permissions Department, 75 Arlington Street, Boston, MA 02116 or fax your request to 617-848-7320.

Between the time Website information is gathered and then published, it is not unusual for some sites to have closed. Also, the transcription of URLs can result in unintended typographical errors. The publisher would appreciate notification where these errors occur so that they may be corrected in subsequent editions.

**Library of Congress Cataloging-in-Publication Data**
Bates, Daniel G.
    Human adaptive strategies : ecology, culture, and politics / Daniel G. Bates.—3rd ed.
        p.   cm.
    Includes bibliographical references and index.
    ISBN 0-205-41815-5
        1. Human ecology.   2. Social change.   3. Ethnology.   4. Economic anthropology.   I. Title.

GF50.B37      2005
304.2—dc22                                                          2004044297

Printed in the United States of America.
10  9  8  7  6  5  4  3  2  1      09  08  07  06  05  04

For Murat R. Sertel
Great scholar, great friend, greatly missed

# Contents

# Preface

A NUMBER OF INSTRUCTORS USING the first edition of *Cultural Anthropology* (Allyn & Bacon, 1996) urged that the sections of the book that deal with human ecology, cultural change, and economic development, and with case studies of diverse societies as they respond to their environmental settings be adapted for classroom use as a freestanding work. *Human Adaptive Strategies: Ecology, Culture, and Politics* is the result of this idea, and due to its success, this is its third edition. It is designed to be used either alone or with other textbooks or case material in a variety of courses that consider human behavior and environmental relationships cross culturally. These courses include cultural anthropology, cultural or political ecology, environmental sociology, cultural geography, development sociology, and human ecology.

A central theme of this book, as in previous editions, is that individuals are active decision makers, continually involved in creating and using their cultural and material environments, however misguided their creations may sometimes be. Hence, the reference to ecology, culture, and politics in the title. Faced with new problems and new situations, people will often attempt to find solutions that go beyond traditional cultural solutions or customary behaviors and received prescriptions. In other words, behavioral innovation and variation constantly exist within as well as between societies. Those variations that prove to be advantageous are often passed on to new generations; they become part of the culture. Some ways of doing things that are useful in one context may prove otherwise in other situations; cultural innovation and transmission are not patterns of cumulative "progress" but processes of continual intergenerational experiment, "filtering," and change—affecting all peoples. In every generation, ideas, technologies, social usages, and even modes of speech

pass through what might be seen as a filter or screen; some, perhaps most, pass though, but not all. Generally, what is transmitted is what seems to work in that particular context. Processes of innovation, the adoption of new ideas and their transmission to others, lie at the heart of cultural variation and are part of broader ecological and evolutionary processes.

*Change* is the word that most accurately captures what is distinctive about humans. Our brief history on earth is one of unparalleled expansion as the early representatives of our species spilled out of Africa to inhabit virtually every region of the globe. This expansion required altering behavior in all domains to meet the demands of very different habitats—in short, the continual interplay between learned behavior and ever-changing environments. Decisions arrived at by individuals, the adaptive strategies of people and societies, and the evolutionary processes of which these form a part are central themes of this book. The approach, then, is essentially an ecological and evolutionary one. However, one cannot slight what might be called the ideational or symbolic aspects of social life—ways of behaving and believing that validate our behavior, form our social identities, and satisfy our aesthetic needs. Nor can one ignore the extent to which individual and group behavior is played out in environments in which the most striking features are other people and other groups. This is, of course, true across the evolutionary spectrum, but it is particularly notable for humans.

In this sense, any understanding of human ecology must consider the politics of group life—factors that determine who gets what, how much, and when. Human populations are often socially far more differentiated than are other social animals. We not only engage in division of labor beyond that associated with age and role in sexual reproduction, but we also create systems of perpetuated inequality, such as caste, class, and other types of difference of economic and political access across age and gender lines. Such inequality has major ramifications for the ways in which we interact with our environments. The fact that there are no physical limits on the accumulation of wealth in a market or capitalist economy, for example, has important consequences for the way that natural resources are exploited. And the fact that the nominal "owners" of resources and the means of exploiting them do not necessarily live and work near them has important consequences for other people who do. Thus, local people may be powerless to prevent their central government from granting rights to a foreign company to cut down the forest they live in. The impact of cultural diversity, exchange, and inequality on humans and on the ways that humans interact with environments has grown with time and with changes in human social organization since the earliest *Homo sapiens* developed tool technology in the Paleolithic period. This is reflected in the growing field of political ecology and is a major theme of this book.

Nor can one ignore the pitfalls inherent in the concept of adaptation, which all too easily can be employed to explain everything and hence nothing. The record of human evolution contains much that is due to chance, misadventure, and error. Further, the ecological and evolutionary perspective includes much more than simply the material aspects of life. Religious and political beliefs and practices, even kinship systems, are as much a part of human adaptation as are subsistence strategies and economic practices. Throughout this text, the many topics customarily treated as basic to an understanding of human society are integrated rather than treated as separate aspects of culture: Politics, economics, and religion are closely intertwined in the adaptive process. I hope that this book conveys some of the excitement and controversy that are part of the contemporary sciences of human ecology and behavior.

## This Edition

This edition consists of eight chapters updated with more than 100 new sources and references. Five of the chapters focus on ethnographic case studies and discussions relating to distinctive forms of human food procurement or subsistence: hunting and gathering, horticulture or low-energy farming, pastoralism, intensive agriculture, and industrial society. This organization reflects a very general evolutionary or historical approach, but it is not offered as a rigid typology or simple sequence of stages of development. In every instance, it is clear that every population today uses a variety of ways of securing their livelihood. The cases, as organized here, do provide a closer look at the anthropological perspective in action; a number of case studies illustrate how anthropologists view long-term cultural change, analyze cultural adaptation, and attempt to understand diverse aspects of social behavior. Most chapters make use of archaeological data to provide richer examples and expanded time frames. Populations whose ways of life and livelihood are as diverse as the San people of southern Africa and the farmers of central California are viewed similarly as people responding to and, usually, coping successfully with the problems facing them. What is emphasized are the costs and rewards of different ways of providing for necessities of life and the relationship of settlement system, mobility, and economic and political organization to other aspects of adaptation. A distinctive feature of all these chapters is that they describe not only different societies but also a wide range of methods and techniques of studying them. This organization is intended to draw the student into interesting ethnographic material and give an insight into methodological concerns. The bulk of the material comes from *Cultural Anthropology* but is rewritten here to focus more immediately on ecological issues. Also, frequent reference is made to current events and topical problems. New discussion on issues related to human ecology and evolution, as well as planned and unplanned change, is presented in Chapters 1, 2, and 8. In response to reader comments, the presentation of material in every chapter has been reorganized to enhance clarity and interest. In particular, important ideas presented in the previous edition as separate case studies and boxes have been incorporated directly into the text. There is a much expanded discussion of basic ecological concepts and ecosystem components and organization. More discussion of population-related issues is also provided in a number of chapters. Numerous new graphics, figures, and maps enhance this edition.

**Chapter 1** introduces general concepts in the study of human social behavior, the concept of culture, and establishes the organization of the book. This edition adds new material to the discussion of culture and gender and expands the discussion of science generally and anthropology specifically. **Chapter 2** outlines the ecological framework on which subsequent chapters build. It offers an extended discussion of evolution, adaptation, politics, decision making, and behavioral variation. The nature of basic systems of food procurement are introduced, although their developmental histories are postponed to subsequent chapters. The emerging field of political ecology is explored, and the importance of gender is again stressed.

Each of the five case study chapters, Chapters 3 to 7, presents at least two long ethnographic cases along with at least two more focused ones. Each has boxes presenting more detailed or technical material. Students are introduced to basic concepts and methods in the course of reading about particular peoples and places. Together, the text, ethnographic examples, and boxes illustrate topics such as kinship and marriage, economic processes, politics and leadership, social control, religion, and cultural change. The case study material is, I hope, lively, timely, and jargon free; the discussion accompanying it draws attention to important issues, including the importance of sources of energy in human society, responding to problems or hazards, innovation and entrepreneurship, and short- and long-term processes of change. The book shows anthropological scholarship in action as it addresses important and immediate human concerns, such as the costs and consequences of human energy requirements, environmental degradation, population pressure, social and economic equity in a changing world, and planned and unplanned social change.

More specifically, **Chapter 3** deals with foraging and differs from the earlier edition in having an expanded discussion of reciprocity and social organization in general. The Batak people, formerly discussed in a box, are now developed as a case study. Each ethnographic case also deals with efforts of indigenous people to keep or reclaim their lands. **Chapter 4** now looks specifically at horticulture or garden subsistence farming rather than at extensive farming generally. It discusses the early development of farming, using recent material. Along with the Yanamamö, the Pueblo are presented as a largely historical case in which the Eastern and Western groups are compared. This is a response to requests for more historical material as well as the need for more from North America. The controversy involving Napoleon Chagnon's work is addressed in some depth as it touches on a number of important aspects of scholarship and research. **Chapter 5,** Nomadic Pastoralism, has a much expanded section on tribal organization as commonly encountered in Africa, the Middle East, and Central Asia. There is also more material on pastoralism and development and the discussion of Mongolian pastoralism has been expanded. **Chapter 6,** or Intensive Agriculture: Feeding the Cities, examines the development of the forms of farming that feed the cities of the world. It then goes on in more detail than the previous edition to look at peasant household economics, small farmers and change, and the rise of increasing inequality. The Mexican village of Cucurpe was

formerly presented in boxed material on land ownership but is now a major focus; the Kofyar of Central Nigeria, based on earlier work by Robert Netting and more recent material by the Stones, illustrates African moves to intensification; and Directions of Change in Rural Egypt draws on the recent work of a number of scholars to explore how the long-suffering Egyptian peasant family is responding to International Monetary Fund–induced "structural readjustment," or the move to farming in a free-market economy. **Chapter 7,** Industrial Society and Beyond: Feeding the World, looks closely at how industrial society and farming in particular developed and the social and ecological consequences. The chapter drops the Japanese village that became a suburb, and has somewhat expanded material on North American agriculture as well as from Bulgaria. Bulgarian agriculture became massively industrialized under socialist rule, but since 1990 has seen this reversed dramatically as land once more was privatized and essentially deindustrialized. In this chapter as in the preceding four case study chapters, graphic figures are provided as illustrations, as well as better maps. Globalization, introduced in Chapter 7, is moved to begin Chapter 8 making for a more concise treatment.

Finally, **Chapter 8** deals with planned and unplanned cultural change, development, and the environmental implications of human activities; it concludes with suggestions for risk assessment as we plan for the future. It begins with a historical case, the Vikings of Iceland, and goes on to treat long-term processes of change. It has new material on the postindustrial world, "globalism," the challenges this poses for people struggling to make a living, as well as for those, who as development experts, attempt to assist them. It concludes with a review of the ethical concerns that must accompany and guide development work or applied social science.

In addition to a list of key terms, suggested readings, and illustrations for each chapter, this book contains a number of unique features, including:

Each case study is presented in a contemporary setting, showing people coping with issues and problems to which the reader can easily relate.

Each case is tied to larger issues of cultural transformation and change.

Cases exemplify a variety of research methods and theoretical approaches.

Each chapter begins with a parallel discussion of energy requirements, environmental hazards, and special problems, the development and significance of the adaptive strategy in human history, and the social organizational concomitants.

Each chapter has boxed inserts that either present recent technical reports in summary form or go more deeply into specialized topics than does the text.

# Acknowledgments

I undertook the first edition of this book using material largely derived from *Cultural Anthropology*, published by Allyn & Bacon, itself the revision of a previous work published by McGraw-Hill. Elliot Fratkin and I coauthor the present edition of *Cultural Anthropology* (Third Edition, Allyn & Bacon, 2003). The responsibility for the present content rests with me. Judith Tucker worked on the project from the earliest stages to completion and made numerous recommendations as to reorganization, style, and presentation. She also made a substantial contribution to the boxes. Ludovir Lozny, who works with me in editing the journal *Human Ecology,* was of great help in working on this edition as many of the new studies used came from *Human Ecology* sources as well as from areas in his own specialization, Old World archaeology. Foremost, of course, I owe a great debt of gratitude to the scholars who carried out the often difficult and time-consuming research on which this book reports. Other academic critics and consultants, in addition to several anonymous reviewers in the United States, include: Marla Buckmaster, David Cleveland, Frank Conant, Gerald Creed, Barbara Dilly, Alan Duben, James Eder, Nancy Flowers, Elliot Fratkin, Bernadette Gallegos, David Gilmore, William Irons, Greg Johnson, Patricia Johnson, Susan Lees, Mike Little, Tom McGovern, Martha Nathan, Sophia Perdikaris, Amal Rassam, Harald Skogseid, Glenn Stone, and Dee Mack Williams. I greatly appreciate their generous help and advice. Reviewers who aided specifically in preparing this edition of *Human Adaptive Strategies* include Joseph L. Chartkoff, Michigan State University; Kathleen M. Heath, Indiana State University; and Cynthia Werner, Texas A&M University. I was, as with other projects, immeasurably assisted in numerous ways by many other people. Peter Bogucki, Tom Dillehay, Romauld Schild, and Karen St. John very generously supplied photos as well as sharing their knowledge. Jennifer Jacobson of Allyn and Bacon, Dusty Friedman of The Book Company, and Frank Hubert did a fine job of producing and editing the final manuscript, while Lech Lozny provided new sketches and George Barile rendered them for this book.

*Daniel G. Bates*
*Hunter College, CUNY*
*and Istanbul Bilgi University*

# Chapter 1

# The Study of Human Behavior

By at least some biological criteria, humans are an extremely successful species. *Homo sapiens,* to give the formal description, are the most widespread and numerous of the large animals, are distributed throughout the world, and live under the most diverse and extreme conditions. Despite the enormous variety of local problems and hazards that humans must deal with to survive, all of the world's peoples are very similar in biological makeup and physique. In comparison with many other animals, we are remarkably homogeneous and even rather a dull lot, lacking plumage and other specialized survival equipment. What accounts for the success of our species, and what can we surmise about our future? Why do humans vary considerably in social life and customs while differing only to a small degree biologically? Such concerns underlie much research in anthropology, human ecology, cultural geography, and other fields.

These fields emphasize the connections between human society and the larger web of life. Only by appreciating the fact that we are subject to the same forces that affect all other living organisms can we come to understand those many aspects of human behavior that distinguish us from other

species. And if we more fully appreciate the extraordinary unity and diversity evident in the ways of life of the world's peoples, we may come to a better understanding of our own society.

A perspective on humankind encompassing nonhuman life forms is relatively recent in European thought. For millennia, Europeans were accustomed to thinking of the world, its peoples, and all other living things as eternally fixed and unchanging. Although similarities among species were widely noted, these similarities were not thought to represent the outcome of a shared and ongoing process of change—the process we call evolution. Instead, each species was seen as a unique entity with its own unique characteristics. No such group was related to another or to anything else. It seemed obvious that the world existed for humans—in particular, for those favored participants in European civilization.

However, by the mid-nineteenth century, the idea of evolutionary change had become respectable in European scholarly circles and soon became familiar to the public, in large part as a result of the tremendous impact of Charles Darwin's famous book, *On the Origin of Species by Means of Natural Selection,* published in 1859. The thesis of

*Charles Darwin's work revolutionized not only biology but also the study of human evolution.*
(©Bettmann/CORBIS)

this book is that species are related to one another by descent, with modifications, from common ancestors. Darwin postulated that such modifications occur primarily through differential reproduction, or the ability of some members of a species to produce more surviving offspring than others. These favored individuals pass on their traits to the next generation, whereas the less favored do not do so to the same degree. Darwin called this process **natural selection** and demonstrated that it can change the characteristics of an entire species over time or even give rise to new species. This is discussed in greater detail in Chapter 2.

The idea that humans may also be a product of a long sequence of ongoing change received support of a rather startling variety: the discovery of humanlike fossils in association with stone tools. Fossils are the naturally mineralized remains of organic matter—earlier forms of plant and animal life turned to stone and thus preserved—very often lying underground for thousands of years until chance discovery brings them to light. During the seventeenth and eighteenth centuries, many such fossil remains of extinct plants and animals were collected and classified, and the similarities and differences between them and living species were duly noted. These discoveries, along with Charles Darwin's theory of natural selection, established the idea that not only human beings themselves, but also societies, were the products of evolution—that is, they developed from earlier forms. Over millions of years, the human body and human societies had emerged from

earlier human and prehuman forms, through a combination of physical evolution (cumulative changes in biological makeup) and cultural evolution (cumulative changes in thought and behavior). The study of contemporary peoples and their social behavior offered here is closely tied to this view of the world: the evolutionary view.

Evolutionary thinking is elaborated on in Chapter 2, but one way to envision the process is to draw on the metaphor suggested by British biologist Richard Dawkins (1995). He likens the development of life on earth, from its origins with very simple organisms capable of reproduction to the complexity of all living things today, to an ever-growing and branching river—a "river out of Eden." In this picture, all living things and all who lived in the past are "vehicles of information," carriers of DNA, or genes, and have the potential, sometimes realized and sometimes not, to replicate themselves so that the "river out of Eden" is a swirling flow in which genes meet, unite, sometimes compete, and when separated by branching, give rise to new species. Central to the Darwinian view of life is the special property that genes have to use material at hand with which to replicate themselves, including such flaws in copying as might arise. This model with its singular but elegant economy of assumptions goes a long way to explain diversity among millions of species, or as Dawkins puts it, "ways of making a living." Although each species, not to mention each working organ of each individual, seems so evidently "designed" to work or "make a living," all are products of cumulative change. Each variation builds on what had developed in the past while using genetic information at hand—a blind process stretching back through geological time. While this blind process inevitably leads to change, it also not infrequently leads to great complexity, as changes in one species reverberate through the "ways of making a living" of others on whom they prey or by whom they are preyed on.

# The Nature of Scientific Inquiry

All science is an effort to describe and explain natural phenomena. The aim of the social sciences, including anthropology, economics, cultural geography, political science, history, sociology, and psychology, is to describe and explain one particular natural phenomenon: *Homo sapiens,* the human species. Scientific inquiry, however complex in practice, rests on two interrelated mental activities: (1) reducing the subject of inquiry to manageable units (that is, to define and describe units of useful data), and (2) once a sufficiency of information is in place, generalizing further about related categories of data or even about expectations of what will be found in the future. Thus, inquiry necessarily proceeds at multiple levels, ranging from the microanalysis of very small units to the macrodescription of entire classes of phenomena.

## The Study of Culture

Much of what anthropologists and other social scientists study in their investigation of the human species lies in the broad domain we call "culture." Often, culture is defined as the primary nonbiological means by which humans adapt to their environments (see Fagan, 2004). This is reflected in the strong emphasis in archaeology on the origins of toolmaking as the most obvious proof of the emergence of humanity. But more than simply using tools as diagnostic of culture, of equal importance is the *transmission of knowledge* regarding their construction and use. Thus, a somewhat broader definition is useful to distinguish our nonhuman ancestors from those more recognizably similar to ourselves.

**Culture** is a system of shared beliefs, values, customs, behaviors, and artifacts that the members of a society use to cope with their world and with one another and that are transmitted from generation to generation through learning. This definition includes not only patterns of behavior but also patterns of thought (shared meanings that the members of a society attach to various phenomena, natural and in-

tellectual, including religion and ideologies), artifacts (tools, pottery, houses, machines, works of art), and the culturally transmitted skills and techniques used to make the artifacts. If an explorer on Mars finds, for example, a seashell, she will know that there was once life on the Red Planet; if she finds shells on a string, she will have discovered that culture had thrived there. In short, culture includes almost any form of behavior that is learned rather than instinctive. The difficulties that may arise in attempts to apply this distinction to antiquity are presented later.

## Holism

All scientists tend to specialize, to reduce their subject matter to manageable proportions. There are hundreds of distinct specializations in the sciences, social sciences, and engineering, and the result has been a prodigious accumulation of knowledge about the world. In 1797, when Thomas Jefferson presided over the American Philosophic Society in Philadelphia, all the scientists in America could have been comfortably seated in the lecture hall; today, their intellectual successors, who now number over 450,000, would overcrowd the city (Wilson, 1998, p. 39). In the eighteenth century, any single scholar would have been broadly familiar with the entire scope of European learning, which they would have viewed as a single corpus. Today, a complex division of labor has paid off in the exponential growth in knowledge about our planet and beyond. The drawback of this extraordinary amount of available

*Education is more than just the teaching of technical skills necessary for survival—it is part of the socialization process. Here a young woman in Eritrea learns to sew from her grandmother and, at the same time, comes to share her social and cultural values.*

(Ed Kashi)

information is that the unity of the sciences has become obscured.

This means that scientific **holism,** or the study and description of the properties of complex systems, is all the more important, including the study of living systems comprised of interacting organisms. But in the study of any system, one has to be careful not to forget that the emergent properties one describes for the totality (for example, the workings of a gasoline engine or even a complex natural system, such as a lake or forest) rest ultimately on individual components. Philosophical holism is thus the view that no complex entity is merely the sum of its parts; scientific holism, while accepting this view, keeps in mind that all organic and inorganic matter does have concrete attributes that can be described, measured, and ultimately related to the larger whole. Although some formulations of holism risk sliding into mysticism by focusing exclusively on the emergent properties of abstract systems, responsible holism considers a hierarchy of interrelated components.

As a principle guiding social research, holism is the assumption that any given aspect of human life is to be studied with an eye to its relation to other aspects of human life. Anthropologists, for example, attempt to understand specific problems or questions of interest within a wider context. Carol Laderman, who has worked with rural Malaysian women in an effort to understand traditional medicine and childbearing and midwife practices, writes:

> The strength of anthropology lies within a paradox. The broad philosophical and theoretical concerns of anthropology must be approached through studies of a particular people, living in a particular place and time. But in order to understand the particular, we must approach it from a generalist viewpoint. The specific nature of our inquiries cannot be allowed to limit our field of investigation. Data must be collected even in those areas which at first glance seem to impinge only peripherally upon the problem. For example, understanding a people's dietary habits requires a knowledge of their economy and ecology, as well as their religious, social and aesthetic ideologies. An analysis of childbirth practices must include an investigation into sex roles, rules of marriage and divorce, and the status and training of childbirth attendants, as well as the medical system of which these practices are a part. (Laderman, 1983, p. 1)

Thus, a researcher studying child nutrition in Brazil will probably consider how the occupations of parents affect family diet, and then how differences in nutrition arise and what causes them to persist. The political implications of nutritional differences among ethnic groups may also be explored. The biological anthropologist studying the evolution of the human brain will take into consideration not only the shape and size of fossil skulls but also evidence in regard to the evolution of language, toolmaking, social organization, and of hunting and gathering techniques, all of which are related to the growth of the brain. Likewise, the archaeologist studying prehistoric stone tools and the linguist investigating the origins of language will take all these matters (and more) into account. Scientists in other disciplines are consulted as well. Geologists, paleontologists, botanists, zoologists, geneticists, physicists, geographers, and specialists in other fields all provide information relevant to these concerns. As biologist E. O. Wilson so elegantly writes, "The greatest challenge today, not just in cell biology and ecology but in all of science, is the accurate and complete description of complex systems" (1998, p. 85). Obviously, the most complex systems of all involve human beings.

## Cultural Relativism

The second important principle in the study of cultural diversity is **cultural relativism**—the ability to view the beliefs and customs of other peoples within the context of their cultural matrix rather than one's own. This ability does not necessarily come naturally. Our perceptions are obviously adjusted to our own cultures. So at first sight, an African man with ritual scars on his face or a Middle Eastern woman in *purdah* (that is, with her face and body largely covered) is likely to appear strange to us. Unfamiliar food preferences may seem revolting. When the practice in question is one that we consider a matter of morality rather than simply one of taste—as, for example, the ritual homosexuality found in some New Guinea tribes or the infanticide practiced by the Yanomamö of Venezuela—our reactions can be far stronger.

Cannibalism, now abhorrent to virtually all cultural systems, was once probably quite widespread among prehuman ancestral populations as well as in a number of *Homo sapiens* groups. The most recent evidence shows the near universal presence of a gene protein whose primary function was to suppress the potential ill effects of the practice (Pennish, 2003). Consuming one's own species can lead to viral infection, such as kuru syndrome, discovered some years ago in New Guinea, when people practicing mortuary cannibalism were found to contract a fatal wasting disease, similar to mad cow disease and scrapies in sheep.

*Rituals such as circumcision must be understood in terms of the particular cultural environment of which they are a part. For the young Maasai male, the year of circumcision, the most important of his life, marks his emergence into manhood.*

(George Rodger/Magnum)

Cultural self-centeredness, the tendency to judge the customs of other societies by the standards of one's own, is called **ethnocentrism**. Ethnocentricism is a major threat to objective observation and evaluation. It is by no means a phenomenon exclusive to Western societies. People in every society tend to view outsiders and their customs with suspicion and often condemnation. If we consider infanticide cruel and unnatural, those peoples who practice it may consider our own custom of shutting old people away in homes for the aged equally appalling.

Adopting a perspective of cultural relativism aids understanding; it allows the observer to see the customs of other societies as ways of solving problems—problems that all societies share to some extent. Throughout the world, for example, people have a desire for sexual activity that outstrips their desire for babies or their ability to support them.

Americans tend to solve this problem by artificial birth control mechanisms and, in some cases, abortion; other societies solve it by enforced sexual abstinence or late marriage; others by infanticide, which, when understood in its cultural context, is seen to be most often an extreme measure taken by parents who, in times of food shortage, sacrifice a newborn infant to secure the well-being of another child. Even so, the concept of cultural relativism does not imply that one condones or justifies any particular behavior just because it occurs; rather, it is a means for understanding why it does occur and its significance for the society in question.

When we can see cultural differences through the prism of cultural relativism, we approach other cultures with open minds and an appreciation for human diversity. We need not and we should not

*A number of native American societies recognize cross-gender roles as a distinct and respected classification. This man is a* berdache. (The National Anthropological Archives/Smithsonian Institute Neg. 85-8666)

surrender our own values and our own ethical or moral standards. We simply adopt an approach that fosters scientific objectivity and at the same time encourages empathy with other peoples: an ability to see things, to some degree, as they see them. These products of cultural relativism—objectivity, empathy, and informed judgment—are indispensable to anyone who tries to understand the customs of another society.

There is, however, a troubling dilemma inherent in cultural relativism—one that is increasingly central in discussions of universal human rights. Can we use cultural relativism to justify the violation of basic civil and human rights? Eugene Hammel has written, with respect to the recent bloody wars in the former Yugoslavia, that when a society with which one is familiar is consumed by the flames of war, the anthropologist must speak out against war crimes, as would any moral person. These crimes, such as politically motivated rape, massacre of civilians, and torture, cannot be justified even if such behavior is considered justified by those carrying it out and perhaps even expected by those on the receiving end (Hammel, 1994). The dilemma is that in extending our own society's value system (for example, concepts of universal civil and human rights), we are in fact imposing our own moral standards on other societies.

As the impact of development threatens to destroy the cultures of indigenous peoples that have traditionally been of concern to anthropologists, more and more action-oriented anthropologists are questioning the notions that a detached, objective stance is possible and that silence on social issues equals neutrality. According to these anthropologists, failure to speak out and refusal to become involved are tantamount to supporting the status quo. These anthropologists see the fieldworker's role as making resources available to the people being studied and helping them to understand possible alternatives and to articulate their own views. They support cultural relativism—as long as it does not become an excuse for inaction in the face of exploitation.

## The Role of Theory

The kind of questions the researcher asks depends largely on the theoretical perspective in which the individual is trained. Theories are the backbone of scientific research. A **scientific theory** is a statement that postulates ordered relationships among natural phenomena and explains some aspect of the world. The theoretical model chosen by researchers leads them to ask certain kinds of questions and helps them formulate some questions as specific hypotheses. For example, a functionalist theory of politics that stresses

social stability and integration will direct a researcher to gather data on institutions that adjudicate disputes, release tension, and promote group solidarity. A Marxist theory of politics that emphasizes conflict and competition among those who control the means of production and those who supply the labor will direct a researcher to study instances of conflict reflecting class or economic divisions.

This is not to say that researchers see only what they are looking for and block out everything else. Still, perception is always selective and tends to be shaped by one's assumptions—in this case, by what one expects or hopes to find. To prevent this issue from becoming a problem, anthropologists should be careful to spell out their theoretical assumptions when they write the plans for their research and later when they report their findings. Thus, their biases, if indeed they have influenced the research, are at least not hidden.

A theory is never tested directly; one tests theoretical expectations by testing specific hypotheses. A **hypothesis** is a statement about relationships that can possibly be shown to be untrue. The statement, "Cigarette smoking is bad," is not a hypothesis because it does not define "bad" or specify the relationship between smoking and anything else. It seems like a valid or logical statement, but a skeptic might argue that the economic, social, or psychological benefits of smoking outweigh the physical harm it causes. The similar statement, "Cigarette smoking increases the risk of lung cancer," is a hypothesis because the risk of lung cancer can be measured among smokers and nonsmokers and a causal relationship between exposure to specific carcinogens in tobacco and smoking can be established. This distinction is important because unless a statement is logically falsifiable by appeal to relevant facts (or subjected to the appropriate test), it cannot enhance our knowledge of the world. If the actual results or observations are consistent with the hypothesis in a significant number of cases, the theory that generated the hypothesis is strengthened and perhaps expanded. But if the observed results of hypothesis testing repeatedly contradict theoretical expectations, the theory is eventually altered or abandoned. In short, theories survive as long as they continue to suggest useful approaches to the phenomena that scientists are trying to explain.

A good example of this process in anthropology concerns the peopling of North and South America. For decades, the prevailing view, suggested by much evidence, was that this occurred quite recently, about 12,000 years ago, with people moving from northeast Siberia to Alaska. Now some evidence from new archaeological sites in Chile and possibly Pennsylvania suggests a much earlier date, possibly

20,000 or 30,000 years ago or more (Adovasia & Page, 2003; Dillehay, 2000; Stanford & Bradley, 2000). But this does not close the debate. Unpublished new data collected from DNA sequences of the Y chromosome of Siberian males indicate that the earliest peopling of the New World from Siberian migrations could not have occurred earlier than 18,000 years ago, probably closer to 15,000. In addition, recent revisions of the dates of a number of archaeological sites in the region have placed them earlier than initially thought (Wade, 2003; Wilford, 2002). The give and take of such debates are the basis of scientific advancement.

A theory may be the product of decades of diligent research. Or as in the case of Darwin, it may be the product of a young scientist capable of seeing through the preconceptions that block the insights of others. Every theory has its blind spots—aspects of a subject that are underemphasized or disregarded in favor of other aspects. And new theories often displace the old by redirecting attention to those neglected areas. Through this dynamic process—the constant challenging and retesting of ideas—the discipline's theoretical framework is refined and developed over time.

## Aspects of Culture

The most distinctive single attribute of our species is that complex but elusive trait we call culture. It is complex in that it encompasses behaviors as diverse as toolmaking, bridal customs, funerary rites, farming, religious practices, art—in short, anything that is based on learning and that is passed on among individuals. Culture is elusive because, while it seems easy to distinguish what is learned from what is innate (for example, how to start a fire as opposed to the emotion of fear we experience when threatened by a fire), in practice it is actually very difficult. This is because all behaviors, learned or otherwise, have a basis in the human brain. Learning English as we grow up—as opposed to Arabic—is clearly a cultural phenomenon, but the ability to learn a language at all is a unique biological property of our species. Since culture encompasses all that we acquire through learning as we proceed through life, it can and does regularly change; after all, we do not think and behave as do our parents.

Cultural behavior also varies greatly among individuals in the same society; not everyone has the same preferences in food and dress or even practices the same forms of sex. Nevertheless, there are apparent limitations to cultural plasticity; human sensory mechanisms, intelligence, emotions, reproductive systems, color recognition, and linguistic ability are universally shared. Pascal Boyer argues very effectively that even what might be termed "acquired culture" (that is, what we learn through indoctrination in social situations), while very much dependent on the context, is nevertheless constrained by the evolved properties of the mind (Boyer, 1998: p. 877 ff). Although his case is beyond our interests here, what is noteworthy is that many aspects of cultural learning seem to follow linguistic

*Turkish pupils in a Muslim-run school in Bulgaria. Here boys and girls study in the same classroom, but for religious instruction, they will be separated. Beyond the official curriculum, they absorb a wider understanding of their expected social roles.*

(Daniel Bates)

models of language acquisition and transmission, which helps account for many similarities in basic cultural themes and representations worldwide. Also keep in mind that people frame biological needs into cultural patterns. For example, we think of discrete mealtimes—breakfast, lunch, and dinner—but for many societies meals, satisfying a biological necessity, may occur at any point in the day. The same holds for food preferences: Americans' extensive consumption of beef may strike others as unappetizing.

Even aspects of social life fall into very familiar patterns among very diverse cultures: Notions of human beauty, the importance of family or kin ties, the importance of "reputation," and the importance of religion and art are part of every human society. Thus, while human culture appears as a wonderfully colorful collage, it has an underlying structure expressing our common humanity, which is rooted in our unique ability to acquire and use language. Despite the many biological traits we share with other species, only humans possess the neurological infrastructure that allows for true language and, hence, culture.

## Culture Gives Meaning to Reality

Culture encompasses not only social behaviors but also ways of thinking. From our cultural training, we learn what meanings to attach to the events of our world, and especially to the behavior of others, so that we can make some sense of those events and know how to respond. The meanings of specific actions can vary with the cultural context in which they are interpreted.

Because meaning is supplied by cultural context and because such contexts differ, people of various societies can view the world in quite different ways. For example, members of societies that speak different languages and follow different religious traditions may make very different distinctions between the natural and the supernatural. For the Australian aborigines, certain rocks, animals, and places have souls that are very much a part of them. The sacred sites of Christianity, Islam, and Judaism have meanings for their adherents that are not shared by outsiders. The beliefs and values of a society are a cultural reality. Whether marrying more than one spouse is treated as a crime or as a preferred form of marriage depends on culturally defined rules of behavior.

Even so, we cannot regard our ability to define reality and to make rules for appropriate behavior as completely open or arbitrary. Although different systems of marriage, mating, or cohabiting are practiced by societies around the world, we can easily think of variations that no society has adopted or

condoned. There appear to be universal constraints on sex roles, as on other areas of human behavior, within which variation occurs (Brown, 1991). As David Gilmore (1990) points out, "All societies distinguish between male and female, providing institutionalized sex-appropriate roles for adult men and women. Most societies also hold consensual ideals—guiding or admonitory images—for adult masculinity and femininity by which individuals are judged as worthy members of their sex and are evaluated more generally as moral actors" (pp. 1–2).

## Culture Creates Gender

There is no society that does not recognize, encourage, and even demand behavioral differences between the biologically defined sexes. Anthropologists generally define "sex" as the biological category determined largely by genital structures and secondary sexual characteristics (see Worthman for a good discussion, especially 1995, pp. 597ff). **Gender** is usually taken to be the behavioral or culturally interpreted dimensions of sexual categories, and the term is employed to avoid confusing cultural (and hence "learned" and presumably malleable) aspects of male/female differentiation with biological or inherited characteristics. The issues are rather more complex than implied by this straightforward distinction. Behavior of all varieties and, most particularly, that associated with sex is mediated or regulated by the body's hormonal systems. Thus, our sexual identities are largely fixed during prenatal development. Generally speaking, this basic identity is not subject to simple variation in socialization or

*Girls are often taught at an early age to defer to their brothers and to accept roles that emphasize child care and home-focused activities. This little Yörük girl is already caring for her infant brother.*

(Daniel Bates)

childrearing. What does seem clear is that there is no evidence of rigidly dichotomized male/female or sex-linked cognitive or intellectual capabilities (Worthman, 1995, p. 607). Put simply, there is no biological imperative determining or limiting either male or female participation in cultural arrangements.

Gender, as we have seen, refers to the behaviors associated with the biologically defined sexes, and this is what varies from culture to culture. Parents in all societies begin to train their children at an early age in the social behavior, or gender roles, considered appropriate to their biological sex. Gender identity is one's feeling of being male or female. Gender identity and gender roles usually develop in tandem. Gender roles tend to be defined by the society and establish the kind of behavior that is appropriate and inappropriate for a male and a female. Children are also socialized to respond favorably to what are perceived as the social tasks or jobs appropriate to their gender.

It is impossible to understand any society in the absence of gender as a category of analysis; at the same time, gender itself requires a cultural and historical context. Although gender is a universal source of individual identity and a pervasive means by which access to resources and political power is structured, generalization in the absence of specific historical or cultural experience is risky. The gender experiences of people vary with historical processes, as reflected in religion, cultural conventions, access to resources, and

---

## Box 1.1

# Becoming Invisible[1]

SOME YEARS AGO, ANTHROPOLOGIST Amal Rassam was in northern Iraq doing fieldwork in and around the city of Mosul. Having obtained her research permit, she hired a taxi and a driver, a native of a nearby village. Her notes read:

*On Tuesday morning, 'Ali my driver came to the hotel to pick me up to go to the village to begin my survey. He was dressed in the traditional garb of his region, which marked him as a rural inhabitant, a qarawi, or villager. I sat at the back of the taxi and we drove off. A few miles outside the city we were stopped at a military checkpoint. The soldier ignored my driver and came around to my side of the car, put his head in the window and asked where I was going. I told him that I was on my way to a village down the road, upon which he asked to see my identification papers. Ignoring both my protestations and my work permit, he made us turn around and go back to the city, claiming that the road was mined and that he could not guarantee my safety. On the way back, I expressed my frustration to 'Ali and my fears that I wouldn't be able to complete my research. Upon some reflection he*

*suggested that we try again in a day or two, but this time he would put on his suit and I should wear the 'abaya (the shapeless black cloak worn by the more traditional women in Iraq). I agreed. When he came back two days later to pick me up he was dressed like an* affendi *(an urban gentlemen) and I was enveloped in the 'abaya. I sat next to him in the front of the car and we took off to the rural countryside. As we reached the checkpoint, the soldier on duty came around this time to the driver's window and asked to see his papers; he asked where we were going, and without a direct glance my way, he waived us on, and we continued on our way to the village.*

The first time that Rassam set out, she was the one in the car who was socially "visible," being clearly a foreigner to the area and a woman traveling alone in the back of a hired car dressed in Western-style clothes and without the 'abaya. Her status was immediately recognized by the soldier, who ignored the driver and asked for her papers. Her dress identified her as a member of the urban, educated society, and the fact that she had hired a car marked her as

someone of potential significance. As it transpired, the soldier chose not to assume responsibility for the presence of a strange woman in his area.

On the second attempt, by wearing the 'abaya and sitting next to the driver, Rassam became publicly invisible; the soldier perceived her as "belonging" to the driver. Moreover, the driver, dressed in his Western-style suit, had acquired both visibility and a certain amount of social standing as well. The confrontation had now shifted to one between the two men, the soldier at the bottom of the military hierarchy and the *affendi* representing the lower bourgeoisie or those who identify with them. The woman in the car ceased to exist in any political sense. This, we might add, is one occasion when being a female anthropologist in the Middle East was an advantage. A male anthropologist would have had to show his identification papers along with those of the driver and, on being found a stranger to the area, would likely have been turned back.

[1]This material is courtesy of Amal Rassam, who is presently back in Iraq assisting in the rebuilding of that country.

education—not to mention the fact that within a complex society, gender experience varies with ethnicity, class, and region (see Box 1.1, Becoming Invisible).

Because gender roles are so intensely socialized and so personal, it is difficult to separate the present from the possible. It is no accident that until recently anthropologists (like other observers of society) largely ignored intercultural variation in gender roles. They took it for granted as a biological given that men and women belonged to different spheres of activity and the female domain was domestic whereas the male domain was everything else: productive, political, ceremonial, and military. Not only was great variability in gender roles overlooked, but so was the fact that even apparent similarities in gender relationships could have very diverse roots. In the West, traditional male power and authority have been largely based in property rights and control of wealth; the classic patriarchy, in Roman law, gave the male head of house final title to almost all property and control over his children (to the exclusion of his wives). Among the Yanomamö, male dominance seems to rest in part on the threat of physical violence. Among other Amazonian peoples (the Mundurucu, for example), male social and political precedence rests on their ability to dominate religious and ceremonial life through control of rituals and ritual objects (Murphy & Murphy, 1985).

Anthropologists have become aware of the shortcomings of ignoring gender, in part because of the recent transformation of their own societies.

There are three interrelated areas that are of primary concern in analyzing gender: gender socialization, gender and work, and gender and power.

*Gender Socialization.* Gender socialization of children begins immediately after birth and generates systematic inequality between the sexes. It is largely in the process of socialization that individuals form their notions of what gender identity means in terms of appropriate or expected and acceptable behavior.

*Gender and Work.* The organization of work in society is critical for understanding gender. Labor is often valued differently for men and for women, with the work done by women often seen as private or domestic (rather than productive) and hence undervalued. Further, even restricting access to nonproductive sectors such as religious ritual and ceremonial leadership differentiates between the sexes. In most cases, it is women who play a secondary role in ritual and public ceremony. There are exceptions, but when examined more closely, it becomes clear that women appearing in prominent ritual, ceremonial, and even political roles are often regarded as honorary men for that purpose. Using gender to create different domains of activity usually contributes to stratification. While gender considerations obviously affect access to resources and contribute to inequality, gender usually has to be viewed along with other sources of identity used to compartmentalize and divide society.

*Market women attend a political rally in Accra, Ghana. Women play a major role in the marketing system and have considerable political influence.*

(The Hutchison Library)

*Gender and Power.* The third area of concern is closely related to socialization and the organization of the work force—that is, gender, power, and access to the political process. Even family life can be seen as political, in that individuals are contending for resources. Moreover, social control operates quite differently on men and women in many instances. In societies where notions of family honor are important in local politics or public life, this may be linked to male control over female sexuality and, by extension, many aspects of female public behavior. Thus, it might be thought threatening to family honor for female members of the family to be seen with nonfamily males. This puts serious constraints on female behavior, sometimes so as to make it difficult for a woman to accept employment outside the home. Outside the household, gender can be seen as an aspect of stratification, particularly in conjunction with race, ethnicity, and class. Women from different ethnic groups in the United States, for example, experience very different rates of poverty, childbearing options, and involvement in community mobilization. Class inequality can be greatly amplified by gender expectations regarding housework and childrearing for poor women.

However gender is understood, it has to be kept in mind that gender relations can and do change; in the final analysis, gender is shaped in society by the activities, beliefs, and values of both men and women. People are not simply passive respondents.

## Culture Is Integrated

The religious, political, and economic institutions of a society are shaped by common adaptive forces operating over long periods of time, and as a consequence, they tend to "fit" with each other. The "fit" is often supplied by language or, at least, by verbally expressed models of the world. We use language to signify the legitimacy of a given political order or religious institution. The language used to justify equality or, on occasion, to justify a revolution is expressed symbolically in special terminology—for example, the words of the U.S. Constitution, the Bible, or the Bill of Rights. We also rely on social rules and symbols such as the shape of stop signs and the colors of traffic lights to provide order to our daily lives.

The many ways in which cultural practices are interrelated gives stability and continuity to cultural evolution; changes are incremental and often occur very slowly. We do not wake up each morning with a burning need to reconfirm the existence of institutions on which we depend or the symbols through which we interpret our reality. It is probably because stability and continuity are so important to our survival that change and innovation are usually so conservative. It is as though humans were generally guided by the maxim "If it ain't broke, don't fix it."

Sometimes we see this tendency toward stability and continuity most dramatically when it is violated by the cataclysmic events of war or other disasters. People who are suddenly cut off from their customary practices and familiar ways of doing things experience stress not unlike what is sometimes called "culture shock"—the feeling of disorientation one may experience when thrust into an unfamiliar cultural setting. In many respects, when an individual is born into a particular society and grows up learning its language, social rules, and expectations, it is analogous to a new employee coming into a long-established corporation. The established ways of doing things is the environment in which the new employee must find his or her way; for most of the employee's career, conformity will be the rule and experimentation the exception. Nevertheless, people do innovate, and out of individual shifts in behavior, major cultural shifts or trends occur.

## Culture Is Adaptive

**Cultural adaptation** encompasses all of the learned or socially acquired responses and behaviors that affect reproduction, provisioning, shelter—in short, survival. Like many other species, humans adapt by learning new ways of doing things. The swelling human population is testimony to how rapidly we can adjust our systems of food production and other technologies. Our ability to learn rapidly and to communicate learning is, in large measure, due to our ability to use language. These abilities have enabled us to develop technologies that allow us to occupy most areas of the earth—something no other large animal can do. In the long run, of course, these technologies may also prove to be maladaptive; we may be a species with a relatively short history. Cultural adaptation involves changes of all sorts that continually affect our relationship to our environment. It results in changes that can never be ideal, as the environment is itself constantly changing. No adaptation or response is a perfect or final solution; each carries with it certain costs and hazards.

Adaptation is always opportunistic: We take advantage of whatever resources are available to us at a particular time (including genetic and cultural materials), often with little regard for future consequences. For example, industrialized societies began to use oil as a fuel at the beginning of the twentieth century in a very limited way. This adaptation soon solved the problem of furnishing an effective, cheap fuel to power modern machinery. Its use was opportunistic in the sense that the oil was there to be tapped and our technology happened to have developed to the point that allowed us to make use of it. In adapting to oil fuel, we made numerous commitments that have altered the structure of our society: We rely on food produced with oil-fueled machinery; we grow crops dependent on fertilizers and pesticides derived from the petrochemical industry; we use rapid transport, cheap electricity, and productive systems too numerous to mention. All these activities are fueled by oil.

But in recent years, the environment has been changing in unexpected ways. We are faced with declining reserves of oil, with the toxic consequences of a highly developed industrial society, and perhaps with long-term changes in the atmosphere—all consequences of extensive oil use. It is also certain that whatever other energy sources we turn to next will be imperfect solutions and will generate a host of new and unforeseen difficulties as well.

Adaptation is at once the solution to a particular problem and the source of unanticipated changes and, inevitably, new problems. Many would liken both biological (or genetically measured) adaptation and cultural adaptation, which need not involve changes in the genetic makeup of the population, to an "existential arms race" in which one defensive or offensive innovation triggers a corresponding response. Not infrequently with humans the two processes work together: Treating tuberculosis in humans with antibiotics is cultural adaptation at work; the emergence of a drug-resistant tubercle bacillus is a biological countermeasure on the part of bacteria that cause the disease.

## Behavior and Learning

Animal behavior (including, of course, human behavior) is seen in terms of a basic distinction: It may be instinctive—that is, genetically controlled—or it may be learned. This is especially true when looking at human social behavior. Learned ways of behaving constitute a very large percentage of human activity, probably far outweighing instinctive behavior. One might visualize this situation by thinking of the difference between the behavior of a very young child and that of an adult in the same family. All animals have some capacity to learn, and learning is important to the survival of most species. But no other animal learns, can learn, or needs to learn as much as the human animal. To function as independent members of our societies, we require not only a long period of physical care but also a long period of training in how to use language, to think and behave; in other words, we need training in a society's system of behaviors—its culture. In short, "childhood lasts, and lasts, and lasts" (Angier, 2002) for biological as well as cultural reasons.

A child born into any society begins to learn behavior, language, and skills appropriate to that culture from the day of birth. The child's toilet training and feeding habits, the encouragement (or discouragement) given his or her first experiments in inter-

*In most societies today, much social learning takes place in the formal environment of the classroom. These children in China learn Chinese characters. They also are acquiring complex cultural skills.*

(Max Monroe)

acting socially with others, the rewards offered for correct deportment—all amount to an intensive training course in how to be a proper person. The child goes on to learn social roles specific to the appropriate sex, useful technical skills, and his or her people's religion and moral codes. This training in one's own culture is sometimes called **socialization** or **enculturation,** and what we become is greatly influenced by the persons who carry out that enculturation and the way they do it. In many societies, a fairly narrow circle of people, primarily parents and kin and community elders, is responsible for the bulk of an individual's socialization. In other societies, as in our own, much of this training is provided by specialists outside the family or immediate community; we send our children to schools, churches, summer camps, and universities. To a considerable extent, our behavior as men and women, our conduct as parents, our expectations, and our attitudes are shaped by this process.

Socialization is by no means uniform for all members of a society. In our own society, for example, some parents raise their children quite strictly, setting clear rules and clear punishments for violations. Others take a more permissive approach, making large allowances for experimentation and failure on the child's part. Nor are the parents the only socializing influences. Each child has a unique constellation of friends, relatives, and neighbors, and hence, each learns a somewhat distinctive version of the culture. Moreover, the exact content of the socialization process varies along gender, ethnic, socioeconomic, religious, and regional lines.

For example, Yanomamö boys are encouraged by their parents to be aggressive and to display anger and rage. Their sisters are not encouraged to behave in this way, although we may assume that their capacity for anger and rage is as great as that of boys. Among the Yomut Türkmen of northeastern Iran, young men are brought up with a high regard for physical prowess and the necessity of defending one's kin and community, by force if necessary. One tribe or descent group among the Yomut, however, is considered holy, and the men do not fight. In fact, it is considered a serious religious offense to strike a member of this holy tribe or to steal their property. Boys in this group are socialized quite differently from those born into other Yomut groups, with little emphasis on fighting or self-defense.

Nevertheless, there are broad similarities in how and what the members of a single society are taught. The members of a given society tend to take such similarities for granted (often marking them up to "human nature") and to notice only the differences. Recent research by two biologists from Israel, Eva

Jalonka and Eytan Avital, suggests that some learned behavior in animals, including humans, follows the same rules as genes: Parents, especially mothers, pass on behavioral traits to their children much as they do genetic ones (Angier, 2002). Thus, children learn at infancy to fancy the behavioral styles of their parents, and these modes of behavior can be passed on over generations. This, they suggest, may account for the fact that there is a decided tendency for people to favor as mates individuals who share characteristics with their parents.

This is not to say that these learned behaviors have no basis in biology; in fact, all behavior is mediated by biological processes and limitations. Our basic physiological requirements—the need for food, water, shelter, sleep, and sexual activity—underlie a good deal of our behavior. Our brains, with their elaborately encoded propensities for liking some things and avoiding others, also channel behavior in ways that are only recently being researched. One fact seems clear: Rather than being a sharply distinct alternative to instinct, learned behavior is often guided by information inherent in the genes. Speech learning is a good example. "Human infants innately recognize most or all of the consonant sounds characteristic of human speech, including consonants not present in the language they normally hear" (Gould & Marler, 1987, p. 82). Some cognitive scientists now propose that human brains may be "wired" with a universal program enabling infants to very rapidly learn the subtle and complex patterns of seemingly drastically different languages (Pinker, 1999; Prince & Smolensky, 1997).

Learned behavior, quite apart from instinct, serves biological purposes because of the practical advantages it confers. These advantages are attested to by our success in reproducing and surviving in virtually every climatic zone on earth. Even our universally shared taste for sweets, fats, and salts, and hence the underlying basis for our dietary systems, is the result of a long evolutionary process. It has been suggested that human systems of knowledge—religion, magic, science, philosophy—are based on a uniquely human, inborn need to impose order on experience. This is not surprising, as pattern recognition (for example, seeing a dangerous situation) is a key means for processing information critical to survival.

The biological basis of human behavior, then, is important. But how we go about satisfying inborn needs and developing successful coping strategies is largely a matter of contextual learning. Whether we feed ourselves by growing yams and hunting wild game or by herding camels and raising wheat, whether we explain a thunderstorm by attributing it

*Language is a crucial element in forming individual and group identity. In Bulgaria, the former Communist government attempted to suppress the use of Turkish by over a million of its Muslim minority. Here religious and other leaders meet to demand recognition of their linguistic and religious rights.*
(Fevzi Omer)

to meteorological conditions or to a fight among the gods—such things are determined by what we learn as part of our enculturation. Enculturation prepares us to function as members of a given society—to speak its language, to use its symbols in abstract thought, and so forth. This ability depends in turn on genetically inherited physical traits, notably a brain of awesome complexity. But even though cultural behavior may be guided by genetically rooted limitations and propensities, it is obvious that we do not inherit genes for speaking English as opposed to Swahili or for training as a doctor as opposed to a pilot. It is more difficult to assess the contribution of our biological heritage to the shaping of very basic aspects of social organization, sex roles, aggression, and family, but clearly, there are limits to the range of variation found in different societies.

## Language, Biology, and Culture

Human language presumably began as a call or gesture system. But **language** as we recognize it differs from such systems in several ways. Animal calls, probably because they are in large part genetically determined, are rigidly stereotyped; the call is always the same in form and meaning. Moreover, animal

**call systems** are closed; that is, elements of one call cannot be combined with elements of another to produce a new message. The calls are unique, limited in number, and mutually exclusive.

Human language is open—the number of messages that can be conveyed is infinite. Indeed, with language, people can and continually do create entirely new messages—sentences that have never before been spoken—whereas call systems can generally convey only a very few simple meanings: danger, hostility, sexual excitement, the availability of food, and so on. As Bertrand Russell put it, "No matter how eloquently a dog may bark, he cannot tell you that his parents were poor but honest" (cited in Fromkin et al., 2002). Human language can be used to communicate a vast range of meanings, from subtle philosophical abstractions to complex technical information to delicate shades of feeling. This flexibility is made possible by the arbitrariness of human language. Unlike animal calls, the sounds of a language have no fixed meaning. Instead, meaning emerges from the way sounds are combined into words and words arranged to make sentences in accordance with a complex set of rules (grammar).

Another distinctive feature of human language is that it is stimulus-free. That is, a linguistic utterance need not be evoked by an immediate situation. We do not have to turn a corner and come upon a tiger in order to say the word "tiger" or talk about "danger." We can discuss things that are not present—things experienced in the past, things that may happen in the future, even things that are not true or not real, such as unicorns and utopias. Little of this sort of communication appears possible in call systems, which lack the dimensions of time and possibility. While animals have been frequently observed to send false signals, generally the use of call systems for deception is limited. It has been said, with some justice, that hominids became truly human when they became capable of telling a lie.

All animals communicate with one another, using various kinds of cries, calls, gestures, and chemical emissions. Such means of communication are usually genetically determined, however, and therefore are much less flexible than human languages. A bird's danger call may be the only call it can produce in a dangerous situation; the bird cannot add any refinements to the call to indicate, for example, the source of the danger or the direction it is coming from. Bees, however, are known to have very sophisticated systems of communication, and in some species, "scouts" are sent out by the hive and return to inform the others of the way to proceed to reach a newly discovered food source. Even so, this pattern is far removed from human language, with its nearly infinite flexibility and capacity to generate new meanings. And though we associate human language with speech, sounds are not a necessary aspect of language; people who cannot hear or speak can acquire and use language. Conversely, when a parrot imitates human utterances, it is not using language the way a human does.

Using language involves structures in the brain that other animals, including closely related nonhuman primates, lack; at the same time, apes, in particular, seem to have linguistic ability at the level of what Bickerton calls "protolanguage" (1995). That is, much like human infants prior to age eighteen months or so, they are capable of communicating emotional states but fall far short of fully developed natural languages.

For many years, it was thought that one barrier to primate language use was physiological. In primates, the pharynx (a tunnel of muscle connecting the back of the mouth to the larynx, crucial to the production of speech) is smaller in relation to body size and is shaped differently than in humans. As a consequence, the earliest experiments that sought to teach chimpanzees spoken language were not successful. To get around the vocal-tract problem and test intellectual capacity, two psychologists, Alan and Beatrice Gardner (1969), in a now-classic experiment, decided to teach their test chimp, Washoe, American Sign Language (ASL).

In four years, Washoe not only learned to use 130 signs. More important, she showed that she could manipulate them creatively. Having learned the signal "more" to persuade the Gardners to resume a pillow fight, she spontaneously used the same signal when she wanted a second helping at dinner. Furthermore, whereas chimpanzee calls are never combined, Washoe spontaneously combined hand signals to make new words. Not knowing the signal for duck, for instance, she dubbed it "water bird."

One of the most successful of the later experiments involved a gorilla named Koko. At age four, she was able to use 251 different signs in a single hour. After five years of training in ASL, she scored between 80 and 90 (the equivalent of a five-year-old child) on an IQ test for nonreading children. Like Washoe, Koko could combine words creatively to name new objects. She was also particularly adept at expressing her feelings. Whenever Penny Patterson, her trainer, arrived late at Koko's trailer, the gorilla would sign "sad." On other mornings, when asked how she felt, she would report herself "happy" or sign "I feel good." This was the first clear instance of emotional self-awareness on the part of a nonhuman primate.

There have also been experiments using, not sign language, but lexigrams—symbols that represent common objects, verbs, and moods (see Byrne, 1999, for good review). Sue Savage Rumbaugh trained two chimps, Sherman and Austin, to use a keyboard to produce lexigrams (Rumbaugh & Lewis, 1994). When they had become fairly fluent, she constructed an experiment that entailed Sherman and Austin having to cooperate to perform various tasks. She found that they spontaneously used the lexigrams to learn from and communicate with each other. Even more interesting is the case of Kanzi, a young pygmy chimpanzee, who surprised the psychologists when he revealed that he had learned to use the keyboard to produce lexigrams entirely on his own by watching his adoptive mother.

It would seem incorrect, however, to conclude that these animals used language in the human sense or even came close (Bickerton, 1995, 2003). First, the languages that the test apes learned were in part iconic—the symbols imitated the things they stood for. There is a geometrical relationship between some of the signs and the things they represent. The ASL sign for book, for example, is two palms pressed together and then opened, much like the geometrics of opening a book. Thus, it seems doubtful that apes have the intellectual capacity to handle a totally arbitrary language such as our own. Second, there is still some doubt as to whether the test apes put together sentences spontaneously or simply by rote, although the lexigram experiments with Sherman, Austin, and Kanzi seem to indicate that the chimpanzees were not merely responding to cues from researchers without really understanding their meaning. Third, even if ape language differs from human language only in degree, the distance separating them is vast. The suggestions of subtle reasoning in the apes' verbalizations are quite intriguing, but they are also quite rare. Finally, teaching language to an ape requires immense effort under highly artificial conditions, whereas human children learn it naturally, without training. Apes may share with us certain faculties necessary for language, but it is clear that these faculties have remained relatively undeveloped in their line.

Because sounds leave no trace, researchers investigating the origins of language have to depend on indirect evidence: studies of the way children acquire language, comparisons of human and nonhuman vocalizations, guesses as to what kinds of brains and vocal tracts might have accompanied fossil skulls, and of course, cultural evidence of the way our early ancestors lived.

The cultural evidence seems to indicate that at least some aspects of a proto-language began to evolve as early as 4 million years ago (Schick & Toth, 1993). It was probably around that period that our early ancestors made a crucial change in their way of procuring food—from individual foraging for vegetable foods to regular eating of meat and vegetables on a communal basis. The new pattern demanded cooperation and the coordination of hunting and gathering activities, for which at least an advanced call or gesturing system seems to have been required. The cultural evidence, in the form of stone tools, may, some say, suggest a very early date for the first rudimentary language skills (Schick & Toth, 1993). The flakes made by these early hominids are far more sophisticated than anything a chimpanzee can make when taught by trainers to do so. Most important, the earliest stone tools indicate by how they were struck that their makers were preferentially right-handed, suggesting that their brains were already lateralized as are modern humans (and unlike other primates).

Of course, there are other perspectives on the same cultural data. Derek Bickerton (1995) argues that the relatively slow rate at which technology changed over the first 4 million or so years of hominid evolution suggests that while an elaborate call system is probable, true language did not appear until approximately 100,000 years ago. For example, he points out that the caverns of Zhoukoudian in northern China were inhabited continuously by ho-

minids from 500,000 years ago until 200,000 years ago, their history of occupation is well known, and yet the tiny handful of artifacts produced underwent no change during a period of 300,000 years. "The people of the caves of Zhoukoudian crouched over their smokey fires, eating half-cooked bats" and made no structural improvements in their habitation or elaboration of a very simple material culture (Bickerton, 1995, p. 46). This degree of cultural stasis, he argues, could not be associated with a population possessing full language.

To speak, early humans had to have more than just the need to communicate. Speech requires physical mechanisms as well, such as certain structures in the brain. These structures allow us to associate incoming auditory messages with remembered messages from other sensory pathways—especially with the memory of the words that we will need to voice our thoughts. They also enable us to signal the muscles of the vocal apparatus to make the movements necessary to produce the appropriate sounds. Current research indicates that these operations are carried out mainly by three specific parts of the brain, all located in the cerebral cortex, the thick rind of gray matter that constitutes the brain's outer layer. It is also the region of the brain responsible for the processing of visual stimuli.

The cerebellum of the human brain, a fist-sized structure just above the brainstem at the back of the head, is a recent development; it expanded rapidly and quite late in hominid history and is distinct from that of other primates. Around the time of the transition to food sharing and meat eating, the early human brain was less than half the size of ours and its cerebral cortex was smaller still, but still larger than modern nonhuman primates. Thus, while it seems unlikely that the language-producing structures of the cortex were fully developed at this time, it is a fair assumption that the structures underlying the conversion from call system to language had begun about 4 million years ago.

By about 100,000 years ago, when the Neanderthals lived in Europe and the Middle East, the cerebral cortex had reached approximately its present size. Quite possibly, these people had the mental equipment necessary for a complex language. Some of the cultural evidence—sophisticated tool manufacturing and, in particular, the deliberate burial of their dead—suggests abstract reasoning and well-developed modes of communication. Still, until recently, it was thought that they may have lacked the physiological equipment necessary for fully human speech.

In addition to the cerebral cortex, as we noted in the discussion of language in other primates, the pharynx is crucial to the production of speech. Until very recently, it was thought that the pharynx developed to the size and shape necessary to produce intelligible sounds only after the Neanderthal period. However, a Neanderthal skeleton excavated in Israel in 1989 with the small bones of the larynx intact appears to have had the physiological capability for human speech. Still, it is possible that truly fluent language is only a very recent achievement in the history of our species.

Firm and striking evidence for this has emerged very recently in the study of hereditary speech impairments in families of English and French speakers, defects that can be traced to specific miscoding on DNA segments. Steven Pinker reports on research by teams in England, Canada, and the United States in which very specific language errors, for example, how regular verbs are formed or inflections handled, are passed on through genetic rather than cultural transmission. In one case reported by Pinker, a 16-year-old girl severely retarded with Williams syndrome was observed to have exceptional verbal skills although her effective IQ was 49; still, she made a few but very specific grammatical errors and all in verb conjugation (1999). A French-speaking child with the same syndrome had similar problems. B. Fowler has laid out what he terms "hard wired" universal grammar rules. Less controversial is the recent discovery of the actual genetic site that is universally present in humans capable of normal speech, the gene FoxP2. This was found through studies of a large London family with many members unable to speak properly (Wade, 2003b) and subsequently established as present in all normal humans.

The use of language is undoubtedly responsible for the archaeologically recent, explosive development of human culture. Groups whose members communicated effectively with one another hunted more successfully, gathered more efficiently, made more sophisticated tools, built stronger shelters, found more suitable locations for habitation, and argued and resolved their differences without necessarily coming to blows. It has been argued that language is really a form of "verbal grooming" (Dunbar, 1997). Just as our primate cousins, the chimpanzees, spend a large portion of each day in mutual grooming exercises, humans devote a great deal of time to gossip. Perhaps as much as 70% of conversation is devoted to sharing observations about others in our social world (Dunbar, 1997). This is so important to our constructing and maintaining cooperative group life that it may be the impetus for the evolution of language. Others argue that language evolved out of facial movements and hand gestures (Eakin, 2002). This point is important

because complex social behavior associated with group living and cooperation entails individuals reconciling their immediate self-interest with their long-term prospects. Language greatly facilitates this, as individuals can negotiate long-lasting relationships of mutual trust and assistance that continue beyond any given event. The concomitant growth of language and culture in turn created strong selective pressures for more complex brains, which made possible the development of yet more elaborate language and culture. There arose, in other words, a feedback cycle: language, culture, and the brain evolved together, each stimulating and reinforcing the development of the others.

Nothing is more striking evidence of the transition to the modern human mind than the cave art found extensively throughout Eurasia and Australia and dating no earlier than 50,000 B.P.[1] In fact, the hunting scenes drawn by the living San and by contemporary Australian aboriginal peoples seemingly have close analogies in early cave art (Fagan, 2004). Their depictions too seem to have religious significance as do the earliest examples in Europe, dated about 30,000 B.P. (Chauvet et al., 1996).

## The Science of Anthropology

Having introduced culture, the chapter now turns to its scientific study. Anthropological investigation involves comparisons of contemporary cultures and investigations of cultural and biological changes over time. Anthropology takes as its object of study all human peoples, across the globe and across time, treating topics as varied as their teeth, their diseases, their ways of getting food and shelter and rearing children, and their ideas about their place in the world. Consider the investigations of the ethnographers Terese and John Hart (1996), who carefully determined the caloric and nutritional values of food resources in the Ituri rain forest of Zaire. Their findings indicated that the Mbuti Pygmies—hunters and gatherers in the forest—could not live independently of the farmers with whom they trade. Elliot Fratkin and Eric A. Roth, working in Kenya among the Ariaal (see Chapter 5), found that the key to Ariaal pastoral subsistence was herd diversity combined with mobility. Families who

---

[1]This book uses a simplified version of the archaeological convention for expressing calendrical and scientific dates. For historically known calendrical dates, we use B.C./A.D. For dates established by other means, for example, by radiocarbon dating, we use B.P., or "before the present," and since the present is constantly changing, by common agreement, it is referenced to 1950 (see Fagan, 2004).

*Ethnographers collect and interpret data on every aspect of social life, including how people relate their own aspirations and points of view. Here anthropologist Elliot Fratkin interviews two* laibon *medicine men in northern Kenya.*

(Jake Fratkin)

had different varieties of livestock could cope with drought far better than those who focused on one. Further, wealthy herders with large numbers of animals were better able to recover from periodic disasters, a fact that amplifies wealth differentials.

## Studying Cultural Behavior: Fieldwork, Data Collection, and Analysis

One hallmark of cultural anthropology is the intensive involvement of the scholar with the phenomena being studied, particularly the intimate contact one develops in the course of living for a long period of time with people in what is often a small, close-knit community. Cultural anthropologists, in carrying out ethnography, are sometimes chided by other social scientists for "knowing a great deal about very little," a reference to the frequent involvement of the ethnographer with small and often marginalized populations. However true this may be, it very often turns out that in the course of acquiring seemingly specialized knowledge we discover widespread patterns or problems.

Dee Mack Williams, carrying out his dissertation research in Inner Mongolia among nomadic pastoralists, discovered something rather unexpected. Usually, economists, animal husbandry experts, and ecologists assume that sand dunes are simply environmental hazards. But when Williams began asking questions, he found that Mongol herders not

only view them as benign, but even prefer to herd their cattle, sheep, and goats among them during certain seasons for specific times of the day. So he launched a survey designed to more precisely describe their environmental perceptions. He took a series of photos of different grazing situations, including sand dunes, and took them from herd owner to owner, asking them to rank the scenes as to quality of grazing, utility for herd management, and to describe in detail how they would use the landscape depicted. He found that the herders felt that even the most barren appearing dune would with time generate future grazing and, more significantly, that large sand dunes were important to maintaining the flocks in several ways. Since sand dunes are poor conductors of heat, they can be used to help animals regulate their body temperature during periods of temperature extremes—keeping them cooler in summer when visited in the evening and warmer in winter when visited during the day. Sandy terrain is also good for the hooves of the livestock—a critical problem in livestock management since many diseases are transmitted this way. Finally, dunes are used to shelter herds during not infrequent storms: They protect animals from excessive wind or snow (Williams, 1997, 2002). In short, Williams, taking data from one very localized population, drew conclusions of interest to a wide group of scholars concerned with livestock production and grasslands management.

Gerald Creed also discovered something interesting while studying a small village in Bulgaria over a number of years that had eluded scholars who thought only of the "big picture" or events at the national level. It was common thinking among most observers that since collectivization had been imposed by force throughout Eastern Europe after World War II, sometimes by violent means, once the Communist system collapsed, people would welcome the destruction of the "hated" collective farm. The opposite proved true. Over the years of mandatory collective farming, people, such as those in the village of Zamfirovo, learned "to domesticate the revolution" to use Creed's words (see Chapter 7). That is, they transformed an initially alien institution into one that suited their local and very specific needs. They had come to rely on the collective farm for a steady income and job security, as a means of organizing what, in effect, were village commons, and even as a source of illicit gain when, for example, people diverted state-owned produce or supplies to their private ends. Thus, they were resentful when the collective was dismantled by the authorities with as little regard for the villagers as when it had been imposed initially. The significance of this resentment became manifest when throughout Bulgaria (and in some other countries) rural voters helped reinstate Communist or socialist politicians in free elections (Creed, 1998).

## Studies in the Field

Regardless of theoretical orientation, cultural anthropology relies heavily on the firsthand observation of human behaviors as a means of gathering data and testing hypotheses generated by theories. Most theoretical approaches are not developed in quiet corners of university libraries or modified through laboratory experiments. They evolve through continual testing among the peoples whose ways of life they seek to explain.

Anthropologists gather data in the field partly through firsthand observation and reporting, living among the members of a group in an effort to understand their customary ways of thinking and behaving. They ask people questions and carefully record their answers. They closely examine the things the people produce: their tools, baskets, sculptures, musical instruments, weapons, jewelry, clothing, houses. Above all, they spend many hours watching the people's daily routines and interactions. From these activities emerge the fine-grained ethnographic descriptions that together constitute an invaluable repository of information about the breadth and variety of human culture. There is more to fieldwork than simple observation, as we shall see, but it is firsthand observation that gives

anthropological reports a distinctive and vibrant quality.

Fieldwork is difficult and requires intense preparation. Today, almost all anthropologists are trained at universities. Graduate programs are designed to give students a thorough grounding in anthropological literature, to make them aware of theoretical disputes and of what is already known about the cultures of a particular area, to enable them to establish a valid sample, and to formulate realistic research questions and organize and interpret the ethnographic data they collect. Just as the development of precision instruments in the natural sciences has allowed scientists to probe previously uncharted areas of nature (the surface of the moon, for example), so improved techniques of field research have enabled anthropologists to explore more systematically the many ways of human life and thus to broaden our understanding of human nature. Methodical observation and interviewing, systematic comparison, and sampling are the primary research tools of the anthropologist today.

But the process of observation is not neat and tidy. From the day the ethnographer arrives in the field to the day he or she departs, the course of research is being shaped by myriad chance encounters—often of a less than benign sort. The would-be researcher may be held up for months getting permission from local officials to visit the area targeted for investigation; lack of all-weather roads may make

*Anthropologist Napoleon Chagnon has studied the Yanomamö of Venezuela for over thirty years. Despite recent controversy, his fieldwork remains among the most detailed and important in anthropology.*
(Irven DeVore/Anthro-Photo)

## Box 1.2

# Fieldwork in Northern Kenya

I INITIALLY WANTED TO STUDY ISO-lated agropastoralist groups along the Omo River in southwestern Ethiopia, and in 1974, with funds from the University of London and the Smithsonian Institution, I flew to Nairobi intending to reach Lake Turkana and the Omo River from the Kenyan side. Driving an old BSA 250-cc motorcycle, I headed north around Mt. Kenya through the deserts of Marsabit District toward Ethiopia. When I reached the small town of Marsabit, however, I learned there had been a *coup d'état* against Haile Selassie in Ethiopia and that the border was now closed.

I sat in a dusty bar in Marsabit town wondering what to do. Marsabit town lies on top of a broad volcanic mountain 1,500 meters high, and although situated smack in the center of a hot lowland desert, is covered in deep tropical forest, home to some of Kenya's largest elephants, protected in a forest reserve. A boy about 14 years old approached and asked if I would like to see the elephants. When I told him "Not today," he thought a minute and asked, "Would you like to come to my village and see traditional African dances?" This was more to my anthropological liking, and I readily agreed.

We drove on my motorcycle 17 kilometers south of Marsabit town on the main road, confronted once by an elephant on a bridge (my fearless guide yelling, "Speed up, he has to back up before he can charge us!"). Miraculously, we arrived in his village of Karare, a large Ariaal community consisting of four large circles of houses surrounding cattle enclosures. I could see there was indeed dancing going on, but this was not a performance for tourists. Warriors with long, red-dyed, braided hair, twirling spears, were dancing in a tight circle, wearing grim expressions and singing deeply. . . . It seems that the age-set leader (*launon*) for Lorokushu clan, a man chosen for his leadership and

*Elliot Fratkin and friend during fieldwork in Kenya.*

(Elliot Fratkin)

skills of negotiation, had been killed trying to break up a fight between two Ariaal warriors. His death was very unpropitious for the clan as a whole, and all Lorokushu warriors

had to repeat the *mugit* (ceremony) and replace the dead *launon*.

I was offered a house to stay in that night, a small oval dome of sisal mats and leather skins tied over a wooden frame. Inside, the house was divided with the cooking hearth and visitors' area near the door, and a sleeping area of leather cow skins in the back half. The house was old, its sisal roof mats black and shiny from the fireplace smoke. I was enthralled by the experience, listening to the quiet voices and ruminating cattle outside, looking at the beaded milk containers and leather storage bags tied to the wall frame, peacefully drifting asleep. Suddenly, I woke up as I felt small stings on my legs and back. They were flea bites, and they were everywhere—on my legs, in my hair, under my arms. And there was nothing I could do about it. I pulled a sheet over my head and fell into a fitful sleep, my fantasies of living in a Rousseauian paradise slipping into nightmares about snakes, scorpions, and spiders.

The next morning I was awakened by the "Samburu alarm clock"—flies buzzing around my head and landing on my face, nose, and ears. I got up quickly and walked outside. It was very misty, one could hardly see to the next house. But I could hear metal cow bells ringing and the sound of women's voices gently singing to their cattle as they milked them.

it impossible to visit a site during a critical period; local conflicts or strife may curtail movement from one community to another. Moreover, the data being collected are constantly affected by the researcher's own social presence. Most ethnographers gain access to a community by associating themselves with a particular family or local grouping. Such an alliance, however tenuous, invariably affects the ethnographer's

relations with others in the community—sometimes favorably, but sometimes negatively. People who are on poor terms with one's hosts tend to be cool or suspicious of the guests.

It is reasonable to ask why so much emphasis is placed on theory, method, and planning for the field when, in the end, things are likely to turn out not at all as one expected. The answer is that command of

Outside one house, two warriors were leaning casually on their long spears. . . . The warriors greeted me, *"Sopa murr'ata!"* ("Greetings, age-mate"). One of them flicked his head and asked me if I wanted to accompany them to water their cattle at the wells in the forest. I was ready to go—I had my walking boots and baggy military pants, my shoulder bag with notebook, pen, and camera. *"Ma'apetin"*—"Let's go!"

We left the village and headed toward the large woods of the Marsabit Forest Reserve. Jogging at first, I petered out after a mile. The warriors could easily have run five miles, but slowed down to wait for me. Soon our path became a winding trail through the mountain woods of tall hardwoods, fig trees, and vines. After some miles we came to *l-chota*, a series of wells with hundreds of cattle and scores of warriors about. Several warriors stopped to shake my hand, while others glared at me with unfriendly faces that told me this was not a good time to take pictures. My companions motioned me to one of the wells, and soon had me working, passing water buckets up from the well in a three-man chain. I enjoyed the rhythm of the work, adding my voice to their singing, to all our delight.

When we finished watering the cattle, my companion flicked a finger on the side of his neck and motioned me to follow him and his two friends. The flick at the neck, I soon realized, meant lunch time, specifically blood tapped from a living cow. We approached a large gray ox (castrated male), and as one warrior held it by the horns, the other tied a long leather cord tightly about the neck, exposing a large jugular vein pulsating on the side of a neck. With a small bow, a short arrow was shot into the vein, popping out immediately as a steady flow of blood poured into a woven bowl. After a liter or so of blood was collected, the warrior released the leather cord and the blood continued its flow back in the animal, which was hardly bleeding at all now. My companion took a swig from the bowl, and smiling in delight, passed it to me. Deciding this would not kill me (I was in strong denial of germ theory at the time), I slowly sipped the frothy blood, surprised at its warmth and salty sweet taste. I had little time to savor the moment. Running quickly into the bushes, I knew I could expect a bout of diarrhea every time I drank blood.

Despite, or perhaps because of, these experiences, I decided I wanted to live and study with these people. For eighteen months, I lived in Lewogoso community (an Ariaal clan living in the lowlands), raising a small herd of goats, sheep and two cows, interviewing people about ritual life, plant medicines, and traditional knowledge of livestock production, enjoying the seclusion and isolation far from my own country. I returned in 1985 accompanied by my wife Marty Nathan and 6-year-old daughter Leah. Other anthropologists have remarked on the advantages (and disadvantages) of having one's family along, and these applied to us. My status as a married elder was now secure, allowing me access to the men's shade tree for extensive conversations about livestock and the complexities of Ariaal life. Moreover, the experiences and interactions of Marty and Leah gave me insights into the society that I did not have before. Marty, as a physician and volunteer with the Kenya Expanded Program for Immunizations, spent much of her time in mission clinics in 1985 and earned her own reputation as a friend and healer among Ariaal.

A seasoned fieldworker, I was now able to obtain information in a few days that previously had taken months to figure out, as I knew what I was looking for and I had prepared questionnaires and interview designs. . . . I continue to revisit Lewogoso and to see my friends of twenty years. Sadly, Lekati Leaduma (my adopted father) died in 1987, but I have remained close to his son (my brother Kanikis), who is quickly becoming the new *laibon* of the Ariaal. In 1995, I provided a wedding ox so Kanikis could marry, something that gave me great satisfaction. Lugi Lengesen has remained my closest friend, and now in his sixties is thinking of settling down on a farm on Marsabit Mountain, although he never stays for long when he visits his third wife, who lives at Kitaruni settlement. I have never regretted my decision to live with and study the Ariaal. I have built a lifetime of friendships and experiences in Africa, which has made cultural anthropology very rewarding to me on a deep and personal level (Fratkin, 1998).

theory or theories enables researchers to be flexible and to ask significant questions no matter what conditions they encounter in the field. The researcher who has a firm theoretical focus can tailor work successfully to accommodate ever-changing circumstances in the field. Fieldwork usually must be preceded not only by theoretical grounding but by training in the language and history of the area chosen and in specialized techniques of sampling, computation, and analysis of data.

Today, more and more field research is problem oriented. That is, the anthropologist focuses on one or more important theoretical issues. Nevertheless, anthropologists investigate so wide a range of problems that they must command an equally wide range of information-gathering techniques. One technique that is basic to almost every piece of field research is participant observation, used in conjunction with interviewing and the systematic collection of economic, demographic, and material culture data.

*Participant Observation.* The method most widely used by anthropologists to collect information in the field is **participant observation,** which begins the moment an anthropologist enters the field and continues during the entire time of residence. In practice, "participation" can range from commuting to the village or neighborhood from a home nearby to almost total immersion in community life. In general, participant observers involve themselves in the cultures they study. Malinowski, a pioneer in this approach, explains why it is essential for anthropologists to participate in the activities of the societies they investigate:

> Soon after I had established myself in [Omarakana, Trobriand Islands], I began to take part, in a way, in the village life, to look forward to the important or festive events, to take personal interest in the gossip and the developments of the village occurrences; to wake up every morning to a day presenting itself to me more or less as it does to the native. . . . As I went on my morning walk through the village, I could see intimate details of family life, of toilet, cooking, taking of meals; I could see the arrangements for the day's work, people starting on their errands, or groups of men and women busy at some manufacturing tasks. Quarrels, jokes, family scenes, events usually trivial, sometimes dramatic but always significant, formed the atmosphere of my daily life, as well as of theirs. . . . Also, over and over again, I committed breaches of etiquette, which the natives, familiar with me, were not slow in pointing out. I had to learn how to behave, and to a certain extent, I acquired "the feeling" for native good and bad manners. With this, and with the capacity of enjoying their company and sharing some of their games and amusements, I began to feel that I was indeed in touch with the natives, and this is certainly the preliminary condition for being able to carry on successful field work. (Malinowski, 1922/1961, pp. 7–8)

Participant observation, then, helps anthropologists to see cultures from the inside, to see people behaving informally and spontaneously. Furthermore, it forces fieldworkers to learn how to behave according to indigenous rules.

Official documents (statistical and historical records) can provide valuable information. Burton Pasternak (1993), working with historical documents and government census materials, was able to document precisely the migration and settlement of Chinese farmers in Taiwan over a century ago. The statistical and historical data, together with genealogical data gathered in interviews with living residents in the villages studied, made it possible for him to reconstruct family histories and to calculate such demographic variables as family size and rates of mortality, fertility, and longevity.

*Surviving in the Field.* Although anthropologists arrive in the field armed with an impressive array of research techniques, they usually find their new world full of surprises from the moment they set foot in it. One of the most basic difficulties is language. Although a knowledge of the native language greatly enhances the quantity and quality of data that can be gathered, it is not always possible for an anthropologist to learn that language in advance. Or there may be important dialect differences between the language learned and that spoken in the community ultimately chosen as the research site.

The first month or so in the field is usually spent making practical arrangements. Fieldworkers have to find a place to live and a way to obtain food and supplies. Generally, anthropologists either rent a house in the community they are studying or live with a family. Some live in a tent or trailer, in a house that local people build for them, or in a school. Others commute from a nearby town. If the researchers intend to live in a remote village, they will have to purchase in advance many of the supplies they will use.

Food can also be a problem for anthropologists who work in remote towns and villages. Eating and drinking with local people may be an excellent way to establish rapport, but it can also present difficulties. Napoleon Chagnon did most of his own cooking but found it an ordeal:

> It is appalling how complicated it can be to make oatmeal in the jungle. First, I had to make two trips to the river to haul the water. Next, I had to prime my kerosene stove with alcohol and get it burning. . . . Or, I would turn the kerosene on, hoping that the element was still hot enough to vaporize the fuel, and start a small fire in my palm-thatched hut. . . . Then I had to boil the oatmeal and pick the bugs out of it. . . . Eating three meals a day was out of the question. (Chagnon, 1983, pp. 12–13)

Sometimes the sex of the anthropologist poses special problems in the field. As men and women often move in very different social circles, a male anthropologist may find it difficult to interview women, collect their personal life histories, or closely observe the portion of their social lives from which men are excluded. Conversely, women fieldworkers may have difficulty moving in male social circles or be constrained by the limits of propriety that the society imposes on female behavior. In the end, such constraints can usually be overcome, though at times some ingenuity may be called for, as shown in Box 1.1, Becoming Invisible.

Fieldwork has always had an element of physical danger, and anthropologists are paying more attention to protecting themselves and their students from hazards of infectious disease, safety within communities as well as on the road, and threats of violence, including robbery and assault. Following the death of her and Richard Lee's son in a Botswana road accident, Nancy Howell (1990) wrote *Surviving Fieldwork* for the American Anthropological Association, describing risks and incidence of problems in the field ranging from poor sanitation to mental illness. Fieldwork can be dangerous, but so can driving a car in Los Angeles, and anthropologists forewarned and knowledgeable can avoid mistakes and unnecessary risks.

## Objectivity and Science in the Study of Behavior

Some students of human behavior argue that, as scientists, they have an obligation to strive for the objectivity generally associated with the sciences. This position is based on the belief that it is possible to suspend one's cultural and theoretical biases in the field and to observe and report, with detachment, what one sees. A researcher's cultural background, academic training, and personality obviously have the potential to influence both what is perceived and what is reported. Some therefore argue that it is impossible to "go backstage," or as Vincent Crapanzano puts it, "We were told not to ask leading questions; as if there were such a thing as a non-leading question" (quoted in Berreby, 1995, p. 46). By pretending to be objective, it is argued, anthropologists are deceiving themselves. Berreby describes Clifford Geertz as having done much to turn anthropology away from thinking of itself as an "objective science" (pp. 44–47). A 2002 National Science Foundation poll found that around 70% of Americans do not understand even the rudiments of the scientific process.

The anti-scientific perspective is seemingly well-entrenched in popular culture as well. In *The Demon-Haunted World: Science as a Candle in the Dark* (1996), the late Carl Sagan, astronomer and popular science writer, describes an anti-scientific attitude prevalent in many areas of contemporary American life, including college campuses. Sagan traces this distrust of science and scientific thinking in part to a fear of technology run amok (accidents at nuclear facilities such as Chernobyl or Three Mile Island), as well as to an abhorrence of wasteful consumerism and technocratic bureaucracy. But he warns that such an "anti-science" framework denies a reality that can be observed and validated, and leaves people susceptible to superstitious and metaphysical explanations and open to individuals willing to exploit this susceptibility. Sagan points to the fact that one third of Americans believe they have made contact with the dead, one quarter believe in reincarnation, and a not insignificant number believe they were abducted by aliens from UFOs (Sagan, 1996, p. 203), even though none of these phenomena have been scientifically observed or documented. He believed that life outside

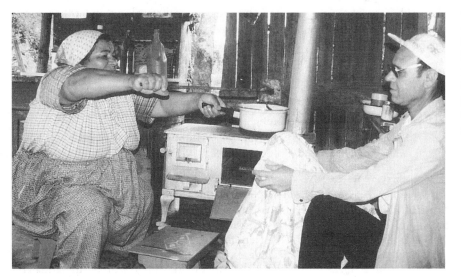

*A well-educated Bulgarian schoolteacher turns to a traditional method of healing (exorcism) to treat his son whom he fears has suffered from the effects of the "evil eye."*
(Daniel Bates)

our planet is indeed possible if not probable, but he laid no claims that contact with such life had ever occurred. Sagan was concerned that Americans are increasingly ready to abandon rational thought and discovery for irrational beliefs and fantasy, which he felt leaves us vulnerable to manipulation by charlatans and dictators.

There are many complex issues involved in thinking of anthropology as science, and they all turn on two interrelated questions. What is science? Can anthropology contribute to it? While usually one contrasts art and science, Steven Reyna, in a provocative critique of contemporary efforts to move anthropology away from its scientific tradition, points out their similarities: "Art, among other things, is a creative, imaginative representation of experience. Science is an art. Like other art forms it is a manner of representing experience. The experience it represents is reality" (Reyna, 1994, p. 556).

This is very similar to the position of E. O. Wilson who argues that it is possible (albeit sometimes difficult) to correct for much of what might be called the "misalignment" of our sometimes emotion-laden perceptions and the real world (1998, p. 60–61). The brain evolved, after all, to survive in the real world and only incidentally to understand it. Thus, it is understandable that sensory perceptions may be flawed, even hugely biased, but if one grants that there is a reality to be described, it can be verified to a tolerably high standard.

To understand how reality is constituted, basic science is explanation; to determine how well we are explaining reality, science is validation. Science is not a quest for absolute truths or the collection of concrete facts. If it were, then anthropologists would be justified in not engaging in the endeavor; in fact, this form of "science" would have little utility for anyone. Science is simply a quest for information about the world.

Anthropology can and does contribute to this quest, even if the researcher is faced with the challenges of cultural diversity. If there are doubts, one only has to look at the state of knowledge about human behavior today in comparison to fifty years ago, when anthropology in Europe and America moved into the post–World War II era. The methods of anthropology—indeed, the methods of science in general—are strikingly similar to processes in nature where individuals (and the populations of which they are a part) respond to experience. Survival, cultural and otherwise, depends on successful responses to experience. Science is not concerned with what is universally true, but with what is approximately true—that is, explanations that are useful until new ones offer improvements. The methods of science are diverse, but all rely on some form of validation—the encounter of explanation and experience. "If one rejects science, one rejects the art of explaining, and validating the explanation, of the experience of reality" (Reyna, 1994, p. 557).

Perhaps what is called for is a matter less of objectivity than of rigor. By using the most rigorous methods possible to evaluate their conclusions, anthropologists guarantee, if not absolute objectivity, at least comparability in the evaluation of theories and ideas. By any criteria, anthropology has contributed a great deal to the understanding of human behavior, origins, language, and cultural history. By any measure, anthropological scholarship meets the test of experience.

The unifying belief among anthropologists who subscribe to the natural science approach is that there are important regularities in human behavior across cultures, as well as diversity, and that these can be accounted for through empirical methods. **Empiricism** refers to the direct experiencing of the reality being described or explained. Obviously, there are limits to direct experience, but direct observation and measurement, implicit in the empirical approach, are central to the idea of anthropology and other social sciences as scientific endeavors (see also Barth, 1994, p. 76; Brown, 1991; Rappaport, 1993).

## Summary

Though anthropologists tend to specialize, they maintain a holistic approach: They assume that any given aspect of human life is to be studied with an eye to its relation to other aspects of human life. Of vital importance to the holistic perspective is cultural relativism, or the ability to view the beliefs and customs of other peoples within the context of their culture rather than one's own. Although everyone is somewhat ethnocentric, judging the customs of other societies by the standards of his or her own, anthropology underscores the need to view other cultures with objectivity and empathy.

A scientific theory is a statement that postulates ordered relationships among natural phenomena. Theory provides a framework for research, directing researchers to certain kinds of questions and leading them to expect certain results, against which they can check the results actually obtained. The many theories that cultural anthropologists have put forth revolve around basic questions: Why do societies differ? How do societies differ? What is the relationship between the individual and society?

Applying the concept of culture, anthropologists make certain assumptions about the behavior, beliefs, and experiences of individuals as members of society: that the human species learns rules of behavior and is dependent on learning for survival; that learned rules of behavior and thinking supply meaning to events and the behavior of others, although each society has its own interpretations; that knowledge is transmitted via language and is to a large degree created out of symbols.

Evolution explains the development of all species as the outcome of adaptation to environmental circumstances through the process of natural selection.

All people are born with certain biological traits that account in part for broad similarities in human behavior. Biology also affects us on an individual level by setting limits—through our health, stamina, and body build, for instance—that cannot be overcome. In addition, biological factors affect certain kinds of individual behavior.

Gender refers to the behaviors associated with the biologically defined sexes, and these behaviors vary from culture to culture. There are three interrelated areas that are of primary concern in analyzing gender: gender socialization, gender and work, and gender and power. Gender socialization begins shortly after birth and generates systematic inequalities between the sexes as boys and girls learn gender-specific notions of appropriate behavior. Second, the organization of work in society is critical for understanding gender. Labor is often valued differently for men and for women, with the work done by women often seen as private or domestic (rather than productive) and hence undervalued. Further, even restricting access to nonproductive sectors such as religious ritual and ceremonial leadership differentiates between the sexes. Third, closely related to socialization and the organization of the work force is access to the political process. Even family life can be seen as political, in that individuals are contending for resources. Moreover, social control operates quite differently on men and women in many instances.

Through social learning, members of a society develop their own ways of behaving or perceiving, which differ from the ways of other societies. Social learning occurs primarily through socialization, the process by which the social group and the family, through formal training and unconscious modeling, pass on skills, knowledge, values, attitudes, and behavior to the next generation. Channels of socialization include childrearing, education, gender- and age-role learning, and rites of passage.

Role learning—adapting to a set of behavioral expectations appropriate to one's position—is an important part of education. While roles channel a person in certain prescribed directions, each individual interprets a given role in a somewhat distinctive way. Both gender roles and age roles are affected by socialization. The form and intensity of the set of distinguishable characteristics associated with each sex—a social construct referred to as gender—vary from society to society.

While all animals apparently communicate through call systems—repertoires of sounds, each of which is produced in response to a specific situation—humans are the only animals that use language. Human language presumably began as a call system. Language differs from animal call systems in that it is open—the number of messages that can be conveyed is infinite. This flexibility is made possible by the arbitrariness of human language (sounds have no fixed meaning) and the fact that it is stimulus-free: An utterance need not be evoked by an immediate situation. The training of apes to use limited sign language has convinced some researchers that their linguistic ability differs from ours only in degree; however, while apes may share with us certain faculties that are necessary for language, it is clear that these faculties have remained relatively undeveloped in their line.

Researchers can only speculate on the origins of language. Cultural evidence suggests a very early date for the first language skills; the physical evidence suggests a later date for the full development of language. It seems likely that the change to language from call systems began about 4 million years ago and proceeded only gradually. It is believed that human language developed through the blending of calls to produce new calls with more complex meanings. This transition is largely responsible for the development of human culture. Language, culture, and the brain evolved together, each stimulating and reinforcing the others.

Languages vary in subtle and complex ways. Human brains may be equipped with a universal program enabling infants to learn the patterns of drastically different languages very rapidly.

This book takes the position that culture and social behavior in general can be studied scientifically. Cultural anthropologists depend heavily on fieldwork, the firsthand observation of people, as their primary means of gathering data and testing hypotheses generated by theories. Most fieldwork today is problem oriented: Scholars study aspects of a given society to test theoretical assumptions. At times, fieldwork can be quite arduous—even dangerous. It is almost always time-consuming—researchers can spend a year or longer in the field. Just as in the natural sciences, great care must be paid to sampling techniques and methodical observation. Common techniques include participant observation and formal and informal interview procedures. Very often, the researchers will conduct some form of census and collect basic demographic and economic data, as well as an inventory of material culture—the technology available to the population studied. Obviously, the selection of a population for study is a major area of concern because it determines the sorts of generalizations the researcher may safely make.

## Key Terms

| | |
|---|---|
| call systems | holism |
| cultural adaptation | *Homo sapiens* |
| cultural relativism | hypothesis |
| culture | language |
| empiricism | natural selection |
| enculturation | participant observation |
| ethnocentrism | scientific theory |
| gender | socialization |

## Suggested Readings

Bernard, H. R. (1994). *Research methods in anthropology* (2nd ed.). Thousand Oaks, CA: Sage. A thorough treatment of qualitative and quantitative approaches in ethnographic research.

Bickerton, D. (1995). *Language and human behavior.* Seattle: University of Washington Press. An important study of the nature of language and its relation to human evolution, behavior, and consciousness.

Chauvet, J-M., Deschamps, E. B., and Hillaire, C. (1996). *Dawn of cave art: The Chauvet cave.* New York: Harry Abrams. An excellent and readable description of the site of perhaps the most important example of early cave art in Europe.

Dawkins, R. (1995). *River out of Eden: A Darwinian view of life.* New York: Basic Books. A short book by a famous British biologist presents contemporary thinking in evolutionary theory in a cogent and readable fashion. He demonstrates how complex design, such as vision, arise through evolutionary processes. It is also a good introduction to how science progresses and how scientists work.

Dillehay, T. D. (2000). *The settlement of the Americas. A new prehistory.* New York: Basic Books. A recent review of the ever-controversial settlement of the Americas by a scholar who has spent many years excavating the arguably pre-Clovis site of Monte Verde in Chile.

Fagan, B. (2004). *Ancient lives: An introduction to archaeology and prehistory* (2nd ed.). Upper Saddle River, NJ: Prentice Hall. A good introduction to archaeology and prehistory.

Fox, R. (1997). *Conjecture and confrontations: Science, evolution, social concern.* New Brunswick, NJ: Transaction Books. A lively exploration of how biosocial anthropology deals with contemporary social and ethical issues.

Gilmore, D. D. (1990). *Manhood in the making: Cultural concepts of masculinity.* New Haven, CT: Yale University Press. Addresses the question of what it means to be a man in different cultures around the world. The author treats manhood as a status achieved through culturally approved stressful, competitive tests.

Lewis-Williams, D. (2002). *The mind in the cave.* London: Thames and Hudson. This well-written book explores the thinking that may have been behind remarkable cave art images that are strikingly similar in many parts of the world.

Pasternak, B., Ember, C., & Ember, M. (1997). *Sex, gender, and kinship: A cross-cultural perspective.* Upper Saddle River, NJ: Prentice Hall. A particularly interesting and readable review of sexuality, gender, marriage, and kinship around the world. It explores such topics as the nature of human sexuality, courtship, the incest taboo, marriage patterns, divorce, and remarriage with reference to competing theories that attempt to explain their occurrence around the world.

Pinker, S. (1999). *Words and rules: The ingredients of language.* New York: Basic Books. This book by one of the foremost American linguists deals with how we learn to speak, why languages change, and what determines how they change. Pinker also has some fascinating ideas about why irregular verbs persist in every language.

Podolefsky, A., & Brown, P. J. (Eds.). (2003). *Applying anthropology* (2nd ed.). Mountain View, CA: Mayfield Press. An introductory reader that emphasizes the practical application of research methods in biological anthropology, archaeology, anthropological linguistics, and cultural anthropology. The articles are timely and interesting; they offer a view of anthropology not available in any other reader. A number of these articles are cited throughout this text.

Wilson, E. O. (1998). *Consilience: The unity of knowledge.* New York: Knopf. A well-known biologist argues that scientific progress will depend on developing a coherent conception encompassing all of the sciences, including the social sciences. The book, certain to be controversial, directly addresses the prevailing reluctance of social scientists to reconcile their perspectives with those well-established in the natural sciences.

Welsch, R. L., & Endicott, K. M. (2003). *Taking sides: Clashing views on controversial issues in cultural anthropology.* New York: McGraw-Hill. This book explores major controversial issues in contemporary anthropology using the writings of the protagonists.

# Chapter 2

# Evolution, Ecology, and Politics

Human ecology is the theoretical orientation that emphasizes the problem-solving significance of culture and behavior, from procurement systems to kinship systems to political and religious life. This chapter explores the rationale for this perspective in greater detail, building on the discussion of evolution in the first chapter. The chapter discusses what is meant by adaptation, the role of variation and decision making in adaptation, and finally, it places evolutionary processes affecting humans in an ecological context.

## The Human Evolutionary Legacy

It is easy to overlook the fact that **evolution** is an ongoing process. Our species, like all others, is continually being shaped by evolutionary forces. While *natural selection* is the major force acting on the genetic composition of populations, any force that causes the genetic composition of a population to change is an evolutionary force. For example, spontaneous change or mutation adds novel genetic material, genetic drift alters the composition of a daughter population randomly (for example, because

of migration and colonization by individuals carrying distinctive traits), and interbreeding, or gene flow that transfers genetic information among populations, is also a major source of both change and unity in human populations. There is almost complete scientific agreement that taxonomically speaking (that is, for purposes of classification) our contemporary species, *Homo sapiens sapiens,* is a quite recent product of evolutionary processes, certainly not much more than 200,000 years old and more likely closer to 100,000. It is also clear that humans and presumably ancestral populations are highly mobile and continually interbreed with neighboring populations. Consequently, we are relatively homogeneous in terms of genetic material in spite of internal variation within every population. In fact, most anthropologists feel it is inappropriate, or at best problematic, to speak of significantly different biological races, as individual differences within large populations are as great as or greater than differences among geographically defined populations.[1]

[1]See Moses, 1997; also see the American Anthropological Association's statement on race on the AAA Web site: http://www.ameranthassn.org/ombmedia.htm.

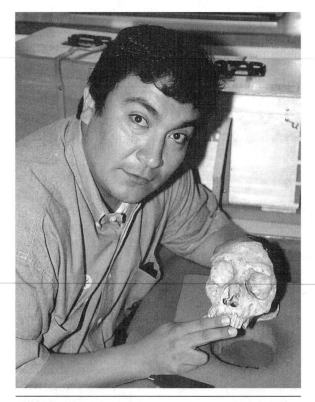

*Paleontologist Sam Marquez with the skull bones of one of the most important archaic* Homo sapiens, *popularly known as "Broken Hill" finds, dating to 300,000 year ago and found in Zambia. Dr. Marquez studied this and other pre-Neanderthal remains in the London Museum.*

(Dr. Sam Marquez)

In 1988, Rebecca Cann, a biological anthropologist, published her work on new techniques of studying the origins, unity, and diversity of our species that do not rely on the examination of fossils or bones, but rather on fetal cell tissues. Based on their analysis of mitochondrial DNA collected from the placentas of babies born throughout Asia, Africa, Europe, and from Native Americans, she and her colleagues, Allen Wilson and Mark Stoneking, suggest that all present-day *Homo sapiens* shared a female ancestor who lived in Africa about 188,000 years ago (Cann, 1988, pp. 127–143).

Mitochondria are important DNA-bearing units lying outside a cell's nucleus, which provide the cell with energy and regulate metabolism. The significance of mitochondrial DNA lies in the fact that it is passed unchanged each generation from mother to daughter and thus is unlike the DNA within the cell's nucleus, which undergoes change and replacement during sexual reproduction. Noting that mitochondrial DNA changes slowly and only by

mutation, the researchers created a "molecular clock" that moved, they estimated, at a rate of change of 1% every million years. Using this yardstick, they concluded that all *Homo sapiens* shared a very recent common African ancestor and that present populations dispersed through migration out of Africa approximately 200,000 years ago. The key to this claim lies in the fact that mitochondrial DNA in African populations displays much more mutation-induced variability, implying that this population must have been antecedent or ancestral to all other human populations.

However, human origins have long been and continue to be the subject of controversy. The "African Eve" hypothesis, as it is often termed, implies that many earlier hominids, such as the Neanderthals widespread in Europe, North Africa, and the Middle East, did not directly contribute to our family line. Also, it would imply that the species *Homo erectus,* clearly ancestral to our species, became extinct everywhere except in Africa, where that branch alone evolved into *Homo sapiens.* What is known? There is little doubt that *Homo erectus* originated in Africa at approximately 1.0 to 1.5 million years ago, evolving from *Homo habilis,* which had itself replaced earlier *Australopithecus* approximately 2.5 million years ago. While australopithecines flourished from about 3.5 million years until their replacement by *Homo erectus,* they do not seem to have spread everywhere in the Old World. The most famous australopithecine fossil is "Lucy," the nickname given a nearly complete female found by Don Johanson and his associates in Ethiopia in 1974, technically classified as *Australopithecus afarensis* and dated to about 3.5 million years ago. Lucy had upright posture and used bipedal locomotion. *Homo habilis,* successor to the australopithecines, is associated with multipurpose tools constructed by splitting suitable rocks to achieve a sharp edge. *Homo erectus,* the generally agreed successor to *Homo habilis,* possessed a significantly larger cranial capacity, some 1,000 cc, a far larger stature, and developed a much more elaborate stone tool repertoire, which, together with the use of fire, enabled them to colonize much of the Old World. While the idea of our ultimate African origins is very well established, until quite recently it remained unclear whether our modern species evolved only there and subsequently spread, or whether our species emerged more or less separately in different parts of the Old World, coexisting and probably interbreeding in places with our close relatives, the Neanderthals (see Stringer & Brauer, 1994; Tattersall, 2000; Wolpoff & Caspari, 1997, for opposing interpretations).

The latter position, argued most forcibly by Milford Wolpoff, is that *Homo sapiens* replaced *Homo erectus* gradually over a 500,000- to 100,000-year period throughout its range all over the Old World. This hypothesis is called "multiregional origins" and is based on the proposition that gene flow (interbreeding) as well as natural selection slowly transformed all regional populations of *Homo erectus* into *Homo sapiens* and that European and Middle Eastern Neanderthals are simply a "peripheral or extreme population within our species."

On the other hand, research by Sarah Tishkoff, Ian Tattersall, and others, relying on DNA information as well as different interpretations of the fossil record, have found renewed support for the out-of-Africa hypothesis (Tattersall 1997, 2000).

A very recent discovery, found in 1997 but not published until 2003, seems to conclusively point to the out-of-Africa origin of *Homo sapiens*. Skulls found at Herto, Ethiopia, are dated to 154,000 to 160,000 years ago, and furnish quite clear proof that anatomically modern humans evolved in Africa and spread out to colonize the entire world (Clark et al., 2003; Gibbons, 2003; White et al., 2003). These skulls predate any similar finds by about 50,000 years and confirm the DNA evidence described earlier. While anatomically identical to modern *Homo sapiens,* their culture as indicated by their tools would not resemble that of any extant population.

It must be kept in mind those features that we often use to describe different peoples of the world—skin color, eye color and shape, stature, and hair—are all the products of very recent and minor adaptations—features that are continually changing in every human population. A closely related issue is the question of how many of our antecedent hominids lived at any given time. Today, of course, there is only one species of hominids, ourselves, but even as recently as 40,000 years ago, Neanderthals are likely to have coexisted, albeit for a relatively brief period, with *Homo sapiens* or modern humans (Tattersall, 2000).

Neanderthals became extinct some 30,000 years ago, but from about 35,000 years ago, another species was present in Europe—the Cro-Magnons, who were much more like modern humans than the short, broad-bodied Neanderthals. In November 1998, at the base of a limestone cliff in the Lapedo Valley in Portugal, the fossilized remains of a boy aged between four and five were discovered (Duarte et al., 1999; Zilhão, 2000). Dated at about 27,000 years old, he lived a few thousand years after Neanderthals were thought to have become extinct and so was presumed to be a modern human. However, further studies have revealed an apparent mosaic of Neanderthal and modern human features: He has a modern chin but the shorter body proportions of a Neanderthal. Another skeleton of a four-year-old child found in Lagar Velho, Portugal, has a skull and teeth like those of modern humans, but his arms and legs are more like a Neanderthal. Some paleoanthropologists believe this skeleton is a hybrid and evidence of interbreeding between Neanderthals and early humans.

For much of our history, however, "we were not alone" in the sense that more than one distinct hominid species abounded before being replaced. The major differences we see between human beings are the products of behavioral or cultural adaptation. As Lewis Binford (1989) writes, "Our species had arrived—not as a result of gradual, progressive processes but explosively in a relatively short period of time. Many of us currently speculate that this was the result of the invention of language, our peculiar mode of symbolic communication that makes possible our mode of reasoning and in turn our behavioral flexibility" (p. 30).

Humans are bound to the rest of nature by evolutionary history—that is, by descent from common ancestors. Our species is kin to every other living thing on earth—not just in a metaphorical or sentimental sense but in a strict biological sense, as two cousins are related by virtue of having the same grandparents. Of course, we are related more closely to some species than to others. Chimpanzees are much closer kin to us than are monkeys, not to mention nonprimates. Varying degrees of kinship are reflected in varying degrees of anatomical and behavioral similarity. Ultimately, however, all living things, ourselves included, are descended from the same forebears: minute organisms that lived 4 or 5 billion years ago in a world we would not recognize.

How, from such beginnings, did we and all the other species of the earth come to be what we are? The answer to this question did not become clear until the early twentieth century. In the eighteenth and early nineteenth centuries, some scientists recognized that species could change over time as organisms adapted to their environments. But they could not visualize how or why such changes occurred. Indeed, most of them did not believe that such changes could actually create new species. Natural processes might produce new "races," or strains within a species, but only God could create a new species. It was not until 1859, when Charles Darwin (1809–1882) published his treatise, *On the Origin of Species by Means of Natural Selection,* that the major mechanism of evolution was finally described in a way that accounted both for change within species and for the emergence of new species without out divine intervention.

## Darwin: Evolution by Natural Selection

Darwin was convinced that new species arose not through acts of divine intervention but rather through natural selection, a blind and mechanical process. He understood that all species of plants and animals tend to produce more offspring than the environment can support and that this results in intense competition for living space, resources, and mates. Only a favored few survive long enough to reproduce. Darwin noted also that individual members of a species differ from one another physically. In a given population of animals, for example, some may have somewhat thicker fur or longer limbs than others, or they may vary slightly in protective coloration, visual acuity, or even social skills. These variations are said to be adaptive if they improve the animal's chances of survival and thereby enhance its chances of producing offspring that survive to reproduce themselves. Needless to say, this process depends on the nature of the demands placed on the organism by its environment and by the changes that environment is undergoing. (Thick fur, for example, could mean a longer life in an increasingly cold environment, whereas it might be a handicap in an increasingly warm one.)

Even features that one might assume would be useful, such as increased intelligence or physical stamina, might in fact prove too costly to the bearer if the payoff is not seen in reproductive success. We take our relatively great intelligence for granted as a "good thing," but our female ancestors paid a heavy price in childbirth mortality for our large crania—clearly, increased brain size must have conferred considerable net advantage to have become established as a distinctive trait. Individuals whose peculiarities give them a competitive edge in their particular environment produce more offspring, and those offspring inherit their parents' peculiarities, so they in turn survive longer and produce more offspring. Thus, with each generation, the better adapted members of a population increase in number at the expense of less well-adapted individuals. In the process, the species as a whole changes.

But an important warning is called for here. "Better adapted" is always a conditional or relative term with respect to the immediate **environment** because no one can predict what the future environment will be. For purposes of thinking about evolution, the environment is not merely the obvious constraints of predators, food, and shelter but consists of every factor that impinges on the life chances of the individual. In this sense, it is sometimes said to be "*n*-dimensional" or ever changing with a nearly infinite range of possible permutations. It also must be emphasized that the process of biological adaptation is absolutely blind and has no goals, no objectives, and no master plan. Although the process may lead to incredible complexity, such as the brains of those reading these words, and is nicely illustrated in the separate evolution of eyesight on at least eight occasions in unrelated species, the same process shapes the design of a single-cell organism and even the ever-changing flu virus. This is the mechanism that Darwin called "natural selection." It served to explain not only gradual changes within a species but also the appearance of new species. For as different populations of a species adapted to different environments, they eventually diverged until the differences in their anatomy or behavior became so great that they could no longer interbreed. According to Darwin, this process—**adaptation** to environmental circumstances—accounted for the great variety of species observable in nature.

Speciation is not in fact quite as simple a phenomenon as is described here. Many species are "ring species," which means that adjacent populations can interbreed but nonadjacent ones cannot. Also, in studying populations of the past, it is not always possible to determine whether or not separate but fairly similar populations could have interbred. The concept of species, however, remains useful as a standard despite empirical problems in applying it.

## Mendel: The Genetics of Natural Selection

A major weakness of Darwin's theory as originally formulated was that he could not explain how favored characteristics were inherited—and such a systematic explanation was needed. The prevailing belief was that each individual inherited a blend of its parents' characteristics. If true, this implied that advantageous variations would be lost by dilution with less advantageous traits long before natural selection could act on them. It was an obscure Austrian monk named Gregor Mendel (1822–1884) who discovered the hereditary basis of natural selection.

In the garden of his monastery, located in what is now the Czech Republic, Mendel spent years crossbreeding strains of peas and other plants in an effort to find out how traits were transmitted from one generation to the next. He discovered that biological inheritance was not an irreversible blending of parental traits. Rather, individual units of hereditary information, later called **genes,** were passed from parent to offspring as discrete particles according to certain regular patterns. In one individ-

*It is hard to overestimate the contribution of Gregor Mendel to evolutionary thinking, and in important respects, he should be considered the founder of the modern science of genetics.*
(© Bettmann/CORBIS)

ual, a gene's effect might be blended with the effects of other genes or even suppressed altogether. But the gene itself remained unchanged, ready to be passed on to the next generation where it might express itself and thus be available for natural selection.

Mendel's work attracted little attention in the scientific community until both he and Darwin were dead. It was rediscovered in the early 1900s, but its relevance to evolution was not fully appreciated until the next generation. By that time, other apparent discrepancies in Darwin's theory had been resolved, and it was finally accepted that the human species, along with every other species, is a product of evolution. Today, evolutionary theory is at the very heart of all research in the biological and natural sciences. With the recent breakthroughs in modern genetics, population biology, and biochemistry, the utility of the "evolutionary synthesis," as it is now called, is established beyond doubt.

While the richness of contemporary evolutionary theory is beyond the scope of this book, it is worth emphasizing some basic ideas. First, any process or force that changes gene frequencies in a population results in what might be called an "evolutionary event," be it ever so trivial, but most would agree that over the long term it is natural selection that has shaped all life forms on earth, including the neural systems we employ to study them. Natural selection is a cumulative process in that it "builds" on what is already present in the form of genetic information. Thus, complex,

highly intricate structures may emerge from very simple foundations. Since selection acts on existing material and in response to specific environmental pressures, it is always "opportunistic"—that is, adapting whatever is available to the exigencies of the day.

Stephen Jay Gould suggests that there are three basic principles underlying the "creativity" of evolution—"the capacity to originate novel structures and functions" (1996b, pp. 43–45). The first he terms "quirky shifts and latent potential," which refer to the fact that since natural selection cannot anticipate the future, organisms, while they "track" their specific environments, are always forced to make do by modifying what they are already endowed with. Thus, features that once served one purpose are adapted to serve novel ones. For example, our large brains did not evolve in order that we might read or write; this was a fortuitous by-product.

Second, "redundancy," both at the functional level of bodily structures and at the level of DNA, offers natural selection a multiplicity of avenues for responding to particular problems. For example, some "redundant" reptilian jaw bones became parts of the ear in mammals, and the air bladders of fish evolved out of the gill and lung double-breathing systems of earlier fishlike creatures.

Third, "flexibility," both as a by-product of selection for other functions and as a result of selection itself, can be important. We will say more about this later, but put simply, there is an advantage to flexibility in problem solving. Hence, in many species, there is a fairly long period of juvenile learning and "play," which retains flexibility for learning. Human culture is perhaps the most striking example of this principle at work because we not only retain the learning period throughout our life, but also make use of what our ancestors had learned throughout theirs and do not simply rely on their genetic contribution.

## Evolution and Human Culture

While agreeing with the premise that humans have to be understood as products of a long evolutionary heritage, cultural anthropologists have generally emphasized the importance of learning and cultural plasticity relatively unconstrained by biological factors (apart from obvious physiological requirements). In the 1980s, however, this position was challenged by new theoretical perspectives on evolution that subsequently emerged from the natural and social sciences—in particular from the areas of neurobiology, population genetics, ethology, and cognitive psychology. The main contention is that genetically controlled biological processes are responsible for shaping a good deal more of social behavior than has been generally acknowledged. The arguments are often controversial. As they have focused much attention on the relationship between biology and culture, we look at them in some detail.

In the last thirty years, new approaches to the study of social or cultural behavior, called variously human behavioral biology, human ethology, evolutionary ecology, and sociobiology, have been propounded (see Cronk et al., 2000, pp. 3–27, for a review). They share the view, brought most dramatically to popular attention by E. O. Wilson in 1975, that Darwinian models of natural selection apply to aspects of human culture and social behavior as well as to animal social behavior. Researchers found a significant percentage of social behavior in nonhuman animals to be under the direct or indirect influence of genes, and they argued that such behavior has adaptive significance. These types of behavior included mate selection, parenting, social relations among kin, food sharing and procurement, and mutual assistance and reciprocity.

Genetic influence does not imply that a specific gene (or genes) controls a particular behavioral complex (say, the love of a parent for its offspring), nor does it imply determinism, as is sometimes charged. In fact, to infer this determinism and to use it as a basis for moral reasoning are well known as the "naturalistic fallacy" (see Cronk et al., 2000, pp. 11–13). Behavior, where genes are concerned, is best seen as an "open program" whereby a behavioral trait or propensity is shaped by the interactions of genes and environmental influences; thus, genetic material and the environment are inextricably linked. An organism continually tracks environmental changes.

The animal whose mating, defensive, and food procurement behaviors work best within its given environment is the animal most likely to survive, reproduce, and rear its offspring to maturity. Organisms have a genetically based propensity to respond to various environmental circumstances in ways that are appropriate—that is, in ways that promote or facilitate individual reproductive success. Some aspects of this approach are well established and not subject to controversy. Certainly, genetically conditioned aspects of animal social behavior are the result of and continually influenced by the forces of natural selection. Much social behavior involves cooperation among close kin (who share much genetic material), as this approach would predict. The genes that control or influence behaviors that contribute to reproductive success are preferentially transmitted through generations, whereas genes that facilitate less adaptive behavior gradually disappear. So well-established is this basic premise that virtually

*Social prestige, wealth, and reproduction can be closely related in traditional societies: Among the Türkmen, wealthy men have numerous children. Here a well-off rural family sponsors a feast with wrestling competitions to celebrate a son's circumcision ceremony.*

(Daniel Bates)

all behavioral research with primates and other social species takes it as a given.

Should this line of reasoning apply also to humans? A variety of studies point to the value of the evolutionary model for an understanding of broad patterns of human behavior: the importance of kinship and family and male–female reproductive strategies. The usual argument for exempting the human species from this line of reasoning is that once humans developed culture (and the behavioral flexibility that accompanies it), they parted ways with the other animals. Our social behavior has certainly come to be based primarily on learning, and our ability to learn can produce behavioral changes much more rapidly than natural selection can via specific genetic codes. Our behavioral repertoire has been passed down to us through our culture rather than through our genes. The behaviors that have survived have been of value less to individuals than to groups, for culture is, in this view, the property of groups.

Even granting these points, those who employ the evolutionary model argue that while culture is transmitted by learning, what is inherited is a built-in propensity to learn and pass on some cultural rules and beliefs at the expense of others. There is no simple resolution to this disagreement. We cannot doubt that lines of continuity run through the behavior of all animals. This line of reasoning has produced a wealth of useful studies (see Cronk, 1991; Smith & Winterhalder, 1992). For example, William G. Irons proposed that in most societies, what is considered "cultural success" (prestige, power, respect) consists of accomplishing things that make biological success probable (1979, p. 258). He tested this on data from the Yomut Türkmen of Iran and found that the wealthier, culturally more successful half of the population had more surviving children. This has been followed up by numerous studies of other populations with results that seem to confirm his hypothesis. Still, there may be other ways to interpret these findings; ways that do not require the assumption that behavior is generally directed to reproductive success (Cronk, 1991, p. 29).

Whatever the results of particular studies, we cannot doubt that human capacity for culture adds a unique dimension to human social life. Much of what social scientists are interested in explaining is not directly addressed by this model; for example, the nature and persistence of inequality, the role of value systems and ideology in social life, and the evolution of contemporary political systems. Nevertheless, any serious inquiry into human behavior will have to consider the complex ways in which cultural and biological processes intersect (Brown, 1991;

Fox, 1994b). Social scientists in such diverse fields as political science, economics, cognitive science, and psychology increasingly draw on evolutionary theory (see Dennett, 1994, 1996; Pinker, 1994, 1999, for accessible examples).

# Human Ecology

In the social and biological sciences, there are a number of themes and interests that bridge disciplines and bring new, often unsuspected, insights to light. Ecology is one example, and its broad subfield, human ecology, is another. Human ecology links the disciplines of anthropology, biology, geography, demography, and economics, to name just a few. Ecologists, whether concerned with humans or other species, are interested in three very broad questions: How does the environment affect the organism? How does the organism affect its environment? How does an organism affect other organisms in the environments in which it lives? The quest for answers to these questions encompasses almost everything ecologists do. What distinguishes human ecology is not so much the larger questions, but the species that is of prime interest: human beings.

Without ignoring the complexity of the issues involved, it is possible to design strategies for research that are at once empirical and consistent with biological models used in studying behavior in general (Smith & Winterhalder, 1992, pp. 4–5). As the term suggests, human ecology combines two approaches: an interest in those features that are unique (or at least distinctive) attributes of humans and the science of ecology, including evolutionary theory on which it is ultimately based.

Human ecology is also distinctive for theoretical reasons. Ecological models designed to study the interactions of other species are often inadequate to fully accommodate our own. Humans hold an unusual position in nature, and their special, if not unique, attributes pose problems for modeling local interactions. As we have noted earlier, humans rely upon and are dramatically affected by our symbolic interpretations and representations of ourselves and other things. Symbols guide the ways that we interact with the organic and inorganic elements of our environments by making them intelligible in ways specific to our cultures—say, by representing what is good to eat and what is not, who may eat what and when and how. Of major importance to humans is the way that we distinguish group differences symbolically, creating cultural diversity among ourselves.

This cultural diversity is often an important element of our social environment, affecting the ways we interact with one another and other elements of our environments.

Our propensity to exchange goods and services and information among individuals and groups in widely separated territories has the effect of vastly extending the range of our resources and of our impacts upon them. It is rare today for a local population to rely entirely on local resources or to be uninfluenced by adjacent or even distant populations.

Ecology is the study of the interplay between organisms (or the populations to which they belong) and their environment. Implicit in this definition is the connection between ecology and evolutionary theory. As we said earlier, evolution operates primarily through the mechanism of natural selection. That is, certain characteristics become more and more common within a population because, within the context of that population's environment, these characteristics give individuals an edge in the competition for survival and reproduction. So a crucial factor in the evolutionary process is an ecological factor—the fit between organisms and their environment.

## The Nature of Ecological Systems

Humans, along with every other form of life, can be visualized and studied as part of a single **ecosystem**—the cycle of matter and energy that includes all organic things and links them to the inorganic. All organisms depend on energy and on matter. Unlike plants, most of the energy and matter that animals use are not taken directly from the sun and the earth. Rather, these are produced by other organisms and cycled among species through feeding—"eat and be eaten" is the rule for all. Humans breathe the oxygen emitted by plants, and plants take in carbon dioxide emitted by humans and millions of other species of animals. Such relationships, taken together, constitute a vast network of individuals exchanging the energy, nutrients, and chemicals necessary to life; humans and bacteria alike are involved in the same process.

## The Components of the Ecosystem

All the energy that flows through an ecosystem comes ultimately from the sun. Depending on their role in the transfer of that energy, the organisms in an ecosystem fall into three categories: producers, consumers, and decomposers. The *producers* are the green plants that convert solar energy and nutrients in the soil into food. The organisms that rely on plants, directly or indirectly, for food are the *con-sumers*. Some of these consumers (herbivores) live on the plants; others (carnivores) live on other animals. A given ecosystem may support several levels of carnivores. The *decomposers* are bacteria and fungi that break down dead organic matter, converting it to nutrients, which are deposited in the soil to be used by the plants. Thus, each of these three groups is dependent on the others. The decomposers provide nutrients for the producers, the producers for the consumers, and the dead producers and consumers for the decomposers.

Both matter and energy are constantly flowing among these elements. The transfer of matter—the nutrients—is cyclical. Producers, consumers, and decomposers process the same nutrients over and over. Energy flow is noncyclical. Energy is constantly being supplied at one end, by the sun, and constantly expended at the other end in nonreusable forms (primarily heat).

The usefulness of the ecosystem concept is, first, that it can be applied to any environment. Second, and more important, the ecosystem concept allows us to describe humans in dynamic interaction with one another, with other species, and with the physical environment. We can chart and quantify the flow of energy and nutrients and specify the interactions critical for the maintenance of any local population. Thus, the ecosystem concept gives us a way of describing how human populations influence and are influenced by their surroundings (Bates & Lees, 1996).

There is usually considerable order and continuity in natural ecosystems. This is not surprising because, over time, the myriad component species of any ecosystem have come to mutually limit one another as they feed, reproduce, and die. The fact that ecosystems appear to persist through time does not mean, however, that they are static. Although most ecosystems are viewed as being in equilibrium or near equilibrium, in fact relations among the component populations are continually changing. One ecologist, C. S. Holling (1973), employs two concepts to describe continuity and change in ecosystems: resilience and stability.

**Resilience** is a measure of the degree of change a system can undergo while still maintaining its basic elements or relationships. **Stability** is a measure of the speed with which a system returns to equilibrium after absorbing disturbances. Systems with high resilience but low stability may undergo continual and profound changes but still continue to exist as a system; that is, their constituent parts persist together even though they take a very long time to return to their initial states. Systems with high stability but low resilience, on the other hand, may show little change when suffering some disturbances but then collapse suddenly.

## Simplified Model of Major Ecosystem Components

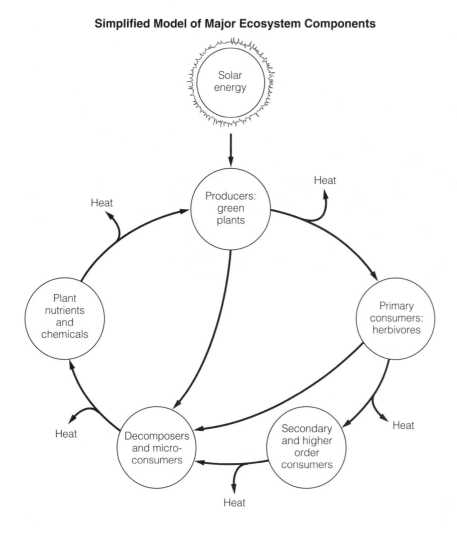

**Figure 2.1.** *Simplified model of a terrestrial ecosystem showing principal components. While not drawn to scale, energy transfers at each junction involve energy loss to the system at roughly the ratio of 10:1. That is, for every kilocalorie of energy stored in the form of a herbivore (say, a cow), ten kilocalories of energy stored in green plants are consumed. Should a carnivore (a human, for instance) consume the herbivore, approximately ten kilocalories would be needed to sustain one kilocalorie of carnivore. Hence, for calories, people tend to rely more on grains than meat in most diets.*

These concepts have considerable relevance for our study of ecosystems. We often assume that, if an ecosystem appears to be in equilibrium or is very stable, it is likely to persist unchanged. As pointed out, this is often not the case. A highly stable system, such as the arctic terrestrial ecosystem, may in fact be very close to the threshold at which it could collapse. The most resilient ecosystems are resilient only to a point—beyond which they collapse. We should bear this in mind when we feel that we are having no serious impact on our ecosystems simply because we see little evidence of immediate changes. For example, the seas around us may appear little changed despite the oil and other wastes dumped into them. Thus, they would seem quite stable. Yet each new addition of oil or waste requires the organisms and microorganisms of the sea to respond in some way, and there are limits to their capacities to continue to do so. The resilience of marine ecosystems is limited, even if the threshold for change is obscured by the appearance of stability.

Anthropologist William Abruzzi (1996) applies ecological models developed from plant and animal research to account for how members of an American religious movement, the Mormons, came to colonize the arid and seemingly inhospitable Little Colorado River Basin in northeastern Arizona. He makes good use of the concepts of stability and resilience as they apply to ecological systems. Although his main focus is on environmental variables such as rainfall, floods, and other hazards to farm life, he shows that settlement was closely linked to the nature of the larger organization—the church. Settlers agreed to come to this then-remote region because of their beliefs, their faith in church leadership, and their fear of persecution; they were able to do so because the church hierarchy made resources available (in particular, what was needed to tide settlements over during droughts or other disasters). The settlers were farmers who, in the late nineteenth century, attempted to settle three distinct ecological zones or habitats: the river basin itself, where dams could be built for irrigation; the middle slopes above the rivers, where runoff water was available; and the upper slopes. As it turned out, the middle slope settlements were the most successful over the long term because they had the resilience to

*Tropical forest ecosystems are dramatic examples of environmental impacts of human activity; of course, most threats to ecosystem resilience are less visible.*

(Carlos Humberto T.D.C./Contact Press Images/PictureQuest)

survive most threats to farming. The upper communities found rainfall too unpredictable and died out; the lower-level communities achieved a high level of production through damming rivers, but this was often punctuated by disasters, as flooding destroyed dams, which then had to be rebuilt. The middle range of settlements were able to construct water storage facilities enabling them to survive both droughts and floods. None of the colonizing would have been possible without the strong, centralized authority of the church, which used members' tithes and contributed skills to assist communities in need.

## Population Ecology

Although the concept of the ecosystem is very useful, much ecological research focuses directly on individuals, populations (groups of individuals of the same species who interact with one another), and communities (diverse populations interacting with one another). Population ecology, or demography, is a field that describes the dynamics of population growth, decline, and change in age and sex structure. In the ecosystem model, energy, information, and material flow through individuals and hence populations and communities. All populations can be thought of in terms of their birthrates and death rates, which when combined with migration in and out, give a measure of rates of net growth or decline, and when calculated according to age-specific fertility or mortality, give a picture of a population's structure. While this may sound somewhat arcane, it actually is quite simple to understand and the implications are often of startling immediacy. Since populations have the potential for exponential growth, even very slight changes in the ratio of births to deaths can have dramatic effects. A 2%

growth rate will cause a population to double in thirty-five years. Thus, with respect to human populations, the demographic dynamics directly affect the number of consumers to be fed and sheltered, the numbers of able-bodied workers, the individuals who by reason of age need to be thought of as dependents, and so on. Countries with high birthrates and even slightly lower death rates can grow explosively relative to resources; conversely, countries, such as many in Europe today, may see a dramatic decline in numbers as low birthrates fail to replace those dying. Rapidly growing populations are usually also characterized by large numbers of relatively young people. Most people living in the Middle East, for example, are younger than eighteen years old. The populations of countries as diverse as Japan, Germany, France, Italy, Russia, Bulgaria, and Ireland with quite low birthrates are aging and face the problem of demands for old-age support and a declining labor force. Japan's work force peaked in 1998 and is now in steep decline. By mid-century, it will have 30% fewer workers and about 1 million people aged 100 (French, 2003). By the end of the century, the present population of 120 million will be halved, according to UN estimates. The relevance of population dynamics holds for all societies.

## The Human Ecological Context

The structure of ecological systems—the flow of energy and nutrients—puts fundamental constraints on the way of life of any human population. Applying the ecosystem model to specific human populations, we can address two major questions. First, what is the population's place in its particular ecological system—that is, what are its relationships with the rest of the living world? Second, how are particular behaviors characteristic of this population related to its place in the ecosystem?

Humans hold a rather unusual position in their ecosystems. First, we occupy a remarkable diversity of such systems. This fact becomes strikingly evident when we look at the **habitats** and the **niches** that our species occupies. The habitat of a species is the area where it lives—its surroundings. Its niche is its "way of making a living," as defined by what it eats, what eats it, and how it reproduces and rears its young. Most animals are limited to a few habitats and a relatively narrow niche. In contrast, we occupy an exceptionally broad niche (think of the great variety of foods eaten by human beings and the many ways in which they are produced), and we live in an extremely wide range of habitats. Indeed, there are very few habitats, from deserts to arctic ice sheets to tropical rain forests, where human beings have not found a way to thrive.

Second, once humans enter an ecosystem, they tend to become its dominant species. This means that we strongly affect the life chances and reproductive rates of the other populations. While we are affected by other species, especially by those that threaten our well-being (such as malaria-bearing mosquitoes), our influence on them is far greater than theirs on us. Our dominance is due to the sophistication of our technology. Other species use tools, but no other species has developed them to the extent we have, and no other species depends on tools for its survival as we do. Our technological expertise has allowed us to transform a vast variety of materials—including some rather unlikely ones, such as fossil fuels—into sources of usable energy. The use of tools has enabled us to create artificial environments, such as farms and cities, in which we maintain very high human population densities by greatly increasing the inflow and outflow of energy,

materials, and information. The use of technology allows us to engage locally in very different lifestyles, very much analogous to speciation and niche formation among other animals.

Human-dominated ecosystems are considerably less resilient than other ecosystems because they can be maintained only by constant expenditure of human energy and ingenuity. Cities depend on surrounding ecosystems for their food, water, and other necessities. In fact, inhabitants of cities tend to organize the countryside around them since they control the capital, markets, and transportation systems on which the rural farming sector depends. Cities also produce large quantities of waste products that the surrounding ecosystem must absorb. When urban ecosystems become large or numerous, the balance between the cities and the food-producing areas that sustain them may break down. In any event, these ecological arrangements depend on massive and costly inputs of energy. With our recent dependence on fossil fuel for energy, the stability of today's urban systems may be severely limited—not only by future fuel shortages, but by problems of waste disposal. Such potential problems are not restricted to the developed or industrialized countries. In Africa, the causes of widespread famines are deforestation, erosion, and soil depletion.

Finally, human populations are socially far more differentiated than are other social animals. This has to be understood if the ecological approach is to have validity, and we return to this important point shortly. We not only engage in division of labor beyond that associated with age and role in sexual reproduction, but we also create systems of perpetuated inequality, such as caste, class, and other differences of economic and political access across age and gender lines. Such inequality has major ramifications

*In 1999, India's population reached 1 billion, 15% of the world's population, and 40% are younger than fifteen. By 2050, UN demographers estimate at current rates of increase India's population will reach 1.5 billion.*

(© Galen Rowell/CORBIS)

for the ways in which we interact with our environments. The fact that there are no physical limits on the accumulation of wealth in a capitalist economy, for example, has important consequences for the way that natural resources are exploited. And the fact that the nominal "owners" of resources (and the means of exploiting them) do not necessarily live and work near them has important consequences for other people who *do*. Thus, local people may be powerless to prevent their central government from granting rights to a foreign company to cut down the forest they live in. The impact of cultural diversity, exchange, and inequality on humans and on the ways that humans interact with environments has grown with time and with changes in human social organization since the earliest *Homo sapiens* developed tool technology in the Paleolithic period.

## Ecosystems and Adaptation

Despite all of our technological advances, we are still as deeply enmeshed in our ecosystems as any other group of organisms. What distinguishes humans from other species in their relation to the environment is the rapidity with which we respond through learning. Different human societies may develop wholly different ways of life as they adjust to their environment and can change rapidly as circumstances require. We can most usefully study the nature of this adaptive process by combining ideas from evolution and ecology.

Although evolutionary research is diachronic (that is, through time) by definition, ecological research tends to be synchronic (that is, primarily concerned with the present). However, both focus on the same phenomenon: adaptation—the process whereby organisms or populations of organisms that live together in a defined environment make biological and/or behavioral adjustments that increase their chances for survival and reproduction. An evolutionary study may trace adaptation backward through time in an attempt to understand major causes of change within a given species as an outcome of natural selection and other evolutionary forces. Ecological studies, in contrast, tend to focus on the present and to look at the outcome of the adaptational process by analyzing the totality of relationships among organisms in a given environment. Evolutionary-ecological research unites these two approaches by studying living organisms within the context of their total environment to discover how their evolved characteristics and strategies for survival contribute to their success within that environment—how they have adapted. Still, culture, or aspects of it, has an identity quite distinct from behaviors that are directly acted upon by such evolutionary forces as natural se-

lection. In fact, traits adopted and favored by cultures may, for a while at least, work at cross-purposes with individual strategies for adaptive success. People enthusiastically embrace beliefs and adopt behavioral traits that apparently have little immediate relevance, either to their own well-being or to that of a larger group or a community.

Sometimes extreme examples are more useful illustrations than are common ones where costs and benefits are obvious. Consider societies that have stressful initiation rites, including in some instances severe genital mutilation. It is hard to understand how such practices, with the attendant risk of death or injury, can benefit the individual (or his or her parents), except in the important context of social relations. Traditional practices of female circumcision and female infibulation (sewing the vagina closed), found in the Sudan and East Africa, and male subincision (cutting open the penis and the urethra), found among Australian aborigines, hardly promote the well-being or reproductive success of the individuals who suffer through them, except as they contribute to the initiates' social acceptability. They also may benefit other members of the society at the initiates' expense. For example, female circumcision aids male control of female sexuality and reproduction, and male subincision enhances older men's control of younger men (Irons, 1995). Such practices appear to be related to the nature of the society itself—the way it forms its cultural identity, defines concepts of sexuality and social maturity, and effects social control. Many anthropologists argue for a "dual inheritance" perspective, from which cultural transmission and change are seen as working simultaneously with a parallel process of natural selection (Boyd & Richerson, 1985; Durham, 1991; E. A. Smith, 2000). This means that we should not expect humans to operate within the narrow constraint of immediately perceived costs and benefits but rather to respond to and solve problems using a wide range of cultural tools. We cannot blame genes for acts of violence, warfare, racism, and similar chilling facets of human social life; what we do know is that we have the biological potential for them to occur, as well as the capacity to limit such behavior (see Gould, 1996a; Wrangham & Peterson, 1996).

We have seen that evolution is a process of cumulative change consequent on the responses of organisms to their environments (adaptation). Adaptation can be an elusive concept because it involves processes that seem to operate on several different levels at once. Furthermore, adaptation can only be observed over long periods.

### Variation: Human Decisions and the Environment.
Variation, whether biological or behavioral, is the

*In Congo, these young Lese and Efe women are undergoing a religious ceremony marking their transition to adulthood.*

(Richard Wrangham/ Anthro-Photo)

key to the process of adaptation. One of the main contributions of recent studies of animal behavior is the recognition that among animals of all sorts, systems of mating, male–female differences, feeding habits, food sharing, social interaction, and the like can be understood as the outcome of behaviors that start as individual strategies. Groups are never homogeneous; all contain individuals who respond somewhat differently to the problems at hand. Seen in this light, patterns of behavior become increasingly interesting. As human culture is elaborated, new solutions that seem to work can be rapidly added to the repertoire of knowledge that is passed on. The acceptance of innovations depends to a great extent on the fact that customary ways of acting are always subject to variation. Individuals constantly make decisions, and decision making gives rise to behavioral variation. There are enough conflicting versions of proper behavior in every society to create some ambiguity, thus allowing for the introduction and acceptance of innovation.

To understand the nature of human decision making or problem solving, we have to consider the environment in which it takes place. We are all too prone to treat the environment as a fixed landscape or static fact and so fail to consider the nature of variation in all environments. Environments are complex and they constantly fluctuate. The environment of any individual or population consists of all external factors that affect it in any way—not only the obvious features of the habitat (the place where the population lives) but also the presence of organisms that transmit disease, competitors, shelter, and climate. It also includes the cultural setting in which the individual must operate. In a society in which male initiation rites are important, for example, this social fact

is part of the individual's environment. The environment also includes the demographic structure of the population; often, the most important feature of an individual's environment is the presence of other members of the same population among whom an individual will find both allies and competitors.

Finally, environments are dynamic. In his classic ecological study, Lawrence B. Slobodkin (1968) argued that four patterns of change underlie the dynamics of all environments: the degree of novelty (how new), frequency (how often), magnitude (how much), and duration (how long) of environmental events of all sorts. The organism with the best chance of success is not necessarily the one most perfectly adapted to its environment at any particular point but rather the one that maintains its ability to respond to the environment in flexible ways. Generally speaking, the most successful response is the one that involves the minimum sacrifice of flexibility. In other words, choices among alternatives are made to minimize risk, not simply to attempt to make large gains.

In general, behavior is fairly predictable and conventional; people tend to arrive at similar decisions under similar circumstances. Were it not so, group life would be impossible. People regularly make major decisions regarding such basic issues of subsistence as whether to plant one crop or another or whether to migrate to new pastures or not; they also make day-to-day decisions such as with whom to socialize or to whom to send a greeting card. The structure of human societies provides the context for, and information concerning, choices among alternatives. As Frederik Barth (1981) has put it:

Social life [is] generated by actors who go about their activity by pursuing their interests fitfully, often thoughtlessly, and generally conventionally. Yet they are concerned about the outcomes of their efforts in so far as these affect themselves. In this concern their judgments are based on values which serve to organize choice and action by providing standards to compare different alternatives and outcomes, both prospectively and retrospectively. When doing so, people tend to maximize the amounts of value they obtain by pursuing benefits and avoiding losses and drawbacks inasmuch as they see a way to do so. (p. 102)

No one would argue that actors are always rational, but it is broadly evident that the values that shape decisions always involve trade-offs and compromises. Decisions to irrigate, for example, involve costs that might even threaten household budgets but promise long-term yield improvements. At the same time, lurking behind this decision is what sociologists and others who study human behavior call "unintended consequences." Thus, some seemingly successful adaptation may look less so in long-term perspective.

*Adapting through Innovation.* It is important to recognize the very important role that variation in behavior plays in societal change, even when that behavior is termed "deviant." Behavior that is said to be strange or outside the established range of variation can in time become widely accepted and, in some cases, the basis for the survival of the group. A farmer may initially be seen as "strange" or abnormal because he adopts a new plant or tries a new system of cultivation—as, for example, in the United States when a few innovative farmers began in the 1980s to farm organically (that is, without chemical fertilizers). While considered eccentric at first, by the end of the century, organic farming had become widespread because of changed consumer tastes and, importantly, its cost effectiveness.

In any society, most people know what is appropriate in a given situation, but they do not always act according to a rigid formula or set of rules. And when we look at the ways in which people break the rules they espouse, an interesting pattern emerges. For one thing, most of us "sin" in more or less the same way our neighbors sin; that is, we deviate in packs. A simple example of this phenomenon is the tendency of automobile drivers to exceed the speed limit, just a little. When the legal limit is fifty-five miles per hour, most people can be found driving at sixty to sixty-five. In fact, most of us look askance at people who obey all the rules to the letter. The rigid bureaucrat who plods through every inch of red tape, refusing to cut corners, is generally considered a deviant. Likewise, though few Americans would openly condone lying, all would agree that in many social circumstances, telling the complete truth would be a mistake; we tell "white lies" or otherwise manipulate the facts to fit our needs.

People everywhere establish rules for acceptable behavior and then proceed to break the rules in more or less predictable ways. The reasons for this behavior are the necessity of making received rules and values fit the circumstances of the individual. Though most people feel a need to do what is "proper," and though their culture provides time-honored definitions of "proper" for them to fall back on, survival nevertheless depends on the ability to solve problems in the immediate environment and adapt to changing circumstances. Once people develop a new solution, they usually begin to argue

*Even modern seed production becomes localized in that each new strain of hybrid seed must be field tested and adjusted to microclimatic and soil conditions. This family-owned firm specializes in matching product to environment in the Midwest.*
(Rudy Bergner)

not that it is new but that it is good—not expedient but proper.

Changing gender roles in our own society are a case in point. At one time, it was not considered desirable for women to work outside the home, and usually, only those who had no alternative did so. In time, certain kinds of work in offices, hospitals, and schools came to be viewed as quite appropriate for women, and families began to invest in the training of their daughters as secretaries, nurses, and teachers. With the advent of World War I, industry and the civil service needed women to fill jobs left vacant by men who had gone to war. Following the war, women not only continued to be employed in large numbers but the right of women to vote was secured. Slowly, the employment of women in wider and wider sectors of the economy came to be viewed not only as legitimate but desirable by a substantial percentage of the population. In recent years, the right of women to be employed in every occupation became established in law, though not necessarily in practice.

Once a new behavior, with its newly acquired moral value, gains enough adherents, it becomes a shared practice that is taught to the next generation as part of "the right way to do things"(Irons, 1991). In time, newer solutions will be adopted, but the rule remains the same: Individual ways of coping, if enough people find them useful, will become part of the system of shared behavior.

# The Evolution of Procurement Systems

Of all the problems people face, securing adequate food is the most fundamental. When ecologists note that "you are what you eat," they mean that the source and variety of foods used by any population, human or otherwise, are critical to its maintenance. While a vast array of adaptive patterns can be found throughout the world, if we concentrate on the central issue of the way a population procures and distributes its food, we will note common strategies. The behavioral strategies that a particular group uses to secure foodstuffs are termed its food procurement system. Within general patterns, the available strategies are so numerous that no two systems are exactly alike. In fact, it is rare to find two individuals within a society practicing precisely the same strategy. However, there are some important generalizations that can be made about food procurement behavior that will help explain the nature of adaptation in this context. Five major patterns of food procurement can be identified:

1. **Foraging** (or hunting and gathering): collecting wild vegetable foods, hunting game, and fishing.

2. **Subsistence agriculture:** a simple form of agriculture (sometimes called **horticulture** or extensive agriculture) based on working small plots of land with perhaps some use of draft animals, plows, or irrigation. In contrast to foragers, subsistence farmers produce food by managing domesticated plants and animals.

3. **Pastoralism:** an economy based on herding. Pastoralists maintain herds of animals and use their products (milk, curds, whey, butterfat, meat, blood, hides, bones) both to maintain themselves directly and to trade with other populations. They also often use their animals to gain mobility that can be used for military purposes.

4. **Intensive agriculture:** a form of agriculture that involves the use of draft animals or tractors, plows, and often some form of irrigation. Intensive agriculture produces far greater yields per acre of land with less human labor than can be obtained by subsistence agriculture. Intensive agriculture is often highly specialized, with farmers relying on one or two main crops.

5. **Industrial agriculture:** food production and manufacturing using machines powered largely by fossil fuels, including modern commercial fishing and marine farming.

As we have stressed, the crucial selective pressures giving rise to the divergence of the human line from that of the apes probably entailed brain-related behavioral changes—the gradual development of a greater commitment to group life and cooperation and language use. The australopithecines, from whom the earliest humans evolved, probably ate meat only occasionally; their main food resources were the plants of the East African savanna, which they ate as soon as they found them (Wrangham & Peterson, 1996). From what we can guess, about 2 million years ago, a few populations of australopithecines, while still relying heavily on vegetable foods, began to supplement their diet with a regular intake of meat that they procured by hunting and scavenging. Further, they probably began sharing their food more extensively, bringing both the vegetables and meat they found to be divided among the whole group. In time, this change in food procurement and consumption patterns produced the behavioral changes and anatomical features unique to the human lineage. One of the behavioral changes was an increased emphasis on learning, as exemplified by the development of toolmaking and use.

*Food procurement is fundamental to all populations. Humans today rely on intensive agriculture for most food; today's populations could not be sustained without the highly industrialized techniques utilized by this American farmer. The agricultural decisions of individuals have implications for the availability and prices of food products in distant countries.*

(John Running/Stock, Boston Inc.)

Anatomical changes included increased brain size and decreased tooth size.

Foraging, or hunting and gathering, has itself changed greatly since the time of the australo-pithecines. However, in one form or another, it continued to be the universal human food procurement strategy until relatively recently. Over the centuries, it was gradually refined. Approximately 200,000 years ago with the appearance of anatomically modern hominids (*Homo sapiens*), almost all of the Old World was occupied by highly successful hunter-gatherer populations utilizing hitherto unknown technologies (see Wrangham & Peterson, 1996). It is likely that this successful adaptive radiation of *Homo sapiens* was related to the fact that they possessed a fully developed language. We can infer this from the morphology of their brains, from their artistic accomplishments, and from indirect evidence of religious beliefs (see Bickerton, 1995). People learned to make containers and digging sticks to help them in gathering, and they developed improved weapons—spears, spear throwers, and eventually, bows and arrows—to increase their efficiency as hunters. By 40,000 years ago, different local populations had also learned to be highly specialized in terms of procuring specific kinds of game and plant resources in very different habitats. As early as 20,000 years ago, European and Asian hunters and gatherers (and probably others as well) were making

and using textiles and basketry, showing a high degree of technological sophistication (Soffer, Vandiver, & Klima, 1995). Mezhirich on the Dnieper River in Russia is a winter camp of Upper Paleolithic big game hunters dated to about 18,000 B.P. (Soffer, 1985). The camp was located in a valley where people could not only find game but gather plants and fish in the river. It is a complex of well-built houses constructed of mammoth bones. Similar houses of mammoth hunters have been found at Dolni Vestonice in the Czech Republic (Price & Feinman, 1997). Also approximately 15,000 years ago, humans crossed the newly exposed land bridge at the Bering Strait and began their rapid dispersal throughout North and South America.

From specialized hunting and gathering, with skills adapted to the exploitation of particular plant and animal species, it is a relatively short step to systematic planting and herding. Although we do not know precisely how or why, we do know that about 12,000 years ago societies in various parts of the world began experimenting with the domestication of plants and animals. However, another 3,000 or 4,000 years passed between the first appearance of agriculture and its widespread use. Not until 5,000 years ago, in the Near East, are we able to find signs of irrigation and the beginnings of intensive agriculture. (In this period, too, specialized pastoralism probably became important.) Over the next 2,000 years, agricultural practices became more efficient and productive in some areas. Large-scale irrigation works were constructed in Mesopotamia and Egypt, making it possible to support larger and larger populations in limited areas. We return to this topic in subsequent chapters.

Finally, as recently as the nineteenth century, certain Western societies developed a new pattern, industrial agriculture, whereby machines began to be used for farming, animal husbandry, manufacturing, and other subsistence activities. As a result of the Industrial Revolution, the family farm was transformed into a highly mechanized and capital-intensive operation, which more recently is being replaced by agribusiness.

Because procurement systems are so varied, most societies do not fall tidily into one or another food procurement pattern. When we refer to foragers, subsistence farmers, pastoralists, agriculturalists, and industrial societies, we are merely pointing out a cultural emphasis on the use of particular food procurement methods. The specific procurement systems that people use involve varying strategies and varied degrees of reliance on the same strategy. People typically combine several methods. In most societies, for example, subsistence farming is supplemented by hunting and collecting wild foods. In others, horticulture (subsistence farming without the use of plows) is practiced alongside plow farming: the former in steep and rocky areas, the latter in flatter areas where plowing is possible. Pastoralism is generally found in conjunction with other procurement strategies—in some cases with hunting and gathering, in other cases with small-scale horticulture. And needless to say, many agriculturists raise animals not only for transportation but also as sources of protein, wool, and hides.

# Adapting to Environmental Problems

The assumption that a given food procurement system is an adaptation to a certain range of environmental conditions still does not explain very much. It is certainly true that the characteristics of environmental zones of different types—grasslands, deserts, tropical forests, temperate forests, the arctic, and the subarctic—place limits on the kind of life that can be sustained in them. One does not farm in the arctic, nor does one herd animals in a tropical rain forest. Yet these broad environmental factors account for only a small portion of the variation we see in procurement systems. They do not tell us why inhabitants of similar regions—indeed, of the same region—often practice widely different procurement strategies or why inhabitants of different regions sometimes practice remarkably similar strategies.

To understand how and why specific procurement systems develop, we must consider them as responses less to broad environmental characteristics than to very specific environmental problems in local areas. Some common problems faced by local populations are fluctuations over time and space in quantity, quality, and availability of resources and the activities of other human groups in competition for those same resources.

It is impossible to list and categorize all of the nearly infinite range of potential environmental problems or hazards, which include such obvious ones as climatic factors that determine the availability or growth rates of plants and animals, and thus the potential human food chain, diseases, predators, and of course, such hazards as floods, extreme storms, tectonic events, and the like. But whatever they may be, it is almost axiomatic that the activities of humans themselves are implicated in a synergetic fashion. For example, disease is a major hazard on every continent, but disease vectors are often determined by human activities themselves. AIDS is an obvious example.

Many diseases have animal vectors, and thus the development of animal husbandry placed Eurasian and African populations in intimate contact with smallpox, measles, influenza, typhus, and bubonic plague, diseases that wreaked havoc among New World populations. In 2003, SARS (severe acute respiratory syndrome) evolved in China in a semidomesticated species used as food, civet cats (no relative to our domestic felines), and spread rapidly in human hosts as far as North America and Europe. Also, agricultural settlements in the Old World, West Africa, the Eastern Mediterranean, the Persian Gulf, and Southeast Asia exposed local populations to mosquito-borne malaria. To all of these diseases, furthered by human intensification activities, humans arrived at adaptational responses at a number of levels. Genetically, many populations developed at least partial resistance, and socially, they developed settlement systems, migration schedules, and even medical and religious prophylactic responses to mitigate negative impacts. Even hazards such as floods and earthquakes have their severity largely determined by such factors as density of population, land use, and construction practices.

## Adapting to Available Resources

Every local environment or habitat has a limited potential for supporting any of the populations within it, both human and nonhuman. This demographic potential is called the environment's **carrying capacity**—the point at or below which a given population tends to stabilize. The most obvious limiting factors may be the availability of food or water. Others include disease, temperature, and even the regularity and predictability of critical resources. The fact that a food source is available during the year, for example, matters less than the ability of the people who rely on it to predict with accuracy *when* it is going to be available. The best way to determine carrying capacity is to observe the demographic characteristics of the population: rates of birth, death, and migration. Researchers may also estimate an environment's potential carrying capacity for a particular population by computing the *minimum* amount of water and of vegetable and animal matter available on a regular basis for human consumption.

A long-term project in East Africa illustrates some of the issues involved in such research. The South Turkana Ecosystem Project is a collaborative effort of scientists from universities in Kenya and the United States, with research interests as diverse as human genetics, demography, rangeland management, plant ecology, nutrition, and ethnology. The lands of the Turkana are subject to extremes of

*A low water supply may limit the number of people an environment can support. In Ethiopia's arid Omo Valley, residents search for water by digging under a dry riverbed.*

(George Gerster/Comstock)

temperature; daytime highs average 87 to 100°F (35–37°C), and highly erratic rainfall varies from 5.8 to 19.5 inches (150–500 millimeters) a year. This low and variable rainfall, combined with intense solar radiation flux, results in a short growing season; farming is limited. Most of the Turkana people of northwestern Kenya, a population of 150,000 to 200,000 distributed among a series of tribes and subtribes, exploit this region by "nomadic movements of their polygynous family settlements and the five species of livestock that they herd—camels, zebu cattle, goats, sheep, and donkeys. Home settlements will move, on the average, one or more times each month" (Little, 1988, p. 697). The Turkana live almost entirely on the products of their animals, and starvation is a constant specter.

As part of the project, one study conducted by rangeland ecology specialists and ethnographers (Coughenour et al., 1985) addresses a key issue in the study of pastoral adaptations to extremely arid lands: How do these people maintain enough animals to sustain themselves without degrading their habitat? Using detailed measurements of energy expenditures, the researchers were able to map plant-animal-human food pathways. They not only studied animal requirements but also measured ground cover and the diets of a sample of nomadic households. They found that the Turkana derived 92% of their food energy from animal products (meat, milk, and blood) and from maize meal, sugar, and other foods that they acquire by bartering animal products. Though their animals produce less milk and meat than American and Australian breeds, they are more resistant to disease, heat, and drought-related stress.

The Turkana can maintain an adequate diet and keep a critical reserve to face unexpected losses without degrading their rangelands because of two factors: (1) the number of animals they can keep is limited by the availability of water holes, and (2) they manage a mix of five species, each with its unique productive qualities. When milk from the cows fails, they turn to their camels; when meat is needed, they can kill small animals such as sheep or goats. Cattle that do not produce milk provide blood, which is nutritionally rich. The livestock is often scrawny by European standards, but if the rains bring a bumper crop of vegetation, the animals put on weight rapidly and their fertility rate goes up.

Another study sheds light on the role of blood as human food in such a system (Dyson-Hudson & Dyson-Hudson, 1982). Turkana cows yield only one tenth the milk of well-fed American Holsteins, but their blood is a more efficient source of energy than meat (which involves much waste and of course requires the slaughter of the animals). Twenty-one pints (9.9 liters) of blood are taken from each 1,000-pound steer every four to six months; smaller amounts are taken from breeding stock and smaller animals. The use of blood in the Turkana's diet greatly enhances the herd's productivity, particularly because it can supplement the diet during the season when cows are not producing milk.

Among the people themselves, Paul Leslie and Peggy Fry (1989) found extreme seasonality in births, with more than half falling between March and June. The rate of conception, then, is highest during the early dry season (July through September), when the food supply has been at its peak for some time. The Turkana claim not to time their children's birth (as some African populations do) and

## Box 2.1

# Risk Management in a Mountain Farming Ecosystem

KENNETH MACDONALD (1998) reports how traditional farmers in the mountains of Karakoram, north Pakistan, view their environment and how their perceptions put them at odds with those who view the production goals of "modernized" agriculture as "normal." What MacDonald demonstrates in a fine-grained analysis of land use and decision making in these formidable mountains is that "rational" behavior is entirely context dependent. Although this seems fairly obvious, it flies in the face of the "one size fits all" policies of development agents who emphasize productivity above all other factors. Specifically, MacDonald looks at such risk-mediating practices as field dispersal, delayed planting, intercropping (that is, more than one crop in a field), and planting multiple variants of the same crop as entirely consistent with the needs of the people to cope with a very uncertain farming habitat. In short, the people have independently arrived at the ecologically sound notion that diversity can reduce risk—and hence are behaving rationally. This is not, however, how local development agents see things.

In many respects, the negative manner in which development planners here view both the mountain habitat of the villagers and their traditional methods can be easily mirrored in other parts of the world where the urban-educated view indigenous knowledge with suspicion—even contempt. The words most commonly used by planners in north Pakistan, coming from a tradition of capitalist intensive farming, to describe the villagers include "tradition bound," "inept, " "ingrained and obstinate," and "community-focused and lack-

ing initiative." MacDonald writes that from this perspective, local village practice is seen as timeless, stagnant, and deeply resistant to "improvement."

However, the view is strangely at odds with both MacDonald's perspective as a geographer and the very earliest reports of European travelers who, in spite of the racial prejudices of their day, were amazed at local ingenuity in managing irrigation and mountain terraces. MacDonald found ". . . [I]n general, much of the operative farming system in Askole [the village he studied in depth] can be interpreted in terms of intentional and unintentional means of mediating acceptable levels of environmental risk." Askole, which had a population of 364 people in forty-two houses in 1990, is some two days' journey from the nearest market town. The economy is subsistence agriculture using mountain terraces combined with vertical transhumant animal herding. Crop land is owned by the households, while pastures are held in common. Due to the altitude, there is a short growing season, and farmers are heavily dependent on irrigation using runoff from winter snow packs. In addition, they contend with early and late frosts, disease epidemics, crop diseases, and windstorms. Nevertheless, they consistently attain high yields—a fact that interventionist agencies seem to ignore.

Local farmers recognize a wide variety of soil types, largely judged according to their ability to respond to irrigation. According to soil type and availability of water, they plant a mix of crops, many of the grains are rotated, and all households have a range of soil types to exploit. While they lose time in moving

from field to field, dispersal gives them a vital hedge in case of crop failure. It has long been noted that mountain villages often are "mixed" in that fields at different altitudes are used. Here most fields are at the same level but do vary significantly in soil. In addition to careful distinctions of soil potential, farmers stagger their planting not to maximize yield but to minimize risk from either a late frost in the spring or an early one in the fall. They intercrop buckwheat and turnips, for example, observing that the latter are frost resistant. Thus, they willingly forego the possibility of a somewhat higher yield to gain security. To further diversify, they plant three different strains of wheat—the mainstay of their diet.

Farmers also make good use of vertical zonality to pasture their yaks and other livestock for dairy products. The mix of animals and how they are pastured contribute to risk minimization and, very importantly, to minimize erosion that might occur should animals feeding on only one grass or shrub be intensively pastured. Animals are herded communally in "stock associations," and this strategy also minimizes any individual interest in pushing production to the point of damaging the commons.

While MacDonald is careful not to represent any given agricultural practice as a specific response to some particular threat, he says that when viewed as a system supporting people, it is one that reduces vulnerability. Local development planners view negatively the reluctance of households to adopt new techniques, such as high-yield grains, but viewed in terms of long-term security, their reluctance is understandable, even rational.

attribute the seasonality of births to the separation of spouses during the pastoral cycle, high temperatures that inhibit coitus, and other factors. Whatever the reason, the human population closely tracks the environmental fluctuations.

These plus other completed and ongoing studies of the South Turkana Ecosystem Project not only contribute to a much fuller understanding of the Turkana people and their ecosystems, but they also have a wider significance for pastoral, ecological, and medical research.

The carrying capacity of an area is affected not only by the total amount of food available but also by the availability and distribution of essential dietary items such as protein, vitamins, and minerals. In other words, the nutritional quality of resources is as critical as their quantity and availability. To avoid chronic malnutrition, humans must somehow adjust to the variations in nutritional value among available foods. While some physiological adjustment is evident among human populations in areas of diverse resources (as with populations occupying extremely high, arid, or cold regions), people generally solve the problem through restrictive dietary practices and in the way they prepare their foods.

A final factor affecting carrying capacity is the human ability to recognize resources. Even the determination of what plants and animals are edible varies considerably among cultures. Goosefoot and lambsquarter, two plants that we consider weeds, were important sources of both seeds and greens among many Native American groups. These and many other plants and animals that we do not now consider edible are staples (and even delicacies) in other societies. Many resources identified as usable in one culture are ignored in others.

As these examples illustrate, an environment's human carrying capacity is not a simple reflection of local resources. Also, as we see in later chapters, carrying capacity depends on the organization of the society and on the exchange of food and tools among populations.

## Adapting to Resource Fluctuation

Populations must adjust not only to the quantity and quality of resources but also to fluctuations in their availability. Effective carrying capacity, as stressed earlier, is the minimum available critical or limiting resource. For example, over a five-year period, an area may produce an average of 100 kilograms (about 221 pounds) of corn per year, but if production drops to 50 kilograms (about 110 pounds) one year, the people must adjust or risk starvation.

The Shoshone Indians, who lived in North America's Great Basin before the coming of the Europeans, provide a good historical example of adjustment to fluctuations in resources. Because of extreme variation in rainfall in this region, the Shoshone were never able to predict with any certainty where or how much plant and animal food would be available from one year to the next. The Shoshone adapted to these environmental uncertainties by relying on a wide variety of resources and pursuing a highly mobile way of life, changing their location and residence patterns according to the kind and quantity of resources available. During most of the year, a Shoshone family traveled alone or with one or two related families, gathering roots and seeds and hunting small animals. Periodically, however, when rabbits or antelope became unusually plentiful, several families might band together temporarily for a collective hunt. And when isolated families heard reports that a resource such as pine nuts seemed promising in a particular locality, they would plan to arrive together in time for the harvest and would separate again after the resources had been collected (Steward, 1972).

People who live by cultivating crops or raising animals generally have a more stable food supply than those who depend on wild resources alone. But these groups are also affected by seasonal and yearly fluctuations and must adjust to them. Since population is more concentrated in these groups than among hunter-gatherers, the effects of food shortages may be even more devastating to them. The Ariaal of western Kenya (Chapter 5) depend on agricultural produce for the bulk of their caloric intake. However, droughts and fluctuations in rainfall can result in crop failure, in which case the Ariaal fall back on their cattle and goat herds for their food supply. Thus, their cattle may be seen as a means of storing energy as much as a means of producing it.

Another example involves an ancient American people that farmed in an extremely unpredictable climate. The Anasazi Pueblo relied on a diverse set of agricultural strategies to minimize risk of crop failure in an area of high aridity. One strategy used in the fourteenth and fifteenth centuries was "pebble mulching"—that is, deliberately adding small pebbles to the soil of their gardens. This served to conserve soil moisture, reduce erosion, and extend the growing season (Lightfoot, 1993, p. 116).

Consumers in our society rarely experience sudden short-term fluctuations in resources because we depend on the products of a huge area serviced by an efficient transportation system. A wide variety of fruits, vegetables, grains, meats, and dairy products

*Ariaal elder with two newborn camels.*
(Elliot Fratkin)

are available throughout the year. This steadiness of supply is due to our technology: Producers have means of storing and transporting food so as to cover shortages, and our technology enables us to minimize some fluctuations in resources (although often at considerable cost).

When a rancher's pasturelands go dry, the rancher feeds cattle by hauling forage and water to them with tractors and trucks rather than by moving the animals. Similarly, a farmer can bring water to crops through irrigation, control insects with chemical sprays, and spread fertilizer to add nutrients to the soil of a depleted field. The farmer can even grow crops in the dead of winter by constructing hothouses. But these techniques have costs that are passed on to the consumer. Modern agriculture depends on machine technology and is thus subsidized by the large-scale use of fossil fuel in the form of gasoline and diesel oil.

Despite the apparent advantages of modern agricultural techniques, we should not make the mistake of assuming that industrialized societies are somehow infallible in minimizing uncertainty in food production. Perhaps the greatest paradox of recent human adaptation is that responses aimed at stabilizing and increasing food production are in many cases having the opposite effect—the famous "unexpected consequence." That is, they are creating a new and more serious threat to the stability of the procurement system. To diminish the threat of drought or irregular rainfall, for example, a community may increase its dependence on irrigation agriculture, only to discover that the increased irrigation has ele-

vated the salt content of the soil to the point where it can no longer support crops. Equally, a rancher who increases herd size to increase profits risks overgrazing the savanna ranges on which he or she depends to an extent that actually reduces their carrying capacity. This is illustrated by recent research on rangeland (mis)management in South Africa presented in Box 2.2, Management and Mismanagement.

Thus, while people in technologically advanced societies may accomplish impressive feats of environmental engineering, they must still remain sensitive to the environment in which they live. Ultimately, the success of a group's adaptation to its resources depends not only on its ingenuity in manipulating its ecological system but also on its care in maintaining that system. As a consequence, the internal distribution of resources among people through social interaction is as important as the resources on which they depend. This is why the objective of most planned development is "sustainability."

## Political Ecology

The type and distribution of basic resources are only two aspects of an environment. Human populations make up another and no less basic aspect. Every society must adjust to the presence and activities of neighboring peoples just as it must adjust to variations in local resources. The study of this adaptive process is important enough to constitute an entire subfield of human ecology: **political ecology**—the

## Box 2.2

# Management and Mismanagement

ANDREW HUDAK (1999) STUDIED two areas of savanna rangelands in north central South Africa that straddle the border of the former *bantustan* (Black homeland) of Bophuthatswana with the Republic of South Africa. Historically, Tswana pastoralists grazed cattle in the area, but the arrival in the nineteenth century of white "Trekboers" of Dutch origin, along with their livestock, dramatically altered the ecology of the rangelands.

Hudak notes that while livestock grazing is, globally, the primary cause of desertification of rangelands, a less recognized but more widespread form of rangeland degradation is "encroachment by generally unpalatable trees and shrubs at the expense of palatable grasses. . . ." The ecology of arid and semiarid savannas is characterized by a continuous grass understory interspersed by a discontinuous woody overstory, and in the

area Hudak conducted his study, the savannas are subject to seasonal drought from April to mid-November and common but unpredictable interannual drought. In years with good rainfall, grass growth is vigorous, which means that the risk of natural fires ignited by lightening is increased. Fire kills the smaller trees while grasses resprout quickly, and several years without fires will allow tree seedlings to become better established. Another element in savanna ecology is the presence of grazing herbivores; the animals that eat grass favor the growth of tree seedlings, while those that browse (that is, eat the woody plant growth) leave more resources for grass growth.

This combination of climate, fire, and herbivore grazing and browsing means that savannas are inherently unstable, although able to withstand quite high variability among these elements at low enough pop-

ulation densities. However, Hudak points out that a combination of heavy grazing and fire suppression over several decades appears to push this unstable, but resilient, system over a threshold into a relatively stable environment of thick, thorny thickets that allow for little or no grass growth underneath. "In summary, bush encroachment [the term used in South Africa for this phenomenon] is a textbook but underpublicized example of a creeping environmental phenomenon, the term coined by Glantz (1994a) to describe many long-term, slow-onset environmental degradations that may proceed to great magnitude before the need for remediative action is realized or remediative action taken" (pp. 58–59).

With the arrival of the Boers in the nineteenth century, their herds of cattle and sheep, which eat only a few grass species and do not browse, replaced the previously diverse herds

study of how people compete to gain access to, maintain control of, and utilize natural resources.

There are many ways in which politics determine how humans interact with their environments and also many environmental factors that affect the political process. Many anthropologists consider most human ecological studies to really be analyses of political ecology because the main determinants for how resources are accessed and distributed are political. This might also be called the "political economy" approach because it considers the ways in which politics and economics intersect (Peet & Watts, 1994). Politics obviously reward some more than others. Among the Türkmen of northern Iran, for example, wealthy and influential men occasionally hire teams of large tractors and set them to plowing arid and only partially arable public lands that the rest of the community uses for grazing. They then seed the new fields and, if they are lucky with the rains, make a handsome profit on the resultant

wheat crops (that are guarded by their hired help); the soils, however, quickly erode and the common pastures are lost to both farming and grazing.

## *Access to Resources: Cooperation and Competition*

Local populations and the individuals within them by necessity cultivate and maintain multiple political and social ties with each other that allow them to cope with uncertainties of all sorts. Until very recently in the West, and still in many parts of the world, local populations depend on local food resources. At the same time, as we have noted, the potential for agriculture or other forms of food procurement is highly variable, with sharp contrasts between highly productive and marginal areas. Even within regions, members of particular societies are often differentiated in terms of access to critical resources and their place in the system of production.

of indigenous grazing and browsing animals that had ranged alongside the Tswana cattle herds. The fence lines erected by the Boers restricted livestock movement, which in turn shortened or eliminated grass recovery periods. Further, boreholes and wells were established to provide cattle with water year round over wider areas, and this also facilitated continuous grazing of grasses adapted to rest during the dry season. Finally, naturally occurring fires were either actively suppressed by the farmers or did not "take" because the grasses that would have fueled them were either eaten or trampled by the cattle.

Unfortunately, farmers' response to the bush encroachment consequent upon these developments was to blame it on drought, and so relief efforts focused on drilling more boreholes—a strategy that, as we have seen, is bound to backfire because creating permanent drinking stations for the cattle exacerbates the destruction of the grasses.

In the 1980s, the South African government bought out, for fair market value, most of the White-owned farms in Hudak's study area, which already showed signs of being heavily overgrazed. In 1991, 60,000 hectares were set aside as the Madikwe Game Reserve. The remainder were divided into South African Development Trust (SADT) Farms, with a 3,000 hectare size limit, and advertised for lease to Black farmers. White farms have no size limitation and often reach 30,000 hectares, so from the outset Black farmers were at a disadvantage. Overgrazing occurs when farmers try to make a profit on smaller farms or by high capital investment in larger farms. White farmers, Hudak found, tended to invest more both emotionally and financially in their farms, while only three of sixty-eight Black farmers in the study actually lived on their farms and made only minimal investments in them. "In summary, the socioeconomic and cultural forces driving cattle farmers to overstock . . . differ . . . but the end result—bush encroachment—is the same" (p. 68).

Meanwhile, in the Madikwe Game Reserve, park managers are working to thin the bush and restore the vegetation "through a combination of fire, browsing, and mechanical means . . ." (Madikwe Development Task Team, 1994). The park managers define fire as "an integral part of the Madikwe system," and Hudak states that its use appears to be successfully thinning bush densities. However, local cattle farmers apparently still do not fully understand the essential role of fire in savanna ecology, although attitudes are shifting among farmers who are following developments in the game reserve. Hudak thinks that educating the Afrikaner farmers, in particular, will be difficult, since ". . . they viewed cattle grazing as not only the best *use* for the [savanna] but also its most appropriate *purpose*" (p. 72).

Hudak concludes that the causes of bush encroachment in South African savannas and the hopeful example of the Madikwe Game Reserve are relevant for rangeland management worldwide. "Grazing management will prove sustainable only once existing ecological knowledge is applied" (p. 74).

---

There is inevitably a great deal of exchange of food items, labor, and other services both within communities and among them; virtually no local population is completely self-sufficient. Pastoral farmers and herding households exchange continually. The pastoral Yörük (see Chapter 5) sell their animal products in markets, the Pygmies of the Ituri Forest in Zaire trade forest products for grain with their Bantu farming neighbors, and so forth. In the settlement of the arid reaches of the Little Colorado River, as we saw with Abruzzi's study of Mormon colonization (1996), the political ties of each community to the central church hierarchy were critical to survival; local communities were supported by the church during lean or disastrous years.

The nature of resources affects political behavior. Competition for resources will arise only where those resources (such as fields or irrigation works) have a high intrinsic value and are in a clearly bounded area. The fields or grazing areas over which people contend are generally highly productive and thus worth defending. Hunters and gatherers, on the contrary, today usually occupy lands where resources are not concentrated; thus, land ownership or control is not a major source of competition.

### Environmental Uncertainty

Environmental uncertainty is another factor encouraging individuals and groups to maintain a multiplicity of political associations. Most communities periodically face conditions of drought, crop and animal epidemics, disease, and the like that necessitate seeking help from others—even from those with whom relations may be strained or hostile. For example, observers of social life in the Middle East have been struck by the great amount of time and energy individuals spend socializing and politicking. Whether it be the ubiquitous teahouses of rural

Turkey, Iraq, and Iran, the village guesthouses of Syria, or the urban coffee shops of Egypt, clusters of men and women meet (usually separately) on an almost daily basis to reaffirm existing ties, to forge new ones, and to keep an eye on the activities of others. Farming and pastoralism in these regions are carried out in an environment that demands close attention to ever-shifting political winds in addition to changing market conditions.

One result of this variability and interdependence is that we frequently find prosperous communities abutting poorer ones; households and groups are simultaneously faced with the need to compete and to cooperate. Peasants and pastoralists may fight for the same well; upstream villagers may fight with downstream neighbors over water rights; communities, neighbors, and even relatives may find themselves in competition even as they rely on each other for help and the exchange of goods. Individuals try to maintain as wide a range of contacts as possible and are continually prepared to shift alliances as interests dictate. Since the most important predator or competitor any local population might face is its neighbors, politics are an integral part of the environmental setting.

## Politics and Access to Resources

To secure resources, a group must have some assurance of continued access to an area where those resources are located. People define and regulate access to productive resources in a variety of ways depending on the nature of the resources and the means available to control and use them.

Most agricultural and industrial societies maintain clear-cut rules that define rights to productive land and other resources. Among most hunting and gathering societies, an individual's rights to use resources are relatively unrestricted. Hunters and gatherers such as the Eskimo and the Dobe !Kung must be able to move according to the seasonal availability of resources; otherwise, they might starve when normal fluctuations in climate deplete the local water supply or alter the distribution of wild animals or plants. The more uncertain or mobile the food supply, the greater the need for flexible boundaries and collective rights of access.

The extent to which people define and defend a territory also depends on the gains versus the costs of maintaining exclusive rights. A group that stakes out and defends territory retains the resource supply in that territory. But to guard a territory requires time and energy that might be spent in other activities. It also involves risk; one can be killed defending a boundary.

Finally, reliance on a restricted area for resources may be disadvantageous, as it would be for many hunter-gatherers. To the degree that costs outweigh the gains, territoriality will be relaxed. To the degree that the gains outweigh the costs, territoriality will be strictly observed. Thus, while hunters and gatherers have territories to which groups lay primary claim and stake out possession of strategic resources such as wells or rich stands of vegetable foods, they do not necessarily defend the boundaries as vigorously as farmers defend their fields (Dyson-Hudson & Smith, 1978). Generally, permission is readily granted to outsiders to visit wells or traverse territories.

The gains/cost formula is well illustrated by the pastoral Pokot of East Africa, a population closely resembling the Ariaal (Chapter 5). The Pokot's sorghum fields are critical to their survival, and they are relatively easy to defend because they are small and located near the people's houses. The fields are carefully guarded against both intruding animals and human thieves. The pastureland on which the Pokot graze their cattle is almost impossible to defend, and it would be unwise to try to defend it. It covers too large an area, and the water resources and the quality of grass vary seasonally in any one area. A well-defended patch of brown grass with dry water holes would benefit no one. The Pokot therefore exercise far less control over grazing land than over fields and farmland.

Maintaining control over a territory, whether loosely or strictly, is only the first step in regulating access to resources. Every society has principles that govern who may use which resources and under what circumstances. One important principle observed in our own society is that of private ownership of property, or freehold. Americans regard land, water, minerals, machinery, and all types of productive resources as things that someone can own. Owners, whether individuals or corporations, decide who has access to their resources and when. They may exploit them in any way they wish; they may also rent or sell them. Of course, even capitalist economies recognize that the concept of private property has limits. Systems that provide essential resources, such as transportation and electricity, are often considered public utilities and are heavily regulated, sometimes even owned outright by the government. Zoning laws further define actual use of private property. And social constraints may restrict the way one disposes of it. Few urban neighborhoods in the United States allow one to keep chickens in the backyard, although not too long ago this practice was widespread.

At the same time, effective ownership may depend on active use: In many European and American cities, squatters have taken over buildings that the owners left unoccupied. In many less developed countries, entire sections of major cities are given over to illegal shantytowns formed by rural settlers who simply erect rough dwellings on vacant land without municipal approval or title to the land. In Turkey, for example, such settlements are called *gecekondu*, or "built in the night." Taking advantage of a customary law that prohibits the destruction of one's domicile, poor people rapidly put up a house and dare the authorities to evict them.

In many nonindustrial societies, groups rather than individuals control the land and other productive resources, along with the equipment necessary for production. The individual gains rights to these resources only by virtue of affiliation with a group. We can see this form of corporate ownership best by looking at the way such groups control land.

*Ownership Versus Use Landholding Systems.* In traditional societies that do not recognize individual ownership of land, the kin group or the community at large either is the landholder or at least has a great deal to say about who uses what resources. Individuals or households may have the right to use these resources for limited periods, but they do not own them; they can neither buy nor sell the land they farm. Such kin group or community landholding rights are often termed "corporate rights." Thus, while people in most industrial countries acquire land and the resources on it through inheritance, purchase, or rental, people in most nonstate societies gain their right to land as a birthright or through marriage to a member of a landowning group. As a member of a band, for example, a Dobe Ju/'hoansi (!Kung) man or woman automatically has the right to hunt and collect wild foods within the area used by that band. The !Kung say it does not matter who owns the land itself because one cannot eat the ground. Rather, each band collectively holds the right to exploit specific water resources and patches of wild plant foods (Marshall, 1965).

With few exceptions, pastoral peoples follow the same rule. Grazing lands are generally treated as a communal asset, open to all members of the tribe—or at least to all members of the large and cooperating kin groups that typically migrate and settle together.

Horticulturists, on the other hand, are generally concerned with allocating rights to use specific plots, for they invest a great deal of time and labor in these plots. Like hunter-gatherers and pastoralists, they acquire rights to land by virtue of group membership, but to retain the right to a particular plot, one must actively use it. Among the Tiv of Nigeria, for

example, the head of the household is allowed to cultivate any unused piece of land within a territory belonging to his lineage. He may lay claim to as much land as his household can handle. As long as the household actively works these fields and keeps them clear, the members are entitled to their exclusive use. When fields revert to fallow, however, rights lapse and the land becomes part of the public domain, to be claimed by other families in the lineage. Nevertheless, a Tiv man always retains the right to some land—if not to one particular field, then to another—simply because he is a member of a certain kin group (Bohannan, 1960).

In other horticultural societies, rights of use may be acquired simply through residence in the village or through the performance of some social obligation, but again, the land must be cultivated if those rights are to remain in force. As with hunter-gatherers and pastoralists, collective as opposed to private ownership of land may be critical to a horticultural group's way of making a living.

*Private Ownership and Commercial Farming.* In areas that were ruled by European colonial powers, European systems of private ownership usually replaced traditional land-use systems. As a result, the economic system became more impersonal and less tied to a larger system of social relationships. Sometimes already-existing discrepancies between the property rights of men and women were amplified. Very often, even in horticultural and pastoral societies, property rights differ by gender; even the egalitarian Dobe !Kung recognize different rights to possession for men and women. When the colonial powers imposed the concept of private property as a means of controlling productive resources, they usually allocated ownership to men rather than to all individuals (Etienne & Leacock, 1988). Among the Buganda of Central Africa, for example, chiefs traditionally allotted portions of their estates to tenant farmers. These grants could be revoked at any time. Once the British took control of this region, they passed a law enabling tenants to do as they liked with their land grants, even pass them on to their heirs without the chief's permission. The aim was to protect tenant farmers from exploitation—and in the process, to bring them more thoroughly under colonial control through land registration and systematic taxation. As a result, in Uganda land is now individually owned.

By different routes, the movement toward private land rights has taken place in many other societies. Private ownership allows a certain freedom for individuals to make a living by using their land for their own exclusive benefit. This freedom, however, significantly alters an individual's ties to the group, along with the psychological and social advantages it once afforded. Under a system of corporate rights, since ownership is collective, the individual has a sense of place—a knowledge of belonging, in perpetuity, to this group and this piece of land. Under private ownership, land is transferable and it may belong to someone other than those who work on it. Individuals who must sell their labor because they do not own the land they farm may come to be commodities themselves, with few economic rights in, and limited benefit from, what is being produced.

Not infrequently, rural people rise up in open rebellion or revolution to assert their perceived rights to land or better conditions. The Chinese Revolution, the Mexican Revolution, and the Cuban Revolution were essentially agrarian movements, although led by urban educated intellectuals. At the present, there is a similar peasant rebellion underway in Chiapas, Mexico.

Of course, private ownership is not the only European model to have been transferred or adopted elsewhere. Various forms of collective farming, essentially products of European socialist or utopian philosophy, are still operating in Russia, South America, Asia, Africa, and China. One common denominator of these systems is that they are usually imposed on peasant farmers by outsiders; thus, in some respects, they contain the most oppressive aspects of absentee landlordism: The people who farm have a limited say in the actual management of their work and must sell their crops at prices set by impersonal agencies.

## Gender, Politics, and Property

The interests of men and women often conflict when it comes to property; the resolution of divergent claims and interests is inherent in the political process. In most of Europe, until relatively recently, the rights of women to own and inherit property (especially land) were limited. This reflected political structures in which most formal political power was vested in males. This is not surprising, since all of Europe was once governed under Roman law in which male heads of households were legally recognized as owners of, and as being responsible for, all household possessions, including wives, adult but unmarried daughters, children, slaves, and other chattel. In the twentieth century, this has changed greatly, but men and women still participate differently in the economy and with respect to control of resources. The move toward greater equality in property rights seems closely linked to the increased involvement of women in wage labor, whereby they gain greater control over household resources. This is not always without conflict. Henry Rutz (1992) has found that in Fiji, a country that has developed wage labor opportunities for women only recently, as women began earning money from wage labor, their fathers or husbands would attempt to appropriate it. This in turn led to elaborate negotiations about how much women should contribute to household or community activities and how much they could spend themselves.

The following example from Kenya illustrates something of the ongoing conflict over property rights in a society where cattle are major economic and prestige items.

## Whose Cows Are They, Anyway?

Regina Smith Oboler was carrying out ethnographic fieldwork among the Nandi of western Kenya (1996). She happened to attend a church wedding and was intrigued to find that the clergyman's sermon focused on the appropriate marital roles of husband and wife. In particular, he harangued against married women who claim to own cattle; once married, all property belonged to the family, and the cows to the husband. This remark was met by nervous laughter; most in the audience knew the ambiguity that surrounded Nandi cattle ownership.

Many Nandi women do claim to own particular cows, but in general, Nandi people, when asked "who owns cows?" will say that men do. With regard to particular animals, a man may claim to "own" a cow that his wife also claims. Part of the problem is linguistic. The term *own* has many connotations among the Nandi; several people can have rights in the same animal at the same time. In fact, Oboler suggests that the concept of ownership is misplaced in speaking of indigenous African property systems; there is no single individual who has the kind of absolute rights that the English use of the term implies (p. 269). Usually, the right of any individual to control cattle is constrained by rights in the same animal held by other individuals (p. 269). Almost everyone agrees that ". . . husbands and fathers do not have the right to use family cattle in ways that are not to the benefit of wives and children" (p. 266). A woman is given rights in cattle when she marries and, since the household is usually polygynous, she expects that her children will ultimately inherit the herd she builds up. Some cattle are also given directly to women as gifts or as part of their bridewealth; such cattle can be used only by the bride or by her full brothers. Some cattle are acquired by men through purchase with cash earned in wage labor; even so, they are expected to use them to benefit equally the houses of each of their wives.

Currently, there is a new element of ambiguity: People are selling traditional East African cattle and replacing them with high milk-producing European dairy cows. These cattle are usually regarded as if men had bought them with wages, even though often they had to sell inherited or bridewealth cattle to purchase them. This seems to threaten the rights of women. Thus, the sermon that Dr. Oboler heard can be seen ". . . as an attempt to put the force of religion behind a new norm, one favorable to the husband's position" (p. 270).

## Summary

EVOLUTIONARY ECOLOGY IS A THEORETICAL ORIENTATION that emphasizes the adaptive significance of culture and behavior, from procurement systems to kinship systems to political and religious life. There are two aspects to this orientation: evolutionary theory and ecology (the study of the interplay between organisms and their environment).

Anthropologists are concerned with the ways in which individuals and groups adapt to their ecological environments. In its simplest sense, adaptation refers to the ways organisms make adjustments that facilitate their survival (and hence, reproductive success), which determines their genetic contributions to future generations. The success or failure of adaptive responses can only be measured over the long term, and the evolutionary consequences of any observed behavior are unpredictable.

We, like many other species, adapt by learning new ways of doing things. No adaptation or response can be seen as a perfect solution; each carries with it certain costs and hazards. Also, any adaptation is opportunistic in that it makes use of whatever is already at hand. Variation, whether biological or behavioral, is the key to the process of adaptation. The recognition of variability draws attention to the process of selection among choices, the process of decision making.

To understand the nature of human decision making or problem solving, we have to consider the environment in which it takes place. Environments are dynamic. One ecologist, Lawrence Slobodkin (1968), has argued that four patterns of change underlie the dynamics of all environments: changes in the novelty, frequency, magnitude, and duration of environmental events of all sorts. The organism with the best chance of success is not necessarily the one most perfectly adapted to its environment, but rather the one that maintains its ability to respond to the environment in a wide variety of ways—to be flexible. A multitude of strategies for coping with different environmental problems are practiced in any human population. Nevertheless, behavior is usually fairly predictable and conventional.

People guide their decisions according to expectations about consequences. To predict the course of future behavior or the way a population may respond to some novel event, anthropologists have to work with certain assumptions about human decisions or choices. Larger patterns or processes are simply the expressions of myriad individual acts and beliefs. Assumptions of rationality and individual self-interest are obviously too simple and too narrow to account for the entire range of cultural behavior. Despite their limitations, however, such assumptions are useful because they allow us to form expectations of behavior with which actual behavior can be compared.

Anthropologists may use the concept of an ecosystem—the flow of energy and nutrients among the numerous species of plants and animals in a particular setting—to describe how human populations influence and are influenced by their surroundings. For an animal species, commitment to its niche (its adaptive strategy in the larger scheme) is relatively binding; the human species is distinctive in its capacity to alter its adaptive strategy and accommodate itself to many niches. However, humans are still subject to the rules established by the flow of matter and energy. We depend, as do all living things, on other species and must adjust our numbers and activities to our environment and available resources. An ecosystem may be in equilibrium—all of its components in balance—or it may not be and thus be changing. All ecosystems are limited in their capacity for change; it is often human activities that place the greatest strain on natural ecosystems. Each local environment also has a limited potential for supporting any of the life forms in it. The point at or below which a population tends to stabilize is called its carrying capacity.

Specific human food procurement systems develop in response to both general environmental characteristics and environmental variables in the local area. These variables include the quantity and quality of available resources, fluctuations in the availability of resources, and the number of other groups competing for the same resources. A population's long-term success in adjusting to its resources may depend on its ability to maintain its ecological system; in this respect, simple societies can be as successful as technologically advanced societies. A vast array of adaptive strategies are employed throughout the world, but within that wide range are certain common patterns. Among food procurement strategies, for example, there are five basic patterns: foraging or hunting and gathering, subsistence agriculture, pastoralism, intensive agriculture, and industrial agriculture.

The type and distribution of basic resources are only one aspect of an environment. Human populations make up another and no less basic aspect. Every society must adjust to the presence and activities of neighboring peoples, just as surely as it must adjust to variations in local resources. The study of this adaptive process is important enough to constitute an entire approach in human ecology. This approach, called political ecology, is the study of how people struggle to gain access to, maintain control of, and utilize natural resources in the face of competing interests. The nature of resources also affects political behavior. Competition for resources will arise only where those resources (such as fields or irrigation works) have a high intrinsic value and are in a clearly bounded area. The fields over which people usually contend are highly productive and worth defending. Hunters and gatherers, on the contrary, generally occupy lands where resources are not concentrated; thus, land ownership or control is not a major source of competition. Most agricultural and industrial societies maintain clear-cut rules that define rights to productive land and other resources. Among most hunting and gathering societies, an individual's rights to use resources are relatively unrestricted.

The interests of men and women often conflict when it comes to property; the resolution of divergent claims and interests is inherent in the political process. In most of Europe, until relatively recently, the rights of women to own and inherit property, especially land, were limited. This reflected political structures in which most formal political power was vested in males. In the last century, this has changed greatly, but men and women still participate differently in the economy and with respect to control of resources. The move toward greater equality in property rights seems closely linked to the increased involvement of women in wage labor and greater control over household resources.

In societies that do not recognize individual ownership of land, the kin group or the community at large either is the landholder or at least has a great deal to say about who uses what resources. Individuals or households may have the right to use these resources for limited periods, but they do not own them; they can neither buy nor sell the land they farm. Such kin group or community landholding rights are often termed "corporate rights." Thus, while people in the most industrial countries acquire land and the resources on it through inheritance, purchase, or rental, people in most nonstate societies gain their right to land as a birthright or through marriage to a member of a landowning group.

## Key Terms

adaptation

carrying capacity

ecosystem

environment

evolution

foraging

genes

habitat

horticulture, or subsistence agriculture

industrial agriculture

intensive agriculture

niche

pastoralism

political ecology

resilience

stability

## Suggested Readings

Abruzzi, W. S. (1993). *Dam that river! Ecology and Mormon settlement in the Little Colorado River Basin.* Lanham, MD: University Press of America. See pp. 68–69. A rich account, using ecological models, of Mormon settlement in the nineteenth century.

Bates, D. G., & Lees, S. H. (Eds.). (1996). *Case studies in human ecology.* New York: Plenum Press. A collection of case studies illustrating many aspects of human-environmental relations, organized around broadly defined procurement strategies.

Boyd, R., & Richerson, P. J. (1985). *Culture and the evolutionary process.* Chicago: University of Chicago Press. Discusses the ways psychological, sociological, and cultural factors combine to change societies. The authors also develop models to analyze how biology and culture interact under the influence of evolutionary processes to produce the diversity we see in human cultures.

Campbell, B. (1994). *Human ecology: The story of our place in nature from prehistory to the present.* Hawthorne, NY: Aldine. This book is intended as a supplementary text for social science courses dealing with our current ecological crisis. It uses the study of human prehistory as a means to understand our present evolutionary and ecological situation.

Cronk, L., Chagnon, N., & Irons, W. (Eds.). (2000). *Adaptation and human behavior: An anthropological perspective.* New York: Aldine de Gruyter. Twenty-one empirical essays that make use of the evolutionary biological paradigm. A first-rate introduction to this growing field in human ecology.

Cultural Survival, Inc. (1994). *State of the peoples: A global human rights report on societies in danger.* Boston: Beacon Press. A selection of papers by both cultural anthropologists and others that describe the urgent threats facing distinctive societies around the world as they adapt to a rapidly changing world.

Eshleman, J. R. (2003). *The family* (10th ed.). Boston: Allyn & Bacon. A fine up-to-date handbook on current ideas about the nature of the family. It offers fine-grained statistical information about all measurable aspects of family life.

Flannery, T. (2001). *The eternal frontier*. New York: Atlantic Monthly Press. An excellent introduction to the use of the ecological perspective that is especially good in describing the human component in North American ecological history.

Gilmore, D. D. (1998). *Carnival and culture: Sex, symbol and status in Spain*. New Haven, CT: Yale University Press. A very accessible and informative analysis of ritual behavior and popular culture in Spain. Carnival is a means of understanding the ways in which Andalusian people interpret and negotiate their world.

Hrdy, S. B. (2000). *Mother nature: A history of mothers, infants, and natural selection*. New York: Museum of Natural History. A primatologist looks at what it takes to be a mother in different species, including our own. She deals with gender roles, mate selection, and parenting, stressing an evolutionary view.

Moran, E. F. (2000). *Human adaptability* (2nd ed.). Boulder, CO: Westview Press. A review of principles of adaptation as well as an introduction to ecological concepts and methodology. This book is the best general review of the topic for anthropologists. The volume is particularly useful for its case study approach to human adaptation in different environmental contexts.

Pinker, S. (2002). *The blank slate: The modern denial of human nature*. New York: Viking Press. A provocative re-examination of the old nature versus nurture controversy. The author attempts to show the ways in which many intellectuals have denied the existence of any form of innate human nature.

Ridley, M. (2003). *Nature via nurture: Genes, experience, and what makes us human*. New York: HarperCollins. A popular writer on science, the author explores the significance of the human genome sequence—that is, how our genes express themselves.

Skolnick, A., & Skolnick, J. H. (2003). *Family in transition* (12th ed.). Boston: Allyn & Bacon. This book offers empirical studies of how contemporary family life is changing.

Smith, E. A., & Winterhalder, B. (Eds.). (1992). *Evolutionary ecology and human behavior*. New York: Aldine. An excellent discussion of the general principles of evolutionary ecology, together with very interesting illustrative case studies.

Stringer, C., & McKie, R. (1997). *African exodus: The origin of modern humanity*. New York: Henry Holt. A fine defense of the out-of-Africa model, which is generally the accepted one.

Tattersall, I. (1995). *The fossil trail: How we know what we think we know about human evolution*. Oxford: Oxford University Press. An up-to-date account of hominid evolution, including a careful analysis of competing models.

Wrangham, R., & Peterson, D. (1996). *Demonic males: Apes and the origins of human violence*. New York & Boston: Houghton Mifflin. A thoughtful review of what is known of ape social behavior and its possible significance for understanding human aggression.

# *Chapter 3*

# Foraging

Humans and their immediate hominid ancestors have lived on the earth for more than 4 million years, and for more than 99% of that time, they grew no food. They lived by hunting animals and gathering the plants that grew wild in their habitats. This adaptation is usually called foraging, or hunting and gathering. This form of subsistence became increasingly complex in the course of human evolution and came to require careful scheduling for collecting many (often hundreds) species of plants and hunting game; detailed environmental knowledge; and sophistication in storing, processing, and preparing food items. Further, in many instances, it involves active management of resources by such techniques as water diversion, building weirs or dams constructed out of branches, and selective burning of grasslands or forests (see Anderson, 1999; Gottesfeld Johnson, 1994).

Anatomically modern human fossils date from about 150,000 years ago in Africa, and between 30,000 and 40,000 years ago, anatomically modern humans appear in the archaeological record in sites across Europe, Asia, and soon thereafter, in North and South America. While there are many theories as to how modern *Homo sapiens* ultimately replaced their most closely related species of Neanderthals,

all seem to agree that it occurred because of major cultural breakthroughs in subsistence technology critical to foraging (Jolly & White, 1995; Tattersall, 1998). The modern hominids, as evidenced from their camps, from butchering sites (where game was killed or butchered), and from remains of stone tools, developed a hitherto unknown sophistication in hunting and gathering that involved the cooperation of many individuals, probably from different groups or bands. They made specialized tools consisting of different parts (such as spear throwers) and bladed instruments using wood, antlers, and ivory; they created sturdier housing and clothing; and they produced art—as shown so strikingly in the cave paintings of France and Spain. The proud moment of the invention of clothing, interestingly enough, can be dated to between 72,000 and 42,000 years ago, as determined by analyzing the evolution of the body louse, which only lives in clothing and which evolved from the human head louse (Wade, 2003a). At this time, we also find the first evidence for long-distance trade as a means of providing toolmaking materials to groups whose environments did not supply them. This could have also facilitated the development of a collective body of knowledge among hundreds of local groups over wide areas. At the same time, there is striking evidence for cultural diversity: In Africa alone, for example, there were at least eight different traditions of toolmaking among early humans.

Today, foraging as a primary subsistence strategy is relatively rare and becoming rarer, not just because local people are quick to adopt new technologies but also because the lands available to sustain people in this endeavor are being encroached upon by outsiders. A review of the approximately 860 historically known hunter-gatherer societies tabulated in the *Ethnographic Atlas* found that only 179 survived into recent times (Ember, 1978, p. 440). Of those 179, far fewer remain today and none are unaffected by close relations with the products of industrialism and market economies. In fact, existing foragers are threatened on every continent where they still attempt to follow their traditional adaptation (see Table 3.1). As seen in Box 3.1, the issue of who speaks for whom in representing the interests of contemporary hunter-gatherer populations threatened by development is a contentious one.

Even though this way of life is rapidly vanishing, hunter-gatherers are well worth studying for several reasons. They help us better understand the archaeological record, or what is called "ethnoarchaeology." This in turn helps us to understand our ancestors' behaviors, for example, mating systems,

leadership and political behavior, and the like. Finally, these populations offer insights into the conditions to which we have adapted over a very long period of time, even if today some of our adaptive predilections are not well matched to current circumstances.

Anthropologists, in describing any society in which they are not actually working at the time they are writing, often employ the convention known as the **ethnographic present.** The term indicates that the information being presented applies to when the data were collected; it doesn't necessarily describe the way the people in question may be living at the time the report is read. All of the peoples we discuss should be understood with this fact in mind, for lifestyles and technologies can change radically from one year to the next.

This chapter looks at three examples of foraging, or hunting and gathering, groups. The first are the Dobe Ju/'hoansi, or !Kung (also sometimes called the Basarwa), who lived, when the first studies were carried out, by gathering nuts, vegetables, and fruits and by hunting wild animals on a semiarid plain in southwestern Africa. In their case, the term "foraging" is certainly appropriate; while they made economic use of hundreds of species, the bulk of their diet was supplied by plants. The second case is a composite portrait of the people whom outsiders

### Table 3.1 Contemporary or Recent Foraging Populations

| Africa | | South America | |
|---|---|---|---|
| San (Angola, Botswana, Namibia, South Africa, Zimbabwe) | 100,000 | Amazon (Ache, Siriono, Huaorani, Botocudo, Aweikoma, Ayoreo) | 2,500 |
| Pygmies (Ba Twa, Ba, Mbuti, Baka, Aka) (Central Africa) | 200,000 | Tierra del Fuego (Alacaluf, Ona, Yaghan) | 1,000 |
| Okiek (Dorrobo) (Kenya, Tanzania) | 40,000 | **North America** | |
| Hadza (Tanzania) | 2,000 | Inuit (Nunamiut, Copper Eskimo, Netsilik) | 100,000 |
| **Asia** | | Aleuts | 30,000 |
| Northern Peoples of Siberia (Yukaghir, Gilyak) | 200,000 | Northern Indians (Kutchin, Kaska, Chipaweyan, Montagnais) | 50,000 |
| Ainu (Japan) | 26,000 | Northwest Coast (Tlingit, Tsimshian, Bella Bella, Kwakiutl, Chinook) | 50,000 |
| Penan (Malaysia) | 20,000 | Californian (Modoc, Washo, Yuki, Wintu, Yokuts, Seri) | 25,000 |
| **Australia** | | | |
| Tiwi, Murngin, Walbiri, Aranda, Dieri, Wikmunkan | 300,000 | Total | 1,146,500 |

*Source:* Compiled by Robert Hitchcock, University of Nebraska at Lincoln.

---

## Box 3.1

# Who Speaks for Whom?

IN 1992, WHEN J. PETER BROSIUS returned to Sarawak to visit the Eastern Penan, he was surprised at the frequency with which they referred to the great loss of medicinal plants as being one of the worst consequences of the destruction of their forest environment (1997, p. 62). In his three years of fieldwork among the Western Penan in the 1980s, he had rarely heard discussion of medicinal plants, even though, based on his experiences among the Pinatubo Atya in the Philippines, he expected to hear more. What accounted for this change?

In the early 1980s, timber companies began moving into the upland areas of Borneo (Malaysia) inhabited by various groups of Penan hunter-gatherers. Since 1987, when the Penan began to actively resist by blockading access, they have become the focus of an international environmental campaign to protect their land rights and preserve the rain forest. All over the world, environmental organizations became involved in various aspects of the Sarawak campaign, although, remarkably, the campaign was never centrally organized but evolved independently as the situation of the Penan became more widely publicized in the media. "In short, the Penan have become icons of [indigenous] resistance for environmentalists worldwide" (1997, p. 48).

Environmentalists (and Brosius includes here both representatives of environmental organizations such as World Wide Fund for Nature and Greenpeace, as well as indigenous rights organizations such as Survival International and Cultural Survival) are concerned with peoples who are "endangered . . . precisely because they, their institutions, and their systems of land-tenure are disvalued by national governments" (1997, p. 64). In the case of the Penan, and similarly for other peoples throughout the world, environmentalists have to demonstrate to national governments, in this case the Malaysian government, and to Western audiences the dire consequences of the destruction of the rain forest and the Penan.

One way Brosius sees this as being achieved in environmentalist texts is the transformation of indigenous knowledge into "wisdom, spiritual insight, or some other such quality" (p. 64). Since accessing indigenous knowledge is not something that can be achieved in a few weeks (or even months, as anthropologists are especially aware), the problem is how to represent the knowledge as valuable without actually understanding it. In linking this knowledge to the sacred, the authors are able to discuss the meaning of a body of knowledge, rather than the knowledge itself, providing what Brosius terms "meta-commentaries." He quotes anthropologist David Maybury-Lewis:

*Western science . . . is only now beginning to understand that*

---

usually refer to as the Inuit, or "Eskimo"; that is, the indigenous populations of the circumpolar regions of arctic Alaska and northeastern Canada. Many of these peoples still support themselves primarily by hunting and fishing (using modern technology to do so) but also increasingly by wage labor in the oil fields. The third case, that of the Batak of Palawan Island, the Philippines, concerns a population of foragers who are increasingly caught up in the larger economy and coming to rely on farming while retaining many of their traditional ways.

In certain respects, the lives of these modern hunter-gatherers, until quite recently at least, probably paralleled the lives of early prehistoric humans. This is one of the reasons they are of such great interest to anthropologists and also are the source of some controversy (Burch & Ellanna, 1994; Lee, 1993; Wilmsen, 1989a, 1989b). The study of recent or contemporary foragers may help us understand why and how some aspects of human culture developed as they did, but it is important to bear in mind that the hunter-gatherers of today are not "throwbacks" or "living fossils." As Wilmsen and others have stressed, every modern population has a long and varied history regardless of whether written records exist and cannot be seen as direct evidence of how earlier populations might have lived (1989a). On the contrary, they are twenty-first-century people with twenty-first-century problems. As Eder (1996) has pointed out in the case of the Batak in the Philippines, hunter-gatherers are quick to incorporate new technologies into their subsistence systems. They deal with governments that have jurisdiction over them and with neighbors whose cultures may be quite different from their own. All hunter-gatherers have been drawn into exchanges with other groups: doing occasional wage labor for nearby agriculturists and pastoralists, buying from and selling to traders from industrialized societies, and even at times receiving welfare from their governments.

*peoples who had no "science" of their own could nevertheless have developed a profound knowledge of their corner of the natural world. This is nowhere more true than in the rainforests, yet it is in the rainforests that the clash between Western arrogance and **traditional wisdom** is most violent.* (Maybury-Lewis, 1992, p. 46. Emphasis added.)

Based on his own published articles on the (Western) Penan (1986, 1988, 1990), Brosius provides a number of examples of the transformation of ethnographic texts into environmentalist texts, and "how, in the process the substantive properties of indigenous knowledge are also transformed" (p. 55). For instance, he discusses the Penan knowledge of the landscape.

*the richness of vocabulary for talking about landforms and rivers, the way in which rivers form the skeleton around which environmental knowledge is organized, and how river names incorporate geographical, ecological, historical, and genealogical information . . . to demonstrate how Penan encode*

*ecological information in the naming of landscape features, and to demonstrate the coherence . . . between the physical landscape, history, genealogy, and the identities of individuals and communities.* (p. 59)

His discussion is transformed by Wade Davis in *Penan: Voice for the Borneo Rainforest* (Davis & Henley, 1990), who states that "For the Penan this forest is alive, pulsing, responsive in a thousand ways to their physical needs and their spiritual readiness" (p. 98). The Penan are skilled naturalists, Davis asserts, because they identify "both psychologically and cosmologically with the rainforest" (p. 99).

Brosius warns of the pernicious effects of imposing meanings on Penan "knowledge" that may be imaginary. The Penan certainly have a sense of the sacred and ineffable, which they express in a range of concepts relating to power, avoidance, and respect, among others. But he maintains, "it is nothing like the obscurantist sanctity Davis and Henley describe" (p. 65). In addition, in describing Penan knowledge as "wisdom" or "spiri-

tual insight," the environmentalist metacommentary deprives them of the diversity that defines them, and transforms them into generic "indigenous people" or "forest people," interchangeable with, for instance, the Mbuti of Zaire or the Ache of Paraguay. In the effort to make the people and their knowledge valuable, "environmentalist discourse . . . has the potential to transform that knowledge into something it is not . . . Thus the rich, if generally mundane, Penan knowledge of the forest landscape, by being transformed into something that is sacred, valued, and thus to be saved, is constructed in terms of categories that are Western in origin . . . Western discourses are transported to the Penan, who again convey them to Western interlocutors" (p. 66).

Brosius concludes:

*As the future of the forests, other biomes, and indigenous peoples is negotiated in the years ahead . . . the issue of who talks for whom and who constructs representations of whom is critical.* (p. 66)

Modern foragers are people for whom some version of this ancient subsistence strategy is still effective in their particular environments. The fact that most hunter-gatherers throughout history lived in areas far more hospitable than those they inhabit today implies that food sources were more abundant and reliable, nutrition better, and population densities higher than we see among current foragers. An examination of some of the methods of food procurement used by hunter-gatherers, their systems of kinship, residence patterns, and other cultural traits will show that these behaviors constitute solutions to the problems of making a living in their particular habitats.

*Archaeological Evidence for Ancient Foragers.* Many archaeologists believe that a hunting and gathering lifestyle must have been determined to a great extent by the environment. For example, the early settlement patterns of foraging peoples of the Americas incorporated several types of sites apparently serving different functions, such as base camps, seasonal camps, butchering sites, quarry sites, and other locales of human activity. Different artifacts and different types of evidence of human activity characterize these sites. Base camps contain evidence for the preparation of food and the construction of shelters and a large variety of tools and toolmaking debris; such sites are usually located close to a permanent source of water and provide evidence for long-term use or reuse. Seasonal camps contain much sparser evidence for human activities; tools are simpler and less worked. Butchering sites (also known as kill sites) show evidence of meat processing activities—broken tools, both crafted and simple, are found in proximity to animal bones. Quarry sites show evidence of the extraction of toolmaking materials such as chert or flint and frequently have caches of unfinished and broken tools. Other sites may not always be easy to classify in terms of their specific function, but they show evidence of human activities. The existence of such a variety of sites confirms that early Americans must have had a very specific knowledge of their environment and must have used their knowledge to make decisions as to the most appropriate sites for their various activities.

# The Organization of Energy

Hunters and gatherers subsist primarily on wild plants and animals. Unlike agriculture, the hunting and gathering economy does not involve as much direct or intensive intervention to regulate the growth and reproduction of the life forms on which people depend. The diet of hunter-gatherers is more strictly determined by habitat than that of other groups. In fact, abundant wild resources are available in any American city but not in quantities sufficient to sustain a population of any great size.

As local environments vary, so do the dietary staples of their inhabitants. Peoples who live in areas where plant life is more abundant or reliable than game depend primarily on vegetable foods—nuts, fruits, and the like. Such is the case, for example, with the Dobe dwellers of Africa's Kalahari. The Eskimo, by contrast, rely much more heavily on meat and fish, for plant life is scarce in the arctic. Whatever its emphasis, however, the diet of hunter-gatherers tends to be highly diversified because it must be responsive to seasonal and annual fluctuations in resources.

If anyone were tempted to characterize hunter-gatherer subsistence as "simple," Scott Cane's (1996) study of the traditional seasonal round of the inhabitants of the Great Sandy Desert in Australia would disabuse them of the notion. His study, conducted over six years with the Gugadja people, meticulously documents the resources utilized and methods of procurement and processing. He assesses the relative nutritional contribution and importance of key foods, providing quantified data on seed collection and processing—a key element in aboriginal diet and one that allows them to exploit a habitat characterized by seasonally extreme aridity. Seeds are stored for the aptly named "hungry season." It has long been known that seeds were important to Australian hunter-gatherers; Cane, however, shows that this is not true in terms of caloric intake. Seeds require much effort in collection, winnowing, and particularly in preparing them for final cooking and consumption. It is because they can be stored that they are vital. By documenting dietary shifts from season to season, Cane demonstrates that it is inaccurate to characterize such economies as primarily based on "hunting" or "gathering"; what people eat and how much effort they expend depend on the season. Within the study area, 126 species of plants were recognized and named and used for 138 different economic, social, and medicinal functions. Edible seeds were collected from forty-two plants. The Gugadja also hunt and they process reptiles, tubers, fruits, birds, and large game. Their subsistence is not, Cane reports, precarious or even difficult on balance; rather, there is a seasonal rhythm. Vegetable foods dominate the winter season and make up to 70% of food consumed; but with spring, their diet becomes much more generalized, utilizing both meat and vegetable foods. Women and men contribute about the same to subsistence, although their roles vary depending on the season.

## *Managing Resources*

This is not to say that foragers do not manage their resource bases. In both North and South America, indigenous foragers use fire to burn forest cover on a regular basis to promote the growth of vegetation supporting favored game animals or favored root tubers or berries (Gottesfeld, 1994). Coincidentally, this periodic burning may be instrumental in promoting the long-term health of the forest as well because it prevents the buildup of undergrowth that can cause dangerous fires or harbor disease.

In fact, much of pre-Columbian North American forest and plains vegetation was a product of human land use strategies engaged in by both native farmers and hunter-gatherers, with seasonal and selective burning being foremost in importance. One recent report documents how critical native practices were in what is now the state of California and most likely for many other regions as well (Anderson, 1999). Anderson's study focuses on the neglected area of basketry. All over the world, and well before the rise of farming, basketry has been prized not only for aesthetic reasons but for its utility; baskets are of vital importance as containers for goods of all types. Basketry generally requires material in the form of straight, supple growth taken from shrubs and trees unaffected by insects, diseases, or accumulated dead growth. Such growth does not occur in abundance in nature but can be encouraged by frequent "light fires" such those used by the Native Americans from coast to coast (Anderson, 1999, pp. 96–97). "Light fires" are fires set before shrubs reach maturity, and thus, they induce both rapid growth of fresh grass as well as an abundance of supple, harvestable branches; old growth, when it burns, results in a catastrophic destruction of root systems and animal life. Modern forestry has come belatedly to understand the value of these ancient techniques.

Hill and Baird, looking at aboriginal use of fire in Queensland, Australia, go so far as to suggest that in systematically burning tropical forests, the native hunter-gatherers were really using fire to "grow" a certain tree seed (*Cycas media*) essential to their diet (2003, pp. 27ff.). Fires were set in patches of rain forest to maximize relatively open plots within larger forests.

Most, if not all, foraging peoples engage in varying degrees of exchange with other societies. The Mbuti Pygmies of Zaire, although often described as self-sufficient hunters, sell antelope and other game to visiting traders and buy the agricultural products and manufactured foods of their Bantu and Sudanic neighbors (Milton, 1985). It is extremely doubtful that they could have survived otherwise (Hart & Hart, 1986). The Dobe people also trade with and work for the Bantu farmers (Wilmsen, 1989a, 1989b). The Eskimo hunt not only for their subsistence needs but also to enable them to trade for the innumerable products of industrial society on which they have come to depend (see, for example, Feit, 1994, pp. 421–440).

An interesting contemporary use of gathering as a source of income in otherwise commercialized economies is the gathering of wild snails, mushrooms, and truffles in many parts of Europe and Asia. In addition, sometimes the income produced by gathering wild products can influence the economic value of areas such as wetlands or woodlands. In Turkey, people in the Karasu wetlands on the Black Sea coast have taken to harvesting wild reeds, which they prepare for sale to florists all over the country. Although the per household income is not great and this is mostly done to supplement the income of the poorest sector of the rural population, taken cumulatively and in addition to income generated from fishing, it is sufficiently significant to tip the economic balance in favor of wetland preservation as opposed to draining and development (Özesmi, 2003).

## Food as Energy

One of the reasons anthropologists find hunter-gatherers especially fascinating is that these people show us how humans can live on a low-energy budget. A **low-energy budget** is an adaptive strategy by which a minimum of energy is used to extract sufficient resources from the environment for survival. All humans, of course, have roughly the same basic nutritional requirements and constraints, modified by body stature and environmental factors such as altitude or climate, for example. What does vary is the amount of energy we expend, directly or indirectly, in support of a particular population. Humans are distinctively adept at extracting energy

from the environment, but we also expend great amounts of energy in doing so. A single sack of potatoes, for example, represents a considerable investment of energy: in manufacturing the fertilizers and pesticides that were used on the potatoes; on powering the machines that planted, fertilized, sprayed, and harvested the crop; in packing and transporting the harvest; and so on. In comparison with other animals, humans—especially in industrialized societies—live on a high-energy budget. Foragers are the dramatic exception to this rule.

In general, the primary source of energy that hunter-gatherers expend in food procurement is that contained in their own muscles. While they may invest energy in building shelters, traps, and even boats or weirs, relatively little effort is directed into the construction of a complicated infrastructure of food procurement—cleared fields, irrigation systems, or fuel-burning machines. As a result, hunter-gatherers spend much less energy to support a single unit of population than do other peoples. And since they generally support themselves rather well in terms of nutrition, leisure time, and general physical well-being, their system must be regarded as remarkably efficient.

They are also efficient in preserving their resource bases. Because of their low expenditure of energy and because they tend to exploit a wide variety of foods, hunter-gatherers place relatively limited demands on any one of their resources. At the same time, their way of life seems to limit their population growth; their numbers tend to remain proportionate to those of the animal and plant species on which they depend. The combined result of this adaptive strategy—low-energy needs, a wide resource base, controlled population—is that foragers interfere relatively little with other components of their ecosystems. Because humans are the most versatile predators in their habitats, they do affect the populations of the species on which they feed. However, their ecosystems appear to be in relative equilibrium, and their resource bases may remain unthreatened, at least in comparison with those of other economic systems. This "conservationist" approach is largely inadvertent and easily altered by new technologies.

A rapid expansion of population accompanied the development of agriculture in most parts of the world. With this development, many foragers became pastoralists or horticulturists, relying on domesticated plants and animals for their subsistence. Later, as new agricultural techniques (such as irrigation and plowing with livestock) were introduced, horticulturists turned to intensive farming, which led to further growth in human populations. Populations in some societies have stabilized, but most are still experiencing population growth as new technologies are introduced. The resulting demand for ever more food encourages people to increase their efforts to produce reliable harvests.

Thus, people come to reshape their environments—digging canals, planting crops, eliminating insects—and in the process, they are locked into a struggle to maintain themselves at the expense of the equilibrium of the ecosystem.

Of course, hunter-gatherers are also quite capable of overexploiting their resources. The Miskito of Nicaragua came close to wiping out the local turtle population. Though turtles are their primary source of protein, they were lured by cash payments from turtle-packing companies to hunt the sea animals to the verge of extinction. Fortunately, the nine-year war with the Sandinistas interrupted the commercial fishing operations, and the sea turtle population recovered. Now the Miskito are actively trying to gain rights to their sea territories so they can again use traditional means to manage this resource. No longer partners in the commercial fishing operations, Miskito communities are now fighting to preserve their valuable resource (Nietschmann, 1995). Likewise, when the native North Americans suddenly found themselves in contact with a European market for beaver skins in the eighteenth century, they hunted nearly to extinction an animal on which they had depended for centuries. In both cases, we see essentially the same process: Once people who have been exploiting a resource for a limited market (themselves) are tied in to an unlimited market, the attraction of short-term gains often leads to the depletion of the resource.

As these examples suggest, those hunting and gathering peoples who have preserved their resource bases have not necessarily done so because they em-

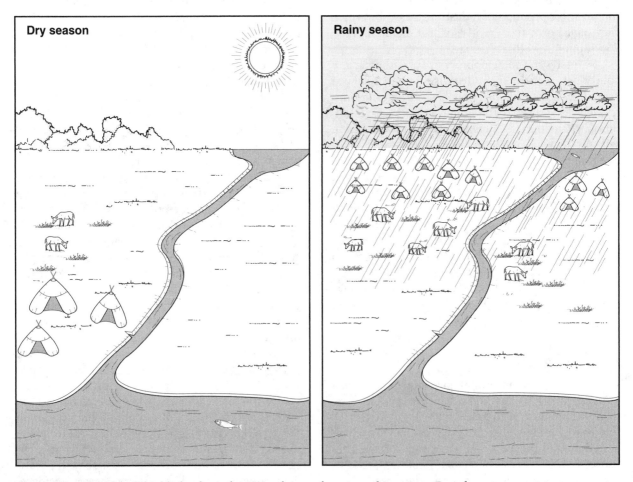

**Figure 3.1.** *This sketch highlights basic features of many foraging adaptations. Populations exploit a wide variety of wild food sources, often thousands of species, and frequently move across landscapes to do so, with marked seasonality due to summer aridity and winter rains. Populations may concentrate more in dry seasons around water sources and disperse widely in smaller groups during rainy periods. Since the availability of game and vegetable foods changes, diets may vary sharply according to season.*

*Hauling a green turtle* (Chelonia mydas) *on board off the Miskito Coast, Nicaragua. Commercial hunting has greatly reduced this once abundant species.*
(Bill Curtsinger)

braced a conservationist ethic, although some may do so (Gottesfeld, 1995). Nor can it be safely claimed that they deliberately limit their population to adjust it to their resources. It appears, rather, that several interrelated factors have operated to maintain these peoples in balance with their resources. These factors include limitations imposed by their storage technology, the absence of a wider market for the food produced, the lack of fossil fuels, and other environmental conditions that constrain population growth. An examination of the Dobe !Kung (Ju/'hoansi), the Eskimo (Inuit), and the Batak of the Philippines will show how people in three societies make a living and how various cultural practices contribute to their adaptation to harsh environments.

## Social Organization

No one type of social organization inevitably issues from any food procurement strategy, including foraging. The way foragers organize themselves politically and socially varies widely. However, since the environments of most recent and contemporary foragers tend to be the less desirable habitats with relatively sparse and highly variable resources, the groups occupying these environments share certain broadly defined attributes of social organization.

Foragers typically live in small groups—camps of closely related families. The size of the camps, and of the society as a whole, is limited by the local supply of natural resources. Unlike agricultural societies, hunter-gatherers cannot easily increase food production to accommodate an increase in population. Their population levels reflect the availability of food during the worst season of the year because, for the most part, they lack the technology for bulk food storage. When food (or even water) cannot be stored, the season in which the least food is available limits population, no matter how abundant food may be in other seasons. And since their lands today are marginal, their population densities are generally low. This, of course, was not true for many earlier populations where abundant and predictable food sources permitted large, settled concentrations of population, such as on the northwest coast of North America.

### Economic Exchange: Reciprocity

A critical factor in the adaptation of modern foragers is the rule of **reciprocity**—that is, the systematic sharing of food and other goods. Central to any economy, in fact to social life in general, is the near constant give and take among individuals. While much of this may be simply passing the time of day, there is also a continual movement of material items from hand to hand. In a more elaborate sense, this is what "economics" is all about: the organization of rights to things, the production of things, and their ultimate exchange. To understand traditional hunter-gatherers, this topic is of vital concern.

Some resources in every society are kept and consumed by those who produced them or procured them, while the rest enter the society's network of exchange. Exchange, a basic part of any economic system, allows people to dispose of their unneeded surpluses against future need and to acquire necessities from other people's unneeded surpluses. At the same time, exchange serves as social cement. Indeed, some anthropologists have argued that regardless of what is exchanged, the very act of exchange is the primary bond that holds societies together.

Reciprocity is the key. While systematic reciprocity is important everywhere, gifts are given more often, in greater quantity, and to more people in non-industrialized settings, and in particular among hunter-gatherers or foragers. The obligation to reciprocate is stronger, and most important, reciprocity

*An aboriginal Australian family group on trek. Few support themselves today primarily through foraging, but many treasure their traditional lifestyle and culture.*
(© Penny Tweedie/Woodfin Camp & Associates)

plays a fundamental part in the actual production process, as it is likely to involve strategic food resources.

Because reciprocity is so crucial to the economies of these societies, it does not always take place in the atmosphere of casual benevolence associated with our familial and neighborly exchanges of favors. Anthropologists have identified three forms of reciprocity, each involving a distinctive degree of intimacy between giver and taker and hence a distinctive measure of formality and goodwill: generalized, balanced, and negative reciprocity (Sahlins, 1965).

Household members, other relatives, and friends usually engage in **generalized reciprocity**—informal gift giving for which no accounts are kept and no immediate or specific returns are expected. The !Kung even have a word for it: *hxaro*. Household members, close kin, and perhaps close neighbors routinely provide services for one another with no calculation of expected return; a mother does not record for future use the cost of the breakfast she feeds her children. Households usually pool all or most of their foods and share in their consumption without close regard to who may be getting the most out of each transaction. Even the most casual form of reciprocity, however, operates with the implicit understanding that goods and services exchanged are to be continued over the long run. Household members assume that they can rely on long-term mutual support; neighbors who "help out" assume that when they need help, others will come to their assistance. So in one important respect, reciprocity is a form of storage or warehousing: You give goods or services to someone

else, and ultimately, even without close calculation, you receive something comparable. This is particularly useful when the goods are perishable and cannot otherwise be stored for future use. Historically, this was almost always the case with foragers—so reciprocity might be called "social storage."

Generalized reciprocity was the characteristic form of exchange among hunting and gathering peoples and was essential to their adaptation. The Dobe !Kung, as we will see shortly, have no means of preserving meat. So they exchange access to meat by sharing. When a hunter kills a sizable animal, he keeps only a small share for his family. The rest he distributes among his hunting companions, who share their portions with their kin, who in turn share with other kin. Tomorrow or next week, the favor will be returned. The result is that despite constantly shifting and uncertain resources, everyone eats (Marshall, 1965). Of course, this is not to say that individual self-interest is lost sight of in these transactions. Melvin Konner, who worked many years with the !Kung, recalled that one respected man in the group approached him with the leg of an antelope he had killed and asked that the anthropologist keep it for him so he could consume it later (1983, p. 375). It was clear that one reason members of this group shared widely was that they had limited means of storage, and it was physically very difficult to keep one's relatives and neighbors from eating one's food or using one's other possessions.

Somewhat more formal than generalized reciprocity is **balanced reciprocity**, gift giving that clearly carries the obligation of an eventual and

## Box 3.2

# Integrating Indigenous Knowledge into Resource Management: Australia and the United States[1]

Only recently has it come to be recognized that much of the land areas of Australia and North America were actively managed by pre-European indigenous peoples. European settlers, with some notable exceptions when their very survival depended on native expertise, viewed these vast regions as "wilderness," or *terra nullius*—land unowned and unmanaged. Although it is now clear that this was not the case, nevertheless, many laypeople and scientists alike assume that the indigenous knowledge relevant to land management is something from the past that disappeared with the arrival of Europeans. But Anne Ross and Kathleen Pickering (2002) argue strongly that in many instances indigenous land-use knowledge has been retained and should be incorporated once more into active management schemes. They take as examples the native people of Moreton Bay, Queensland, in Australia and of the Puget Sound region of North America.

The peoples of Moreton Bay, known collectively as the people of Quandamooka, exploited and actively managed their marine and terrestrial resources. Mullet were prized but very difficult to catch from canoes in open sea. In pre-European days, the mullet would stream into the waters of the bay, led, the aborigines said, by their "elders." For this reason, they never harvested the mature or older fish until the end of the season so as not to disturb the migratory pattern. Once in the bay, the people used dolphins to help herd the fish toward shore, where they could be easily caught. Shellfish were another bay resource and were grown on artificial reefs built up over long periods of time. Fresh water creeks were managed to keep the beds clean, and new oyster beds were regularly built to ensure year-long harvests. Dudongs, large marine mammals, were hunted in a

manner tightly restricted by ritual procedures, and village elders limited the numbers taken to maintain the dudong population as an ongoing resource. Following the arrival of Europeans, the aborigines lost control of the bay and its resources.

The twenty tribes of the Puget Sound area include the people of Squaxin Island. Traditional subsistence was heavily focused on fishing, especially for salmon but also for shellfish. The yearly calender was divided into stages corresponding to the salmon life cycle. As with the mullet fishing of Moreton Bay, the focus was on sustained yield: Gill nets had large holes to allow immature fish to pass through, nets were placed only one third of the way across rivers, and most important, fishing stopped once food needs were met. As for shellfish, elders regulated when and which banks could be harvested to ensure a year-round harvest.

The coming of European settlers changed more than just the numbers of stakeholders exploiting the two regions in question. The newcomers commercialized the local resources with no regard to native subsistence use and with little long-term thought to sustainability. Europeans implemented "scientific management" practices without regard for preexisting systems of usage. In Australia, by far the most egregious example, few native rights to land and resources were recognized until quite recently, and there was little or no consultation with indigenous stakeholders. The waters off Queensland were heavily fished, and mullet no longer come in significant numbers to the bay. The oyster reefs are no longer managed and have declined. Dudong numbers are in decline because of habitat loss: The grassy beds on which they feed are degraded, and they are also being drowned in commercial nets. In Puget Sound, commercial fishing and dams on rivers

have had a negative impact on resource availability. In both Australia and the United States, indigenous people are actively organizing to reclaim some of their voice in resource management where they live. They are not concerned with returning to the past but rather are interested in adapting modern technology to traditional practices to promote conservation, and they are certainly not averse to the use, for example, of hatcheries and fishing regulations to advance their goals.

One important difference exists between the strategies available to native conservationists in Australia and the United States. In Australia, there are no treaties between the government and the aboriginal peoples. In the United States, the myriad treaties entered into by the successive governments are recognized as the law of the land so that litigation has been the main vehicle for native peoples to take control of their resources. In Puget Sound, the Boldt Decision of 1998 required that a Native American resource management body be established with recognized rights. In Australia, native rights have been advanced mainly by direct negotiation, and successes have been more limited. In practice, Australian aborigines have little interaction with federal regulators, unlike Native Americans, who deal with the Bureau of Indian Affairs, a federal agency, as well as with state and township authorities. In spite of the legal obstacles, the Australian aboriginals, like their North American counterparts, are incorporating a strong environmental note into their struggle for recognition and local self-rule.

[1]Largely based on Ross and Pickering (2002), The politics of reintegrating Australian aboriginal and American Indian indigenous knowledge into resource management: The dynamics of resource appropriation and cultural revival. *Human Ecology*, 30(2), pp. 187–214.

roughly equal return. This form of reciprocity normally takes place between more distantly related individuals, friends of roughly equal social or economic status, or formal trading partners. The expectation is explicit: What is given must be balanced by a return of something comparable. As with generalized reciprocity, what is returned may be quite different from what is received, and the return gift or favor may be given later.

Exchanges between enemies or strangers are generally impersonal transactions, with each side trying to get the better end of the bargain. Such exchanges, classified as **negative reciprocity,** involve an effort to get something for nothing or for as little as possible. They can range from unfriendly haggling to outright theft. The Mbuti Pygmies, for example, find it expedient to exchange meat and their own labor for the produce and metal of their horticultural neighbors, but these exchanges are marked by a good deal of mutual antagonism. The villagers use threats and bribes in an effort to get as much from the Mbuti Pygmies as they can, while the Pygmies do their best to work as little as possible.

Sometimes the lines between the different modes of reciprocity become blurred. Among the settled hunter-gatherers of the northwest coast of North America, there was a distinct form of reciprocity called the **potlatch.** Here reciprocity was manipulated to gain social or political advantage. Chiefs or important individuals would, on occasion, give away vast quantities of goods—blankets, furs, copper, and of course, food. This was "balanced" reciprocity in that over the years the feast giver would have received similar munificence, but it was also somewhat "negative" in that it could be highly competitive and loaded with political significance as men strove for political recognition and power.

## Power, Influence, and Social Control

Some members of a hunting-gathering band will have more influence than others, and men tend to have more influence than women, but it is rare for anyone to have institutionalized power—that is, an office authorizing one person to make decisions for others. Decision-making power is spread rather broadly among all the families in the group. Those who disagree are likely to move away.

Systems of **social control** in foraging groups also tend to be informal. Order is maintained on a day-to-day, consensual basis rather than through adherence to codified laws enforced by an administrative hierarchy. Codes of conduct and their enforcement are integral parts of the group's traditions, myths,

and religious ideology. Both the definition of crime and the appropriate punishment reflect the consensus within the group at any given time. Some Eskimo, for example, had "dueling songs" to resolve all disputes except those involving murder (Hoebel, 1954). The two disputants, with their families serving as choruses, perform songs to express their side of the story and to vent their anger, and the winner is chosen by the applause of those attending the song duel. No decision is made as to who is right or wrong in terms of a body of law existing apart from public opinion. The most important thing is that the parties feel that the complaint has been raised and laid to rest; they then can resume normal social relations.

In extreme cases, individuals who repeatedly violate rules and social expectations in foraging societies may be ostracized by the group. But most commonly, the dispute is between two parties, and if it cannot be resolved, the disputants and their families simply move apart.

This type of social organization, characterized by great fluidity, flexibility, and equality, is by no means inherent in the hunting and gathering way of life. When food resources are regularly available in relative abundance, foraging can support a highly structured cultural system accompanied by high population density. There is archaeological evidence in the Old and New Worlds that some foraging societies of the past (much like fishing communities to-

*The* potlatch *was an important social and economic institution among the people of the pacific Northwest until it was suppressed by the U.S. and Canadian governments.*

(Archive Photos Getty Images)

day) had large year-round settlements numbering several hundred members, with considerable inequality of status and wealth (Hayden, 1994; Price, 1981). Indeed, various groups of Native American hunter-gatherers lived in permanent villages, had chiefs and hierarchies of other officials, and observed rankings of wealth and power—all predicated on a complex division of labor that involved castes and slavery. They traded with other groups, conducted warfare, incorporated captives into their labor force, and so on. In such complex foraging societies, competition among individuals and groups was intense and, as Hayden suggests, very closely related to the fact that certain resources were abundant, concentrated, and capable of being stored or transformed into political power and prestige. In short, they very much resembled advanced agricultural societies.

## Settlement Patterns and Mobility

A major concern of anthropologists who study human-environmental interaction is the manner in which people distribute themselves over the landscape. What is the nature of the settlements they occupy? How frequently, if at all, do they move? How are such decisions affected by the variability of resources from place to place and from time to time? Forager groups today tend to be nomadic. Their seasonal migrations on their home ranges are adjusted to the availability of resources in different places at different times. Once again, the limits of storage and transport technology are important. Most foragers deal with variability in resources by moving people to the food rather than by moving food to the people.

Often, the camps of related families form larger groupings, called **bands,** within a territory. The members of a band may come together at one or another of these camps for ceremonies, or the band may simply be an aggregation of people who regularly intermarry. The bands are strikingly flexible in their composition, expanding and contracting in response to fluctuations in resources. When certain resources are scattered, the members of the bands also scatter. Later, when game converges in one area or when large permanent water holes offer the only available water, camping groups come together again to exploit these resources jointly. Social habits also play a part in the flexibility of the bands. Groups are continually re-forming as families visit or entertain their kin, move away from bands with which they do not get along, or move into bands

that are short on people or long on resources and fellowship. Generally, foragers exhibit a territorial system of land use; that is, they identify a particular tract of resources as belonging to a particular local group with outsiders having limited access (Gottesfeld Johnson, 1994). The main source of variability in this is the degree to which usage is exclusive and the willingness of the putative owners to defend their territory by force.

Although most contemporary foragers make use of mobility to track seasonal food sources, more sedentary patterns can be found. The Kwakiutl of the American northwest coast, the Chumash of southern California, the Ainu of Japan, and the Andaman Islanders of India are foraging groups whose members lived in large, sedentary villages. In such cases, the key factor seems to be the availability of large quantities of stable and storable resources. Especially important are environments containing great quantities of fish and shellfish, which are often fairly concentrated, predictable, and abundant. Also, as seen in our discussion of the Batak foragers of the Philippines, one should not be too quick to generalize about the relationship of sedentism to foraging or farming.

## Resilience, Stability, and Change

Of all the adaptive patterns, that of foragers interfered the least with the resilience of their ecosystems. While interaction and exchange occur, ties of dependence between families (and especially between groups) are minimal. These people adjust to the environment by making use of any local resource that is abundant. At the opposite extreme are societies such as our own, which use a vast array of chemical and mechanical strategies to control the environment irrespective of changing conditions.

The viability of the hunter-gatherer strategy is based on the limited degree to which environmental problems are transmitted from one group to another. Some groups succeed; others fail. Yet this is the food procurement strategy that humans employed as they became the dominant species on earth. It is interesting to note one circumstance in which this form of adaptation came into direct competition with a technologically more advanced system of procurement. As explained in greater detail in Chapter 8, the Vikings of Norway settled Greenland in the tenth century and maintained colonies whose economy was based on farming, seal hunting, and fishing. They did not, however, adopt the patterns of hunting used by the indigenous Eskimo, whom they feared and despised. The Viking practices were not well-adapted to the environment in Greenland, and the settlers were unable to secure food in sufficient abundance to support themselves. Eventually, the colonies died out, leaving Greenland once again the exclusive domain of the Eskimo (McGovern et al., 1988, 1996; Pringle, 1997).

The superiority of the indigenous hunter-gatherer adaptations to the European technology introduced into Greenland is not an isolated instance. In 1846, Sir John Franklin and his entire expedition (two ships, 200 men) starved to death in the heart of Netsilik Eskimo territory, presumably because they could or would not use Eskimo food procurement techniques (Cyriax, 1939). The Burke and Wills expedition of 1861 attempted to cross Australia from south to north and return; all but one explorer starved to death as they refused to forage or accept assistance from the aborigines until it was too late (Moorehead, 1963).

The following three foraging populations illustrate the points we have been stressing. Keep in mind, though, the warning regarding the rapid changes that such peoples everywhere are undergoing. The three societies we will explore are those of the Dobe Ju/'hoansi, or !Kung, of southwest Africa, the Inuit (or as they are still commonly referred to, the Eskimo) of Alaska and northeast Canada, and a shorter discussion of the Batak of the Philippines.

## The Dobe Ju/'hoansi

The Ju/'hoansi are one of five culturally related groups of southern Africa who are known collectively as the San. The San are something of a historical mystery.[1] An educated guess is that they once occupied most of southern Africa but were eventually displaced by successive waves of Bantu and European invaders. Those who were not killed or absorbed into the invaders' populations were gradually forced back into the arid wastes of the Kalahari Desert and its surrounding areas in Botswana, Namibia, and Angola. Most of the estimated 50,000

San who still live in and around the Kalahari are slowly being absorbed by the surrounding agricultural, industrial, and pastoral communities, although they still maintain their distinct cultural and linguistic identity. In fact, the Khoisan speakers of South Africa and the Hadza of Tanzania, also hunter-gatherers, have been shown by geneticists to be the earliest known populations to have split, perhaps as early as 50,000 years ago (Wade, 2003b). Since both of their languages, while very divergent, use a rarely employed sound—a click made by sucking the tongue down from the roof of the mouth (notated as an exclamation mark, as in !Kung)—it may be that the world's very early ancestral language also used such a sound.

The several hundred Ju/'hoansi San who live in the Dobe area, on the northern edge of the Kalahari, are an exception. Although the Dobe Ju/'hoansi have been in contact with Bantu and Europeans since the 1920s, share water holes with Bantu pastoralists, and sometimes work for them, the majority (over 70%) were almost self-sufficient hunters and gatherers at the time they were first studied by contemporary anthropologists. Since their way of life has changed dramatically, our description will begin with how they once lived and conclude with their present situation. In the mid-1960s, when Richard B. Lee lived with them, they had no interest in agriculture, herd animals, or firearms. They neither paid taxes to nor received services (except for smallpox vaccinations) from the government of Botswana. They traded with neighboring Bantu pastoralists but worked for them only occasionally. Thus, although the Dobe Ju/'hoansi are not isolated, until recently they were largely independent—mainly because they occupy territory that no one else wants.

Until 1992, they were in the middle of an international power struggle among White-ruled South Africa, Angola, and Namibia, a newly independent state. As a consequence, the Ju/'hoansi's traditional freedom of movement was severely curtailed beginning in the early 1970s. A massive chain-link fence can still be seen on parts of their territory. Many Ju/'hoansi were employed by the South African army as scouts, and all, willingly or not, are involved in the processes that are transforming this once remote land. Their situation is changing rapidly, and in all likelihood, the life we describe will soon be transformed beyond recognition. As Richard Lee has remarked, those working with the Ju/'hoansi in the 1980s and 1990s find it hard to visualize the society that he found and described in 1965 and thus came to conclude that he had misinterpreted what he had witnessed (1993). We will refer to both early

---

[1]Until recently, they were known as Bushmen, a name given to them by the Dutch who settled in South Africa in the seventeenth century. Africanists, however, now prefer the term San, which means "original settlers" in the Cape Hottentot dialect. The population described here was often referred to as the !Kung; Richard Lee, who has worked with them since 1962, advocates referring to them as they prefer to call themselves—which is the Dobe Ju/'hoansi (pronounced "doebay zhutwasi"). To confuse matters further, the preferred usage of the Botswana government is Basarwa. The "click" language they speak is called Khoisan.

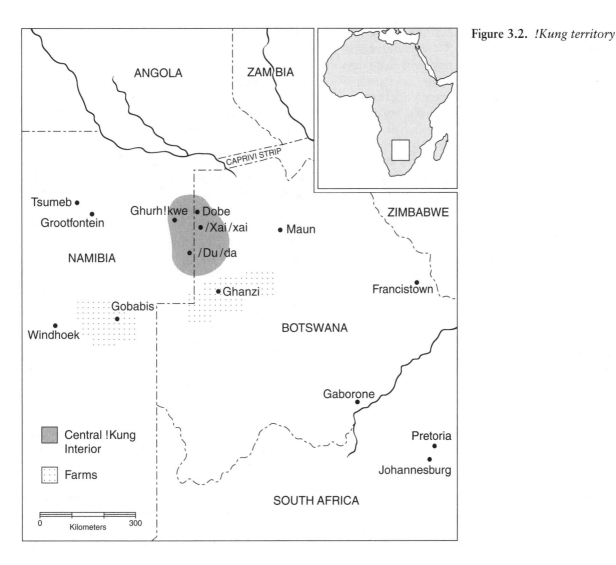

**Figure 3.2.** *!Kung territory*

and recent accounts, beginning with an account of their way of life when Lee first encountered them.

## Climate and Resources

The Dobe area is an inhospitable environment for humans, a fact that has protected the Ju/'hoansi from invasion and assimilation, if not from contact. Dobe is a transition zone between the Kalahari Desert to the south and the lusher regions, inhabited mainly by agriculturists and pastoralists, to the north. It consists of semiarid savanna with a scattering of trees and grasslands and very few permanent water holes. The temperature ranges from below freezing on winter nights to 37°C (100°F) in the shade during the summer. Even more variable than the temperature is the rainfall. For six months of the year, the area is completely dry; during the other six months, there are heavy rains. Furthermore, rainfall varies considerably from year to year.

In 1967–1968, for example, rainfall in the area was 250% greater than it had been in 1963–1964 (Yellen & Lee, 1976). Such variation in rainfall, along with the sandiness of the soil, makes agriculture impossible. Nor is the area an ideal hunting ground; because the vegetation is scattered, it cannot support large migratory herds.

Nevertheless, the Ju/'hoansi manage a livelihood in this habitat, in part because they exploit such a wide variety of resources.[2] Despite the extremes of climate, Dobe supports about 500 species of plants and animals. Of these resources, the Dobe Ju/'hoansi

[2]In the mid-1960s, their population was 466–379 permanent residents and 87 seasonal visitors (Lee, 1968, p. 30). This discussion relies heavily on the preliminary work of Richard B. Lee and Irven DeVore, along with the more recent writings of the rest of their Harvard team, many of which are collected in *Kalahari Hunter-Gatherers* (1976), edited by Lee and DeVore. We also use Lee's monograph, *The Dobe Ju/'hoansi* (1993), Wilmsen's book (1989a), M. Shostak's *Nisa* (2000), and Lee and Daly (2000).

use about 150 plants and about 100 animals, and they eat approximately 100 species of plants and 50 animals (Yellen & Lee, 1976). They gather wild nuts (chiefly from mongongo trees), berries, melons, and other fruits; dig for roots and tubers; collect honey in season; and hunt everything from warthogs, kudu, and leopard tortoise (three favorites) to springhare, guinea fowl, and rock pythons. The larger animals, such as the antelope and kudu, are shot with poisoned arrows. The Ju/'hoansi hunt the smaller animals with dogs or trap them in ingenious snares. Very young animals, inept at running, are sometimes simply chased and snatched up. Although the Dobe Ju/'hoansi definitely prefer some of these foods to others, their versatility in using a wide range of resources ensures that they are seldom without something to eat.

Most of their other needs are also easily supplied by the resources of the area. Their huts are constructed of branches and grass found throughout the area. Ostrich eggshells, also readily available, make ideal water containers. A wooden digging stick, whittled in an hour, lasts several months. A bow, arrows, and a quiver, which take several days to make, last years. The people's few luxuries—ostrich eggshell necklaces, thumb pianos, intricately carved pipes, and children's toys—are likewise made from materials readily at hand. Indeed, there is only one important resource that the Dobe Ju/'hoansi traditionally obtain through exchange with other groups: iron for making tools. But even in this case, they exercise a certain independence: They collect scraps of metal from the Botswana Veterinary Station fences to make arrowheads.

Limited in their needs and resourceful in filling them, the Dobe Ju/'hoansi have little difficulty obtaining food and raw materials. The scarcity of water is the major problem, and it is this factor that in large part makes the Dobe Ju/'hoansi a nomadic people.

## Settlement Patterns

As rainfall determines the availability of water in the Kalahari, it also determines the people's settlement patterns. During the dry season, from June through September, the Ju/'hoansi congregate in relatively large camps of about twenty to forty people around the large permanent water holes, the only available sources of water (Yellen & Lee, 1976). In this period, the people rely primarily on roots and tubers found within a day's walk (about a six-mile radius) of their camps. The cool, clear weather makes for good tracking and hunting, and small groups of women periodically hike to the mongongo forests to collect nuts. By August, however, many of the preferred local foods have been eaten and rising temperatures make hunting and long gathering treks hard and uncomfortable. At this time, the Ju/'hoansi turn to less desirable foods—gums and the larger, bitter-tasting roots and melons that they passed up a month or two earlier.

But this period of austerity does not last long. In October, the rains begin, filling the hollow trees and the standing pools in the upcountry with fresh water and transforming the parched landscape into a lush green, thick with new plant and animal life. This is the season of plenty. The Ju/'hoansi now separate into groups of perhaps two or four families and scatter over the land to take advantage of the new crop of fruits, melons, berries, and leafy greens and the new generations of birds and animals that follow the rains. For seven to eight months, the small groups move from camp to camp, staying an average of about three days in each spot and returning periodically to the permanent water hole. This pattern continues through April, when the pools of water begin to dry up. In May, the wandering upcountry groups return to the permanent water hole to set up new camps, and the cycle begins again (Yellen & Lee, 1976).

The Dobe Ju/'hoansi, then, are an extremely mobile people. Accordingly, their goods are the kind that can be moved easily or left behind. Even houses fall into this category. When a group sets up camp, in a matter of two or three hours each woman constructs a small hut (perhaps 1.5 meters—about 5 feet—in both height and diameter) for her own nuclear family. The huts are arranged in a circle around an open space where the camp activity takes place. Very little goes on in the huts. Indeed, it is unusual to find anyone inside a hut, except perhaps a person who is taking a nap or seeking shelter from a storm (Draper, 1976). A hut serves simply as a storehouse and as a marker, a sign of a family's residence in the camp. When the camp is broken up, the huts, representing little investment of time, energy, or material, are abandoned. Each member of the Ju/'hoansi group can pack all of his or her possessions into a pair of leather carrying sacks and be ready to move in a few minutes (Lee, 1993, p. 43).

## Social Practices and Group Composition

The Dobe Ju/'hoansi are very gregarious people; they spend about a third of their time visiting other camps and another third entertaining guests. (The size of the camp Lee studied on his first trip varied from twenty-three to forty persons in a single

*The !Kung are extremely mobile. They construct huts in two or three hours and can abandon them in minutes.*

(M. Shostak/Anthro-Photo)

month.) This tradition of conviviality, along with fluctuations in the availability of resources, keeps the Ju/'hoansi on the move. The two factors should not be thought of as independent. In fact, the habit of visiting is probably an adaptation to the necessity of adjusting the populations of camps to local resources. It also facilitates exchanges of information about game and other matters of concern to the dispersed local groups. Both Lorna Marshall (1961, 1965) and Richard Lee (1993) describe the constant babble of voices at night in Ju/'hoansi camps, when residents and visitors exchange notes on rainfall and water holes, ripening vegetables and fruits, and animal tracks in what amounts to a debriefing.

Ju/'hoansi social customs provide not only for short-term visits but also for much lengthier stays. When a couple marries, for example, the husband moves to the wife's camp for an indefinite period of **bride service**—payment for his bride in the form of labor—and he may bring his parents or a sibling with him. Usually, he stays with his wife's people until the birth of their third child (about ten years). At that point, he may return to the group into which he was born (perhaps taking some of his wife's kin along), stay where he is, or move to a camp where one of his brothers is doing bride service or where his wife's siblings have settled. Bride service may also have evolved as a way for parents to keep their brides, who can be as young as nine or ten, at home for a longer period of time (Lee, 1993, p. 66). Since people are marrying later today, this service is also changing.

Such shifts are not limited to bride-service graduates. Any Ju/'hoansi family may leave their group and move into another group where they have kin. Kinship is interpreted very broadly. The Ju/'hoansi recognize ties among all individuals who share the same name and address all of that person's relatives by kinship terms. Because the number of names used among the Ju/'hoansi is limited, a person is quite likely to find a name-mate in camps where he or she has no relatives and be welcomed there too. Thus, the Ju/'hoansi have considerable freedom of choice with regard to residence. Lee (1968) estimates that every year about a third of the population makes a shift in group affiliation.

These changes in group composition, like the rounds of brief visits, help the Ju/'hoansi to tailor the populations of their camps to local resources. At the same time, the flexibility of the group helps to prevent quarrels from turning into serious fights, which are carefully avoided. The Ju/'hoansi are keenly aware that they all possess poisoned arrows and that fights have been known to end in killing. To avoid such an outcome, families that cannot get along together simply separate—one or both of them moving to another group.

## Reciprocity

The Ju/'hoansi have a saying, "Only lions eat alone." One of the characteristics that distinguish human beings from other animals, they say, is sharing and exchange. Though all humans share periodically, the Ju/'hoansi system of distributing goods is characterized by continuous giving and receiving of gifts. General reciprocity, or *hxaro*, is the basis of their

domestic and local economy and much of their social life as well (Lee, 1993). *Hxaro* is practiced daily
as adults hunt and gather over a wide area. Working
individually or in pairs, they find a variety of foods
that they share with the entire camp.

It is easy to overromanticize the altruism of this
system. The appropriate distribution of food is a
common cause of quarreling among the Ju/'hoansi.
The way the day's take is divided depends on a variety of factors. In some cases, as when someone has
brought in a large animal, the distribution is rather
formalized. The owner (the person who owns the fatal arrow, whether or not he actually killed the animal) divides the meat into portions according to the
size of the hunting party. The recipients then cut up
their shares and distribute them among their relatives and friends, who in turn give pieces to their relatives, and so forth, until everyone has eaten.

The size and distribution of shares of meat are
matters of individual discretion, but the Ju/'hoansi
take care to meet their families' needs and to repay
past generosity. Smaller animals and vegetables are
distributed more informally. A family may invite
someone standing nearby to sit at their fire, send children to neighbors with gifts of raw or cooked vegetables, or take fatty bits of meat and nuts with them
on a visit. Thus, each family's dinner is a combination of the food its members collected and the food
they are given. The exchange of food constitutes an
effective system that permits each family to store up
goodwill and obligation against times of need.

The various artifacts used or enjoyed in daily life
circulate in a similar manner. When a person re-
ceives an arrow or a dance rattle as a gift, he keeps
it for a few months and then passes it on to someone
else with the expectation of receiving a gift of more
or less equal value in the future. As with food, the
giver expects no immediate return, nor is there any
systematic way to calculate the relative worth of
gifts or to guarantee that the other person will reciprocate in kind. The Ju/'hoansi consider bargaining
and direct exchange undignified, and although they
trade with the Bantu, they never trade among themselves. Food sharing and gift giving are based on
norms of reciprocity that are understood and accepted by all Ju/'hoansi; as they put it, "we do not
trade with things, we trade with people" (Lee, 1993,
p. 104).

## Quality of Life: Diet and Nutrition

We have briefly described the Dobe Ju/'hoansi's way
of life. Before Lee and his colleagues began their
study of these people, it was widely assumed that the

*Medical anthropologists learn much from traditional
healers such as this Dobe !Kung woman.
A knowledge of indigenous medical practice is
important when attempting to deliver modern
medical services.*
(Irven DeVore/Anthro-Photo)

Dobe Ju/'hoansi (indeed, all foragers) waged a constant struggle for survival, battling hunger and poor
nutrition from day to day. After all, the Ju/'hoansi
live in an area where game is scarce, their weapons
are unsophisticated, and they have no way of storing their food. On the surface, they seem to lead a
precarious hand-to-mouth existence. Yet as Lee established through his painstaking research in the
1960s, the appearance bears little relation to the reality. In comparison with some other groups, the
Dobe Ju/'hoansi lead secure and easy lives (Lee,
1969, 1993; Lee & DeVore, 1968).

From July 6 through August 2, 1964, Lee kept a
diary of subsistence activities at an average dry-season camp. (Remember that this is a period of relative
scarcity.) Each day, he recorded the number of people in camp, the number that went out to hunt or
gather, and the hours each spent acquiring food. He

weighed all the animals the hunters brought back to camp during this period and all the bags of nuts and other foods that the women acquired in the course of each day's foraging. He even counted the number of mongongo nuts the Ju/'hoansi cracked and consumed in an hour. By dividing the population of the camp in a given week into the total amount of meat and vegetable foods acquired and then into the total number of hours devoted to their preparation, Lee was able to calculate the Ju/'hoansi workweek and daily consumption of food. The results were surprising.

Lee found that the vegetable foods the women gather account for the bulk of the Ju/'hoansi diet by weight; the meat that the men bring in amounts to only 20 to 25%. Meat, then, is a delicacy for the Ju/'hoansi, not a staple. The reason is obvious: A man who spends four hours hunting may kill one animal (this is the average), whereas a woman who goes out to gather vegetable foods always finds something for her family to eat, even if it is not an especially choice item. Lee estimates that gathering is 2.4 times as productive as hunting in the Dobe area. One man-hour of hunting brings in approximately 800 calories; one woman-hour of gathering, approximately 2,000 calories. Thus, the success of the hunt is not the critical variable in survival that it was once thought to be. It is vegetable foods, not meats, that form the basis of the Ju/'hoansi diet—and it is the women, not the men, who are the chief breadwinners in Ju/'hoansi society.

Drought-resistant mongongo nuts are the Ju/'hoansi staple, making up 50% of the vegetable diet. The average daily consumption (about 300 nuts) provides an individual with 1,260 calories and 56 grams of protein—the equivalent of 2.5 pounds of rice or 9 ounces of lean meat. In addition, everyone in the camp Lee studied ate an average of about 9 ounces of meat per day. Together mongongo nuts and meat gave each person 2,140 calories and 92.1 grams of protein per day—well over the U.S. recommended daily allowance (1,975 calories and 60 grams of protein) for small, active people such as the Ju/'hoansi.

Not only do the Ju/'hoansi eat well, but they do so with little effort. By counting the numbers of hours each person devoted to acquiring food during the twenty-eight—day period, Lee discovered that by Western standards the Ju/'hoansi invest relatively little energy in the quest for food. Typically, a man will spend five or six days hunting and then take a week or two off to rest, visit, and arrange the all-night dances that the Ju/'hoansi hold two or three times a week. Furthermore, it is not at all unusual for a man to decide his luck has run out temporarily

and take a month's vacation. The women also have considerable leisure. In one day, a woman collects enough food to feed her family for three days. Household chores take between one and three hours. Plenty of free time is left to rest, visit, and entertain. Lee calculated that the average Dobe Ju/'hoansi adult spends only six hours a day acquiring food, two and a half days a week—a total of fifteen hours a week.

## Demography

The workweek figures are all the more surprising when one considers Ju/'hoansi demography. It was once thought that few people in such societies lived beyond what we consider middle age. This assumption too has proved to be unfounded—at least for the Dobe Ju/'hoansi. Lee found that 10% of the Dobe residents were over sixty years old. These old people do not participate directly in food procurement. Neither do the young, who constitute another 30% of the population. Unlike other African foragers, Ju/'hoansi children do not actively contribute to subsistence activities; they are kept in camp or with their mothers until adolescence, a fact that puts a greater strain on those who actively provision the family. (Ju/'hoansi do not expect young people to work regularly until they marry, usually between ages fifteen and twenty for women, twenty and twenty-five for men.) Thus, 40% of the population are dependents who live on the food that the young and middle-aged adults bring in. Such a proportion of nonproducers is surprisingly high, resembling that in agricultural communities.

At first glance, these figures may suggest that if the Dobe Ju/'hoansi worked harder, they could support a much larger population. This is not the case, however, for while the people as a whole could certainly spend, say, twice as many hours collecting food, the Dobe environment could not produce twice as much food for them to collect or twice as much water for them to drink.

This observation brings us to a factor that seems crucial to the Dobe Ju/'hoansi's way of life: the control of population growth. The well-being of any group, human or otherwise, depends in large part on the ratio of population to resources. For hunter-gatherers, this ratio is especially critical because, unlike agriculturists, they cannot increase their resources.

The Dobe Ju/'hoansi are particularly interesting in this regard, for their fertility is unusually low. On the average, Ju/'hoansi women do not become pregnant again until four years after the birth of the previous child. The Ju/'hoansi do not have a long postpartum taboo (that is, prescribed abstinence from sexual intercourse after childbirth), nor do they use chemical or mechanical birth control devices. The women of Dobe attribute their low fertility to "the stinginess of their god, who loves children and tries to keep them all to himself in heaven" (Howell, 1976, p. 147). Prolonged breast-feeding is probably a factor. Because they have no soft foods on which to wean infants, Ju/'hoansi mothers nurse their babies for at least three years, until the child is able to digest the tough foods of the Ju/'hoansi diet (Draper, 1976). Breast-feeding is not a guaranteed birth control technique, but it does inhibit ovulation to some degree. Nancy Howell has suggested that gonorrhea, probably introduced through contact with Bantu and Europeans, may have reduced the fertility of some Ju/'hoansi women. Of course, infant mortality, including occasional infanticide, is also a factor in the wide spacing of Ju/'hoansi siblings. Twenty percent of infants die in their first year (Howell, 1976).

This factor of controlled population, along with other factors that we have discussed (high mobility, flexibility of group membership, reciprocity, and a low-energy budget), allows the Ju/'hoansi to strike a balance with their environment. This is not to suggest that the foraging life does not have its own hazards and limitations. Climatic and other disturbances can cause hunger, even starvation. By keeping their numbers and their energy needs low and by operating on the principle of flow—flow of groups over the land, flow of people between groups, flow of resources among people—they are able to fit their needs to what their habitat has to offer from day to day. As a result, they live a relatively easy life; they eat well, work only in their middle years, and have time to rest and play. They are also well-prepared for hardship. In times of shortage, Bantu pastoralists fare worse than the Ju/'hoansi, and Bantu women turn to foraging with the Ju/'hoansi to feed their families. Though the Dobe Ju/'hoansi may not qualify as "the original affluent society," as Marshall Sahlins has termed the early hunter-gatherers, their adaptive pattern is still remarkable in that it yields them such a stable and comfortable existence within such an austere habitat.

## The People of the Dobe Today

In 1963, three quarters of the Dobe area people had been relying on hunting and gathering, and there was a virtual absence of institutions associated with the state and a market economy: stores, schools, clinics, feeding stations, drilled wells, or airstrips. In 1967, the first trading post opened near the region

(although the Ju/'hoansi had no money), and a fence was erected that cut them off from their nearest neighbors, the Nyae-Nyae. Since foraging was greatly restricted by the fence and since the government offered assistance in starting cattle herds, many began to build semipermanent mud-walled houses near cattle kraals (enclosures). Many too became dependent on government feeding programs, a problem made worse by the game laws of the 1980s that limited their rights to hunt. Even the shape of the village changed, reflecting a changed social order (Lee, 1993, p. 156). Instead of houses drawn up in a circle, the new ones are all in a line and focused on their private property, the herds. While formerly their diets had made them a population with remarkably low levels of serum cholesterol and a general absence of heart disease, this has changed (pp. 156–157). Their present diet is dominated by

*Traditional diet in the Dobe area relied heavily on nuts, roots, and grass seeds gathered by women.*
(M. Shostak/Anthro-Photo)

refined carbohydrates, together with heavy tobacco and alcohol consumption. Many men were induced to sign up with the South African Army during its long war in Angola, dramatically increasing the cash in circulation.

John Marshall, an anthropologist who, with his wife, Claire, has lived with the neighboring Khoisan on and off since 1951, established the Nyae-Nyae Foundation to assist those living in or near game parks, where, by 1997, they had become something of an attraction—thanks to the popularity of the films *The Gods Must Be Crazy* and *N!ai: The Story of a !Kung Woman*. But the situation is complicated by the fact that illegal hunting using guns and horses has depleted the game, and many are living in squalid settlements where alcoholism, disease, and crime are prevalent (McNeil, 1997). Employment opportunities are limited; some work for tourist camps, others herd cattle, and many live on handouts or petty crime. The Nyae-Nyae Foundation by 1997 had itself become divided and disorganized. Some argue, as does Marshall, that the only future for the !Kung is to shift to cattle herding, but others in the foundation want the !Kung to retain their traditional ways even if only to serve as tourist guides (McNeil, 1997). As Marshall has put it, "Anything that rests on this fantasy that people can still live by hunter-gathering is bound to flop" (quoted in McNeil, 1997, p. 3). In neighboring Botswana, the condition of the Kalahari dwellers is even grimmer (Daley, 1996). The last 1,000 people dwelling on Central Kalahari Game Reserve are under mounting pressure to abandon their traditional hunting territories and move to settlements where there is little prospect for employment. While independence has brought many benefits to the people of both Namibia and Botswana, they are not evenly distributed: The Khoisan peoples, some 50,000 in all, have become marginalized in their own lands.

However, not all has changed; when Richard Lee and others returned, they found familiar faces and people caring for each other and sharing in the manner they recalled from the 1960s. Moreover, the people have retained their dignity and cultural self-identity. Lee attributes this to what he calls their "communal mode of production" and egalitarian spirit (1993, p. 174). This has enabled them to persist in the face of integration into the contemporary market economy. People still take care of one another, and while eager to accumulate consumer goods, they take care to do so within limits. Care for the elders and the infirm is seen as natural—their entitlement—and not a burden. There are lessons for us here, Lee concludes.

# The Inuit, or Eskimo

Until quite recently, the Eskimo peoples[3] who lived on the vast treeless plains (or tundra) and along the changing coastlines of the arctic were isolated from the rest of the world by their formidable environment. Like the Dobe Ju/'hoansi, they occupied land that no one else wanted, and so for centuries, they remained self-sufficient hunters and gatherers, relatively uninfluenced by the agricultural and industrial societies that grew up to their south in the more fertile regions of the North American continent. The Inuit Eskimo language family, dialects of which are spoken by the dispersed people we describe, is distributed over a vast area, from northwest Alaska and Canada to the coasts of eastern Greenland and Labrador. For this reason, we shall refer to them as Inuit (Burch, 1994a).

Since the beginning of the twentieth century, the isolation of the Inuit has slowly broken down. Money has become an important factor in their relationship with their environment. While most Inuit groups are fully settled today, some are still hunter-gatherers and in some ways resemble the Dobe Ju/'hoansi. At the same time, because of cultural changes resulting from their buying and selling in the world market and because of their residence in the United States and Canada—not to mention their unique habitat—they provide an interesting contrast to the Ju/'hoansi.

## The Arctic Ecosystem

If the Dobe seems an inhospitable environment, the arctic circumpolar region of North America seems almost uninhabitable. Throughout much of the region, from October through July, the waters are locked in ice while the land lies frozen and almost bare of plant and animal life. During this period (the local population's fall, winter, and spring), arctic animals, with the exception of seals and walruses, either migrate south or hibernate. By midwinter, the ice is six to seven feet thick. Temperatures during the

---

[3]This discussion is based primarily on Asem Balikci's now-classic study (1970, 1989) of the Netsilik Eskimo of northeastern Canada and Ernest Burch's study of the Inupiat in northwestern Canada (1994) with reference also to William B. Kemp's study (1971) among the Baffin Island Eskimo, a summary and synthesis by William Sturtevant and David Damas (1984), and to the work of Emilio Moran (2000). Keep in mind that the various groups described are widely separated and that among the Eskimo there are many variations in language, custom, and ways of making a living.

eighteen-hour Arctic nights may drop from a mean of –16°C (–30°F) to –27°C (–50°F). Forty-mile-an-hour winds with gusts up to seventy miles an hour are common. In the Hudson Strait area, forty-five–foot tides build walls of broken ice along the coast, making navigation extremely hazardous.

In most years, the freeze continues into late July. Then this land on top of the world enjoys a brief summer. Temperatures rise above freezing, and daylight lasts as long as twenty-two hours. Lichens, mosses, shrubs, and tufted grasses sprout on the tundra, attracting a variety of wildlife: herds of caribou, musk oxen, polar bears, foxes, rabbits, and migratory birds. Seals and walruses bask in the sun; whales may appear; large schools of salmon run downriver to the sea in July or thereabouts, returning to inland lakes in August. But this arctic summer lasts a short six to twelve weeks. The sea begins to ice over in late September, and the long freeze begins once again.

Foraging in this environment is quite different from living off wild foods in the Dobe area. Except for the summer berries, there are no vegetables, edible roots, or fruits in the arctic; the long, dark winters, incessant winds, poor soil, and short growing season discourage plant life. The Inuit's subsistence strategy is centered on animal life—on hunting, fishing, and to a lesser extent, trapping and gathering of duck eggs, clams, and the like. And whereas the availability of water largely determines the migrations of the Dobe Ju/'hoansi, it is the availability of animals and fish that structures the Inuit's patterns of movement.

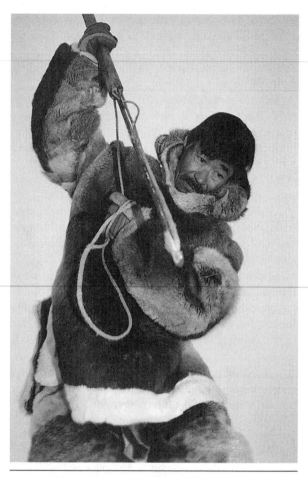

*Most Eskimos have turned to modern high-powered rifles, but they complain that these weapons have destroyed the mutual trust between animals and humans.*

(Gordon Wiltsie/Peter Arnold Inc.)

## The Seasonal Migrations

Like the Dobe Ju/'hoansi, most circumpolar populations are to some degree nomadic people, changing the sizes and locations of their camps as their resources change with the seasons. The pattern of these migrations is essentially the same as with the Ju/'hoansi: dispersal in small groups in the season of plenty, concentration in large groups in the time of scarcity. Again employing the ethnographic present, we will examine the pattern of livelihood and social life of one population, the Netsilik Eskimo, and then turn our attention westward to their distant relatives in Alaska.

In the summer, when food is abundant, the Hudson Bay Netsilik Eskimo traditionally form small groups of twenty to thirty people consisting of one or more extended families and move inland to take advantage of fish runs and caribou migrations. Each August, for example, the Netsilik carry their be-

longings up the waterways to the stone weirs (circular dams) they have built to trap schools of salmon. Some of the fish are eaten raw, on the spot; the rest are dried and stored for the winter.

Toward the end of the month, the group packs up once again and moves farther inland to await the coming of the caribou. Depending on the terrain, the Netsilik may construct knife-lined pits in the caribou's paths (which are well-known to the Inuit) or stalk them with guns, much as in earlier days when they hunted with bows and arrows. Another common technique is to stampede the animals into a trap. Howling in imitation of wolves, a few men drive the herd into a narrow valley where hunters lie concealed or into a river where the hunters wait in kayaks. Caribou provide not only meat but also another crucial resource, skins for clothing. In 1970, Balikci estimated that a family of four needs about thirty skins to see them through each winter. In October and November, the Netsilik live primarily on food stored during the caribou hunts, supplemented by occasional fresh fish and musk oxen. The most important activity in this period is making winter clothing, a job performed by the women.

In December, the scattered Netsilik come together once again in their winter camps along the bays and straits, where fifty, sixty, or as many as one hundred people join forces to hunt the major cold-season resource—seals. Although some seals migrate south for the winter, others remain in the arctic, digging breathing holes up through the sea ice. (Seals need air every fifteen to twenty minutes and dig several holes.) Hunting seals in midwinter involves hours of silent, motionless waiting at the breathing holes, harpoon in hand. For much of the winter, seals plus an occasional fox are the only sources of fresh food.

In May or June, when the ice begins to melt, the Netsilik move to tents on solid ground. Hunting seals is easier and more productive in these months, for the animals often come out of the water. By July, the ice starts to crack and seal hunting becomes dangerous, so the Netsilik camps divide once again into smaller groups for their annual inland treks (Balikci, 1989, chap. 2).

The Inuit's seasonal round is similar to that of the Dobe Ju/'hoansi, but there are important differences between the patterns of the two groups. For one thing, the Inuit, unlike the Ju/'hoansi, can store food. When fish are running and game is abundant, they collect as much as they can and smoke or store the surplus in stone or ice caches. However, the cold also requires the Inuit to work on a higher energy budget than the Ju/'hoansi. In such a climate, simply to stay alive (to say nothing of hunting) requires a relatively high-calorie diet. Furthermore, the Inuit have to invest a good deal of energy in the task of protecting their bodies from the cold: building shelters (traditionally, igloos in the winter and skin tents in the summer), making clothing (multilayered garments, boots, and mittens), and heating their shelters (with seal-oil lamps or kerosene stoves). And they have to feed their sled dogs, a vital component of their traditional nomadic way of life.

These activities require not only considerable energy but an accumulation of material goods. While the Ju/'hoansi travel light, the Inuit, with their dogsleds and snowmobiles, motorboats, tools, rifles, clothing, lamps, and stockpiles of food, have a good deal to carry around. Furthermore, their tents and igloos, unlike the Ju/'hoansi's disposable huts, take time to build and cannot be lightly abandoned. Hence, even during the summer season, the Inuit change camps much less often than the Ju/'hoansi.

## Demography

From what we can gather from early explorers' and ethnographers' accounts, this way of life did not enable the Inuit to support sizable numbers of dependents, or at least not in bad years. Old and sick individuals who could not keep up with the group were occasionally left behind to manage for themselves—in other words, to die (Balikci, 1970). Furthermore, the unequal sex ratio in some Inuit groups at the turn of the twentieth century suggests that they also limited the number of the dependent young through female infanticide (see Balikci, 1970, 1989; Freeman, 1971).

In some cases, population controls were probably quite deliberate attempts at family planning. The threat of hunger is a recurring theme in Inuit conversation, even in communities where the evidence indicates that hunting accidents have caused many more deaths over the years than hunger (Kemp, 1971)—and one way to stave off hunger is to limit the number of nonproducers to ensure that at least some children survive. The archaeological record does contain evidence of some large and formal villages that were exceptions to this pattern, but they appear to have been short-lived.

The ratio of population to food resources may become a more realistic worry in the near future, for Inuit populations are rapidly increasing. With improved health care supplied by the United States and Canadian governments, the mortality rate has declined steadily in recent years. At the same time, their fertility rate has increased. In the Inuit community of Wainwright, Alaska, for example, the average woman gives birth to nine or ten live children in the course of her reproductive years. The average Dobe Ju/'hoansi woman, on the other hand, has five. As a result, the population of this group is growing at a rate of 3% a year (Milan, 1970), six times the 0.5% rate of the Dobe Ju/'hoansi. Other groups are expanding at similar rates, putting a strain on their ecosystems.

## Social Relationships

The Inuit, like most other hunter-gatherers, have extensive networks of kin, but the most important social unit is the extended family. This is considered to be the "real family." Jean Briggs notes in her study of the Uktu in Hudson Bay (neighbors of the Netsilik), "Whenever possible, it is with their 'real family' that the people live, work, travel, and share whatever they have. Moreover, it is only with their 'real family' that they appear to feel completely comfortable and safe" (1970, p. 39). These extended families are organized into larger kin groups that generally camp and work together. Like the Dobe Ju/'hoansi, however, Inuit families have considerable latitude in choosing the people with whom they will camp. It is common for everyone in an Inuit society to be considered kin to everyone else—if not by blood, then by marriage, adoption, or shared names (a practice that we have already seen among the Ju/'hoansi). These extensive ties allow families to shift about on short-term and long-term visits and thus enable the Inuit to adjust the makeup of their groups according to the availability of resources and personal preference, especially in the scattered inland camps during the summer and fall.

In their personal relationships, the Inuit place great value on restraint. Demonstrations of emotion are frowned upon. Briggs (1970) noted that Uktu husbands and wives and their older children never kiss, embrace, or even touch one another in front of anyone else. Even more unwelcome is a show of negative feelings, especially anger. To these Inuit, the ideal personality traits are shyness, patience, generosity, and an even temper.

It is no surprise that many local populations traditionally had no formal group leadership. Though a man with a reputation for wisdom or expertise in hunting may come to have some influence in decision making, anyone who tries unabashedly to impose his will on others is regarded with deep suspicion. Likewise, the Inuit have no formal code for dealing with people who violate social norms. Stingy or bad-tempered individuals are not directly criticized or punished; rather, the others will try to soothe or tease them out of their folly. If this strategy does not work, the offender is simply avoided. The worst punishment that Inuit societies can inflict is ostracism, a very serious threat in harsh arctic conditions.

## The Impact of Modernization

After Balikci's investigation, William Kemp (1971) made a careful study of energy use in one of the last all-Inuit communities on Baffin Island, to the north of Netsilik territory. The value of his observations lies in his documentation of the effects of new technology on energy use. These were changes that have transformed all Inuit communities, including the Pella Bay community studied by Balikci.

The village Kemp studied consisted of four households whose total population varied from twenty-six to twenty-nine over the period of the study. Three of the families lived in wood-frame tents covered with skins and old mailbags that the people had sewn together and insulated with a layer of dry shrubs. These tents were heated by traditional seal-oil lamps. The fourth family lived in a prefabricated wood house supplied by the government and heated by a kerosene stove.

This house was not the village's only sign of industrial technology. Among them, the villagers owned two snowmobiles, a large motorized whaling boat, and a twenty-two–foot freight canoe with an outboard motor, along with several large sledges and thirty-four sled dogs. In 1971, hunting was still the most important subsistence activity, but they were also hunting with rifles as well as harpoons. The younger men spent only part of their time hunting; they also mined soapstone and carved it into statuettes for export, and some of the young men left the village periodically to work for wages at government construction sites. In one year, village members earned $3,500 from carvings, $1,360 from animal skins, $1,225 in wages, and $670 in government subsidies.

***Energy Flow among the Baffin Islanders.*** Kemp's 1971 analysis of energy flow in this small community was similar to Lee's study of the Dobe Ju/'hoansi's subsistence practices and standard of living. But Kemp had to take into account the use of fuel as well as muscle power, the hours spent working for wages as well as foraging, and the acquisition of store-bought as well as wild foods. To calculate the energy flow, he reduced both the number of hours individuals spent at various activities and the various foods they acquired and consumed to the common denominator of kilocalories (thousands of calories). This procedure enabled him to analyze in considerable detail the sources of energy, the routes along which it flowed, and the uses to which it was put.

Kemp calculated that over the fifty-four weeks during which he kept records of village activities, the Inuit expended some 12.8 million kilocalories of human energy in hunting, mining, and carving; working for wages; taking care of household chores; traveling; and visiting. In addition, they used 885 gallons of gasoline, 615 gallons of kerosene, and 10,900 rounds of ammunition. During the same period, they acquired 12.8 million kilocalories in wild food for human consumption (plus 7.5 million kilocalories in food for the dogs) and 7.5 million kilocalories in store-bought food. Thus, important sources of energy lie outside the local economy, and indeed, the Inuit are as dependent on industry and fossil fuels as is the rest of North America's population. They may spend more time and energy in hunting, but such activities as wage labor and soapstone

*An Inuit woman shopping in a supermarket in Baffin Island, Canada. Even though all now purchase most of their food from shops, hunting remains culturally and nutritionally important.*

(Kevin Fleming/Woodfin Camp & Associates)

carving force them to depend on critical inputs of imported energy.

When observed, the Inuit ate well. Game—primarily seal but also whale, caribou, and other animals—remains their dietary staple, accounting for 85% of their food. In Pella Bay, the villagers have given up seal hunting and rely mostly on caribou, which has a better taste and does not involve traveling far from the settlement. The Baffin Island villagers rarely bought canned meat and vegetables, though they did purchase sugar, powdered milk, quantities of flour and lard for bannock (a pan-baked bread), and small amounts of such delicacies as peanut butter and honey. Kemp estimates that this combination of wild and store-bought food provides each adult with 3,000 calories a day. The Inuit's calorie intake, then, is about 50% higher than that of the Dobe Ju/'hoansi. Their protein intake, accounting for 44% of their calories, is also quite high—a reflection of their heavy dependence on game. Of their remaining foodstuffs, 33% are in the form of carbohydrates and 23% in fat. Such a diet fortifies them for the exertions of arctic life. Kemp noted, however, that when the men of one household abandoned hunting for a month to work for wages and the family ate only store-bought food, 62% of their diet consisted of carbohydrates and only 9% of protein—an unhealthy balance. Such a diet resembles that of the poor in North American cities, who rely heavily on factory-prepared snack foods.

## Changes in Settlement and Hunting Techniques.

The products of industrialization—motorized vehicles, high-powered weapons, store-bought foods—have affected the relationship between the Inuit and their environment throughout the circumpolar region. Almost everywhere, the people have become sedentary, living in year-round villages or towns. Settling in towns has meant that Inuit children can attend schools near their homes; attending high school no longer means that a student has to move to a distant boarding school (Burch, 1994a). Snowmobiles and boats enable hunters to travel to their hunting grounds in a relatively short time, so it is no longer necessary for the whole village to pack up and move. Store-bought food provides the insurance against hunger that was once provided by seasonal moves to exploit a wide variety of game. However, caribou is still an important food item among the Inuit (Burch, 1994a), and it is easily hunted with new high-powered rifles.

Although many Inuit value the introduction of the rifles, some complain that it has destroyed the mutual trust between humans and animals (Kemp, 1971). Seals are wary of the rumbling motors and rifle reports; only young animals can be coaxed within shooting range. Also, when guns were first introduced in the late nineteenth century, they led to the near-extinction of native caribou herds. Today, however, caribou have been reintroduced and are now regulated by the U.S. government (Burch, 1994a).

The Inuit point out that rifles are not necessarily better than their old weapons. In the spring, for example, seals fast, losing their winter layer of fat; when melting snow reduces the salinity of the water, the animals are less buoyant. Unless an animal that has been killed by a rifle is immediately secured with a harpoon, it will sink—a fact that renders long-range weapons useless. Kemp notes that in one thirty-hour session of continuous hunting, the Inuit killed thirteen seals but retrieved only five.

Kemp observed that, in the fall, the hunt yielded enough food to last through the winter, so the villagers were able to spend more time visiting than hunting in February, March, and April. Although they might have used this time to collect extra skins for trading (and perhaps dangerously reduce the seal population in the process), they chose to travel instead. Whether this choice was based on conservationist concerns is debatable. The people may have been conscious of the need to preserve the supply of wild game. They may also have decided that the returns on hunting were simply less than those gained from the time spent on craft production, wage labor, or even than the rewards of visiting friends and

*The contemporary Inuit settlement of Igaluit, Baffin Island, Canada. Recent changes in Canadian law that give native peoples control over their resources have transformed Inuit society in recent years.*

(Bryan & Cherry Alexander)

relatives. Practices that limit hunting—visiting days, the soapstone industry, even the custom of observing Sundays as a day of leisure—help the Inuit maintain a balance between their needs and their resources.

Adaptation is not simply a matter of the direct interplay between technology and the environment. Rifles and snowmobiles do not inevitably spell ecological disaster, for social customs intervene between technology and the uses to which it is put. The need to earn money through carving takes young men away from the hunt. And the same snowmobiles that enable them to kill more sea mammals give them the option to forgo hunting and visit distant kin when they have enough to eat.

*Surviving in the Modern World.* The Inuit ethic of sharing is evident in the way the Pella Bay Inuit adapted to the introduction of the mission store. As the Inuit became more integrated into the wider market economy, the original store was replaced by a cooperative store, owned and managed by the Inuit to serve the community. This proved to be a successful operation, not only addressing the needs of those who wanted to buy and sell goods, but also providing an interface between the community and the government, negotiating for government contracts and the like. The co-op became "the principal economic integrator of the community and the mediating agency between the community, the government and the Euro-Canadian economic system in all matters of commerce and economic enterprise" (Balikci, 1989, p. 253).

While modernization has transformed the lives of the Inuit, they have managed to retain elements of their traditional culture. Despite the physical distance that now exists between members of a kin group, they maintain ties through telephones and CB radios. In the Inupiat territory, in northwestern Alaska, where 74% of the population is Inuit, the Inuit language remains in use and is taught in schools, and traditional food is still preferred by most.

*Claiming the Land.* In Alaska, there has been a profound transformation in the economies and ways of life of indigenous peoples in the course of the Cold War and in the aftermath of oil exploration. During the long period of rivalry with the former U.S.S.R., the U.S. government considered Inupiat territory on the Beaufort Sea a front-line area. While building bases offered a certain amount of employment, traditional patterns of hunting and fishing were disrupted by the appropriation of 4,500 acres (as an air base) and all of Barter Island—causing forced relocations (Chance, 1990, p. 141). Later, following several years of planning in which the Inupiat were not invited to participate, the Atomic Energy Commission, with the support of the Alaskan state government, announced a plan to detonate one or more atomic weapons in Inupiat territory to create an artificial harbor (Chance, 1990, pp. 140–143). This occasioned such local outrage that people organized in opposition, thus for the first time creating a united Inupiat political organization devoted to securing their aboriginal land rights—a movement that came to cooperate with other Native American political action committees (Chance, 1990, pp. 140–143). Soon they were able to defeat the proposed harbor project and, more important, set in motion a political mechanism—the Alaska Federation of Natives—for dealing with nonindigenous forces—namely, the state and federal bureaucracies, oil companies, and business interests. This organization was soon to become a significant political voice.

After years of litigation, Inupiat and other Alaskan populations have received substantial allocations of land as well as a percentage of oil and gas royalties. While welcome to many, it is for others scant compensation for what they have lost—their autonomy. Oil wealth has transformed life; the village of Katovik, where Norman Chance had lived in 1958, now has modern housing, a new school with an indoor pool, government offices, and shops (1990, pp. 200–201). While subsistence and nutrition are still based on fishing and hunting, the Inupiat use three-wheelers and snowmobiles to check their nets and take game. While the older generation retains the old skills, the younger, educated members of the community do not have the self-reliance of their parents. They are, however, being educated in modern facilities, they travel widely, and they are finding employment in the larger U.S. economy. This in turn has given them a new perspective on their personal needs—one that is much like that shared throughout the American population. The dilemma facing the Inupiat—indeed, all of us—is how these new needs can be satisfied in the face of unequal distribution of wealth and without even greater environmental risks being taken (Chance, 1990, p. 218).

In September 1988, the Canadian government passed legislation giving the Inuit and other native peoples of the Canadian northern territories formal title to their extensive and potentially resource-laden lands. The economic and social future of the Inuit appears to be far brighter than that of other contemporary hunters and gatherers.

# The Batak Foragers of the Philippines

It has been generally assumed that as hunting and gathering societies take up farming, they are almost immediately incorporated into the wider society and make a sharp transition from mobility to a sedentary lifestyle. In other words, as hunter-gatherers become more integrated with (and often dependent on) the wider social system, it is assumed that they settle down.

James Eder, who conducted research among the Batak of the Philippines, a tropical forest foraging people, extends this line of reasoning. He postulates that the nature and direction of the changes a hunter-gatherer society undergoes as it becomes increasingly connected to the wider society are to some extent determined by its own cultural characteristics (Eder, 1996). Using historical accounts, interviews with the oldest Batak, and comparative observations of other hunter-gatherer societies, he has examined how Batak hunting and gathering practices have altered over the past hundred years as they incorporated other practices into their subsistence system. He also found that the Batak are becoming more, not less, mobile as they become more integrated in the wider society.

The Batak inhabit the mountains of central Palawan Island and are distributed in eight groups, each associated with a particular river valley. The number of households in each group range from

*Batak family camping near their swidden fields, Palawan Island, The Philippines.*

(James Eder)

three to twenty-four, and the groups are located between three and ten kilometers upstream from coastal Filipino villages. Like other contemporary hunter-gatherer societies, the Batak no longer rely exclusively on hunting and gathering for subsistence, although foraging still provides about half their basic needs. They are still able to provide for their subsistence exclusively by hunting and gathering for extended periods of time, even a year or more, as they did during World War II and during an unsuccessful government attempt to relocate them in 1970 (Eder, 1996). Nevertheless, trade, horticulture, and wage labor are also part of their current economy. In fact, trade and horticulture are probably not at all new to the Batak, but wage labor emerged more recently, with the arrival of the first lowland settlers during the latter half of the nineteenth century. As the Batak became more involved with the settlers, their desire for lowland foods and manufactured goods increased and patron–client relationships rapidly evolved, tying individual Batak to individual settlers. An even more recent development has come in the form of foreign tourists, who have discovered the Batak and now provide them with a minor source of income as guides.

Another change wrought by the arrival of settlers was in the Batak settlement pattern. When root crops were still the mainstay of Batak horticulture, periodic visits to swidden fields (partially cleared areas in the forest) were part of a pattern of year-round residence in temporary forest camps. However, today, the Batak plant their swidden fields exclusively with upland rice, and during the agricultural season, it is from their field houses that they make periodic foraging trips to the forest.

A further change in settlement pattern dates from the early twentieth century, when government officials encouraged the Batak to come down out of the mountains and settle permanently on the coast. In 1930, five of these coastal settlements were declared reservations exclusively for Batak use. The legal disposition of the land was never clear, and in any event, the settlements were too small to provide the Batak with adequate subsistence. Thus, although the Batak did build houses on the reservations, they never occupied them full time. In fact, by the 1950s, the reservations were overrun with non-Batak settlers, and the Batak, in a pattern of movement that still continues, began relocating their settlement sites further up their respective river valleys, leaving themselves relatively isolated but conveniently situated for access both to the lowland areas and the forests (Eder, 1996).

Eder uses seven criteria against which to measure changes in Batak hunting and gathering practices: seasonality, encampment duration (mobility), encampment size, resource utilization, division of labor, hunting technology, and length of workday.

*Seasonality.* Eder's data show that forest camps were used more frequently during the first six months of the year (when the weather is dry and not suitable for agricultural pursuits) than the latter six months (which are mainly rainy and swidden oriented). Since the Batak do most of their hunting and gathering from forest camps, his data suggest a marked seasonality in contemporary foraging. Although he concedes that this may always have been the case, his own view is that it is a more recent development. The tropical monsoon forest in which the Batak live has a distinct dry season that would promote growth of edible plants; in addition, the Batak themselves maintain that they once lived off the land and state that in any season at least a few of the eight species of wild tubers they utilize are available (Eder, 1996, p. 44).

*Encampment Duration.* According to Eder's informants, in the past, forest camps would be occupied for periods of up to three to four weeks. Today, the occupation periods are considerably shorter, usually a matter of two to seven days. The reason is that individuals now must balance the demands of hunting and gathering against those of cultivation and participation in the market economy. Occupation periods are now shorter, and forest camps are left, not for other camps, but to return to swiddens and settlement houses. Although the encampment duration is short, the Batak spend 40% of their time in camps of one sort or another—indicating that they now have a greater rate of residential mobility. However, the shorter duration of encampments makes travel to and from camps more costly in terms of energy—energy expended over several days rather than weeks. The Batak also do not make their camps as far away from the settlements and from one another as they did in the past, and thus, resources are more quickly depleted in regularly visited areas. The energy costs of round-trip travel to camps are further increased because today the Batak bring along a lot more baggage: pots and pans, flashlights, radios, and so on.

*Encampment Size.* Eder found that it was rare today for more than seven households to camp together, whereas in the past thirty to forty households would commonly join forces. In part, this is due to demographic changes; there are simply fewer Batak today. However, more significantly, Eder traces the change to the same scheduling conflicts that affect encampment duration. Each household has a differ-

*Batak family on the move between their settlement and a forest camp.*
(James Eder)

ent swidden location, the timing of their agricultural cycle differs, and each has a different set of ties to lowlanders. "Not everyone, in effect, can get away to the forest at the same time."

*Resource Utilization.* Eder offers two explanations of why the Batak today utilize a much narrower range of plant and animal resources than in the past. First, wild resources are seasonally available and cannot be used if their availability coincides with the planting or harvesting season. Second, not only are the Batak aware that the lowlanders consider them "primitive" because of the forest foods they use, but they also regularly obtain many lowland foods (sugar, coffee, etc.), which may have changed their preferences for traditional foods.

*Division of Labor.* Eder found that there have been subtle changes in the division of labor as a consequence of certain foraging activities being discontinued, the depletion of game, and the fact that from August to October the women harvest the rice fields while only the men occupy forest camps. This latter development has had the consequence that today, over a period of a year, husbands sleep separately nearly 10% of the time—a new phenomenon among the Batak.

*Hunting Technology.* Traditionally, the Batak hunted with blowguns. However, the use of blow-

guns ceased after World War II, and now the chief weapons are spears, used in conjunction with hunting dogs, bows and arrows, and homemade guns.

*Length of Workday.* Although he has no time-allocation data from the past with which to compare his own observations, Eder concludes that contemporary Batak work longer hours. He bases his conclusions on the fact that at least some foraging now is for trade as well as subsistence and that the women are now involved in making articles for use in agriculture, such as harvesting baskets and rice-drying mats.

Eder concludes from his study that despite the fact that the overall returns of hunting and gathering for the Batak today should be higher than in the past—fewer Batak forage in the same location, and they stay for shorter periods of time—they are in fact lower. Because the Batak are now engaging in a range of economic activities, none will be as remunerative as they would be if pursued full time. Not only has Batak hunting and gathering ceased to be as successful as it once was, but Batak horticulture, because it is pursued only part time, also does not create the returns that, for instance, the lowlanders' farms do. On the other hand, they are successfully maintaining themselves and have been quick to incorporate new technologies into their subsistence system.

In the light of these findings, it is necessary to re-examine many anthropological theories regarding the relationship of hunting and gathering societies to the wider social systems into which they are becoming integrated. One should not assume that change is a simple process whereby traditional hunter-gatherers are absorbed or quickly overwhelmed by contact with farming populations. Also, one need not assume that increased participation in agriculture is inevitably associated with increased sedentism and decreased mobility. People are resourceful and innovative, and hunter-gatherers are no less so than others.

According to Eder, there have recently been some interesting and rather positive developments for the Batak, in particular, concerning their efforts, augmented by the work of non-governmental organizations (NGOs) on their behalf, to secure some of their ancestral lands against further encroachment (Eder, personal communication). The Philippine government has enacted some quite progressive legislation making it possible for indigenous peoples (actually, "indigenous cultural communities," since the legislation is written in terms of social forestry and community-based natural resource management concerns) to apply for and obtain Certificates of Ancestral Domain Claim in return for drawing up a community-based resource management plan that emphasizes conservation. On the local side, a variety of Batak-related NGOs, some with international funding, for example, the International Union for the Conservation of Nature (IUCN), have sprung up to assist the Batak (and other tribal peoples) with this endeavor. The result has been that some, but not all, local groups of Batak sometimes become more sedentized and in larger groups as NGOs send in local project staff to work with them on land concerns and a set of "sustainable development" efforts, such as the planting of tree crops, to help secure the land claims. But again, these developments have not affected all Batak settlement areas equally, and even in the two with the most conspicuous NGO presence, it is still not clear how enduring the effort or the changes will be. Also, the ancestral domain claims are writ large, so people can still pretty much move around as before.

## Summary

THE FORAGING ADAPTIVE PATTERN, WHICH HAS BEEN dominant for much of human existence, is illustrated in this chapter by the Dobe Ju/'hoansi of the Kalahari Desert, the Inuit of northeastern Canada, and the Batak of the Philippines.

Foraging peoples traditionally have been self-sufficient, but they are becoming less so as they become less isolated from the dominant societies around them. Unlike societies that cultivate their food resources, hunter-gatherers eat what nature provides and diversify their diet to accommodate fluctuations in resources. Survival necessitates an adaptive pattern that balances resources, the group's technology, and its social organization.

Foragers typically live in small, flexible groups that can scatter when natural resources become scarce and converge when resources again become plentiful. Some hunter-gatherers move regularly from campsite to campsite as resources become available in various locations; others occupy a permanent settlement from which they move to temporary camps to exploit seasonally available resources. Their kinship system creates ties over large areas so that people can move in and out of groups as resources fluctuate. Reciprocity—the sharing of food and other goods—also allows hunter-gatherers to adapt to fluctuations in resources. Their systems of decision making and social control tend to be informal.

One reason for the success of hunter-gatherers is their low-energy budget. They invest relatively little energy in the quest for food resources and obtain substantial returns. Their traditional adaptive strategy of low-energy needs, a wide resource base, and a controlled population results in minimum interference with their ecosystem. Hunter-gatherers risk wiping out their resources when they attempt to exploit them for an unlimited world market.

The Ju/'hoansi San occupy the Dobe area on the northern edge of Africa's Kalahari Desert. They are able to satisfy their needs and live comfortably in this inhospitable region by exploiting a wide variety of resources. Seasonal migrations are necessary because of fluctuations in the availability of water. The nomadic Ju/'hoansi possess only goods that can be moved easily or left behind. Social practices contribute to the mobility of the Ju/'hoansi and the flexibility of their groups. The Ju/'hoansi enjoy visiting kin in other camps, and bride service can take families to other groups for indefinite periods. Flexibility in group composition helps tailor population size to local resources and also helps reduce friction among group members.

Although meat (hunted by men) is a prized resource, vegetables and fruits (gathered chiefly by women) are the staples of the Ju/'hoansi diet. The quality of the Ju/'hoansi's life is apparently quite high; their diet is nutritionally sound and procured with relatively little expenditure of energy, and they enjoy a great deal of leisure time. A low birth rate is crucial to the Ju/'hoansi adaptive pattern.

The Inuit have traditionally depended on a seasonal quest for animals to provide food, clothing, tools, and fuel. Contact with the world market, however, has eroded the isolation and self-sufficiency of the Inuit.

The arctic environment dictates the adaptive patterns of the Netsilik of northeastern Canada and the Baffin Island Inuit. These people change the sizes and locations of their camps as their resources change with the seasons. In the summer, they disperse to take advantage of abundant food, and in the winter, they come together to hunt seals. Unlike the Ju/'hoansi, they are able to store food for the long winters, but their climate forces them to adopt a higher energy budget than that of the Ju/'hoansi and to accumulate material goods (such as heavy clothing, snowmobiles, lamps, and rifles) that reduce their mobility. In the past, the Inuit have kept their population level in harmony with their food resources, but now their population is rapidly increasing, with a resultant strain on their ecosystem.

Extensive kinship ties allow the Inuit, like the Ju/'hoansi, to move easily in and out of groups, but the most important social unit is the extended family. The Inuit frown on shows of emotion or of negative feelings. They have no formalized leadership or code of social control.

A study of the Baffin Island Inuit revealed that their intake of energy is high and their output low. They hunt seal, caribou, and other animals and catch fish in weirs (circular dams) they have built of stone. Their natural resources are supplemented by store-bought food, particularly the ingredients to make bannock (unleavened bread baked in a shallow pan), and such items as snowmobiles and kerosene stoves.

Industrialization is changing the life of all Inuit. Seasonal migrations are no longer necessary, as they can quickly travel to their hunting grounds by snowmobile, and store-bought food provides insurance against hunger. The introduction of high-powered weapons almost led to the destruction of the Inuit's traditional resource base, but the U.S. government intervened and the caribou herds have returned. Today, most Inuit live in villages with most of the amenities of contemporary North American life. Still, they retain their languages, social identities, and many traditional food preferences.

The Inupiat of Alaska illustrate some of the problems contemporary U.S. native peoples face as well as how they have organized to take at least some political control over their own destinies.

The Batak of the Philippines confound the prevalent assumption that as hunting and gathering societies take up farming they become more integrated with, and often dependent on, the wider social system almost immediately and that they make a sharp transition from mobility to sedentism. However, the changes the Batak are experiencing as they increasingly interact with the wider Philippine society seem to have been largely determined by their own cultural characteristics. They have eagerly incorporated new technologies into their traditional subsistence system, and they now engage in a range of economic activities. And while they are successfully maintaining themselves in this way, because they are not pursuing any of these activities full time, they have in fact become more mobile.

## Key Terms

| | |
|---|---|
| balanced reciprocity | low-energy budget |
| bands | negative reciprocity |
| bride service | potlatch |
| ethnographic present | reciprocity |
| generalized reciprocity | social control |

## Suggested Readings

Aldona, J. (1999). *The Yuquot Whalers' Shrine*. St. Louis, MO: Washington University Press. This fascinating book explores the collection of northwest coast religious artifacts gathered by Franz Boas and George Hunt in 1905.

Bailey, R. C. (1991). The behavioral ecology of Efe Pygmy men in the Ituri forest, Zaire. *UMMA Anthropological Papers, 86.* Ann Arbor: Museum of Anthropology, University of Michigan. A detailed volume of Efe foraging activity with a focus on time allocation and hunting returns, using a socioecological approach.

Burbank, V. K. (1994). *Fighting women: Anger & aggression in aboriginal Australia*. Berkeley: University of California Press. Contemporary and controversial, this book focuses on the aggressive behavior of aboriginal women in Australia and offers an interesting perspective on domestic violence.

Burch, Ernest S., Jr., & Ellanna, L. J. (Eds.). (1994). *Key issues in hunter-gatherer research*. Oxford: Berg. A collection of articles based on research among contemporary hunter-gatherers, with an introduction and concluding sections dealing with the general state of such research and its prospects.

Chance, N. A. (1990). *The Inupiat and arctic Alaska: An ethnography of development*. Fort Worth, TX: Holt, Rinehart & Winston. A detailed account of how one population has coped with a changing political environment and successfully gained control of much of their traditional lands.

Condon, R., with Oguia, J., & Holman elders. (1996). *The Northern Copper Inuit: A history* (The Civilization of American Indian Series, V. 220). Norman, OK, and London: University of Oklahoma Press. A historical reconstruction and ethnographic account of the Northern Copper Inuit written in collaboration with leading members of that society.

Fondahl, G. A. (1998). *Gaining ground? Evenkis, land, and reform in southeastern Siberia. Cultural survival studies in ethnicity and change*. Boston: Allyn & Bacon. The Evenkis are reindeer herders and hunters of southeastern

Siberia who, having survived the coming of the Russians in the seventeenth century and often the harsh rule of the Soviets, now have to contend with yet a new set of problems as they attempt to retain some control over their resources.

Freeman, M. M. R., Bogoslovskaya, L., & Caulfield, R. A. (1998). *Inuit, whaling, and sustainability* (Contemporary Native American Communities Series). New York: Sage Publications. An interesting account of Inuit whaling from their perspective; a highly charged subject.

Hemley, R. (2003). *Invented Eden: The elusive, disputed history of the Tasaday.* New York: Farrar, Straus, Giroux. This very readable book reviews the complex history of the Tasaday of the Philippines, who were "discovered" in 1971 and promoted as a living example of a "Stone Age people." But it was soon alleged to be an elaborate hoax. This book suggests that while not a hoax, the Tasaday are simply an isolated hunting population who separated from agricultural kinfolk about 100 years ago to take up foraging and who were exploited by the government and the media.

Hessel, I. (2003). *Inuit art: An introduction.* Vancouver, BC: Douglas & McIntyre. Inuit art has gained a prominent place in the world of art, and this is an excellent introduction.

Hill, K., & Hurtado, A. M. (1996). *Ache life history. The ecology and demography of a foraging people* (Foundations of Human Behavior). New York: Aldine de Gruyter. A splendid account of both the Ache people and the authors' long-term research involvement with them.

Lee, R. B. (1993). *The Dobe Ju/'hoansi.* Fort Worth, TX: Harcourt Brace College Publishers. A broadly oriented case study on the hunter-gatherer way of life of the Ju/'hoansi of the Kalahari Desert, exploring topics such as subsistence techniques, kinship, religion, and environment.

Schrire, C. (Ed.). (1984). *Past and present in hunter-gatherer studies.* Orlando, FL: Academic Press. This collection of papers attempts to understand both the past behavior and current ways of life of hunter-gatherers by focusing on the history of their interactions with other peoples.

Shostak, M. (2002). *Return to Nisa.* Cambridge, MA: MIT Press. Shostak describes what has become of Nisa, the !Kung woman whose life she had earlier chronicled in a now classic book. (This book was completed by her husband after her death.)

Smith, A. (2000). *The Bushmen of southern Africa: A foraging society in transition.* Columbus: Ohio University Press. A well-written historical overview of the peoples of the Kalahari from prehistory to the present.

Turnbull, C. (1961). *The forest people.* New York: Simon & Schuster. An intimate view of the Mbuti Pygmies of equatorial Africa that explores the relationships of the people to the forest and to their horticultural neighbors. Now a classic.

Wilmsen, E. N. (Ed.). (1989). *We are here: Politics of aboriginal land tenure.* Berkeley: University of California Press. An anthropological investigation that explores the issues of aboriginal relations to land and territory.

Winterhalder, B., & Smith, E. A. (Eds.). (1981). *Hunter-gatherer foraging strategies.* Chicago: University of Chicago Press. A collection of ethnographic and archaeological analyses that apply optimal foraging theory.

# Chapter 4

# Horticulture: Feeding the Household

Horticulture, or simply gardening, is a very basic but still vital form of food production. In Zimbabwe, a man and his sons burn trees and brush to open a circular field on which they will plant millet; in Brazil, a woman pushes seed yams into the soil of her irregularly shaped garden; in Peru, a family works together to place stones to form a terrace that they will plow in order to plant corn. These mundane, everyday acts, taken cumulatively, sustain many of earth's some 6.5 billion people. This chapter looks at societies that practice agriculture relying primarily on localized inputs: human labor, locally made tools, and if used at all, animals for traction (plowing, pumping, and transport). Such forms of agriculture are often termed **horticulture** or **subsistence agriculture;** production, even if traded, sold, or bartered, is primarily aimed at household provisioning rather than investment.

Food production, however simple or complex in terms of technology, is the very foundation of contemporary human existence. Foraging, as we have seen, involves the collection of naturally occurring food resources in a given habitat with relatively little intervention or management. Agriculture involves the domestication and management of edible

species that characteristically cannot survive or reproduce without human assistance. There is no direct evidence that people who lived in prehistoric times consciously or unconsciously tried to influence the reproductive cycles of the species on which they depended, but since they were intelligent, experiments certainly occurred. Over the ages, however, as people and animals and plants interacted, selective pressures changed the reproductive success of the animals and plants favored by humans.

These changes need not have resulted from a conscious manipulation of a species by the people who used it. Such changes could have come about as inadvertent by-products of the way people were altering their environment—being selective in the killing of members of a particular population, for example, or harvesting grain in such a way as to change the genetic makeup of seeds by selectively retaining some and discarding others. Even the use of fire could be a stage in the domestication of some plants (see Hill & Baird, 2003). Such selective pressures eventually led to **domestication,** the process by which people began trying to control the reproductive rates of animals and plants by ordering the environment to favor their survival—protecting

them from pests, predators, and competitors, for instance, and supplying them with water and nutrients. Ultimately, these efforts led to agriculture, one of the most significant achievements of the human species.

The development of agriculture irrevocably affected the course of human cultural history. The full impact of these changes can be seen in the societies that practice intensive agriculture (discussed in Chapter 6), the most productive and technologically sophisticated form of food production. But the contrast to the hunting and gathering adaptation can be seen clearly even in societies that practice a modest and comparatively simple form of agriculture: horticulture.

**Horticulture,** meaning "garden cultivation," is almost always accompanied by some reliance on hunting, fishing, and collecting wild plants. However, unlike hunter-gatherers, horticulturists depend primarily on domesticated foods, especially plants; and unlike intensive or industrialized agriculturists, they raise these plants in small plots using relatively simple methods and tools. Agricultural techniques, along with other forms of behavior, vary widely from group to group. Yet the shared procurement strategy—production of food crops primarily for personal consumption—creates certain broad similarities in settlement patterns, social organization, and interactions among groups. First, this chapter will examine how the strategy developed and its general features. Then it will focus on two specific groups of farmers: the Yanomamö of Venezuela and Brazil and the Native American populations usually referred to as the Pueblo. While the traditional agricultural practices of Pueblo communities are preserved more as a means of keeping continuity with the past, Pueblo identity and culture remain vibrant. In the case of the Pueblo, the material presented is largely historical, while the other case reflects the more or less contemporary scene—keeping in mind the rapid pace of change affecting people everywhere. Although these cases represent very different technologies, they share the fact that human labor is the main input. Horticulturists can produce most or all of the tools they need for farming, and their households are highly self-sufficient.

## The Horticultural Adaptation

### Prehistoric Origins of Agriculture

Agriculture is truly a human global achievement in that, with the exception of Australia, every continent has made a significant contribution to the world's mix of domesticated crops and animals. It is unclear which region of the Old World witnessed the first independent experimentation with domestication, with South Asia and the Middle East seemingly developing apace, but Africa and the New World only marginally later. While native Australians did not have agriculture prior to European rule, they did practice very sophisticated resource management along the rich coastal areas and most likely would have moved soon to full domestication had not Europeans arrived (Diamond, 1999; Hill & Baird, 2003). The multiple independent origins of agriculture and domestication in Africa, the Indus Valley of India and Pakistan, and China as well as in Mesoamerica and South America have long been recognized. Two areas where agriculture was thought not to have developed in antiquity are Australia and New Guinea. Now, however, evidence has come to light of the deliberate planting of two valuable food crops, taro and banana, in New Guinea dating as far back as 6,950 years ago (Denham et al., 2003). What remains puzzling is why this region did not undergo the subsequent development of intensification seen elsewhere.

Since the archaeological record for the Middle East is currently the most accessible, it is useful to look to this region rather than to attempt a global review. Although humans have lived in the Middle East for tens of thousands of years, history in one sense begins with the period known archaeologically as the **Neolithic,** or New Stone Age. The Neolithic, which roughly dates from about 10,000 years ago and extends until the rise of states and cities at approximately 5,000 years ago, is often regarded as a watershed in the development of human culture. It was during this era that domestication of plants and animals took place, thus setting in motion profound changes in human society.

Anthropologists recognize that people do not usually "discover" something as complex as agriculture; instead, it must be regarded as the culmination of a long series of interrelated events, even accidents. People slowly, and often without realizing it, react to specific problems in ways that only later will be seen as significant. The question we have to ask is why people in the Middle East changed their mode of subsistence to emphasize agriculture and domesticated animals. As prehistorians put it, "there had to be *opportunity* (that is sufficient populations of the prerequisite plants), *technology* to use the plants effectively, a *social organization* that could cope with 'delayed return' economies, and *need* before people would alter their habits of acquiring food" (McCorriston & Hole, 1991, p. 46). McCorriston and Hole in fact go so far as to assert exactly when and where these conditions came together to produce agriculture—in the Jordan Valley around

**Horticulture**

Figure 4.1. *The horticultural adaptation, like foraging, often exploits numerous wild food sources as well as cultivating gardens. In some cases, the gardens are fenced or barricaded to keep out animals, domestic or otherwise. Housing is usually more substantial than with foraging peoples because populations are more sedentary. Generally, horticulturists live in nucleated settlements or villages, often for reasons of defense but also because reliable food production allows for larger year-round community size.*

lakes that were receding due to increased aridity around 10,000 years ago, give or take only a few hundred years (p. 46).

The natural habitat for the wild ancestors of wheat and barley is not in the lowlands but seems to lie in the higher areas of the Levant and the Taurus and Zagros, which might suggest that the early experimentation with domestication took place far from the centers of early civilization that followed in the riverine lowlands. In fact, wild barley and wheat can still be found in the Zagros uplands. Jack Harlan, a botanist, demonstrated in 1967 the great abundance and productivity of wild wheat in southeastern Turkey. Using a primitive stone sickle, he hand-harvested six pounds of wild wheat in an hour and estimated that a family of four could gather a year's supply of food in approximately three weeks.

Early foragers in the area must have found such wild grains a good source of food, and it is likely that a number of pre-Neolithic foraging populations

came to depend on them as their staple. Recent archaeological evidence indicates a long preagricultural tradition of village life based on wild grain and animals. Archaeologists refer to this cultural period as the *Natufian*, and it was then that people began making and using pottery, living in fixed dwellings, at least for significant portions of the year, and using stone mortars to make flour from wild grains.

At the same time, it is likely that not all populations had equal access to these naturally abundant grain areas. Some must have been living in areas with a limited or erratic food supply. McCorriston and Hole suggest that it was among these marginally located populations that had settled in the Jordan Valley that early experimentation in domestication is more likely to have occurred. Because domesticated grain represents a genetic change from the original form, it is possible that the pressures that precipitated this change were inadvertently engineered by humans attempting to use grains where they normally did not

## Box 4.1

## Red Rice out of Africa

THE GREATEST SERVICE WHICH can be rendered any country is to add an useful plant to its culture.

*Thomas Jefferson.*

From the sixteenth to the eighteenth centuries, there occurred a period of intense crop exchanges between the Old and New Worlds known as the Columbian Exchange. Researchers have long emphasized the centrality of economically valuable crops originating in the Americas, Asia, and Europe in this exchange and the role of Europeans in their global diffusion. This view thus emphasizes the diffusion of crops to, rather than from, Africa. Judith Carney (1998) states that two factors account for this focus, "the minor role of African domesticates like okra, cowpeas, yams, pearl millet, and sorghum in food and plantation economies, and the long-standing belief that rice was solely of Asian origin" (p. 526). However, recent historical and botanical

scholarship challenge this perspective and lend support to the view that indigenous African rice (*Oryza glaberrima*), rather than the higher yielding Asian *sativa* varieties, was the first type of rice grown in the plantations of the eastern edges of the Americas as well as to the fact that West African slaves, being familiar with its cultivation, "played a crucial role in adapting it to diverse New World environments."

It was only in the twentieth century that the discovery that rice domestication occurred in West Africa independently of Asia was made; it is now known that rice domestication occurred more than 3,000 years ago in the region stretching from Senegal to the Ivory Coast. Arab and European sources from the eighth to the sixteenth centuries mention rice cultivation along the West African coast and the inland delta of the Niger River. Early Portuguese mariners are known to have purchased rice on the West African coast, and during the At-

lantic slave trade, rice surpluses provisioned ships bound for the New World. Despite this evidence, until quite recently, scholars assigned an Asian origin to this rice and attributed its diffusion to Arab and Portuguese traders.

During the 1920s, French scholars intensified their research on *glaberrima*, in part in response to France's concern over growing food shortages in its West African colonies. They showed that Asian rice had not yet reached the Nile and Egypt by the first century A.D., making it extremely unlikely that its diffusion across the Sahara could account for the frequent mention of widespread rice domestication in West Africa in Arab commentaries from the eighth century on. In the 1970s, the French botanist Portères identified the African center of rice domestication primarily in the inland delta of the Niger River, with secondary centers along the flood plains in Senegambia and the mountains of Guinea Conakry. As

grow. For example, Hole, Flannery, and Neely (1969) describe the planting of wheat and barley close to edges of swamps at Ali Kosh, an archaeological site in southwestern Iran. Because these grains do not normally grow wild in marshy areas, the native vegetation must have been cleared away to make room for them. Here, suggest Hale et al., we see some of the first steps in the deliberate modification of the Middle East landscape by human hands. Early efforts such as these must have ultimately led to a full-time commitment to agriculture.

Even though our understanding of all the events leading to the domestication of plants and animals in the area is still very limited, it is certain that within 1,000 years agriculture had spread widely and that by 7000 B.C. villages based on domestic plants and animals were becoming increasingly common. Evidence from this early period suggests that early agriculturists practiced dry farming and utilized domesticated sheep and goats. Certainly, by 6000 B.C., village life replaced nomadic foraging as

the dominant pattern throughout most of the Middle East. Jarmo, a site in northeastern Iraq excavated by Robert Braidwood and now considered to be of particular importance, was a village of approximately twenty-five mud-walled houses, each with its own courtyard, storage pit, and oven. Sickle blades and grinding stones, found together with barley and wheat, indicate an ongoing commitment to agriculture. Finds elsewhere—for example, in Turkey, Iran, Syria, Israel, and Jordan—suggest that the case of Jarmo is not unique.

Although a modern visitor to ancient Jarmo would find its inhabitants unlike any living group in the Middle East today, certain features of their general life would be familiar. The people of Jarmo, like many contemporary rural Middle Easterners, practiced a mixed economy combining grain production with animal husbandry. In an environment of unpredictable climatic variability, it is advantageous for people to hedge their bets by diversifying their subsistence base. Moreover, the presence of individ-

Carney describes it, the legacy of this research culminated in 1974 in the publication of two "path-breaking" books: Polish historian Lewicki's *West African Food in the Middle Ages,* based on previously untranslated Arab sources, documented the antiquity of indigenous rice cultivation in West Africa, and U.S. historian Peter Wood's *Black Majority* argued for the strong probability that rice cultivation on plantations in South Carolina was of African origin.

Wood noted that rice cultivation appeared in South Carolina in tandem with slavery from the earliest settlement period between 1670 and 1730. Further, the early English and French Huguenot planters were not familiar with rice cultivation techniques, and over 40% of the slaves imported into colonial South Carolina were from the region in West Africa where *glaberrima* rice was cultivated. Wood therefore concludes that the West Africans were crucial to the establishment of the plantation rice system in South Carolina. Carney points additionally to the fact that at the beginning of the Atlantic slave trade there were three major rice cultivation

systems in use in West Africa: rain fed, inland swamps, and tidal flood plains. All three systems are documented as existing in South Carolina by the 1730s, "within decades of the crop's introduction to the colony" (Carney 1993, 1996, 1998). Another feature of the rice plantation system in South Carolina, the task labor system, may also provide evidence for the African origin of rice cultivation there. The task labor system, found only on rice plantations, assigned a daily field task to be completed so that healthy slaves who could work faster would have a shorter day. In the more common gang labor system, slaves worked daily from dawn to dusk on one or a series of tasks. Carney comments, "The unusual appearance of the distinctive task labor system on rice plantations perhaps represents the residue of a complex pattern of negotiation in establishing Carolina rice plantations in which slaves provided the know-how to grow rice in exchange for circumscribed demands on their daily labor" (p. 531).

Two further items add weight to the argument: Until the advent of water-powered mills during the

eighteenth century, rice milling was done by hand in the traditional African manner with a wooden mortar and pestle; and the hulls were removed through winnowing in fanner baskets woven in the same way as those used for the same purpose in the West African rice growing regions. An interesting note on the latter is that Native American baskets were plaited and twilled, whereas those used for winnowing were coiled, identical still to those used in the West African rice regions (Rosengarten, 1997).

Carney concludes:

> *A focus on the environmental aspects of rice cultivation and the material culture . . . thus brings new insights to the recovery of perhaps a significant narrative of the African diaspora. . . . Trying to recapture elements of that history centuries later demands a multidisciplinary perspective, particularly additional research in botany, historical archaeology, and the archives of countries of the Americas where rice cultivation developed.*

ual domiciles and granaries in Jarmo suggests another similarity to modern farmers in that the household, then as now, was an extremely important social and economic unit. Everywhere in the horticultural world, the household is still the primary unit of production and consumption.

This development was closely paralleled in Asia and Africa as well. By about 9,000 years ago, there were signs that people had begun to plant and harvest crops and to domesticate various animal species. This shift in adaptive pattern is of great interest to anthropologists because it ultimately set in motion greater changes in social life and technology than had occurred over the preceding millennia.

While the earliest evidence of cultivation and herding appears in the Middle East, where wheat and barley were the first staple crops, horticulture also appeared early in China and Southeast Asia. Surprisingly, millet, not rice, was the primary crop in early Chinese cultivation. The origin of rice, one of the world's most important crops, is still poorly

understood. We do know now that dry field rice originated in West Africa (see Box 4.1) (Carney, 1998). While our knowledge of the domestication process in Africa is incomplete, there is evidence for the cultivation of sorghum, millet, and a variety of other plants that dates back some 4,000 years. One very common African food crop is the banana. The Ugandan word *matooke* means both food and banana. The average person in Uganda consumes 350 kilograms of bananas a year (*The Economist,* 2003b). Bananas and plantains are the fourth most important food crop by value in Africa. What is different about the banana is that it is not grown from seeds but is cloned—that is, grown from shoots from the parent plant. Wild bananas, which do produce seeds, are inedible, and it is a mutant form, discovered in antiquity, which is now propagated by people. The problem, now being addressed by new genetic research, is that the banana plants as clones are especially prone to disease. There is little genetic diversity among bananas compared to seed crops.

In Mesoamerica and South America, cultivation appeared thousands of years later than in the Old World. Corn, beans, and squash were the important crops cultivated in higher altitude areas; manioc was grown in coastal zones.

Some archaeologists have suggested that agricultural experiments began when humans noticed plants growing from seeds in their garbage dumps. There is evidence that hunter-gatherers were well aware of the relationship between plants and seeds, and it is possible that horticulture began with tending useful herbs. The interesting question is why hunter-gatherers would give up a stable existence for one that requires substantially more work.

However one judges the record, it is clear that people came to exercise more control over their environment. Ultimately, they chose more productive resources, stored seeds, selected from among the seeds those most likely to generate productive plants, and altered the conditions under which the plants were growing by removing weeds and supplying additional water.

### Early Farming in Poland: An Archaeological Example.

Subsistence farming emerged in Europe between 7,000 and 5,000 years ago. At about this time, farming villages had spread northward from the Carpathian Mountains into what is now Poland. For several seasons, Peter Bogucki of Princeton University and Ryszard Grygiel of the Archaeological Museum in Lodz excavated the site of Oslonki in north-central Poland, focusing their research on the earliest farmers of the north European plain. Excavations revealed a large village, dated between 4300 and 4000 B.P., with thirty trapezoidal longhouses and fortified with a ditched enclosure surrounded by a palisade. Bogucki and Grygiel have excavated more than eighty graves at the site, and in some they found evidence that the village may have had a social hierarchy; one grave contained an extraordinary amount of copper, including a diadem that may have been a symbol of rank. Another grave contained an archer with five bone arrow points in a quiver. The quality and variety of artifacts found at the site make it one of the richest archaeological finds in central Europe.

The people who settled Oslonki undoubtedly changed the local habitat significantly. They would have cut forest for timber for building and firewood, cleared land for crop cultivation, and grazed their livestock on the land surrounding their village. In addition, they hunted wild animals and waterfowl and fished in the nearby streams and lakes. Satellite settlements have been found which appear to have been established for specific purposes such as tending crops grown away from the village and as bases for hunting expeditions. Oslonki was occupied at the same time as the nearby settlement of Brzesc Kujawski, and the residents of both communities most likely cut trails through the forest, further altering the landscape. Both villages were abandoned about 4000 B.P., but it is unclear whether this was because of resource depletion or as a consequence of some other humanmade or natural event. Bogucki and Grygiel hope that further excavation and research will throw more light on this question.

*Neolithic "flexed" burials found at Oslonki. Grave goods indicated that the villagers may have had a social hierarchy.*

(By permission of Peter Bogucki)

## Population and Pressure on Resources

Despite many regional differences, the common thread underlying the development and spread of agriculture is that it was paralleled by population growth or, at least, pressure on resources and the instability that accompanied it. The most common early strategy for solving the problem of food procurement was to move to a new location, but as population levels became high in relation to available resources, this alternative became less feasible and more settled patterns of existence resulted. This new pattern of sedentism probably upset the balance between human groups and the resources on which they depended. When mortality, fertility limitations, or migration were not sufficient to keep a population within acceptable limits, some groups began to manipulate the natural availability of resources (by planting and so forth). This strategy made it possible to sustain a larger number of people without depleting their resources. As these groups grew and spread, other groups imitated their practices. Because they could increase the carrying capacity of their environment in ways in which hunter-gatherers could not, horticulturists, farmers, and herders became more predominant.

It is important to emphasize that the initial expansion of horticulture did not occur because it was a universally superior adaptation to hunting and gathering. Horticulturalists often had to work harder. Analyses of skeletal material from the time periods suggest that overall health decreased, and disease and malnutrition increased. But the increased productivity and reliability of the food supply provided the basis for further population growth, a cycle that has continued to the present. Both depend on the elaboration of methods of cultivation.

Another point that is important to keep in mind is that even prehistoric hunter-gatherers often incorporated significant horticultural production into their adaptation, just as predominately farm-supported populations also foraged and hunted. Marla Buckmaster, an archaeologist working in the Upper Peninsula of Michigan where farming today is very limited, has documented just how elaborate this can be. She has discovered extensive evidence of systematic field preparation by people whose settlements were small and temporary and whose first line of food support was foraging and hunting. The northern people, long before the Colonial Era, carefully prepared clusters of parallel furrows organized in a checkerboard fashion, which extended two kilometers along the Menomenee River. They lined the furrows with rocks. The rocks are, she believes, an ingenious mechanism for retaining enough heat in the soil to grow an annual crop of corn, as evidenced in plant remains, in a zone marking the northern limits of farming at the time. These sites also show how populations, whether fully or partially dependent on agriculture, tracked changing microclimates and extended even a limited farming system northward as far as possible at about 1405–1450 B.P. (Buckmaster, 1999).

## Energy Use and the Ecosystem

The objective of any form of agriculture is to increase the amount of predictable or reliable energy that a given unit of land can yield for human use. Although horticulturists usually extract far fewer food calories or other products per acre than do plow farmers (let alone modern intensive farmers), they also expend less labor than intensive agriculturists. They use neither their land nor their labor to the fullest. Simply producing enough to feed the family takes much less work than people are capable of doing; thus, many of the able-bodied (such as adolescents) may not have to work at all while those who do work may do so intermittently and spend more time hunting or in other activities. That is not to say that horticulturists are lazy. They may simply have more options as to how to use their time. A comparison of four populations in the Brazilian Amazon finds that while all hunt to acquire needed protein, those who live in the best horticultural areas hunt the most. Meat is a desired luxury and the men can afford the time to seek it (Werner et al., 1979, pp. 303–315). Horticulturists have time left over after the minimum required subsistence tasks to devote to elaborate food preparation, ceremonies, and the acquisition of luxury items beyond their basic needs.

In general, the lower the energy demands a human group makes on its environment, the less the group alters that environment. Clifford Geertz, in an early and very influential discussion of the subject, has argued that many farmers in the tropical lowlands do not so much alter their ecosystem as create "a canny imitation" of it (1969, p. 6). Their ecosystem contains a remarkable diversity of living things packed in a small area; that is, the ecosystem is generalized rather than specialized. Although tropical soil is often thin, it can support this dense variety because the nutrients are rapidly recycled rather than locked up in deep soil. The dense canopy of trees prevents this layer of rich organic soil from being washed away by rain or baked hard by the sun.

The plots of such farmers copy these qualities of the tropical forest. Unlike the specialized fields of most intensive agriculturists—all rice or all toma-toes—the plot contains a jumble of crops, from roots and tubers to fruit trees and palms, flourishing pri-marily in a bed of ash. Like the trees of the uncultivated forest, the domesticated trees of the plot form a cover that filters sun and rain, thus protecting the soil from erosion or parching and at the same time reducing the encroachment of undergrowth. And within a few years, this plot reverts back to forest.

Horticulture differs from intensive agriculture in several ways. First is the relatively simple technology associated with this type of farming. Only small and often scattered plots of land are cultivated at one time, and they are usually worked without the help of plows or animal traction, to say nothing of ma-chines. The only tools used are simple hand tools: knives, axes, digging sticks, and hoes. In other words, horticulturists, like hunter-gatherers, still rely mainly on the energy stored in their own mus-cles to procure their food.

Second, in comparison with intensive agricul-ture, horticulture provides a relatively low yield per acre of land; for this reason, it is frequently catego-rized as **extensive agriculture.** For every unit of en-ergy produced, horticultural methods require much more land than intensive agricultural techniques. The amount of energy horticulturists extract from the land is enough to sustain them, but they gener-ally do not produce large food surpluses for the pur-pose of trade. Although trade is often of concern to horticulturists, usually it is for the acquisition of items produced by another population. Exceptions occur when horticulturists are in close contact with hunter-gatherer groups from whom they may ac-quire animal products. The Mbuti Pygmies of north-eastern Zaire, for example, are a hunting people that supply their Bantu-speaking horticultural neighbors with meat and honey from the forest (Hart & Hart, 1996; Peacock, 1984).

Third, in general, horticulture allows for house-hold self-sufficiency. Each group, and in most cases each household, is capable of producing most of the food it needs. Most important production decisions are made at the household level. Horticulturists need not depend on other groups for food because they cultivate a wide variety of crops with an exceedingly modest technology. This orientation toward self-suf-ficiency is one of the reasons that the production of horticultural societies remains low.

## Horticultural Cultivation Methods

Most contemporary horticulturists occupy marginal territories: either tropical regions, where soil is thin, or arid regions, where the water supply is a constant

*Farmer burning vegetation in Rondonia, Brazil preparing forest lands for farming. Massive areas of tropical forest are lost worldwide due to pressure by farmers as well as commercial logging.*
(© Stephanie Maze/CORBIS)

problem. In this respect, they resemble hunter-gath-erers. They often have been excluded by competing groups from more favored lands where intensive agriculture is possible. In such circumstances, they cope with the challenge of agriculture in several ways. They may concentrate on crops that make few demands on the soil. They may plant next to rivers or in areas that flood in the rainy season. They may plant in several locations so that if one field fails, an-other may still feed them, or they may shift their fields regularly to avoid depleting the soil. Many horticulturists use several of these techniques. The last, however, which in its present form is called **slash-and-burn agriculture,** or **swidden agriculture,** is the most common.

*Slash-and-Burn Agriculture.* Slash-and-burn agri-culture is a method of farming in which fields are cleared, the trees and brush are burned so that the soil is fertilized by the ash, and the fields are then planted. Each field is used for perhaps two or three years and then it is left to regenerate for about ten years while the farmer moves on to other fields.

Swidden agriculture was practiced in Europe until the beginning of the Christian era and in North America until about the seventeenth century. (Indeed, it has been suggested that one reason for the success of the European colonists in North America was that they imitated the slash-and-burn techniques of the Native Americans.)

Unfortunately, all too often, traditional horticultural plots are being consolidated into open-field farms and ranches in environments unsuited to such enterprises. The Amazon rain forest is being burned and bulldozed at an ever-increasing rate to make way for ranches and open-field farms, whereas horticulturists such as the Yanomamö (whom we will meet shortly) have managed to exploit the rain forests without harming the environment. With more intensive land use in the same areas, the thin soil rapidly erodes.

The slash-and-burn technique demands a fine sensitivity to the environment. Swidden farmers must know exactly when to move their fields and when to replant a fallow field. They must also make rather precise calculations as to when to burn—on a day when there is enough wind to fan the fire but not enough to spread it to the rest of the forest. Horticulturists in general (swidden and otherwise) know an enormous amount about their environment, including minute details about different kinds of soil, about the demands of different kinds of plants, and about the topography and microclimate of their habitats. This knowledge is the key to their survival.

*Polyculture Versus Monoculture.* The mix of crops, or **polyculture**, can vary considerably among swidden cultivators even in the same general region, as studies in the Amazon have shown (Coimbra et al., 2002; Flowers et al., 1982, pp. 203–217). Earlier studies have emphasized the diversity of crops and the apparent helter-skelter aspect of horticulture—a complex mix of plants and trees that is as ecologically diversified as the forest itself. Recent work shows that very often the people rely on one or two main crops but intersperse them with useful trees; the planting is not done in a random or unplanned fashion but is carefully patterned so that as the garden ages different crops become available in turn (see Beckerman, 1983; Boster, 1983; Flowers et al., 1982). Thus, even the return to fallow is carefully regulated, each stage providing some product to the cultivators.

All agricultural systems, at least temporarily, simplify specific portions of their natural ecosystems. It is also claimed that fertility is sustained by the complementary characteristics of different plants, the nutrient enriching tendencies of some balancing the nutrient robbing tendencies of others.

Polyculture (the interplanting of different crops in one field) has long been considered the key to ecological stability and sustainable, reliable yields in traditional horticulture, whereas monoculture, as practiced in intensive systems of agriculture, has often been linked to major disasters such as the Irish potato famine of the 1840s and even the Sahelian famines of the 1980s. One of the chief criticisms of monoculture, and one that is associated in particular with the use of modern hybrid varieties of crops, is the loss of biological variability. Unfortunately, monoculture is usually the easiest way to increase

(a)  (b)

*Horticulture or polyculture in Nyeri, central Kenya (a), and monoculture near Kisumu, Kenya, on fields established by European settlers (b).*
(Daniel Bates)

yields—something that is desperately needed in many countries. For years, many researchers have argued that polyculture is more natural than monoculture in that the mix of different species in a field parallels the diversity of the forest and thus acquires a great resistance to diseases that might threaten a single species. More recently, there has been evidence that the same effects can be achieved in monocultures by means of interplanting different varieties of the same species.

## Social Organization

Horticultural or extensive farming societies, however varied, tend to share a number of very general characteristics when compared with low-energy budget foragers. One is **sedentism,** the practice of establishing a permanent, year-round settlement. Whereas hunter-gatherers invest time and energy in moving from place to place to find food, farmers invest their energy in increasing food production in one place—their fields.

Population density is also generally higher. In a group that is not on the move constantly, infants, old people, and sick people have a better chance of surviving. The fertility rate may go up, for when men are no longer called away to the hunt, they spend more time with their wives. Similarly, storage, which equalizes the distribution of resources through the year, is easier in a permanent settlement. Sedentary groups, then, tend to have higher population densities than nomadic or seminomadic groups.

Both these conditions—sedentism and increasing population density—result in a more complex society. Agriculture is a group effort, involving considerable cooperation in clearing fields, planting, harvesting, and storing crops. The crops and fields have to be protected from predators, including the threat of theft by others. At the same time, since agriculturists invest time and energy in the land, organization is required to regulate access to the land and to resolve disputes that inevitably accompany life in a large residential grouping. Finally, a group that contains many people, interacting on a permanent basis, needs to order the relationships of group members: to determine who owes loyalty to whom, who can marry whom, who must give in to whom in a quarrel, and so forth.

Hunter-gatherers have fewer such problems. They can work individually, they own the land collectively, and when disputes arise, they can simply pack up their belongings and move. The horticultural life presents more social challenges that must be met through a more complex social structure. Horticulturists, for example, frequently consider land to be

the property of the group. However, individual households have exclusive access to the crops they produce on a given plot. Though farmers may move when disputes break out, once they have invested in a plot, it is harder to do so.

*Relations within the Community.* The basic unit of a society heavily dependent on farming is the **household,** a small group of people closely related by marriage and kinship who work together to produce food, share in its consumption, and cooperate on a day-to-day basis. Thus, it is a unit of production and consumption analogous in many ways to a small family firm in our society. These family-based households, as we have mentioned, are relatively self-sufficient because their gardens or fields allow them to produce almost everything they need. Nevertheless, they cannot afford to be completely independent of one another, for agriculture creates vulnerability. Once a family has invested its energy in a plot of land, crop failure or a raid by another group can wipe out its livelihood in one stroke. Therefore, as insurance, households must make alliances and integrate themselves into a larger social unit: the community. They achieve integration primarily through kinship ties and participation in community-wide religious or political groupings. In some respects, collective land ownership by kin groups or small, closely knit communities is reinforced in the horticultural communities of the tropical lowlands by the practice of having long fallow periods. These long periods during which families cease to cultivate their plots to allow the forest to regenerate do not encourage individuals to assert exclusive control over any given plot. Also, in most circumstances, the fact of collective ownership limits incentives for long-term investments in the agricultural infrastructure such as constructing terraces or systems to control the flow of water.

Kinship is often (though not invariably) the basis for recognition of individual rights to the use of land. Kinship is almost always the basis of extensive gift exchanges that establish reciprocal ties and obligations throughout the community. By regularly sharing surplus produce among friends and kin, horticultural families ensure that they will not be stranded if they fall on hard times. Indeed, it might be said that gift exchange is the horticulturist's way of storing food or ensuring future assistance, just as among hunter-gatherers.

After kinship, the second integrating force is political organization. While differences in wealth are usually slight or nonexistent in most horticultural groups, there are differences in power. Farming communities tend to have better defined leadership roles than do hunter-gatherers, although the authority of the leaders varies from group to group. As we shall see, the headman in a Yanomamö village is simply a man with influence; he has no formal office and no right to coerce others. Whatever the allotment of power, the headman serves to integrate the horticultural community by helping families settle their quarrels, arrange their marriages, and so forth, and by leading them in feasts, religious rituals, and raids.

*Relations among Communities.* As social organization within communities becomes more structured, so do relations among communities—whether friendly (as in the case of exchange) or hostile (as in the case of conflict). Both of the groups we will be describing engage in some trade. The Yanomamö acquire metal tools from neighbors, government officials, and missionaries. Their involvement in trade is expanding each year as they are increasingly drawn into the national economies of Venezuela and Brazil.

Yet self-sufficiency is still important among many extensive agricultural communities, and much of their intergroup exchange is a form of gift giving rather than impersonal monetary trade. A Yanomamö man gives a man in another village a dog; some months later, the second man gives the first a bow. Neither party necessarily depends on what the other gives: Both can acquire dogs in their own villages and make their own bows. What they do need is each other's support, either in warfare or in obtaining a wife. Thus, just as gifts passed within groups serve to foster goodwill, so gifts passed between groups help to create and cement alliances; exchange is as much a social as an economic transaction. Arranging marriages with other groups is the ultimate expression of solidarity among the Yanomamö and many other tribal agriculturists.

The kula ring is a unique system of exchange linking dispersed island communities of horticulturists that traditionally did not have a common overarching political structure or market system. The Trobriand Islanders, off the east coast of New Guinea, are a matrilineally organized horticultural society inhabiting a large number of islands—some of which depend on trade for food. The **kula ring,** described originally by Malinowski, is a highly complex system for trading two varieties of shell ornaments, the white armbands called *nwal* and the red shell necklaces called *soulava.* Paralleling the ceremonial trade, conceptually separate essential goods are also exchanged. Ornaments are never traded for food and so forth, nor are essential goods used to buy ornaments. They occupy different **spheres of exchange.**

A Trobriand Islander who possesses a group of kula ornaments has the option of making a trading expedition to another island. After deciding to make the trip, the islander must abide by the strict rules governing trade. The islander can only offer the valued kula ornaments to one of his lifelong trading partners with whom there exists a relationship of trust. Trading partners are located on all of the islands where trade takes place. An old chief may have as many as 100 partners to the north and an equal number to the south, while a young commoner might have only a handful of partners. In addition, the kula ornaments must travel through the islands in a special direction: The red shell necklaces move in a clockwise direction, and the white shell armbands move counterclockwise. Thus, the kula ornaments continually move around the chain of islands, passing from one partner to another. The objects do not remain in any individual's hands for much more than a year.

Every part of the expedition is steeped in custom and ceremony; now travel is by modern transport, but formerly, canoes would be overhauled and elaborate preparations made for the trip. The individual trader always goes with a party from his community. Once the trade party arrives, trade partners go through an elaborate exchange of kula ornaments,

*Trobriand Islanders set out for a kula exchange in traditional attire worn for the occasion. The ceremony has retained its importance.*
(Andre Singer/The Hutchison Library)

following the principle of balanced reciprocity. When one partner gives an ornament as a ceremonial gift, he can expect to eventually receive a roughly equal gift. At the same time as the ritual exchange, the trade partners begin exchanging utilitarian items that may be vital to the individuals involved. The kula ceremonial exchange provides a kind of "social cement"; the existence of trading partners throughout the islands helps maintain lines of cultural and political communication. It is also a means by which men, in accumulating partners and ornaments, gain prestige and political influence.

Although the kula ring has received the most attention, Trobriand women have their own exchange system based on balanced reciprocity (Weiner, 1976). Following a death, women from nearby hamlets bring gifts of food to the people in mourning. Women associated with the deceased prepare bundles of banana leaves and weave fiber skirts to give in return. Husbands assist in this accumulation necessary for the final, major mortuary ceremony, which is held by the women. Much like a potlatch, each senior woman in mourning tries to distribute as many bundles and skirts as possible, perhaps over a thousand bundles and dozens of skirts. This is balanced reciprocity because the givers have in the past received comparable gifts as well as food and other services. A woman can gain socially from this competitive gift giving, just as do men.

Social organization among farmers is decidedly different from that among most hunter-gatherers. Hunter-gatherers residing in areas which sustain only low population densities form small, relatively amorphous groups whose resources and members flow back and forth in such a way as to blur boundaries between subunits. The nuclear family remains intact, but it is not a distinct economic unit; the economic unit is the band as a whole. A farming society by contrast is a complex structure made up of well-defined and largely self-sufficient households within relatively stable and self-sufficient communities. These communities in turn are likely to have relatively formalized relationships with one another, often mediated by a system of kinship-based groups, each with its own territory and insignia.

## The Yanomamö

Napoleon Chagnon, who has worked periodically among the Yanomamö for twenty-five years (for a cumulative period of field research adding up to more than sixty months), believes them to be one of the largest unacculturated tribes in South America, numbering about 20,000 members (1992, 1997). When Chagnon arrived among the Yanomamö people in 1964, missionaries had already established posts in two villages, but many of the Yanomamö knew of the outside world only indirectly from the metal axes and pots they obtained through trade. Today, interaction with outsiders in missionary settlements and through work for ranchers and government agents has brought the Yanomamö into far greater contact with the external world. There are now few if any Yanomamö who have never seen a non-Yanomamö. Thus, this discussion is first presented in the ethnographic present (as the Yanomamö appeared when anthropologists first began to work with them) and updated to show them today.[1] However, before taking up this study, mention must be made of a controversy involving Napoleon Chagnon, whose research has become the lightning rod drawing much of the ire of those who oppose studying human behavior in a biological or ecological context—in particular, using evolutionary models.

Patrick Tierney's *Darkness in El Dorado: How Scientists and Journalists Devastated the Amazon* (2000), excerpted ("The Fierce Anthropologist," *New Yorker,* October 9, 2000) prior to publication, raises serious allegations of ethical misconduct by scientists studying the Yanomamö, particularly Napoleon Chagnon and geneticist James Neel of the University of Michigan. Tierney accuses Chagnon, with his collaborator, Neel, of causing, or at best doing nothing to stop, a deadly measles epidemic that resulted in the deaths of thousands of Yanomamö in early 1968. Tierney accuses Neel and Chagnon of purposely spreading measles among the Yanomamö by using an early measles vaccine known as Edmonston-B, which Tierney claims has the capacity to itself cause measles or result in extremely high fevers leading to death. In addition to the charges of causing the measles epidemic, Tierney claims Chagnon, through the course of his own long-term fieldwork among the Yanomamö, interfered massively with the lives of his subjects. He charges that Chagnon bribed children to reveal the names of dead relatives, much against the wishes of the Yanomamö, who never speak of their dead kin. He also claims that Chagnon encouraged villages to fight each other, particularly during the filming of his documentary, *The Feast*, and further, that Chagnon staged the events depicted in his film, *The Axe Fight*. Tierney and many of Chagnon's critics maintain that

---

[1] The material on the Yanomamö, unless otherwise noted, is from Chagnon's updated book, *Yanomamö, the Last Days of Eden,* San Diego, CA: Harcourt Brace Jovanovich (1992) and 5th ed. (1997).

Chagnon's behavior in the field was insensitive, bullying, and exploitative, and ultimately created a fiction about the Yanomamö's purported predilection for violence.

The fallout from Tierney's allegations was substantial. Two cultural anthropologists, Terrence Turner, former head of the American Anthropological Association's (AAA) Special Commission to investigate the Brazilian Yanomami (1990–1991), and Leslie Sponsel, former chair of the AAA Committee for Human Rights (1992–1996), co-signed a letter to the AAA in which they endorsed these charges.

Responding to this statement, others in the field provided a dramatically differing perspective. At the University of Michigan, Provost Nancy Cantor reported on their investigation, point-by-point refuting the major claims of Tierney's book (Report to Deans, Department Heads, and Faculty re "Darkness in El Dorado" University of Michigan, November 13, 2000). John Tooby likens the attacks to "witchcraft accusations" (Tooby, 2000, p. 8). James Neel's field notes for the 1968 work in Venezuela, as well as his written consultations with the Centers for Disease Control (CDC) in late 1967 in preparation for the program in measles immunization he planned to undertake, presented evidence quite at variance with Tierney's charges. Specifically, Neel had Venezuelan government permission to carry out the vaccine program; had consulted a CDC expert on measles about the vaccine; had included gamma globulin with all the vaccines he administered, keeping meticulous records of names of persons immunized; and having heard about the outbreak of measles on January 20 when he was in Caracas, did not administer any vaccine until January 25. There is no evidence that Neel discouraged anyone from dispensing treatments. He also provided penicillin and Terramycin® to curb the effects of the epidemic and spent two weeks administering the vaccines and antibiotics and worked out a plan to control the epidemic. Medical scientists are unanimous that measles has never been shown to be transmissible from a vaccine recipient to a susceptible contact.

Many anthropologists, including this author, believe that Chagnon and Neel have been unjustly maligned and that much of this "debate" is ad hominem and motivated by ideology rather than based on scientific observations or evidence. Although many anthropologists disagree with some of the underpinnings of Chagnon's theoretical positions and challenge his conclusions, most agree that Chagnon has made a very substantial contribution to the discipline of anthropology and, in the meticulousness of his long-term fieldwork, to enriching our understanding of Amazonian cultures. Moreover, the specious claim that vaccinations can spread measles may itself prove very detrimental to public health if it encourages people to keep their children from being vaccinated.

## Farming in the Jungle

The Yanomamö live in villages of 40 to 250 inhabitants (the average is 70 to 80), widely scattered through the dense tropical jungle in southern Venezuela and northern Brazil. For the most part, the land is low and flat, with occasional rolling hills and mountain ridges. It is crossed by sluggish, muddy rivers that become rushing torrents in the rainy season. Palms and hardwoods create a dense canopy over a tangle of vines and shrubs. The rain pours down two or three times a day, increasing in intensity between May and August. The humidity rarely drops below 80%, intensifying what to us would be uncomfortable year-round temperatures of 26° to 32°C (80° to 96°F).

This habitat provides the Yanomamö with a variety of wild foods. They collect palm fruits, nuts, and seed pods in season; devour honey when they can find it; and snack on grubs, a variety of caterpillars, and roasted spiders. They fish by a rather ingenious method known among many nonindustrialized groups: They dam a stream, pour a drug in the water, wait for the stunned fish to float to the surface, and then scoop them into baskets. They hunt monkeys, wild turkeys, wild pigs, armadillos, anteaters, and other species with bows and poisoned arrows. A survey of their hunting practices and game brought into the villages indicates that their intake of protein is approximately seventy-five grams per person per day, well above the thirty to fifty grams necessary to support an adult (Chagnon & Hames, 1979).

Wild foods alone are not abundant enough to support the Yanomamö at their present population level. Fruits and tubers are seasonal. Animals are small, many are nocturnal, and most live singly so that they are difficult to hunt (Good, 1995, pp. 59–60). Chagnon notes that although on one occasion he and a group of Yanomamö hunters killed enough game to feed an entire village for one day, on another occasion, five days of searching did not yield enough meat to feed even the hunters (1992). Moreover, Yanomamö technology does not allow them to exploit the rivers as they might. Their bark canoes are too awkward to navigate upstream and so fragile that they are generally abandoned after one trip downstream.

Even though they hunt from necessity since they do not raise animals, they tend to engage in hunting

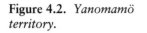

**Figure 4.2.** *Yanomamö territory.*

much more than is required from a nutritional perspective; they go on hunting treks because they enjoy doing so (Good, 1995, pp. 59–63). Even though it is the men who hunt, it is not unusual for the entire community to set off on a month-long trek to the coolest portion of the untouched forest. Also, meat is the only item that is shared villagewide and is therefore of great social importance; sharing creates important bonds among families, and not to share can disrupt normal relations (Good, 1995, p. 61).

Thus, the Yanomamö depend mostly on their gardens, which provide 85% of their calorie intake. The most important crops are plantains and bananas (which together make up 52% of their diet in calories); manioc, a root crop used to make flour for cassava bread; sweet potatoes, taro, and maguey; and peach palm trees. Less important crops are maize, avocados, squash, cashews, and papayas. The Yanomamö also cultivate cane for arrow shafts; cotton for hammocks, belts, and cords; hallucinogenic drugs; and a variety of "magical" plants. One of these plants (cultivated by men) makes women sexually receptive, another (cultivated by women) calms male tempers, and others cause miscarriages and similar calamities in enemy villages. Finally,

every Yanomamö garden has a sizable crop of tobacco, which is highly prized and is chewed by men, women, and children.

Like other people of the South American jungles, the Yanomamö practice slash-and-burn agriculture. To clear land for a garden, they first cut away the undergrowth and small trees with steel axes obtained from missionaries and through trade (or from anthropologists). They let the cut vegetation dry in the sun and then burn it off on a day when the wind is right. This task done, they set about felling the large trees, which they leave in the fields to mark boundaries between individual family plots and to chop for firewood when the need arises. The most difficult part of planting a new garden is carrying cuttings from plantain trees in the old garden to the new site. This is an arduous job, for a single cutting can weigh up to 10 pounds (4.5 kilograms). Planting other crops involves little more than making a hole with a digging stick and depositing seeds or small cuttings. Gardens are individually owned while they are being tended, and each man plants a variety of crops on his land.

Newly established gardens produce in spaced cycles. Thus, at the beginning, there are alternating periods of scarcity and plenty. Then, after two or three years, the gardens mature, and overlapping plant cycles produce a constant supply of food (Chagnon, 1997).

The Yanomamö do most of the heavy work of clearing the land during the rainy season, when swamps and swollen rivers make it impossible to engage in visiting, feasting, or fighting with other villages. Once established, a garden takes only a few hours a day to maintain. Men, women, and children leave for their plots at dawn and return to the village around 10:30 A.M. (if the men have decided not to hunt that day). The women also gather firewood and supervise the children playing nearby. No one works during the midday heat. Sometimes a man will return to the garden around 4:00 P.M. and work until sundown. Most men, however, spend the afternoon in the village, resting or taking drugs, while the women go out to collect more firewood and haul water.

Cleared land in a tropical forest will not support crops indefinitely. Once a garden has been cultivated continuously for two or three years, the farmer gradually begins to shift it. Every year he abandons more land at one end of the plot and clears more land at the other end, transplanting crops to the new addition. The garden "moves" in this way for about eight years, after which time the weeding problem becomes insurmountable and the soil unproductive. The plot is then abandoned, and an entirely new site is cleared. Left fallow, the old plot recovers its natural forest covering in about ten years. It should be noted that the Yanomamö are somewhat unusual in their swiddening. Most horticulturists use their plots for longer periods and carefully supervise the long fallow period, going back regularly to harvest wild fruits and other resources as they appear.

## Village Life

The Yanomamö live near their gardens in circular villages they call *shabono.* Each man builds a shelter of poles and vines for himself, his wife or wives, and their children. These homes are arranged around a central courtyard, and the spaces between them are thatched to form a continuous roof with an open space over the courtyard. The shabono, then, is roughly doughnut-shaped. For safety, most Yanomamö groups also construct a high pole fence around the shabono, with a single opening that can be barricaded at night.

What authority there is in the village rests in the person of the **headman,** an individual who has proved his superiority in combat, diplomacy, hunt-

*A Yanomamö man uses a hoe to cultivate his garden plot in a clearing in the Brazilian jungle.*
(Robert Harding Picture Library)

ing, or some other skill. Headmen have no official right to order others around; they lead only to the extent that people respect or fear them. Kaobawä, the headman of the village in which Chagnon lived in 1964–1965, is probably typical. Kaobawä had demonstrated his fierceness in numerous raids and quarrels. He also enjoyed a large natural following: five adult brothers and several brothers-in-law, who were under obligation to him for the sisters he had given them in marriage. Having established his superiority, he simply led by example. People came to him of their own accord for advice, which he dispensed with an air of quiet authority.

Most members of a village are related to one another either by blood or by marriage. Kinship among the Yanomamö is reckoned by **patrilineal descent;** that is, it is traced through the male line. Both men and women belong to their father's lineage. Typically, a village consists of two patrilineages whose members have intermarried over several generations. Within a single lineage, all males of the same generation call one another "brother," and all females call one another "sister." For a man, however, the really important ties are not with his "brothers" but with the men of the lineage from which he can acquire a wife. Wives cannot be chosen according to fancy. Yanomamö marriage rules specify that a man must choose a woman from a lineage other than his own. In practice, his choice is narrowed to a small group of women in the village's one (or two) other lineages. This form of marriage[2] is well known in many societies, horticultural or not, but what distinguishes the Yanomamö is how competitively males manipulate the rules to marry women who would otherwise be prohibited (Chagnon, 2000, pp. 125ff). Men who call each other "brother" as they grow up may begin to use the term "brother-in-law" to set the stage for marrying their companion's sister. Women do not manipulate kinship terminology, since their marriage is a certainty.

Neither the composition nor the location of a Yanomamö village is permanent. Villages move every few years. Sometimes the group relocates for the purpose of acquiring fresh lands, but as a rule, there is plenty of land to cultivate in the immediate vicinity because villages are widely separated. As with many other horticulturists, a growing shortage of firewood is an important reason for movement. However, the Yanomamö also move because hostilities make it impossible for them to stay where they are. Sometimes internal feuds divide a village into two factions, which then go their separate ways. More commonly, a village moves because warfare with other villages has escalated to such a degree that the only way to survive is to flee. Kaobawä's group, for example, had made sixteen major moves in seventy-five years. One move was motivated by the need for fresh land, one by a desire to acquire steel tools from a group of foreigners newly arrived downstream, and the remaining fourteen by either bloodshed within the group or warfare with neighboring villages (Chagnon, 1983, pp. 174–177).

## Warfare and Violence

Violence in fact is a salient feature of Yanomamö social life; internal hostilities are exceeded only by external hostilities. Intervillage duels, raids, ambushes, and kidnappings are almost daily fare. Why is there so much conflict? According to Chagnon (1997), the reason that is given by the Yanomamö is women. Other observers have alternative interpretations. Some feel that while the Yanomamö may explain their actions in terms of conflict over women, there are other underlying causes. Brian Ferguson views Yanomamö conflict, internal as well intergroup, as arising out of the impact of external forces, notably the governments of Venezuela and Brazil, which have altered tribal territories and destabilized social relations among populations far from centers of

power (1995a, l995b). We will consider these interpretations as well as Chagnon's.

*Unbalanced Sex Ratio.* The only forms of family planning the Yanomamö practice are a long **postpartum taboo**—a woman may not have sexual intercourse while she is pregnant or while she is nursing a child—and infanticide. If, despite the taboo, a woman does become pregnant while she is still nursing her last child—a practice that itself decreases the likelihood of pregnancy—she will kill the new baby rather than deprive the older child of milk. A woman is also likely to kill her first baby if it is a girl, for her husband of course wants a son, and displeased Yanomamö husbands can be brutal, even murderous. The practice of selective female infanticide creates a sexual imbalance among the Yanomamö. The boys of a given village invariably outnumber the girls, sometimes by as much as 30% (Chagnon, 1992). The fact that older, more powerful men usually take second and third wives makes the shortage of women a particular problem for the younger men. Chagnon has reported that men who have been successful in raiding and who are known to have killed enemies are far more likely than other men to have two or more wives, further exacerbating the situation. This has been confirmed by John Peters, who has worked among the Brazilian Yanomamö for more than thirty years (1998).

The unbalanced sex ratio increases conflicts within and between villages. Competition for the limited number of women eligible as brides under the marriage rules turns biological and classificatory brothers into potential enemies. Suppose there are ten young men in a lineage, only seven young women eligible for them to marry, and older men take two of these girls as brides. The men grow up knowing that only five of them will be able to marry within the village. Somehow they must outshine or disgrace the competition, and this necessity tends to undermine whatever solidarity might develop among them as brothers. (A young Yanomamö may seek a bride in another village, but most are reluctant to do so because they would have to undertake years of bride service.)

In addition, the shortage of women increases the temptation to commit adultery—a temptation to which married men succumb as readily as bachelors, especially during the four years or so when their wives are taboo. If a man succeeds in seducing another man's wife and is caught, the husband will retaliate with all the ferocity he can muster. Club fights over women are the major cause of villages splitting up. After they split, hostility between the two groups tends to continue on its own momen-

---

[2]Technically referred to by anthropologists as "prescriptive bilateral cross-cousin marriage," it is basically a simple exchange of mates between groups.

tum, each group taking turns avenging wrongs inflicted by the other group.

Warfare between totally separate villages follows the same pattern. Fights over women may precipitate the conflict, or one village may suspect that its crops are being pilfered by a neighboring village. If a child falls sick, the illness will be blamed on sorcery emanating from another village. (The Yanomamö may invoke evil demons to steal the souls of children in enemy villages.) Whatever the original causes, contests over women are usually part of the ensuing hostilities. Typically, a raiding party will kill one or two men and abduct any women they can lay their hands on. This raid precipitates a counterraid to avenge the murders and recapture the women. The retaliatory raid in turn triggers another and so on.

Eventually, the members of one village will be put to flight. Abandoning their gardens and homes, they take refuge in another village until they can plant new gardens. This arrangement, while necessary for the group's survival, further exacerbates the woman-shortage problem, for the hosts are almost certain to take advantage of their guests' weakened position to demand temporary or permanent access to their women.

Thus, the Yanomamö, according to Chagnon's accounts, are locked into a vicious cycle. The more the men fight over women, the more eager they are to have sons who will help in the fighting, the more female infants they kill, the fewer women there are, and the more they fight. Moreover, the men encourage their sons to be suspicious, hot-tempered, and quick to take violent action against the slightest offense. Teasing fathers often provoke small sons to hit them and then reward the boys with laughter and approving comments on how fierce they are becoming. By raising their sons in this way, the Yanomamö perpetuate hostilities in the effort to defend against them.

Chagnon's explanation for Yanomamö warfare is not without its critics. Marvin Harris (1984) and Daniel Gross (1983) state that underlying the frequency of warfare is a shortage of game and other

*Horticultural societies are not entirely peaceable. In fact, violence is a salient feature of Yanomamö social life. These Yanomamö are preparing to depart on a raid.*

(Napoleon Chagnon/Anthro-Photo)

sources of protein. Although the Yanomamö grow more than enough produce to fill their stomachs and have miles of virgin forest to clear for new gardens, the foods they cultivate do not provide large amounts of protein. To meet these protein requirements, they must hunt and fish. Harris suggests that at some point the Yanomamö began to intensify their agricultural activities and that their population level rose accordingly. As the population grew, they killed increasingly larger numbers of wild animals, thus depleting their game resources. Today, Harris argues, there is not enough protein to go around and what the Yanomamö are fighting over, albeit unwittingly, is hunting territory. However, although warfare may indeed serve to preserve hunting territories, it does not appear that this is the immediate or conscious objective of the combatants (Chagnon, 1992; Chagnon & Hames, 1979). Such different observations, while difficult to resolve, provide new and innovative directions for research.

*Political Alliances.* In this hostile social environment, the Yanomamö devote considerable time and resources to cultivating alliances with neighbors. Overtures begin cautiously, with parties of visitors bearing gifts. The gifts are not free, however; the takers are obliged to reciprocate at some point in the future with gifts of equal or greater value. If visiting goes well, specialization in craft production may begin: One village may rather suddenly abandon the making of pots and the other the manufacture of arrow points so that they become dependent on each other. These contrived shortages express growing trust; all Yanomamö have the resources and skills to make everything they require.

After a period of trading, one group takes the next step toward alliance by holding a feast for the other group. They harvest and cook great quantities of food, amass goods for exchange, and prepare elaborate costumes and dances. Because giving or attending a feast implies a higher level of commitment, the occasion must be handled with caution and diplomacy. The dances and songs are essentially displays of strength. Each side tries to impress the other with the fact that it does not really need allies and probably never will.

Almost invariably, disputes break out and the toughest men of the two villages challenge one another to contests of physical strength: chest-pounding duels, in which two antagonists take turns socking each other squarely on the chest, and side-slapping duels, in which the contestants take turns hitting each other on the flanks. The object is to stay in the game until your opponent withdraws or is knocked unconscious. If tempers get hot, these fights can escalate into club fights, full-scale brawls in which the men of each village beat one another over the head with eight-foot poles.

An occasional club fight leads to full-scale violence, destroying the alliance altogether. Usually, however, these carefully graded levels of hostility allow the Yanomamö to vent their ever-present aggression, display their fierceness, and still finish the feast on a friendly note. If all goes well, the fighting ends in a draw and gifts are exchanged. The guests depart peacefully, the hosts can expect to be invited to a return feast, and each group assumes it can count on the other for refuge and food in times of trouble.

The final step is an exchange of brides between the two groups. This step is not taken unless the villages are convinced of each other's good intentions or unless one is so weak it has no choice. Villages that exchange women usually can expect support in their raids and skirmishes with other Yanomamö. But even alliances based on marriage ties are tenuous; no village honors a commitment when it sees some advantage in breaking it.

In sum, the Yanomamö are great fighters and poor allies. Consequently, their social world is one of chronic suspicion and hostility. The human costs are high. Warfare accounts for at least 30% of all male deaths; approximately two thirds of people aged forty or older have lost at least one close biological relative, a parent, sibling, or child (Chagnon, 1992, p. 239). This figure seems startling, but it is comparable to those of New Guinea tribes and of Native American societies that feuded regularly.

The problem, as Brian Ferguson points out, is not so much whether or not the Yanomamö fight but whether this is a long-established feature of their way of life (1995b). No one, including, of course, Chagnon, argues that the Yanomamö are the "living embodiment of a violent evolutionary heritage" (Ferguson, 1995a, p. 62). But the interpretation of their level of conflict depends on the extent to which this is caused by forces outside their immediate habitat, which is the view argued by Ferguson (1995a, 1995b). While it is obvious, as we shall see shortly, that the Yanomamö are greatly affected by contemporary developments in Venezuela and Brazil, what is not so plain is how deeply they have been affected by outside events over the last 300 years.

Outside influences began when the colonists arrived in the early seventeenth century and began raiding for slaves; the ensuing conflicts wiped out a number of societies in the Yanomamö region and destabilized others. Most important, apart from direct contact, was the competition among groups that developed as trade goods were introduced. This competition often was played out in warfare (Ferguson, 1995a). Rather than a pristine example of tribal warfare, Ferguson suggests, "The Yanomamö case shows the extraordinary reach and transforming effects a centrally governed society or state (here the states of Venezuela and Brazil) may have, extending way beyond its last outpost" (1995a, p. 63).

## Future Prospects for the Yanomamö

The Yanomamö at the end of the twentieth century were in a much more precarious position than at any time in their history. Generally, anthropologists describe what happens when two cultures impinge on each other as **acculturation,** which leads to changes in both cultures. In particular, the politically or technologically dominant society exerts the greater impact. This process is transforming all the native tribes of the Amazon rain forest and resembles what was experienced by native populations throughout North and South America in the early days of European colonization. They have been abruptly brought into contact with a technologically advanced and alien cultural system. However, the case of the Yanomamö is so extreme that Chagnon refers to it as "catastrophic change" (1992, p. 243).

When Chagnon arrived in 1964, the villages closest to European settlements had seen only a handful of Whites and those of the interior none at all. Trade goods had been reaching them, passed on through intermediate groups, but no extended contact had occurred between the Yanomamö and the outside world. Since the period of first contact, roads have been built to provide access to the Amazon region. With the completion of the first road, change has occurred rapidly and often against a backdrop of misery and misfortune.

The arrival of the roads brought an immediate adaptive response. The Yanomamö nearest the road arranged themselves alongside it to beg and barter for shorts, shirts, food—doubtless it seemed like an easier way to make a living than their traditional horticulture and hunting. Some went to work on farms and sawmills; for twenty or thirty days' work, they received a little money (not more than $2 or $3) and some cigarettes and used clothes. They tried to emulate the ways of the Brazilians (*civilizados*) and not to appear to be *indios bravos* (wild Indians).

The "roadside" Yanomamö came to differ from the unacculturated villagers of the interior. They adopted Brazilian haircuts, took up smoking cigarettes, bought canned foods and candy, and added lots of salt to their food. In fact, their traditional diet was superior to that of the average Brazilian farmer; with contact, their diet declined in terms of calories earned per unit of labor expended. But because they wanted to appear like the Brazilians and to interact more with them, they adopted as many Brazilian practices as they could. Not only did they adopt such utilitarian items as aluminum pots and pans, steel axes, shotguns, and other tools that facilitated subsistence activities, they also came to depend on large numbers of consumer items that tied them ever more closely to their Brazilian suppliers. As John Saffirio and Raymond Hammer (1983) write, it is doubtful that they would have embraced this alien culture so wholeheartedly if they had understood that in so doing they were losing their political autonomy and entering Brazilian society at the very bottom of the social and economic hierarchy.

Along with contact have come diseases to which the Yanomamö have no immunity. They have been decimated repeatedly by epidemics; one disastrous influenza epidemic in 1973 killed a quarter of the population in the villages sampled (Chagnon & Melancon, 1983, p. 59). These scourges have had a severe impact on traditional social organization; ritual specialists have died before passing on their knowledge and skills, kin groups have been broken up and forcibly resettled, and leaders have succumbed to these new diseases.

While Yanomamö territory has been exploited for twenty years by lumbermen cutting down their rain forest, the most serious assault came in 1985 with the discovery of gold in the Amazon. This discovery, which coincided with the completion of the Perimetral Norte highway that cut through the heart of the Yanomamö territory, precipitated a gold rush into the Amazon. Since 1985, over 50,000 miners have invaded Yanomamö territory (Gorman, 1994). Once again, epidemics took an almost instant toll: Villages studied soon after the road was constructed had lost between 30 and 51% of their populations (Chagnon, 1992). The mining operations have further ravaged the fragile environment, damming rivers and polluting water. Even though the land rights of the Yanomamö were protected in the Brazilian constitution, the government made no effort to enforce those rights.

However, the plight of the Yanomamö did not receive international attention until four Indian men were killed when they wandered into an illegal mining village. Ironically, the public outcry that resulted was not in response to the killing but in response to action taken by then-President Sarney. He ordered all journalists, missionaries, anthropologists, medical workers, and international workers out of the territory and embarked on a plan to reduce the Yanomamö territory from 37,000 square miles to 12,000. This announcement led to a four-year battle for the preservation of the Yanomamö land rights

---

## Box 4.2

# Indigenous Brazilians and the Environmental Alliance

BRAZIL IS HOME TO MORE THAN 200,000 native people, speaking 180 languages and living under very diverse conditions (Conklin & Graham, 1995). Most live in the Amazon region but differ as to the degree of their contact and interaction with the national populations. All, however, share the fate of their lands being increasingly coveted by outsiders (Conklin & Graham, 1995).

For years, the rights of indigenous people have been defended by a relatively small group of committed activists, as we have noted earlier. Anthropologists have been prominent among them and have argued on behalf of indigenous populations largely on grounds of basic or universal human rights and the intrinsic value of maintaining cultural diversity. At the same time, naturalists and biologists argued to save the rain forest because of its biological diversity. In the last decade or so, this apparent divergence of interests has changed significantly, as Conklin and Graham report. What has emerged is a new alliance of indigenous native leaders and a new cast of Brazilian and foreign advocates, which is using a new rhetoric—that of environmentalism and conservation.

Both native leaders and advocates of indigenous rights have decided to "go green" and to present indigenous peoples as a vast repository of environmental knowledge. (See also Box 3.1, p. 00.) This approach also tends to characterize traditional practices of indigenous peoples, regardless of their geographic location and actual behav-

ior as, at their heart, conservationist and protective of the habitats in which they live. This has helped bring in the support of the numerous nongovernmental agencies (NGOs) trying to protect flora and fauna as well as pharmaceutical companies seeking new medicines. They saw that alliances with indigenous rights activists, such as Cultural Survival, as well as with specific native leaders would further their interests in preserving natural forests and other biomes threatened by commercial development. Saving the people has become almost a by-product of saving the rain forest.

However, there have been numerous benefits from these alliances. Indigenous populations such as the Xavánte and the Kayapo have been visited and had their plight publicized by thousands of "eco-tourists," including rock stars and royalty. Companies such as The Body Shop and Ben and Jerry's Ice Cream have promoted their cause in the course of promoting their own products (although these commercial arrangements have not been without their critics).

International and domestic public opinion has forced Brazil's government, for example, to pay attention to environmental issues that also impact the native population. The Kayapo and the Xavánte have gained legal title to a territory the size of Scotland (Conklin & Graham, 1995, p. 780). Their leaders have visited the United States and European countries for high-level talks, and international conferences continue to publicize the issues.

But some fear that the alliance may rest on shaky foundations to the extent that support for indigenous peoples is based on the unrealistic assumption that they are somehow "uncorrupted" or "natural conservationists."

As discussed elsewhere, the practices that contribute to conservation and sustainable growth are not usually rooted in an enlightened sensibility regarding the environment relative to that prevailing in the industrial world. Rather they are the unintentional outcomes of low population densities, disease vectors placing limits on exploitation, limited storage and extractive technology, and lack of access to markets and consumer goods. Once empowered, Kayapo leaders supported by segments of their population, for example, have shown themselves to be quick to capitalize on ecologically short-lived and destructive but very lucrative logging and mining contracts, and some have greatly enriched themselves (Turner, 1995, pp. 109–110).

The alliance between human rights advocates and environmentalists has produced useful results in Brazil for many indigenous peoples, but one should not romanticize or idealize any society. There are no generic "indigenous peoples." Successful campaigns for the rain forest, for example, and those who live in it should perhaps be best based on an awareness of long-term benefits of sustainable yields and of human dignity.

---

fought by international rights organizations as well as Brazil's own Indian protection agency. Finally, in November 1991, the new president, Collor, authorized the official demarcation of 36,000 square miles of Yanomamö territory, providing $2.7 million to physically and legally implement this demarcation. Soon after, a demarcation order was also issued for the Kayapo (Rabben, 1993).

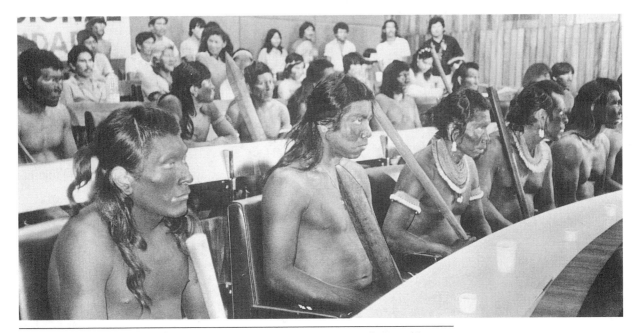

*Kayapō Indian leaders attend a 1988 meeting of the Constitutional Assembly in Belem, Brazil. The assembly was voting at that time on the rights the central government would grant to the Indians.*
(Marlise Simon/NYT Pictures)

Despite these gains, the future of the Yanomamö is still in question. Miners continue to operate illegally in their territory, and there are reports of continuing violent confrontations between the native people and the miners. In 1993, Chagnon was part of a team that investigated a massacre of Yanomamö women and children. According to Chagnon, this was in retaliation for earlier killings of miners by the Yanomamö. Apparently, some Yanomamö men had shot two Brazilian miners after they had killed five Yanomamö men near an illegal mining site (Chagnon, 1993).

## The Pueblo of North America[3]

Historically, the Pueblo tribes of the American Southwest differ considerably from the Yanomamö in the environment they inhabit, the agricultural techniques they employ, and the way their societies are organized. Furthermore, whereas the Yanomamö until recently lived in almost total isolation from the outside world, the Pueblo have always been in contact with populations pursuing very different ways of life. Prior to the arrival of Europeans, they were on the periphery of the great empire of the Aztecs, and for the last several centuries, they have been interacting closely with often competing populations—Spaniards, other Native American tribes, and settlers from northern Europe. Indeed, *pueblo* is the Spanish word for "village," and the groups comprising the Pueblo differ culturally and linguistically.

The picture presented here is largely historical, but this should not obscure the fact the Pueblo are very much contemporary U.S. citizens, thriving along with others in Arizona and New Mexico. Before the coming of the *Castillas,* or Spaniards, in the mid-1500s, there were over 100 villages in New Mexico alone; now there are nineteen Pueblo groups speaking five languages.

The Pueblo are the cultural and biological descendants of hunter-gatherers who migrated to the American Southwest more than 10,000 years ago. The ancestors of today's Pueblo were skilled basketmakers, weavers, potters, and above all, architects. They are famed (and named) for their pueblos—dwellings of three and four stories honeycombed by interconnected rooms, some of which open onto a protected inner courtyard, where a *kiva*—a round ceremonial chamber—is sunk into the pavement.

[3]This case study was originally drafted in collaboration with the late Fred Plog, an archaeologist specializing in the American Southwest, but also draws the works of Fred Eggan, E. P. Dozier, and A. Ortiz.

**Figure 4.3.** *Pueblo territory.*

Such compact structures housed entire villages of as many as several thousand people.

Historically, the diversity among Pueblo settlements was greater than it is now. However, after the decimation of up to 80% of the Pueblo peoples by diseases brought by the Spanish conquistadors—measles, smallpox, plague, influenza—to which Pueblo peoples had no resistance, two basic patterns remain. One of these patterns, the eastern Pueblo adaptation, is based on complex irrigation works. This was the most common pattern of prehistoric times, but in the last few centuries, it has survived in only a few areas, most of them on the Rio Grande in New Mexico. The western Pueblo adaptation, found in eastern Arizona and western New Mexico, is based on the simpler techniques of rainfall and floodwater farming. The eastern Pueblo region of New Mexico was the first area to be settled by the Spanish in 1598 and the site of the second European settlement in North America. It was also the locale for the first uprising against colonial rule when, in 1599, a religious leader in the Tewa-speaking San Juan Pueblo by the name of Popé led an uprising that some call the "First American Revolution." While the Spanish returned some twelve years later, they were forced to grant treaty rights and land grants that are still legally in force and that have helped the Pueblo to preserve their lands and self-rule.

Thus, we see an unmistakably horticultural adaptation in the western Pueblo and the beginnings of intensive agriculture in the eastern Pueblo. This contrast was most marked immediately before and after colonization by Spain; this is the period described here. Since that time, the industrial economy of the United States has grown up around the Pueblo, transforming many aspects of their world. Even so, the basic technological and social features of the eastern and western adaptations survive today. Horticulture continues to have great cultural importance in the lives of many, and there is a commitment to continue indigenous farming techniques and crops, today often organized around cooperatives, and to sustain themselves by the sale of farm produce and processed native foods to outsiders.

## Two Environments

*The Western Pueblo.* The western part of Pueblo territory, a landscape of semiarid mesas and canyons, seems an unlikely spot for farming. The growing season is short; the frosts begin as early as September and can persist through May. There are few permanent streams, and rainfall, sometimes in the form of sudden torrents, averages only about twenty-five centimeters (ten inches) a year. As in most arid environments, climatic variability is a more important factor than aridity itself. Records obtained from tree rings show that the predictability of rainfall has varied greatly from year to year and that rainfall is very patchy; one valley may be quite wet during a given growing season while another remains dry.

In some prehistoric epochs, the environment of the area was wetter, the rain less patchy and more predictable. Archaeologists find scant evidence of Pueblo ancestors during such periods. The inhabitants then followed a more mobile hunting and gathering strategy. During periods of variability, ancestors of the modern Pueblo peoples developed sedentary strategies intended to counter such fluctuations in the food supply.

The western Pueblo developed several techniques to cope with variability in rainfall, the most important of which was floodwater farming. Essentially, floodwater farming is the practice of planting crops in areas that are flooded every year in the rainy season, the floodwaters thus providing natural irrigation. Despite erratic rainfall, the western Pueblo's crops stood a chance of surviving, for the flooded soil could hold enough water to see them through the growing season. They also stood a chance of being uprooted and carried away in the violent rainstorms typical of this area. Or the rain might be too late or too scarce to provide adequate flooding for the growing season.

To protect themselves against these contingencies, the western Pueblo supplemented floodwater farming with other strategies. They did some irrigation farming in areas where it was feasible. They planted their maize in deep holes dug into the dunes, where the soil was wetter during the early part of the growing season and where the young plants would be shielded from sandstorms. Some people planted their crops in clusters, thus reducing the water requirements of the field and ensuring that in the event of heavy winds, at least the plants at the center of the cluster would survive. They chose their soils carefully, favoring spots where water was likely to seep into the ground rather than run off the surface.

Above all, they avoided placing all their eggs in one basket: Each village planted its crops—maize, beans, squash, and cotton—in three or four locations, chosen so that whatever the pattern of their climate in a given year, it could not affect all locations equally. In a year when rains were especially torrential, crops planted at the bottoms of gullies might be washed away, but those in a flat sandy area would still come through. In a year of sparse rainfall, the crops in the gullies survived; fields in the drier lowlands might be parched beyond help, but those at higher elevations would still receive adequate rainfall. In a wet year, the productivity of high or low elevations was reversed. As further protection, many western Pueblo planted early and late crops within about a month. If a late-spring frost ruined the late crop, the early crop would survive.

Nevertheless, to ensure the success of the strategy, they had to plant three times the amount of

The late summer harvest is a time for feasting and family reunions. These men and women are performing the corn grinding dance at the western Pueblo of Santa Clara.

(John Running/Black Star)

crops they needed during any one season. One had to expect that only one third of the crops would be successful in any one year, that crops would generally be successful in only one of every three years, or that the two outcomes would be combined.

In sum, the western Pueblo responded to a high-risk environment by diversifying their planting methods as widely and as ingeniously as they could. They knew that even in a normal year some crops would fail, and they took this factor into account when they devised their strategy. Consequently, despite the vagaries of their climate and their extremely simple technology (digging sticks, wooden shovels, and stone axes), they proved to be quite successful at farming. In good years, they stockpiled enough food to last through the next growing season and sometimes the next two—necessary insurance in case of drought. For variety, nutrition, and further drought insurance, they hunted, kept turkeys, gathered small amounts of wild food, and harvested some wild plants that they left to grow undisturbed in the fields.

***The Eastern Pueblo.*** Because of differences in environment and technology, the eastern Pueblo were less subject than the western Pueblo to the vagaries of nature. Both frost and rainfall are more predictable in the eastern region. Soil is richer, retains moisture better, and drains more easily. Valleys are smaller and more enclosed so that the effect of violent winds is reduced. In all these respects, the territory of the eastern Pueblo was more suitable for farming. Most important of all, the eastern groups, unlike those of the west, had a permanent water source: the Rio Grande.

The Rio Grande permitted the eastern Pueblo to regulate the flow of water to their crops through irrigation works. Near the river, they cleared their garden plots, sometimes grading them into terraces to control the flow of water and prevent erosion. Then, at elevations somewhat higher than the fields, they tapped into the river with canals, through which the water flowed downward into the fields. Climatic variation, floods, and insect pests created their own problems for the eastern Pueblo, but overall, climatic variation was less extreme.

Until the Spaniards arrived, the eastern Pueblo cultivated the same major crops as the western Pueblo. And like the western groups, the eastern groups raised turkeys and did some hunting and gathering. In addition, they traded for buffalo meat and skins with neighboring hunter-gatherers. In general, however, while the western Pueblo poured their energy and ingenuity into diversifying their livelihood, the eastern Pueblo focused their efforts on water control, ditches, terraces, and other such devices. Aside from planting and harvesting, there were dams to build, ditches to maintain, and fields to clear, level, and grade. These substantial chores required the cooperative effort of the entire village. The subsistence strategy of the eastern Pueblo, then, was as concentrated or specialized as that of the western Pueblo was diversified. And this difference is reflected in the social organization of the two groups.

## Two Social Patterns

Archaeologists working in the Southwest have shown that the social organization of the Anasazi ancestors of the Pueblo was highly varied. At different times and places, groups were more or less mobile, smaller and larger, more or less stratified. Significant evidence now suggests that before contact with Europeans, larger villages and groups with greater differentials in individual and family wealth and power were more common. These more stratified organizational forms appear to have been destroyed by environmental change and, more important, by the dramatic decline in the population following the arrival of the Spaniards. Thus, these people's organizational patterns are less complex than they were in the past.

***The Western Pueblo.*** Floodwater farming is a family affair, requiring ingenuity and patience but a relatively small input of labor and no major cooperative effort. The typical western Pueblo village was divided into extended families whose membership was determined by **matrilineal descent**—that is, kinship is traced through the female line. Daughters usually stayed in their mothers' households for life. Sons moved to their brides' households, but they continued to regard their mothers' houses as home and returned to them regularly to participate in rituals. The women and girls of each extended family tended the group's vegetables, prepared the meals, hauled the water, made the baskets and pottery and clothing, and cared for the children. The men and boys farmed and hunted for the family, collected fuel for fires, spun and wove cotton, and tanned leather for clothes. Each family, then, was relatively autonomous with respect to domestic and agricultural responsibilities.

Yet families were far from independent of one another. On the contrary, they were bound together into higher level social units of equal if not greater significance. These were the **clans,** groups that claimed descent from a common ancestor—in this case, a female ancestor. The clan owned the houses, fields, seeds, and stored food used by its members.

More important, religious societies were the property of the clan. The eldest woman of the clan was recognized as its ceremonial head and her household as its religious center. Among one western group, the Hopi, each clan owned the rituals and ritual paraphernalia associated with a particular *kachina*—an ancestral spirit symbolized by a dancer wearing a distinctive and quite beautiful costume. Membership in kachina societies, however, was drawn from the community at large, regardless of clan affiliation. Individuals chose to join one society or another because they felt a calling or were dedicated to it; for everyone except the clan head, participation was voluntary. This cross-cutting of clan boundaries within the societies had the important function of creating ties between members of different clans. In this way, nearly all members of a pueblo were related—if not by clan membership, then by society membership. This arrangement helped to prevent villages from dividing along clan lines under normal conditions.

Religion was central to the lives of the western Pueblo—a fact that may be related to the quality of their environment. Constantly plagued by the uncertainty of the rains, and therefore of their livelihood, they turned to the supernatural to explain and influence nature. Efforts to bring the divine forces over to their side were largely the responsibility of the kachina societies (Dozier, 1970). In the kachina ceremonies, masked dancers assumed the roles of the supernatural beings, who were petitioned to favor the crops. The western Pueblo believed that if they made these ceremonies as elaborate as possible and if they participated in them in a state of harmony with nature, harboring no ill feelings toward anyone or anything, the spirits would send them rain. But the job of appeasing the spirits was not left to the kachina society alone. Other societies also petitioned for good weather. Even the medicine societies concerned themselves more with rainmaking than with curing.

Religious societies helped the people adapt to a marginal environment in another way as well. During important rituals, stores of food were brought out and shared among all the participants. As a result, families that had a lean harvest did not go hungry if others had surpluses.

Although the western Pueblo invested considerable time and energy in their religion, leaders of the kachina societies did not exercise control over other aspects of people's lives. They were religious leaders, not chiefs. When they met periodically, they confined their deliberations to ceremonial matters. The western Pueblo had no formal political leaders and no formal means of social control: no laws, judges, or trials. Gossip and ridicule—institutional-ized in the so-called clown cult, which mocked deviants—kept most people in line.

The weakness of large-scale political integration and the strength of the clans were probably responses to a highly variable and unpredictable resource base. If times grew hard, a clan could simply break off from the village to seek its fortune elsewhere. Since government, religion, property, and community affairs were already organized around this social unit, the clan provided the ready-made core of a new village.

*The Eastern Pueblo.* As we have just seen, many aspects of western Pueblo social organization can be interpreted as a response to the unpredictability of their livelihood. Eastern Pueblo life was not so unpredictable; their irrigation works ensured a relatively stable harvest from year to year. But the irrigation works posed other problems. Above all, they encouraged the development of centralized authority. In many areas, large labor forces had to be mobilized. Furthermore, decisions had to be made that would affect the entire community and require its cooperation: How was the water to be allocated? who would build and maintain the canals? and so forth. This situation worked against a social organization based on strong independent clans. If the clans tried to work separately, the efficiency of the irrigation system would be reduced. The social organization that arose among the eastern Pueblo in fact was the reverse of that of the western Pueblo: relatively weak subvillage social units united under a strong centralized political leadership. This tendency was augmented by closer contact with Spanish colonizers than was characteristic among the western Pueblo. The Spaniards imposed a system of village leaders.

The eastern Pueblo tended to concentrate domestic and agricultural responsibilities in the nuclear family. In some areas, they shifted from a matrilineal to a patrilineal kinship system. Thus, the bedrock of organization, the matrilineal extended family, gave way; the clans became less and less important in eastern Pueblo society.

As the clans dwindled in significance, the kachina societies became more important. The function of the eastern Pueblo societies was as much secular as sacred. Because of the security that the eastern Pueblo derived from their irrigation works, they did not petition the spirits continually to water their crops. Their religious ceremonies were aimed more at persuading the spirits to send them health and well-being. But it was their nonreligious functions that made the cults significant. They took over the administrative powers that in the west belonged to the clans.

*Street in San Juan, New Mexico, an Eastern Pueblo, taken in 1927. While today, of course, the people of San Juan are as fully integrated into the electronic era as their neighbors, the distinctive architecture of the Pueblo has been largely preserved, as have many aspects of traditional social life.*

(Library of Congress. Edward S. Curtis 1868–1952.)

When society leaders of the eastern Pueblo met, it was not only to arrange religious activities but also to organize war ceremonies and to coordinate communal hunts, planting and harvesting, work on the irrigation system, and maintenance of the kivas. Hence, power came to rest in the society leaders. Together, they made the community decisions and provided its leadership.

A formal system that divided the community into **moieties** arose. The term *moiety*, which originally meant one of two equal portions, is used by anthropologists to refer to one of the two subdivisions of a society with a dual organizational structure. Every individual in an eastern Pueblo community was a member of one of two groups, each of which ruled the settlement for half of the year. Membership in an eastern Pueblo society was optional, but obedience to the societies' leaders was not. Medicine men, backed by war chiefs, exercised considerable influence—in some cases, great power—over the eastern Pueblo. A family that could not discipline one of its members turned to these big men. Not infrequently, a group that disagreed with the medicine men's views was simply expelled from the pueblo and their holdings confiscated.

Thus, whereas power was diffused among clans and families in the western groups, in the eastern groups, it was centralized in highly structured, quasi-religious associations, with authority over the entire village. In fact, the village was the basic unit of eastern Pueblo society; all other social units—the family, the kin group, the clan—were subordinated to the needs of the community as a whole.

## Summary

FARMING SOCIETIES DEPEND ON DOMESTICATED FOODS, especially plants; that is, people try to control the reproduction rates of their food resources by ordering the environment in such a way as to favor their survival. Human labor and simple tools are the primary means of working the land, and extensive farmers do not produce consistently large surpluses for others' consumption. Their subsistence economies make both the group and the individual household largely self-sufficient and independent. Yet trade with neighboring groups is an important feature of their survival strategy and is integrated with their agricultural activities, as are some hunting and gathering activities.

Since contemporary horticultural societies generally occupy marginal territories and do not use major technological aids, they have developed a variety of techniques to exploit their environment. The most common technique is slash-and-burn (or swidden) agriculture. Trees and undergrowth are cut and burned to form a layer of fertilizing ash. Several varieties of plants are cultivated for several years, and then the area is left to lie fallow and new land is cleared. The success of swidden agriculture, and of horticulture in general, depends on an intimate knowledge of the environment.

Subsistence farmers can support more people per unit of land area than can hunters and gatherers, but in comparison with other agriculturists, they operate on a low-energy budget. They do not have to use their resources or labor to the fullest in order to subsist.

Among the social conditions that normally accompany a dependence on agriculture are increased sedentism—the practice of establishing a permanent, year-round settlement—and increased population density. These conditions tend to increase social complexity and interdependence.

The household is the basic unit in horticultural societies; the integration of families into a community is achieved primarily through kinship ties and political organization. Kinship networks are often the basis for both recognition of individual rights to the use of land and extensive gift exchange throughout the community.

Relations with other communities may be peaceable or warlike or somewhere in between. Trade, alliances, and intermarriage foster peaceful relations; competition for resources, raids, and exploitation provide excuses for war.

The two farming societies discussed in this chapter are the Yanomamö of Venezuela and Brazil and the Pueblo of North America. As the two peoples inhabit different environments, their adaptations have taken very different forms.

The Yanomamö hunt and gather in addition to practicing swidden agriculture in their dense tropical jungle. Authority in their villages rests with the headman, who leads by example rather than by institutionalized power. Kinship is reckoned by patrilineal descent (through the male line), and a typical village consists of two lineages that have intermarried. Strict marriage rules specify that a man choose a wife outside his lineage.

Villages normally move every few years, mostly because of internal feuds or warfare with other villages. The Yanomamö social world is one of chronic suspicion and hostility. Political alliances are cautiously negotiated by the exchange of gifts, followed by trading, feasting, and exchange of brides, but even alliances based on marriage ties are tenuous.

Some anthropologists attribute the hostile social environment to a shortage of sources of protein. Marvin Harris believes that Yanomamö warfare is concerned—unwittingly—with hunting territory, and Daniel Gross holds that the settlement pattern of widely dispersed mobile villages is a strategy for preventing the overexploitation of game in any one area. Yet Napoleon Chagnon, who has studied the Yanomamö longer and more intensively than anyone else, finds no evidence of protein deficiency among them. Chagnon attributes their bellicosity to intense competition for women, caused by their practice of female infanticide and the custom of powerful men to take more than one wife.

The subsistence strategies of the Pueblo fall into two basic patterns. The eastern Pueblo adaptation is based on irrigation works. Because of their relatively stable environment and permanent water source (the Rio Grande), the eastern Pueblo were able to concentrate their efforts on the use of irrigation and terracing. The western Pueblo adaptation is based on the simpler technique of floodwater farming, or the practice of planting in areas that are flooded in the rainy season so that floodwaters provide natural irrigation. To compensate for the vagaries of their climate, the western Pueblo diversified their planting methods as widely and as ingeniously as possible. The basic features of these adaptations survive today, despite the Spanish conquest and the encroaching industrial economy of the United States.

Different subsistence techniques led to different social organizations. The floodwater farming of the western Pueblo is associated with extended family work groups, matrilineal descent (through the female line) and clans, and kachina societies that are ceremonial in purpose and focused on rainmaking. The strength of both the kachina societies and clans may be attributed to the uncertain environment. The religious societies represent attempts to influence nature through supernatural means; the clans provide the nucleus of a new village if a move is necessitated by a lack of resources.

The irrigation works of the eastern Pueblo required large forces, central authority, and cooperation. In response to these needs, the eastern group developed strong political leadership and shifted toward patrilineal kinship. Societies that dealt with both religious and secular concerns took on administrative responsibilities. Each community came to be formed into moieties, or two subdivisions, each of which ruled the settlement for half of the year.

## Key Terms

| | |
|---|---|
| acculturation | Neolithic Revolution |
| clan | patrilineal descent |
| domestication | polyculture |
| extensive agriculture | postpartum taboo |
| headman | sedentism |
| horticulture | slash-and-burn (swidden) agriculture |
| household | |
| kula ring | spheres of exchange |
| matrilineal descent | subsistence agriculture |
| moiety | |

## Suggested Readings

Chagnon, N. A. (1997). *Yanomamö: The last days of Eden.* San Diego: Harcourt Brace Jovanovich. A distinguished albeit controversial anthropologist reviews his work among the Yanomamö, answering those who have criticized his analyses in the past while stressing the problems the Yanomamö face today.

Coimbra, C. E. A., Jr., Flowers, N. M., Salzano, F. M., & Santos, R. V. (2002). *The Xavánte in transition: Health, ecology, and bioanthropology in Central Brazil.* Ann Arbor: University of Michigan Press. A rich discussion of bioanthropological, ecological, and epidemiological data collected over a period of forty years of field study.

Damas, D. (1994). *Bountiful island: A study of land tenure on a Micronesian atoll.* Ontario: Wilfrid Laurier University Press. This book examines the land tenure system in an atoll society and its relationship to population densities and land ownership.

Grinker, R. R. (1994). *Houses in the rainforest: Ethnicity and inequality among farmers and foragers in central Africa.* Berkeley: University of California Press. A groundbreaking ethnographic study of a farmer-forager society in northeastern Zaire and its complex social relations.

Lepowsky, M. (1994). *Fruit of the motherland: Gender in an egalitarian society.* New York: Columbia University Press. An ethnography of the Vanatinai of New Guinea that contradicts the ideology of universal male dominance by exploring gender roles, ideology, and power.

Maybury-Lewis, D. (1997). *Indigenous peoples, ethnic groups, and the state.* Cultural survival studies in ethnicity and change. Boston: Allyn & Bacon. An important statement by the head of Cultural Survival, a nonprofit organization devoted to indigenous rights, which outlines how populations come to be marginalized and subjugated. Examples include peoples on all continents and all traditional modes of tribal life.

Milliken, W., & Albert, B., with Gomez, G. G. (1999). *Yanomami: A forest people.* Kew, UK: Royal Botanic Gardens. A scholarly and very interesting account of the tropical forest habitat of the Yanomami and of their intricate knowledge of their environment.

Oates, J. F. (1999). *Myth and reality in the rain forest: How conservation strategies are failing in West Africa.* Berkeley: University of California Press. While many development projects explicitly claim to benefit conservation, a primate ecologist finds otherwise. Abject poverty has disastrous consequences for wildlife, and community development programs can do little to alleviate it; large-scale political, social, and economic reform is required.

Peters, J. F. (1998). *Life among the Yanomami.* Peterbrough, Ontario: Broadview Press. A close observer of the Yanomami of Brazil since 1958, when he first visited them as a missionary, anthropologist John Peters gives rich details of how their traditional beliefs and practices have changed with contact. He also gives a valuable insight into how the Yanomami themselves perceive outsiders, including missionaries.

Reed, R. (1997). *Forest protectors: Indigenous models for international development.* Boston: Allyn & Bacon. This is an excellent account of the indigenous knowledge and historical experiences of the Guarani, a population occupying a subtropical region across parts of Paraguay and Brazil.

Sahlins, M. (1968). *Tribesmen.* Englewood Cliffs, NJ: Prentice Hall. A now-classic discussion of the economic arrangements, social structure, and ideologies of tribal societies, most of which are horticulturists.

Whiteley, P. M. (1988). *Deliberate acts: Changing Hopi culture through the Oraibi Split.* Tucson: University of Arizona Press. A detailed portrait of the history and social organization of a Hopi village that focuses on social change over a 100-year period.

# Chapter 5

# Nomadic Pastoralism

**P**astoralism is **animal husbandry**—the breeding, care, and use of herd animals such as sheep, goats, camels, cattle, horses, llamas, reindeer, and yaks. When animal husbandry is pursued as a primary adaptation, it is a highly specialized strategy of land use that in certain respects resembles hunting and gathering. Pastoralists operate in habitats that are marginal or removed from centers of settled life. They incorporate movement in their seasonal round of productive activity. They must cope with great topographic and seasonal variability, and extensive environmental knowledge is required for success. In terms of productivity, however, pastoralism is more comparable to farming, even intensive farming. Like most hunter-gatherer groups, pastoralists use lands whose vegetation they only minimally manage: They graze their animals on wild grasses, shrubs, and sometimes fallow croplands. Like agricultural populations, pastoralists invest time and energy in the management of productive resources—their livestock.

Most pastoralists are *nomadic,* moving their herds from pasture to pasture on a seasonal schedule within a well-defined territory. The degree of mobility varies from group to group, and even from year to

year within a group, depending on such environmental factors as rainfall, vegetation, and the availability of water holes. Economic and political constraints also affect the pattern of nomads' movements. Pastoralists must deal with the demands of other groups—even governments—to gain access to pastures and to the markets where they can exchange animals and animal products for clothing, tools, weapons, and food.

The extent of **specialized pastoralism,** the adaptive strategy of primary reliance on animal husbandry, varies with environmental and market conditions. Few groups rely exclusively on their herds for day-to-day subsistence. To do so would entail heavy risks in two respects. To keep their animals alive, pastoralists have to adjust to the vagaries of the environment: snow-blocked passes, lack of water, lack of pasturage, drought, and so forth. At the same time, they must coexist with other groups with whom they may be in competition. Given these complications, it is no surprise that when the environment permits, pastoralists tend to pursue a more generalized subsistence strategy, raising at least some crops along with their animals.

In fact, most pastoralists, no matter how specialized, subsist more on grains

*Camels in Saudi Arabia are rapidly being replaced by trucks, which have become the primary means of desert transport. Raising camels is no longer profitable, so most are being slaughtered for meat and are not being replaced.*

(William Strode/Woodfin Camp & Associates)

than on animal products. The camel-herding Bedouin of Arabia greatly prize their independence but are now, and always have been, linked by numerous economic and social ties to the larger sedentary society. Even before the arrival of trucks, camps in Arabia were regularly visited by merchants laden with wares to trade for camels. The merchants would set up shop in distinctive white tents (in contrast to the black tents of the nomads), and it was a breach of the codes regulating warfare to rob or harm these visitors, so important were they to the well-being of the pastoral community. Today, of course, most Bedouin households have trucks or jeeps and can drive to the nearest town to shop.

Before looking closely at two pastoral societies, the chapter discusses how pastoralism developed and what its social consequences are for groups that pursue it.

## The Pastoral Adaptation

### Development

The archaeological record for the Middle East, at least, indicates that mixed farming based on a combination of domesticated plants and animals preceded specialized pastoralism. Mixed farming was a multifaceted strategy that provided a hedge against droughts, crop failures, diseases, and other natural calamities. For farmers, livestock not only provided valuable material (skins for clothing and shelter) and food products, but the animals themselves were a means of storing food against future use—a freezer

on the hoof. At the same time, if the animals died, the crops were there. Diversification provided both the alternatives and the reserves necessary to survive fluctuations in the food supply. Such diversification is still common in many parts of Africa, Europe, and the Middle East, particularly in mountain villages.

Despite the many advantages of diversification, changes in agricultural practices, especially the development of canal irrigation and intensive agriculture, created the preconditions for specialized pastoralism. Increased productivity based on canal irrigation made possible population growth and the expansion of settlements, with a consequent increase in land devoted to intensive farming and a decrease in land available for animals. It also stimulated interregional trade. Grazing areas were pushed farther from the settlement region into territory where forage was not so lush. To get adequate food and water for their herds, animal owners had to expend more labor and travel greater and greater distances. Furthermore, the animals were more vulnerable to predators and especially to raiders. Thus, care of the animals began to drain energies away from agriculture. At the same time, agriculture became more time-consuming, for farmers now had to clear, tend, and repair the canals in addition to working the fields. The increased demands of each of these strategies may have led to a divergence, with certain households specializing in increasingly intensive agriculture and others concentrating on animal husbandry, or pastoralism.

Pastoralism, then, may have developed hand in hand with intensive agriculture. Whatever the reasons for its development, pastoralism is a strategy usually predicated on agricultural surplus and on regular interaction between herders and farmers. Pastoralism may be an alternative to agriculture, but it is almost never independent of it.

## Early Pastoralism in North Africa: An Archaeological Example

Early pastoral sites are rather rare due to problems of preservation of artifacts from low-density populations who move frequently. One of the very earliest set of pastoralist sites is in the Nabta Playa basin in the eastern Sahara about 100 kilometers west of the famed Abu Simbel monuments. Here archaeologists have uncovered not only extremely early sites but, in a series of excavations, have been able to establish a long history of pastoralist activity. Much of the work has been carried out by Fred Wendorf of the United States and Romuald Schild of Poland together with their students and associates (see Wendorf & Schild, 2001).

The environmental setting then was very arid, although not as extremely arid as today. When occupation began about 9500–9000 B.P., estimated rainfall averaged 100 to 200 millimeters per year, but the climate seems to have been unstable with frequent droughts. Botanical evidence suggests that during the early occupation of the region, there were ten species of trees and shrubs, as well as 117 varieties of grasses and other plants, providing very dense plant cover for most of the period. Faunal evidence indicates few wild species, predominantly hares and a few varieties of small gazelle.

The archaeological data indicate the existence of small and scattered camps; their numbers and density suggesting frequent relocations. There are, however, a few larger settlements with extensive cultural deposits and even architectural remains, such as houses, storage pits, and structures that may have had ceremonial functions. These larger settlements are located at the bottom of the Nabta basin, close to a water source. Wendorf and Schild think that the basin was supplied with water during the wet season by runoff from a large catchment area and that surface water existed in the form of seasonal lakes lasting for several months. They also assume that people dug wells at the bottom of the basin and thus were able to obtain water through most if not all of the dry season.

Using data from several Nabta basin sites, including more than 20,000 specimens of edible floral remains representing 127 species (among them wild varieties of sorghum, millet, legumes, and tubers) and sheep/goat remains dating to approximately 7100 B.P., Wendorf and Schild constructed the following three-phase chronology.

The first phase was cattle domestication by about 9000 B.P. By 8000 B.P., a subsistence pattern had developed that was heavily reliant on domesticated cattle but supplemented by gathering wild plants. Groups were mobile and settlements were small and seasonal but reoccupied frequently.

The second phase, 8050–7300 B.P., is marked by the appearance of deep water wells, large bell-shaped storage pits, evidence of extensive gathering of seeds, fruits, and tubers, and the probable cultivation of wild sorghum (sorghum and two kinds of millet were very common). Oval and round huts

*Camels have declining economic importance in Arabia but are still vitally important livestock in East Africa and the Sahel, where water is a scarce resource. Here Ethiopian herders water their herds.*

(Woodfin Camp & Associates)

with several hearths inside were found at larger sites; pottery was commonly used, and lithic materials for tools and weapons were imported from a distance of 70 kilometers. Cattle do not appear to have been numerous but would have been used for milk and blood as they are by East African pastoralists today.

The third phase, 7100–6600 B.P., sees the rise of social complexity in a mixed herding economy based on cattle and sheep/goats. Pottery is very abundant in this period, although large settlement sites are rare. Most settlements seem to have been short-term camps with simple brush or skin huts and few artifacts but a high frequency of cattle bones. There is some evidence of trade with agriculturalists in the Nile Valley, and the presence of numerous grinding stones indicates that grains were consumed. One site, where cattle remains were found associated with complex stone structures, was probably a regional ceremonial center.

## The Organization of Energy

Like horticulture, pastoralism is more productive than hunting and gathering. Hunters do not try to increase the numbers of animals they hunt or use the products of living animals. They may, as we have noted, hunt in a conservative fashion in an effort not to eliminate their prey altogether, but they do not practice animal management. Pastoralists, on the other hand, do invest labor in breeding and caring for their animals and so increase their reproduction and survival rates. Apart from reindeer herders, pastoralists are usually concerned with the production of milk, hair, blood, or hides, and with traction—using animals as vehicles or sources of work energy. Meat production is almost incidental with one or two notable exceptions. By investing human labor in the production of milk rather than meat, the herder gains a greater net return: The animal need not be killed to be useful. In fact, successful herders can generally increase their holdings at a faster rate than farmers, for as the animals reproduce, the offspring can be incorporated into their herds. Of course, this advantage is partially offset by the precarious nature of herding in most areas. Animals are susceptible to disease, drought, and theft, any of which can reduce a rich household to poverty overnight. In Mongolia, Ethiopia, Rajasthan (India), and Baluchistan (Pakistan), severe drought conditions in 2000 killed millions of livestock and impoverished many thousands of pastoral families.

Full-time pastoralism may be less efficient than farming in areas where cultivation is possible. People can produce approximately ten times as much food, measured in calories yielded per acre of land, by raising grains rather than livestock. But in areas where agriculture is risky or impossible, pastoralism is a useful strategy for converting forage—sources of energy that humans cannot use directly—into milk, blood, and meat. These foods are stored in the form of animals until the people need them either to eat or to trade for agricultural foods, clothing, and other items they cannot otherwise obtain. Furthermore, the fact that animals can move themselves permits herders to move the production system to the resources.

By using a strategy of simultaneously exploiting more than one environment, pastoralists have found a relatively efficient way of extracting energy from an environment not suited to agriculture. For example, the herds of most East African pastoralists are mixed and include not only zebu (oxen distinguished by a hump, much like a camel's) but also large numbers of goats, sometimes sheep, donkeys, and in very dry areas, camels. The importance of the mixed herd lies in the fact that each species has its own feeding preferences so that not one but several environments are exploited. However, since pastoralism produces much less food energy per acre of land than agriculture, specialized pastoralists necessarily have low population densities.

## Nomadic Movement

In nonindustrial societies, **sedentary pastoralism,** or animal husbandry that does not involve mobility (ranching, say, or dairy farming), is relatively rare. The practice more generally followed is **nomadic pastoralism,** the adaptive strategy of moving the herds that are one's livelihood from pasture to pasture as the seasons and circumstances require. Land that is rich enough to support a herd indefinitely in one location will yield far more output if it is given over primarily to crops. By taking advantage of the mobility of herd animals and their own ability to group and regroup, however, pastoralists can adapt to marginal areas by moving as conditions dictate. Mobility is the key that unlocks widely dispersed resources and allows a population to gain a living from an environment that could not sustain a settled community.

The main reason for pastoralist migrations is to secure adequate grazing on a year-round basis, but this is not the only reason. William Irons (1975) has pointed out that the Türkmen pastoralists of northern Iran move to maintain their political and cultural independence as well as to seek grazing lands. In the past, they also frequently raided non-Türkmen sedentary populations and caravans. If they were pursued by a more powerful force, they could simply disperse with their animals into inaccessible areas. Though they were "pacified" by the Iranian government in the early twentieth century, they have managed until recently to retain considerable control over their own affairs. They did so by using the one skill they had developed far beyond the abilities of other populations—moving.

In antiquity, several great empires arose in Eurasia based on the military prowess of nomadic warriors. Around 1000 B.P., two inventions greatly enhanced the military capacity of already highly effective horse-mounted fighters: the compound bow, which by combining different materials (woods and/or bone) generated much more lethal power, and the stirrup, which provided a more secure ride. These innovations allowed mounted warriors to let off deadly shots in all directions while riding at top speed. Great armies, such as those of the Scythians, Huns, and Mongols, that were so equipped formed on the steppes of Central Asia and on several occasions occupied or terrorized large swaths of settled Europe and Asia. Genghis Khan (d. 1227 A.D.) and his immediate descendants conquered an area extending by 1280 A.D. from the Korean Peninsula across most of today's China, Russia, Hungary, Poland, Rumania, the Middle East, and Pakistan. Living evidence of this empire has recently come to light through a rather unusual genetic discovery. An Oxford geneticist, together with colleagues in several countries formerly ruled by the Mongols, collected blood samples over ten years from sixteen populations (Wade, 2003a, p. D3). They found that 8% of the males, or 16 million individuals, bear a distinctive Y chromosome characteristic of the Mongol ruling dynasty. The evolutionary significance of this finding is that a relatively small lineage can affect a disproportionately large number of descendants; Genghis Khan and his sons are historically known to have fathered prodigious numbers of offspring. From a cultural or historical vantage point, Genghis Khan's accomplishments illustrate the often-underestimated abilities of predominately pastoral nomadic populations to mobilize great forces capable of defeating agrarian states.

Today, even within the boundaries of contemporary state bureaucratic systems, mobility often allows nomadic pastoralists to maintain greater political autonomy than settled communities enjoy. With continuing political uncertainty in Iran, both nomadic and settled Türkmen are reasserting their claim to a separate identity, and the nomadic groups are apparently the more successful in their efforts. In other countries, nomads may be able to avoid onerous civic duties such as military conscription and taxation.

The economic strategies of individual households within a given population of pastoralists often vary considerably. Such variations are sketched very clearly in the ever-changing composition of the camp group and in individual decisions on migration. Some groups among the Türkmen of Iran, for example, may move frequently one year and be largely sedentary the next. Regular patterns often underlie this variability. In Turkey, Yörük households with many animals may move early in the spring to pastures in the mountains, braving cold weather to get to the first grasses. Others with smaller flocks may feel they cannot afford the risk of losing even a few animals to the cold and so move later in the season. In general, though, the variability of movement patterns is due to the variation in types of herds, quality of grazing lands, climate, and availability of water. An area of rich pasture land and mild climate does not require as many moves as one dominated by poorer quality pastures (Barfield, 1993).

There are two basic systems of nomadic movement, despite much variation. One pattern, plains or **horizontal migration,** is characterized by regular movement over a large area in search of forage, a necessary strategy where no particular area is capable of sustaining a herd for a long period of time. The Bedouin of the Arabian Peninsula exemplify this form of nomadism; members of Bedouin tribal groups are dispersed over hundreds of square miles as they make use of the scant vegetation of an extremely arid region. Although they gather in larger encampments around seasonal water holes, the density of population is strikingly low. This pattern has been widespread throughout the cattle- and goat-keeping portions of Africa, the deserts and steppes of Central Asia and the Middle East, and in later times, the plains of North and South America.

The second pattern is that of seasonal movement of livestock between upland and lowland pastures, or **transhumance.** The Yörük case to be discussed shortly exemplifies this pattern. This form of nomadism has been found throughout the mountainous zones of the Middle East, parts of Eastern Europe, Switzerland, Central Asia, and again in later times, North and South America. Transhumant nomads often camp together for extended periods of time in two major grazing areas: summer pastures in the mountains and winter pastures in the valleys. During the migrations between seasonal encampments, the roads and trails are crowded with people and animals on the move.

Despite the fact that most pastoral populations adopt a nomadic lifestyle, we often see individual families giving up herding altogether for other pursuits. This is what families in the Middle East tend

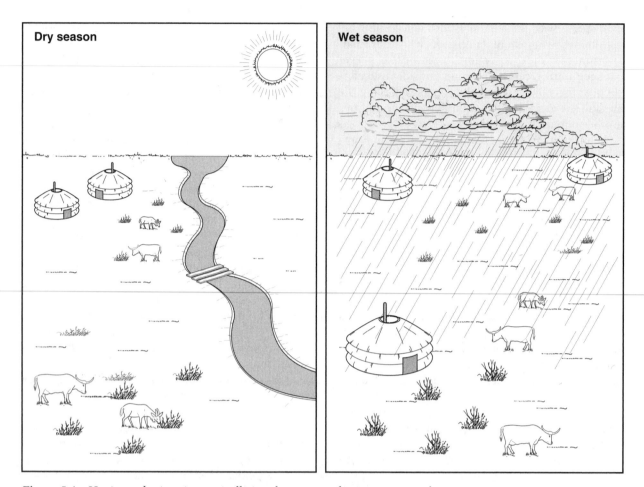

**Figure 5.1.** *Horizontal migration typically involves seasonal migrations much like that of foragers. However, the use of domesticated animals both as transport and food means that they can range farther afield and carry more substantial dwellings and possessions. Most pastoralists also rely on agricultural produce such as grain whether they grow it themselves or acquire it through trade.*

to do when they have accumulated enough wealth to invest in a more secure form of capital, such as land or a shop, or when their herds have become so small that they can no longer support the household. In many regions, settlement, followed by a return to herding, is a regular process. On the other hand, agricultural households may shift to herding if they consider it advantageous. Thus, most of the people described as pastoralists have strong cultural ties in sedentary communities and usually have relatives there as well. The Bedouin of the Negev in Israel, for example, have been largely forced to settle for political reasons but still keep as many animals as they can manage.

However we may think of nomadic pastoralists, we should not fall into the trap of perceiving them as inflexibly committed to a single way of life. Nomadism is a strategy, a means of making specialized animal husbandry work. A group can be more or less nomadic depending on conditions. People can organize themselves into sizable groups and stay together for extended periods when they gain advantages from that strategy, but they will work separately when that approach is more productive. Although we often speak of "group cohesiveness," "corporateness," and "economic stratification" as characteristics of a society, we should not lose sight of their ultimate origins in individual behavioral motivation. What we see as patterns of social organization are the outcomes of the strategies individuals adopt as they cope with their problems and evaluate their opportunities.

## Social Organization

There is no single form of social organization that is peculiar to nomadic pastoralists; such adaptations

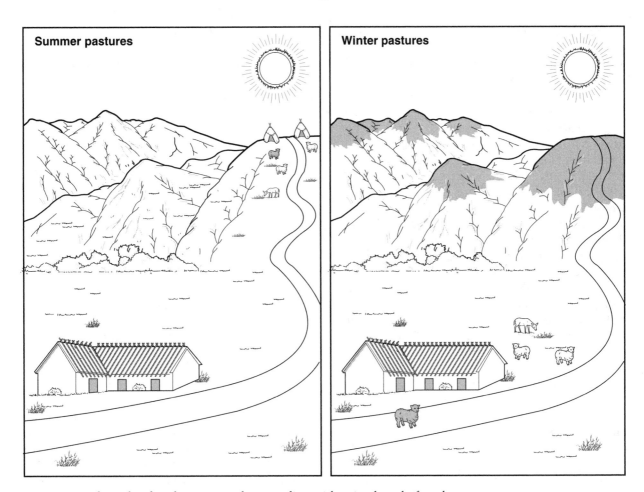

**Figure 5.2.** *These sketches depict vertical seasonality, with animals and often the entire human population as well moving from valley villages or camps where they stay in the winter to upland pastures in spring as the snow melts and grasses appear. Often, transhumants make use of stored hay or other animal fodder in the winter.*

occur in varied environmental, political, and cultural contexts. The social life of Lapp reindeer herders may closely resemble that of neighboring Finnish communities. The Bedouin of Arabia may be culturally similar to tribal villagers in Iraq. Still, most researchers who have studied or worked with nomadic pastoral societies see certain aspects of social organization related either to the necessity (or capacity) for mobility or to the requirements of the animals they tend.

Virtually all nomadic pastoralists are organized in tribes, sociopolitical communities whose members are bound by ties of kinship—most commonly by presumed descent from one or more common ancestors. Such groupings can easily encompass many thousands of individuals through the expedient of recognizing subgroups defined by degree of kinship: clans, lineages, or even large family clusters. Such groupings do not depend on a definition of commu-

nity that rests mainly on residence in a territory or locality; a member of one's tribe is a relative.

## Tribal Structure

It is interesting to look at some of the commonly encountered "basal" components of tribal society as often seen among pastoralists in the Middle East, Central Asia, and Africa, keeping in mind that this is a bare sketch and not an effort to fit very diverse peoples into one framework. The basic unit of tribal society, like that of society at large, is the individual household. This term subsumes a number of closely related persons living under the same roof or in the same compound who are dependent on one another for their livelihoods. The Türkmen description illustrates the meaning of household or this level of organization; they say the household is simply those people "whose expenses are one." Another idiom is "those who share the same cooking pot." These folk categories come very close to those used by demographic census takers—that is, a grouping in which expenses and consumption are shared.

A number of households whose heads share an immediate unilineal relationship to an ancestor two to five generations back constitute a second level of organization, which is often called a lineage or clan by anthropologists.[1] A clan is a group that claims but cannot precisely demonstrate descent from a common ancestor. A lineage is a descent group whose members can usually trace or remember genealogical ties. It is at this point that the tribal idiom defines a group that has potential political significance. Members of the same lineage or clan may share a sense of collective responsibility for property and person and may possibly own property in common. The households of such a group are likely to be linked to one another by a history of close interpersonal relations, including, in some instances, ties of marriage, and by the sharing of a common name. They may also share a common reputation expressed in the code of honor. In theory, both men *and* women remain identified throughout their lifetimes with the lineage into which they are born. Should women marry outside their lineages, they nevertheless consider themselves members of their father's group, and should they be repudiated or divorced, they return to it.

A number of those lineages, again claiming descent from a yet more distant common ancestor, may form a larger unit, usually glossed in the literature as *clan* or *tribal section*. Using the same idea of a common ancestor, a group of clans or sections may form a tribe or the maximal unit of political identity. It is the existence of a number of levels of organization of varying degrees of inclusiveness, all formed by the same principle of descent, that distinguishes tribal society. Moreover, these different levels of organization have different political and economic significance for the individual member of the tribe. For example, in a nomadic pastoral society like al-Murra of Saudi Arabia, those tents that camp and move together are most likely to belong to the same lineage, or as they would say, *fakhd*. In times of serious conflict with outsiders, more inclusive levels of tribal organization may become operant, bringing together distant relatives who would rarely see each other on a daily basis. In forming and consolidating ever-larger groupings, there is one

dominant principle, which is expressed in the Arabic proverb, "I against my brother; I and my brother against my cousin; I and my brother and my cousin against the stranger."

This saying expresses an ideal of how things should be in principle—namely, that closely related individuals and groups should automatically unite and that claims of blood take precedence over other commitments. In fact, it is recognized everywhere that patterns of cooperation and alliance are not automatic. Lineages and tribes are as apt to be rent by factions and disagreements as are any other communities. The precedence of blood and the idea of solidarity derived from shared patrilineal descent are fundamental principles of organization. They constitute the norm against which behavior is measured and loyalty is judged.

The model for understanding tribal organization was first formulated in 1940 by E. Evans-Pritchard for the nomadic cattle-herding Nuer of Sudan and is known as the principle of **segmentary lineage.** Since then, it has been widely used and argued over by anthropologists interested in understanding the political processes of tribally organized peoples. The segmentary lineage principle tries to answer the important question of how order is maintained in the absence of central power. It does so by positing the principle of complementary opposition, illustrated in the proverb cited earlier. According to this, segments of the tribe or group are expected to ally themselves or coalesce with other groups of the same level according to proximity of descent. It is assumed that all segments or lineages at the same level are roughly the same size and strength and that all individuals in the tribe are equal in status. If this were the case, then it would follow that there would always be a balance of power within the tribe that would dampen disputes and prevent them from ramifying through the group.

Demographic fluctuations, internal factioning, and infighting or even warfare can easily result in substantial differences in lineage size within a particular tribal system. When the lineage controls land or pasture, smaller lineages may simply be absorbed by their more powerful neighbors. When control of resources does not depend on the power of the local segment—for example, when land titles are enforced by the state—small lineages may easily coexist alongside larger ones (see Lancaster, 1997).

Najwa Adra (1985) provides a concise description of the nature of the tribal mode of organization in central and northern Yemen and a clear statement of how this ideology is supposed to work as a model. "Segmentary organization provides mechanisms for the bringing together of increasingly larger groups

[1]Most Old World pastoralists employ patrilineal descent ideology, with the Tuareg, who are matrilineal, and the Lapps, who trace descent from both father's and mother's sides (cognatic descent), as the principal exceptions.

according to need without endangering the autonomy of each segment. At each level there are distinct segments, the members of which may be called upon to cooperate with each other or with members of other segments in situations where there is a perceived need for common action. The system is held together by ideological ties of common responsibility . . . genealogy, geography, and political or administrative expediency combine to determine the loose segmentary organization of the tribes of the central and northern highland" (pp. 275–286).

The principle of segmentary lineage is an ideal or theoretical construct used by people to describe their own social order. It is not an accurate reflection of behavior. Complementary opposition is likewise an ideal statement expressing the primacy of kin loyalty. It is also a statement about the contextual nature of loyalty and alliance. It signifies that alliances among people and groups are impermanent and shifting, as allies are brought together according to the circumstances of the particular situation and especially the relationships that exist among the people involved. In a way peculiar to tribal politics, professions of loyalty and alliance contain an important caveat: subject to prior claims.

*Hierarchical Tribal Organization.* While pastoralists' camp groups may resemble the fluid camps of hunter-gatherers, most such societies have a more complex sociopolitical organization that unites the constituent households and camping groups in tribes. Some nomadic tribes, such as the Bedouin of Arabia and the Mongols of Central Asia, have strong leaders. Undoubtedly, the existence of such roles reflects the fact that these peoples were in close contact, even regular conflict, with agricultural communities and lived within the boundaries of nation-states. The Qashqa'i of Iran, for example, have an elaborate hierarchy of leaders, each part of a fairly well-defined chain of command (Beck, 1986, 1991).

A hierarchical tribal organization often has highly specified membership criteria (as by patrilineal or matrilineal descent) and is composed of well-defined subgroups. Such an organization allows for more than just communication across great distances. It is a means of coordinating large-scale migrations, gaining access to grazing land, holding and defending territory, and even on occasion gaining control over sedentary farming populations.

A study by Arun Agrawal of nomadic shepherds, the Raikas of western India, shows how this works. The Raikas are the largest group of nomadic pastoralists in India, migrating from settlements in Rajasthan and Gujarat with their flocks of sheep for more than two thirds of the year. Generally, shepherds move to a new camp location almost every day; there are several hundred thousand sheep on the move. Their mobile camps—*dang*—have as many as eighteen herds (or up to 7,000 animals) and over one hundred men, women, and children. "Daily movements of fifty to one hundred human beings and their animals demand critical collective decisions" (Agrawal, 1993, p. 263). They achieve this by delegating decision making to three groups in each tent.

*The household, strongly identified with the patrilineal descent group, is the basic unit of Bedouin society. Here a group of men from the same lineage gather to socialize.*

(Robert Azzi/Woodfin Camp and Associates)

The first is the *nambardar*, who is the senior leader because of his wide experience, wealth, and contacts with leaders of other camps. He spends his time scouting possible routes and visiting other camps. The second leader, the *kamdar*, makes decisions while the *nambardar* is away from camp and participates in the council of five elders, made up of men representing a broad spectrum of Raikas's interests. The third level of decision making is the *mukhiya*, a man who is the leader of the individual herders in the camp and who intimately knows the needs and characteristics of the herds. The leaders are chosen on the basis of experience, age, wealth, and kin relationships. The *nambardar* makes most decisions about migration, marketing, campwide shearing, and campwide management; he is the best informed about the possible routes and camp sites. The *kamdar* serves to manage internal relations in the camp during the *nambardar's* frequent absences and to coordinate with the council of elders—thus maintaining a check on the *nambardar's* authority. Finally, decisions having to do with herding, labor, and when to bring the animals home rest with the *mukhiya*, who best knows flock management (Agrawal, 1993, p. 270).

### Camp Groups and Household Organization. Individuals and households in herding societies frequently change their patterns of movement and the groups with which they camp. They move in response to changing economic and political conditions and also to new social circumstances. Individual households camp with people with whom they enjoy good relations, and such people are most often kin. There appear to be strong constraints on the number of households that can readily coordinate their activities in an egalitarian society that lacks strong leadership roles. Two observers have noted considerable uniformity in the average size of nomadic camps or migratory groups—usually in the range of 100 to 300 persons (Johnson, 1983, p. 176; Tapper, 1979, p. 81).

When Gregory Johnson examined a large number of nomadic societies whose people lived together by choice rather than by coercion, he found that a camp group comprised on average six households or clusters of very closely related households, such as father-son groupings (1983, p. 183). If conflict were to occur in the camp group, often the easiest solution was for the antagonists to move apart. In many respects, the shifting composition of nomadic camping-and-herding groups resembles the camps of nomadic hunter-gatherers. People use mobility to minimize conflict and to associate with those they find congenial.

## Wealth, Inequality, and Status

In many traditional pastoral societies, livestock constitutes the sole form of economic wealth. Rights to animals are held by individual households and are passed down from father to son. Because some may inherit more than others or may have more success in managing their herds, the numbers and quality of the herds vary from household to household. However, everyone is subject to loss of livestock through disease, theft, drought, or bad luck; a wealthy household may be reduced to poverty in one season. Thus, in many pastoral societies where there is no market for livestock, periods of wealth and poverty are temporary and tend not to create permanent disparities in economic status.

However, it is probably safe to say that distinctions of wealth are more evident among pastoral populations than among the horticulturists discussed in Chapter 4. Among the Komanchi sheep herders of Iran, for example, Daniel Bradburd (1990) found not only great disparities of wealth among households but also systematic exploitation of poorer households by wealthy ones. Such disparities are reflected in marriage arrangements and in many other areas of social life; the poorer households have a limited opportunity to improve their lot. This case may be extreme, but economic differentiation among households is common. Among the Ariaal of Kenya, to be discussed shortly, drought tends to kill off a larger percentage of the wealthy herders' animals because they are not cared for as carefully as the animals of small stockowners (Fratkin, Galvin, & Roth, 1994; Fratkin & Roth, 1996). But since the rich have more animals, particularly drought-resistant camels, they survive periods of drought with far less risk of being impoverished and forced to settle permanently in one location.

## Pastoralism and Market Relations

Camel herders, like all who specialize in animal husbandry, however much they may prize their independence, are still closely linked by numerous economic and social ties to the larger society. This is true for all pastoralists, whether they live and raise their animals in close proximity to villages and towns or whether they range far into regions of no permanent settlement. Pastoralists in the Middle East raise animals for sale in markets where they acquire most of the food they consume, not to mention clothing, cooking utensils, weapons, jewelry, and many other items of household and personal use. The integration of pastoralists into the larger market economy is a point that cannot be emphasized

*In the late 1960s, Yörük entrepreneurs established mobile dairies that follow the herds, collecting milk and processing it into cheese for urban markets.*

(Daniel Bates)

too strongly. In fact, the existence of specialized pastoralism and the number of people who can be supported in this endeavor at any given time are directly related to the ability of the pastoralists to trade with or otherwise acquire the products of sedentary communities. Moreover, these exchanges, for the most part, are cash transactions.

There is very impressive documentation of the balance of exchange among pastoralists and non-pastoralists in western Iran. Dan Bradburd collected and meticulously analyzed data covering 160 years of trade and production (1996). In examining a number of populations for which data were available, he was able to calculate the rate of return from a herd of 100 sheep and, to his surprise, found that the values of commodities purchased, to the extent that they had changed at all, had actually changed in favor of the pastoralists, particularly in the twentieth century. This means that in recent decades a herder could purchase more commodities than in the previous century, even though their personal consumption also went up, in particular the use of sugar, tobacco, tea, and coffee. Given this finding, Bradburd notes, one has to look to other factors to explain rates of sedentarization, such as government policies, the political environment, and changing employment opportunities (1996).

Two studies from the Negev point to what these might be (Ginguld et al., 1997; Marx, 1999). In the North Negev, in Israel, Bedouin persist in pastoral production, sometimes simply to maintain their claim to land, but also for reasons of cultural identity and, of course, to make a living. But this is increasingly difficult, not because animals are no

longer valuable commodities, but because herding activities are greatly restricted by rules and regulations imposed by the government. While herding can be profitable using cheap labor, the best economic strategy for a household involves "intensifying" production through feeding livestock in addition to open grazing. Nevertheless, their access to resources is severely hampered by relations with the Israeli army, restrictive or discriminatory land use laws, and the like—in short, politics.

Governments in the Middle East are often critical in determining local patterns of land use and how local communities interact, even in areas remote from centers of power. A government may not be able to effectively administer certain territories within its national frontiers on a day-to-day basis, but nevertheless, it can usually intervene in local disputes in such a way as to determine their outcome. Because nomads are most commonly found in regions of low population density, remote from urban centers and in terrain difficult to control militarily, it is sometimes assumed that national politics are irrelevant. This is not and never has been the case. A study by an Israeli geographer and a long-term observer of the Bedouin of the Negev clearly illustrates the sociopolitical transformation of a Bedouin population as they cope with the dual impact of Israeli policies and the changing market environment. Meir's (1997) work documents the thorny relationship between the Bedouin and Israeli administrators and the processes that led to the isolation and marginalization of the Bedouin.

Modern technology has, of course, greatly reduced the military advantage of mobility that pastoralists have traditionally enjoyed. Modern governments take care to maintain their monopoly over military armament, and even where tribal groups may be well armed, they are usually vulnerable to air attack and to the ability of the government to bring in large numbers of troops by truck. Such large tribal groups as the Basseri, the Türkmen, and the Qashqa'i are far from being autonomous political entities. However, even when such nomadic groups are able to keep the bureaucracy at arm's length, they still have to contend with a state that can play off one leader against another, interfere in factional disputes, and on occasion, launch large-scale punitive expeditions.

One large region where pastoralism predominates is Mongolia, or Inner Asia—the vast steppes between the Ural Mountains of Russia and the plateau of Tibet. Here in modern-day Mongolia, a country the size of France and Spain combined, some 27 million livestock (horses, yak, sheep, and recently, cows) are herded by a third of the country's households, or 275,000 (*The Economist,* 2002d). Unfortunately, many were impoverished by the bad weather conditions of 1999 and 2002, and the overall prognosis for animal husbandry is poor due to a post-Soviet collapse of marketing and transport networks and the effects of uncontrolled overgrazing.

## The Social and Symbolic Value of Livestock

In addition to the fact that livestock are central to the pastoral economy, they also have considerable social

and symbolic value. For example, some Bedouin tribes keep small herds of pure white camels; others maintain special racing camels. Today, as most camels are being replaced by trucks, their continuing value resides in their significance as a cultural symbol marking their identification with the past and with familial honor (Barfield, 1993, p. 89).

Among the horse-riding pastoralists of Central Asia, horses are prized far beyond their utilitarian value. In fact, sheep and goats have much more value in subsistence terms. However, while horses were never the primary focus of these people, they endowed their riders with the speed to facilitate communication and cooperation and the mobility and power to triumph in battles. Thus, they symbolize military and political power.

In East Africa, cattle have a paramount and pervasive symbolic value. Melville Herskovits (1924) long ago identified this focus on cattle as the "East African **cattle complex**": a socioeconomic system in which cattle represent social, not economic, wealth. They were exchanged as part of marriage ceremonies, ritually slaughtered at other ceremonial events, given as gifts, and prized for their beauty. According to Herskovits, the possession of large herds was such an important status symbol that cattle were neither traded nor used as a regular source of food. This symbolic explanation was used to account for an excessive number of cattle in a culture that did little trading.

However, further research has revealed that, while cattle are clearly central to the social life of

*Archaeological workers in Egypt's Western Desert unearthing a neolith ceremonial structure (ca. 4800 BC). The Nabatia Playa site offers some of the earliest African evidence for domesticated cattle used in a ceremonial context as well as being central to the local economy of that period.*

(R. Schild)

these herders, they also have an economic function. First, the cows' main contribution to the subsistence economy is milk, which is the primary pastoral product. Since the cattle that can survive in the harsh environment of East Africa aren't very productive, large herds are necessary to satisfy subsistence needs. Also, although eating beef except on ritual occasions was forbidden, these ritual sacrifices occurred often enough to suggest that beef was a significant source of food. Keeping great numbers of cattle was also part of a subsistence strategy that divided and dispersed herds over a wide area as a kind of insurance against loss of all one's cattle in one place to raiders from a neighboring group or to disease.

We shall consider two groups of pastoralists, each with a distinctive adaptive pattern. The first

A Yomut Türkmen elder on his prized horse. Horses were formerly an important key to Türkmen military prowess, as well as a source of prestige.
(Daniel Bates)

group, the Ariaal of northern Kenya in East Africa, are among the African tribes for whom cattle are economically and culturally important. Yet they also keep camels as well as sheep and goats—whose products they consume or trade for grain, tea, and sugar. Even though they are pastoralists, they eat meat only occasionally. Milk, blood, and a porridge made of sorghum and other grains form the basis of a diet won from a harsh and unpredictable environment.

The second group, the Yörük of Turkey, raise their herds for the purpose of exchange with other groups. Traditionally, the Yörük cultivated no crops, preferring to use the income from their stock to buy grain and other foodstuffs from the agriculturists of their region. Nor did they have permanent settlements; they moved regularly and on a tight schedule to get adequate pasturage. Economic factors have caused them to change their pattern somewhat in recent years, however, and the majority now live in towns and villages.

## The Ariaal of Northern Kenya

In 1974, Elliot Fratkin stopped his unreliable motorcycle in the dusty market town of Marsabit, unable to continue to Ethiopia, where he had planned to carry out fieldwork among pastoralists: The border was closed because of a coup against Haile

Figure 5.3. *East-African Pastoralists.*

Selassie (Fratkin, 1998, p. 11).[2] Sitting dejectedly in a bar and considering the problem of what to do next, he was approached by a young man who invited him out to a settlement ten kilometers to the south to see a dance. He accepted, and thus he began a study of the Ariaal that has continued until today. The dance that he witnessed was not a tourist show; over 300 warriors were in the middle of a ritual lasting several days that was held to minimize the disharmony caused by the recent killing of one of their leaders. He remained two years; he returned in 1985 for more work and again in 1990, 1992, 1994, and 1996. Thus, Fratkin has been able to see how Ariaal society has changed: how they have coped with the many intrusions into their earlier way of life and, in particular, how the development projects that were meant to assist them actually worked out. Well-intentioned efforts at relieving famine and drought often have had unintended negative consequences.

The Ariaal probably number some 7,000 persons living in Kenya's most arid and least densely populated district; other pastoral populations nearby include the closely related Samburu (70,000), the Rendille (15,000), and the more distantly related Maasai (350,000) who live to the south.

## The Origins of the Ariaal

Although ethnic identities often seem fixed and timeless, it is important to keep in mind that social identity is always being transformed with the passage of time: New formations arise and others disappear. The Ariaal are a good example of this process. Today, they strongly stress their unique identity and the ways in which they differ from their neighbors. Still, there is good evidence that this identity has its historical origins in groups of refugees from the Samburu, Rendille, and possibly Maasai groups who came together as a result of intertribal warfare and drought. Over the years, they coalesced as a distinctive population with its own approach to pastoralism. The last quarter of the nineteenth century was a turbulent era for pastoralists in Kenya. Not only was there a prolonged period of drought, but a number of epidemics devastated many herds. It was in this context that warfare broke out as pastoralists raided each other's herds, particularly among Maasai groups. Impoverished groups of Samburu, whose herds were ravished by rinderpest, fled to Rendille

territory where they formed mixed Samburu/Rendille communities subsisting on camels, sheep, and goats.

They were, by necessity, confined to fringe areas that neither the main elements of the Samburu nor the Rendille exploited. However, as is often the case with the impoverished or socially marginal groups, they soon came to prosper by adopting practices from each population and developing their own distinctive pastoral strategy. They made careful use of a wide range of resources—raising camels as well as cattle and small stock, strategically deploying labor—and maintained close relations with their more populous neighbors. The Ariaal speak Samburu (a Nilotic language related to Maasai) and most are also fluent in Rendille (an Afro-Asiatic language related to Somali); they intermarry with both; and they share some religious and social customs with each (but in their own unique mix).

## The Ariaal Adaptation

What really distinguishes the Ariaal, apart from their own assertions of identity, is their approach to animal husbandry. They inhabit the plains and slopes around Mt. Marsabit and the Ndoto Mountains—an ecologically marginal region that they successfully exploit by using a highly diversified system of husbandry based on large inputs of household labor. Unlike the Samburu (whose economy is based on raising cattle and small stock) and the Rendille (who raise camels and small stock), the Ariaal utilize all three animals, thus using a broader spectrum of resources and affording greater economic security.

The complexity of the terrain and the variety of resource potentials it offers provide the key to their subsistence strategy. The Ariaal live in a semidesert environment with low and variable rainfall and marked seasonality; they "use their domesticated animals to convert patchy and seasonal vegetative resources into a constant supply of food in the form of milk, meat, blood, and a surplus with which to trade for grains, tea, and sugar." Water is clearly the factor that determines much of the Ariaal's herding activity and patterns of movement. The Ariaal have almost 10,000 square kilometers in which to herd, but this region is among the most arid in Kenya. The highlands receive an average of less than 500 millimeters (20 inches) of rainfall per year and the lowlands average 250 millimeters. The rainfall is erratic and irregular so that one cannot predict its occurrence or intensity. However, most rainfall occurs in two seasons: the "long rains" between March and May, and the "short rains" in October and Novem-

---

[2]The following account of the Ariaal is based on Elliot Fratkin's 1998 book, *Ariaal Pastoralists of Northern Kenya* (Boston: Allyn & Bacon).

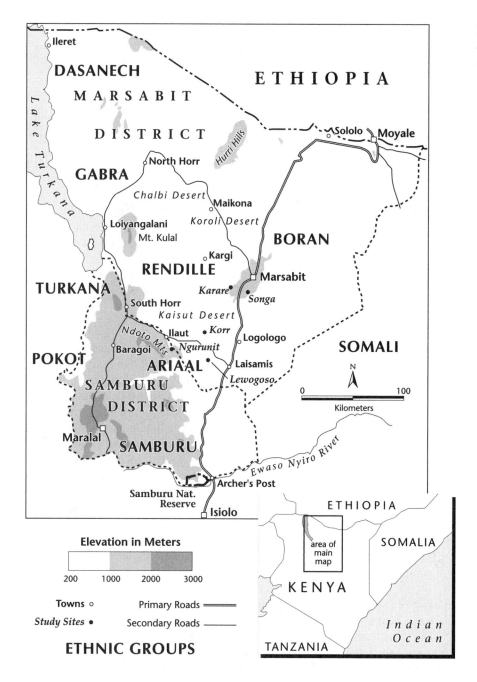

**Figure 5.4.** *Territory of the Ariaal, Samburu, and Rendille.*

ber. The periods between the two rainy seasons are called, very appropriately, the "long hunger" and the "short hunger."

During the wet seasons, provided the rains come as hoped, the Ariaal can use surface water in temporary floodplains, in pools, and in transient rivers. During the dry seasons, they must rely on hand-dug wells around the base of the mountains and a limited number of mechanized wells. They cannot, however, live or camp too near the water sources or their herds will destroy the vegetation.

The key to survival is herd diversity and mobility. Herd diversity allows a family to use different pastures and ensures against loss due to epidemics (p. 68); mobility is an effective adaptation to their arid environment, where rapid deterioration of vegetation for grazing requires regular herd movement. Moreover, vegetation is only rich in nutrients during the limited growing season.

***Diversity in Livestock.*** Ariaal herds generally consist of cattle, camels, and small stock such as sheep

*Elliot Fratkin with his field assistants Patrick Sunewan and Larian Aliayaro.*
(Elliot Fratkin)

and goats. Cattle, which are grass eaters and require water every two days, need to be kept in the highlands. Desert-adapted camels can go for days without water and eat leaves and shrub stems that do well when grasses are in decline. Sheep and goats do well in the desert but must be kept near water sources to meet their need for water every two days. Because of these different requirements, the animals are divided into domestic herds, which are kept near the settlements, and camp herds, which are taken great distances in search of grazing and water. The domestic herd usually contains stock that produces milk (cattle and camels), a few male camels and donkeys for transport, and some sheep and goats for meat and trade. The camp herd will contain the balance of the nonmilking animals.

In this harsh environment, a high rate of livestock mortality is a constant problem. In some years, the Ariaal may lose half their animals. The Ariaal have adapted, as have many East African pastoralists, by keeping a large number of diverse livestock. This is in contrast to many herders in better endowed regions, who generally prefer to concentrate on few species and to maintain their number at a lower level so that each animal is well fed. The Ariaal prefer female animals due to their reproductive and milk-producing capabilities. After a drought, females can replenish the diminished herd. Females also can supply the Ariaal with milk, which constitutes about 70% of the diet in the wet season. The balance of their diet is supplied by meat, purchased grains, and occasionally blood tapped from living animals.

Camels are the primary milk producers, particularly during the dry months when they continue to produce (unlike cattle, sheep, or goats). Unfortu-

nately, they are very slow to reproduce, and up to one third of their offspring may die. Like many East African herders, the Ariaal keep the East African breed of zebu cattle, which have a back hump to enable the animal to store calories in the form of fat. They cannot survive in the lowlands, and their milk production (in this very arid environment) is half that of camels. Still, they reproduce at least twice as fast as camels. One important function of cattle is to serve as exchange goods, particularly for wives, and as ritual sacrifices at weddings and so on. Cattle also are a major source of cash when sold to purchase store-bought maize meal—ground cornmeal, which is a crucial food item when milk is scarce.

The value of small stock cannot be underestimated in the household economy; some households have as many as 300 goats and sheep. Poor households tend to have proportionately more small stock. Camels and cattle, which are considered prestige items, are slow to reproduce and are expensive to buy. The Ariaal tend to prefer goats to sheep because they do better in the intense heat, but both animals reproduce rapidly and are easily sold or traded if the family needs cash. They are also a ready source of meat.

*Seasonal Movements.* Ariaal herding camps, in their search for graze and browse, disperse over a large area, particularly in the dry months of the year (October through February or March). In the driest months, the household breaks up into two quite different units. In one, the domestic settlement, the younger cattle, along with a few camels and goats and sheep, are maintained by older married men, women, and adolescent children of both sexes. Because the domestic herds have to be given water every two or three days, these settlements are often near trading centers and permanent sources of water.

The second unit, the stock camp, keeps the mature nonlactating cattle, camels, and some small stock far out on the plains or up in the Ndoto Mountains. The stock camp is staffed by young unmarried men, members of the warrior age grade, and older boys, who are faced with the dangerous and exhausting task of tending the camp herd. The herd must be continually moved over long distances during the day and guarded at night against human and other predators. The stock camp's personnel and their livestock may be drawn from as few as one or two households or as many as a dozen or so if a number of households lack sufficient labor to tend their own.

The cattle in the dry-season stock camps are mature animals strong enough to withstand the rigors of being herded to distant grazing areas and to require watering only every three days or so. Camels are usually herded separately in the desert plains. The fact that camels and goats browse on leaves and branches not only widens the resource base to include shrub land but very likely also keeps the thornbush from spreading at the expense of grass. In many of the drier parts of East Africa, thorn shrubs and trees of the genus *Acacia* are dominant over the grasses; by keeping the acacias in check, the browsing activities of goats help make possible the grazing activities of cattle (Conant, 1982).

The consumption of blood drawn from living cattle and other livestock is common in East Africa. Among the Ariaal, blood is regularly taken from all livestock. Men and older boys are responsible for bleeding cattle by shooting a blocked arrow into the jugular vein; the blood is then caught in containers. In the settlement camps, blood is usually mixed with milk, as women are not supposed to drink pure blood; the pure blood is consumed largely by the warriors in the stock camps, where there is little milk. Up to four liters may be drawn from a mature camel or oxen every three to four weeks.

The remote camps place the herders at some risk from raids by neighboring groups, who, much like the Ariaal themselves, are always searching for grazing and water resources in a region where both are diminishing. The neighbors of the Ariaal who might be in competition include the Turkana and the Boran. The Samburu and the Rendille are traditional allies, and their frequent sharing of water and grass resources is facilitated by gift-giving and marriage exchanges. It is when the dry season is prolonged that the risk of conflict or the weakening of established ties is greatest.

## The Household: Organization and Status

The economy and social life are rooted in the household. Fratkin puts it this way: "An Ariaal household can be defined as the smallest domestic group with its own livestock and which makes decisions over allocation of labor and livestock capital. Daily life and social interaction are focused on the household and the settlement in which it is located" (1998, p. 99). The settlement consists of independent households who, whether temporarily or not, live together; usually, the settlements are composed of patrilineally related men and their families.

Households are typically headed by a married male stock owner and include his wife or cowives, children, and occasionally a dependent mother-in-law or married daughter who has not yet joined her husband's village. Each married woman is responsible for building and maintaining her own house; consequently, an individual household may consist of three or four houses including two cowives, a widowed mother, or a poor affine (in-law) and their children. While household maintenance takes some time, most settlement life revolves around animal care. Just as in the distant herding camps, animal care in the community involves a great deal of cooperation in watering and grazing the animals.

From one season to the next, each household can drastically alter its herding strategy and change herding partners. A large household (one with several wives and married sons) may split up into smaller units, which then scatter over thousands of square miles of rangeland. Ties of kinship are obviously more difficult to maintain and manipulate among pastoralists than they are in the more densely populated and far more stable farming areas. In such circumstances, people tend to establish extra-descent group ties through the device of **age grades**. An age grade consists of people of the same sex and approximately the same age who share a set of duties and privileges.

Among the Ariaal, there is a great deal of variation among households due to the domestic cycle, and this is amplified by variability in inherited wealth. Some men gain larger herds than they can manage with their labor. Others may not have enough to support themselves and be forced to work for other households to buy animals and build up their own herds.

## The Age Grades and Age Sets

The Ariaal age grade and age set systems, like those of many other East African peoples, are highly complex institutions with multiple functions. These systems are widespread throughout East Africa and are particularly prominent among such pastoral groups as the Ariaal, Rendille, Samburu, Turkana, and Pokot. Among the Ariaal, the age grades serve primarily to organize labor and structure politics. Men pass through different age grades as members of named cohorts or **age sets** that are formed every fourteen years.

Males are divided into boys, warriors, and elders; females into young girls, adolescent girls, and circumcised (by clitoridectomy) married women. Each age grade has its distinct insignia and rules about what it can and cannot wear, what foods it may consume, and with whom it may associate. Each grade is also associated with particular rights, duties, and obligations. Age grades determine the formal political structure, and the system is based on the primacy of elder males over younger males and men over women. Elders are the heads of households and function as the leaders of the tribe.

The warriors are responsible for herding and spend approximately fourteen years as herdsmen caring for animals in the stock camps. They grow their hair into long red-dyed plaits and may not eat food that has been even seen by women. When young men between the ages of eleven and twelve are initiated into the warrior grade together, they will mark this by being circumcised as a group and given a group name that they will use for life, and which will, even subsequent to the death of the last member, be used to identify historical periods.

Adolescent girls are responsible for tending the small stock near the settlements and are forbidden to associate with any married men—even their own fathers. When they move into the "married woman" stage, they become dependent members of their husband's household and lineage. Adolescent boys and married elders may milk camels, but women and warriors may not. These and many other ritual prohibitions, rights, and duties sort society into specific work groups.

The Ariaal rise through the age grades with a specific cohort of their contemporaries that is separately named and that stays together for life. Progression through the age grades is automatic, and it is assumed that each member of an age grade will be able to perform the age-appropriate role. The age grades through which age sets pass are effective ways to organize labor. Age sets also provide the basis for exchanges and alliances that cut across the boundaries of patrilineal clans and lineages. Men, for example, form close friendships with age set mates and exchange gifts of cattle and small stock; they may even take up residence in a settlement belonging to another clan by using the age set connection.

*Ariaal share the same age-set system as Samburu. Here, members of the warrior age-grade dance outside their clan settlement.*

(Elliot Fratkin)

## Gender Roles and Power

Clearly, social and economic roles are allocated according to gender as well as age among the Ariaal. The division of labor starts very early and lasts until death. By age two or three, girls and boys are encouraged to participate in symbolic activities that quickly become gender-specific tasks. Girls play at such chores as gathering sticks for fuel, carrying water, milking, and gathering food. Boys play at tending livestock, hunting, making spears and bows and arrows, and being warriors. By the time they reach age four or five, their play has become work. The small amount of water children can carry and the help they can give in managing livestock soon become measurable contributions to a household's energy budget. The children soon add the care of younger children to their tasks. Although women are responsible for their own infants, almost all child care is in the hands of slightly older children and of some elderly men and women.

Ariaal women and girls commonly milk all of the domestic cattle, sheep, and goats. Women supervise or carry out gathering the firewood, the grass for thatching, and the thornbush needed to build and repair houses and fences. They haul water to the homestead, while men dig the step wells. Among the Ariaal, the men exclusively tend camels, as well as all animals sent to distant pastures. Men are also responsible for butchering livestock. The Ariaal cut the throats of goats, but cattle are often killed with spears in the context of a ritual.

Women play critical roles in economic life; indeed, their labor and reproduction are essential to the household's well-being and the social standing of its male head. This is reflected in both the idealization and practice of polygyny. More than half the households contain cowives. At marriage, a woman's father is given a customary "bridewealth" payment of eight cattle. Shortly thereafter, she joins her husband, who is of another lineage and thus another settlement. If her husband dies, she will still live with her husband's lineage and may bear children fathered by his younger brother (this is called *levirate fatherhood*). It is very hard for a woman to return to her natal settlement should she wish to divorce or move after a husband's death; her family would have to return the cattle they had received.

Ariaal women are virtually powerless in the formal political arena. They may not participate in public discussion, where decisions affecting the group are usually made consensually by elder males. They also have very little economic power. Although her husband will "give" her a herd of milking stock to tend, she may not sell or dispose of them. She does

Ariaal woman milking her goat. As with many East African people, small animals are predominately the concern of women.
(Elliot Fratkin)

control the house itself, since she builds and repairs it. All animals are male-owned; all food, in principle at least, is controlled by her father or husband. She will not inherit either from her father or husband. All livestock passes to the male children. Thus, the work a young man does for his elders is eventually paid for in the form of gifts or inheritances. Women receive no compensation for their labor.

## Can the Ariaal Survive Development?

Until quite recently, the Ariaal lived in a situation of benign neglect as far as the outside world was concerned. Ariaal pastoralism traditionally was dependent on the local ecosystem, constrained by the availability of water and the range of environments that could be exploited by mixed herds of goats, cattle, and camels. They had close relationships with the Rendille and Samburu, with whom they intermarried, traded, and sometimes competed. Until Kenya attained independence from Great Britain in 1963, the Ariaal were fairly self-sufficient, trading with neighbors when necessary. Responses to external events were relatively rare. But since independence, such external factors as government-provided health and education services, famine relief, and the construction of wells and roads have forced basic changes in their way of life, especially among those living near administrative centers and missions. Many missions have opened schools with the explicit

## Box 5.1

# The Situation of Pastoralists Today

PASTORALIST SOCIETIES FACE MORE threats to their way of life today than at any previous time, and it is not clear what form that way of life will take, if indeed it survives, in this century. Population growth, loss of herding lands to private farms, ranches, game parks, and urban areas, increased commoditization of the livestock economy, outmigration by poor pastoralists, and periodic dislocations brought about by drought, famine, and civil war are increasing in pastoralist regions of the world. However, pastoral populations continue to herd their animals in the world's arid regions, and in China and Mongolia, pastoral production is increasing as these economies decentralize and expand their markets.

There has recently been more attention paid to pastoralist and livestock production by international development agencies including the World Bank and USAID, as livestock is recognized as an important and valuable commodity in the world's markets. Moreover, in regions such as Africa, livestock is seen as an important resource to feed the rapidly growing human population. Western development planners, however, see communal herding over large open areas as deleterious to the range, leading to overgrazing and environmental degradation. Many development projects attempt to limiting herd size by increasing livestock marketing, using Western models of individual commercial ranches. Although these policies have benefited some individual ranchers, they have

been harmful to societies that relied on open or communal grazing systems, such as the Maasai of Kenya and Tanzania.

*Maasai Pastoralism.* Few African societies have been as romanticized and popularized by Europeans and Americans, while simultaneously neglected and underdeveloped, as the Maasai. Despite their image as "free and noble warriors," the Maasai have seen their grazing lands continuously reduced by colonial appropriation, the creation of national game parks, the steady incursions of agriculturalists, and most recently, by the creation of private titles to individual ranches that are dividing the remaining land.

The Maasai are a population of over 350,000 residing in Kenya and Tanzania, herding their large herds of cattle in the broad savanna regions that are also home to Africa's largest herds of wildebeest, giraffe, and lions. Never a single political entity, the Maasai are composed of a dozen independent groups, including the Kisongo of Tanzania, and Purko, Loita, Matapato, Kaputei, Sikiari, Loitokitok, Damat, Keekonyukie, ilKankeri, and Lo'odokilani Maasai of Kenya (Spear & Waller, 1993).

In the nineteenth century, Maasailand stretched in an hourglass shape from present-day northern Kenya to central Tanzania. Colonial intrusion cut Maasailand between British Kenya and German Tanganyika in 1885, and again in 1911 when the British pushed the Kenyan Maasai south of Nairobi

on to a single reserve in southern Kenya, as European settlers took the most important Maasai water and grazing lands for their farms and ranches. Confined to 35,000 square kilometers in Kenya and 60,000 square kilometers in Tanzania (60% of their precolonial range), the Maasai were further restricted from grazing their cattle in the large game reserves including the vast Serengeti Park and Ngorongoro Crater in Tanzania and, in Kenya, the Nairobi National Park, Amboseli, Tsavo, Mara Masai, and Samburu Game Parks.

The Maasai also faced competition for land by both expanding agriculturalists and commercial enterprises that were creating grain and dairy estates, particularly after independence in Kenya in 1963. Poor Kikuyu and Kamba farmers, displaced by European farms in the highlands, moved onto Maasai lands, while large wheat growing or commercial beef ranches took large areas of Maasai lands in both Kenya and Tanzania. The increased commercial activity in both Tanzanian and Kenyan Maasailand is leading to an increased polarization between rich and poor, with a wealthy few able to purchase land titles and cattle while many poorer and landless Maasai end up as herding laborers or migrants to urban areas. Today, the Maasai are seeing their land steadily reduced by expansion of farmers and game parks as Kenya and Tanzania seek to increase their foreign revenue earnings, at the expense of traditional grazing rights by Maasai and other

aim of separating children from their traditional religious beliefs (and hence their native culture). Missions and national and international agencies have all intervened in ways that threaten the delicate balanc-

ing act that has so long enabled the Ariaal to survive droughts and epidemics.

Since the Kenyan government opened the region to foreign missionaries in the 1970s, dozens of

pastoralists (Galaty, 1994; McCabe et al., 1992).

Lack of education is also a major problem. As with the Ariaal and other East African pastoralist groups, Maasai youths win respect by doing "warrior service" guarding livestock, and until recently, it was customary to send the brightest Maasai boys into the bush to tend the herds because it takes considerable skill to find water, fend off predators, and keep track of the animals; the rest are sent to school. Consequently, barely one Maasai in ten can read. This, together with dwindling pasture and fewer and fewer livestock to tend, puts the Maasai at a significant disadvantage in the "Information Age." However, a group of educated Maasai are now organizing informal classes in the bush. In one district, 1,800 boys and youths have been taught basic literacy, Swahili, English, and math. Of these, about 100 have gone on to the formal education system, and the rest are now able to read instructions in English on packages of veterinary drugs and other items (*The Economist,* 2002a). In a situation where there are frequently more herders than animals, many young men now aspire to jobs in the wider society.

*Mongolia.* A different situation of market integration is emerging in the formerly socialist economies of Mongolia and China. Recent changes, including decollectivization of pastoral property and increased market participation, have led to radical transformations in livestock pastoralism, including the revitalization of presocialist forms of organizations and the reintroduction of private ownership of livestock resources.

Mongolia is a vast (1.6 million square kilometers) but underpopulated country in Central Asia of 2.2 million people owning 25 million animals including camels, goats, sheep, cattle, yaks, and the famous horses that made the Mongols a world power under Genghis Khan in the twelfth century. In the last century, Mongolia became the world's second Communist state following a revolution in 1921, receiving technical, financial, and ideological support from the Soviet Union. Following a disastrous attempt at forced collectivization that was quickly abandoned, communal cooperatives (*negdel*) were encouraged on a voluntary basis in the 1950s. These cooperatives were welcomed by wealthier stock owners who had large labor needs and where herding households were enabled to pool funds to bore wells, buy haymaking equipment, and build winter shelters for animals.

Until decollectivization in 1991, half of the Mongolian population lived in the capital of Ulan Bator and a few other towns as state employees. But pastoralism provided over half of the GDP (gross domestic product) and 40% of the total exports of the country in the 1980s, and domestic milk and meat consumption is among the highest in the world (Potkanski, 1993).

Following the collapse of the Soviet Union in 1991, Mongolia underwent significant economic and political reform. The state retreated from direct involvement in production, and prices were freed from previous controls. Following World Bank recommendations to increase privatization, *negdel* cooperatives transformed into joint stock companies, which quickly fragmented into privatized companies and

household enterprises. With increased sales of beef and wool to China, the pastoral economy grew. Urban wage-earners, many no longer employed by state bureaucracies or enterprises, moved back to the countryside to join their pastoral families. Where in 1990 state collectives owned 68% of all livestock, by 1994, 90% of the animals were privately owned (Mearns, 1996).

This period has seen a renewed strengthening of the *khot ails,* prerevolutionary herding groups of two to ten households, related by kinship and who act again as a basic social and economic group in Mongolian society. The *khot ail* acts as a social safety net for poorer rural households, providing forms of mutual assistance and pooling risk between households, including sharing food resources as well as long-term loans of livestock. Mongolians have also developed grassroots organizations (*khorshoo*), which are neither customary nor state-inspired institutions, but marketing cooperatives seeking transport and trade with China and elsewhere (Potkanski, 1993).

Although pastoral production is firmly back in the hands of independent household groups, pastoral land is specifically excluded from private ownership. Of Mongolia's total land, 79% is under pasture and is the largest area of common grazing land in the world (Mearns, 1996). This continued public ownership of grazing resources, combined with private ownership of livestock, distinguishes Mongolia from other pastoralist regions, particularly in Africa and the Middle East.

Christian mission stations have appeared. The government and the missionaries, despite very different ideologies, share the view that pastoralism is a primitive, backward way of life and that people should be settled in towns (Fratkin, 1998, p. 111). Although the missionaries wish to make converts, the government's policy is based on the notion that pastoralism is incompatible with a modern society and maintaining tight control over its citizens. Whatever the goals, moving pastoralists to towns is problematic in an arid region that cannot support an agricultural subsistence pattern.

One means by which the pastoralists are brought into larger settlements is through food subsidies or handouts. This is a practice used to gain converts in many parts of the world by many different religions. The insidious aspect of this approach is that people quickly incorporate the cheap or free food into their domestic economy, soon becoming dependent and losing their traditional self-sufficiency. As a result, many Ariaal families are camping near mission stations. Often, households split, with one wife and her children living near town and the second wife staying with the husband in the traditional settlement.

Paradoxically, a further problem involves efforts to promote conservation. Many people automatically blame nomadic pastoralists for overgrazing and the spread of desertification. In fact, the Ariaal system of production prior to the settlement of communities near the missions and administrative centers was entirely conservationist in effect. Animals were moved regularly to follow the major peaks in vegetative production; they were not kept on declining pastures or browses, which would be counterproductive. However, the handouts and restrictions on land use have led to overgrazing of land near mission- and government-created towns.

Elliot Fratkin, although pessimistic about the future of the Ariaal people's traditional economy, does see hope in their natural resilience and ability to respond to changing circumstances. He has some practical suggestions that, if adopted, could improve their chances as Kenya continues to develop a modern infrastructure.

1. Development planners need to appreciate the sophistication of adaptive systems, which, like those of the Ariaal, have developed over long periods of time.

2. Planners should concentrate on assisting animal production through veterinary services and pest control, rather than trying to curtail production to reduce herd size.

3. Grazing restrictions should be lifted because they interfere with herd dispersal, the ecologically and economically sound practice of grazing many herds over a wide area.

4. The market economy would be enhanced by improvements in transportation, auction facilities, and information and by deregulating animal prices.

Lugi Lengesen, Fratkin's close friend among the Ariaal, sums up his prospects for the future. "This is not good land to grow corn or raise gardens. That is something people in the south know how to do very well. But we Ariaal know how to grow our cattle and camels, we know this land because it is our farm. Give us veterinary medicines for our animals, medicine for our infants, schools to educate our children in livestock and health, and markets and transportation to sell our animals. Then places like Korr can become beautiful."

## The Yörük of Turkey

The Yörük are transhumant sheepherders who move their flocks back and forth between two grazing zones in southeastern Turkey. In winter, they camp on low plains on what is geographically an extension of the Syrian steppe. In spring, when the weather warms, they move the herds inland some 100 kilometers (62 miles) to craggy, mountainous summer pasturelands. Traditionally, the Yörük kept camels to transport their belongings during migrations; their economy was based on the sale of sheep and sheep products (Bates, 1973). Today, the nomadic Yörük use trucks and tractor-drawn wagons to move their flocks and possessions. The Yörük's sheep, unlike the Ariaal's stock, serve almost exclusively as the capital basis for market production. Although the nomadic Yörük do eat some of their animal products—milk, butter, cheese, and yogurt—for the most part these products, along with wool and male lambs, are sold. And with the money they receive, the Yörük buy their necessities—chiefly the agricultural products that constitute most of their diet.

This, then, is not a subsistence economy. The Yörük are completely dependent on a market economy not only to sell their animal products and buy their food but also to rent the lands on which they graze their sheep. They actively use the market system to increase their holdings in livestock, to accumulate cash to buy consumer goods, and even to acquire land or urban houses. As a result, even relatively small fluctuations in market prices can bankrupt a household—or make it rich.

When wealth and poverty were relatively temporary conditions, and when each household expected to increase its herds over time, the society was relatively egalitarian. By and large, no one family or elite group held substantial economic or political power over others. This is the situation among many herding peoples because the volatility of animal capital works against the long-term perpetuation of rule by a special class within their society. Today, the situation among the Yörük is changing. Poverty is no

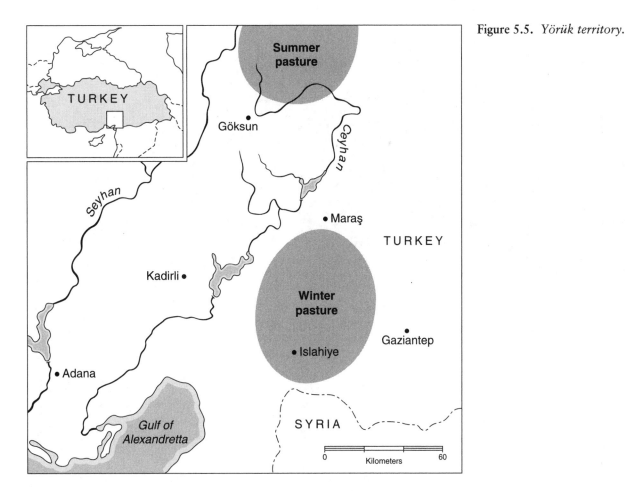

**Figure 5.5.** *Yörük territory.*

longer a temporary condition among herders, and the group of well-to-do merchant families who have emerged in recent years may constitute a distinctly privileged group.

## The Market Economy

The market economy is part of the Yörük way of life. All transactions are made on the basis of established market values, even when goods and services are bartered. If a Yörük family trades wool for tobacco, for example, the exchange is made according to the relative market value of each item. Supply and demand within a particular area can alter the values, of course, but such variations only restructure market prices to fit local conditions. The vast majority of transactions, however, involve cash or promissory notes. Often, a herd owner will contract to supply animals or milk at a future date, accepting an advance payment in cash. Fluctuations in the market prices of animal products, of the foods the Yörük buy, and of the land they rent become significant problems to which they must continually respond.

While the Yörük are dependent on the market, they are just as dependent on other groups: the condition of the crops grown by those other groups, their needs, and the value they place on their own and the Yörük's goods. For the Yörük, the presence of other groups constitutes an all-important environmental variable that shapes their economic decisions at every turn.

Probably the most significant feature of such interactions is the Yörük's reliance on other groups for pastureland. Unlike the Ariaal, for example, the Yörük do not own or even have traditional claims to the pastures they use; they must rent them. In some cases, they also have to pay for access to lands along the migration route, although not when they move the animals by truck. Thus, although the outer limit of their migration schedule is established largely by climate and topography, political and social factors help determine the actual schedule. When Yörük herd owners want to move their animals, they must take into account the wishes of the people who own the land that the animals must cross. This land is predominantly agricultural. The pastoralists would prefer to keep the animals longer in the lowland

*In the 1960s traditional Yörük marriage customs began to change, reflecting changing in the larger Turkish culture. The two couples here reflect this in their attire and lifestyles.*
(Daniel Bates)

plains, but herd movement too late in the season would cause extensive crop damage. They would prefer to return to the plains earlier in the fall if they did not have to wait for the harvest.

As one might expect, disputes often develop between pastoralists and agriculturalists over crop damages. In recent years, the Turkish government has intervened to regulate the herd migrations and to see that all claims for crop damage are satisfied. Without governmental regulation, some agricultural lands would probably have to be abandoned because damage would be too frequent and too costly. This was a common problem in the past. Each annual migration, then, is a complex strategy determined by the availability of grass, planting or harvest schedules, and the restrictions set by the government.

## Social Organization

As with the Ariaal, the composition of Yörük camp groups changes regularly. As many as twenty households or as few as two may camp together; larger clusters generally gather in the summer pasture areas. Although in some pastoral societies (such as the Ariaal) the labor of herding is pooled among members of a camp group, the Yörük household is in effect a self-contained producing unit: It relies almost exclusively on its own labor. The rental of pasture-

lands is an important function of the larger camp group. Though the families that make up the camp do not generally pool their labor, they do pool money to rent their grazing lands jointly.

The composition of a camp group depends on several factors but not on the same kind of rigid rules that govern Ariaal camp groups. Kinship is one such factor. The Yörük place great emphasis on patrilineage, and often, families that camp together are patrilineally related. Some households, however, camp with people more closely related to the wife than to the husband. Sometimes this arrangement simply reflects the woman's wish to be with her sisters or brothers for a season or two. Or it may be a way for the family to secure better grazing than they could get by cooperating with the husband's patrilineal relatives. In other cases, family quarrels may be the determining factor. Thus, while kinship to some degree determines the camp membership, sentiment and economic strategy keep such communities flexible.

## Adapting to a Changing Economy

Since the mid-1990s, the Yörük have had to face a variety of new situations. One major problem is inflation, which has affected the entire country. Although rental fees for pastures have gone up rapidly, so have the prices of animal products. This development has resulted in a significant transformation of Yörük society. Generally speaking, small animal husbandry has enabled them to cope with a changing economy better than most other groups. At the same time, new developments in mechanized transport and in the opening of new markets in the oil-rich Arab world have created new possibilities for some Yörük.

*New Strategies.* The Yörük today practice three adaptive strategies: nomadic pastoralism, sedentary agriculture, and trade or shopkeeping in town. The nomads have developed a very specialized adaptation, engaging in animal husbandry and trading in animals and animal products. At the same time, entire villages of settled Yörük now engage in agriculture, shopkeeping, and commerce. The ability of the Yörük to adapt to their changing environment is evident by looking at some of their activities. Some, for example, operate mobile dairies and follow the herders, buying their milk and converting it to cheese for urban markets. During the Iran–Iraq war in the 1980s, those that owned trucks transported goods to the war-torn countries. Today, some Yörük have become brokers, buying large numbers of animals and shipping them to distant markets in Arab lands where meat is in great demand. Very frequently, entrepreneurs engage in several of these activities simultaneously, coordinating their ventures in town and only sometimes camping in tents.

One point must be stressed. Yörük society, like most others, is changing rapidly, and the challenge to the ethnographer is to describe a way of life without implying that what is observed is a timeless pattern. I first went to southeastern Turkey in 1968, but few of my initial economic observations still hold today. Culturally, too, the Yörük are changing. In 1968, patterns of male–female interactions, recreation, and socializing were very different. Now even pastoral households have access to television sets, refrigerators, and other modern appliances. They usually keep them in village or town dwellings, where they spend part of each year and where children of school age live while attending school.

While the nomadic herders and the new class of businessmen and farmers are economically distinct,

*In spring, the Yörük move their animals and camps to high mountain pastures. Today, this move is usually made by trucks carrying both sheep and herders.*

(Daniel Bates)

they differ little in cultural identity and there is no antipathy between them. After all, they are all Yörük. Some of the strategies are actually complementary. The town-based businessmen often depend on the herders for their trade, while the herders depend on the small businessmen for the credit they need to continue herding in a volatile market economy. The different strategies are also interrelated in that families move from one to another as circumstances warrant. Many people who were settled in a town when I revisited the area in 1978 were once again living in tents in 1983. While they had liked town life, they decided they could make more money raising livestock than selling shoes. Today, wealth or access to capital determines whether a household herds or settles down to other endeavors.

In 1978, and later in 1983, I found that the herders who were using trucks to transport their animals between pastures no longer migrated as a group. Herding had become a form of ranching, where the "ranch" consists of many pastures used sequentially, as sheep are trucked among them. The contemporary Yörük household stays behind in a town or village, leaving herding to the menfolk or hired shepherds. In fact, by the end of the century, some herders were making so much money from animal export that they could afford to rent wheat fields and turn them into pastures and thus could spend most of the year in one place.

Today, far fewer families are being supported by pastoralism, and those few are the better-off members of the society. The majority of households that had been nomadic in 1968–1970 have settled in villages and towns as laborers and tenant farmers, unable to continue making their living in the traditional way because of the rising costs of pasture and feed. Some are living precariously; those who had invested what they had in a shop or some other business have generally prospered.

The adaptation of the Yörük, then, is a matter not simply of accommodating to the physical environment but of finding a niche in a larger social system. To understand even their pastoral economy, we must take into account who owns what. Likewise, it is impossible to discuss the specialization of nomadic pastoralism among the Yörük without reference to other specializations within the larger society on which the Yörük depend for trade. Thus, the effective environment of the Yörük has a political and social dimension as well as a physical and biological one.

*Increasing Stratification.* Wealth is no longer spread evenly among the Yörük. The new economic system has transformed a generally egalitarian society to one that is decidedly stratified. The poorer herders, those with just enough animals to make

herding viable, are often in debt and seldom have the ready cash they need to rent pastureland, pay for winter grains, or more recently, hire truck transport. To pay debts accumulated during the winter, they are forced to shear their sheep at the beginning of spring. But early shearing leaves them at a disadvantage in the migration to high pastures: They must wait longer before leaving, as shorn sheep are vulnerable to disease in snow and extreme cold. When they finally do leave, they may travel over lands already grazed by sheep belonging to wealthier herd owners who could afford to forgo an early shearing. The poor grazing leaves the last flocks tired and hungry by the time they reach summer pasture. The sheep of the poorer herd owners are more likely to die during migration than those of the wealthier ones. The affluent herders not only have healthier sheep, but they are also able to transport animals to choice but distant grazing areas.

Even after selling their spring wool, many Yörük herders do not usually have the cash necessary to rent summer pasture. Needing an additional source of income or credit, many supplement their income by selling milk to the mobile dairy tents that follow the flocks. Many of these dairies are owned by the wealthier herders, who have established dairies and have bought stores and land in an attempt to diversify. Just as there is a limit below which a flock is not economically viable, there is an upper limit as well. Huge numbers of animals require a large deployment of labor, so the wealthy can only increase their wealth through diversification once their herds reach an optimal size.

The dairies are rather sizable enterprises with a ready supply of capital that enables them not only to buy the herders' milk but to purchase it in advance. Such milk futures are purchased at a relatively low price, but they give the poorer herders the money they need for pasture rental. Once the dairymen have the milk, they process it into cheese and sell it for a substantial profit in urban markets. Thus, the dairies allow the herders to fend off bankruptcy at the same time that they yield high profits to the dairymen.

It is easy to see that such a system encourages **economic stratification**, the creation of increasingly fixed classes of rich and poor. In the past, the Yörük had no such permanent economic groups. As long as the people remained herders, they could expect to go from rags to riches and back again several times in the course of their lives because animals are such a volatile form of capital. But once the temporarily wealthy began to invest in more fixed forms of capital such as farms, shops, and dairies, their wealth ceased to be temporary, and indeed, it began to increase. The increase in wealth enabled them to settle down. The traditional way of life—nomadic,

## Box 5.2

# Resourceful Pastoralists:
# Building an Oasis

ALTHOUGH WE HAVE DISTIN-guished pastoralists from farmers, from an economic point of view many local populations had both farming and pastoral communities, such as the Baluch, Qashqa'i, Türk-men, and others. Even families, as we have noted, may shift back and forth between pastoralism and farming. Emmanuel Marx (1999) gives an interesting account for the Negev and incidentally shows how oases themselves come into being.

We usually associate the Bedouin with nomadic pastoralism, but in reality, most Bedouin today are sedentary farmers. Also, many regularly alternate between herding, farming, and wage labor depending on market conditions, availability of work, and political security. In the South Sinai, for example, tribally organized Bedouin, today numbering some 10,000, in addition to herding have long been highly skilled horticulturists, specialists in well-digging, grafting and pruning fruit trees, and expert in pollinating date palms (Marx, 1999). They not only inhabit the oases of this geographically complex and varied re-

gion, but they also create them. As Marx explains, the oasis is a human artifact, established for particular purposes. He distinguishes five varieties, including large ones, with settled year-round residents, similar to those found in North Africa and in Arabia, those established primarily for purposes of smuggling, and still others that are little more than small orchards visited only periodically by families who rely on wage labor or herding.

Although the pattern of land use has changed greatly in recent years, in large part due to the Israeli occupation, which ended in 1982, the Bedouin have a long history of horticulture, probably acquiring their skills while employed by the monks of St. Catherine's monastery, which is itself a major oasis dating back to the sixth century A.D.

Today, most Bedouin families have claims to orchards, even though few rely exclusively on them for income. Each tribe has a known territory within which members are free to develop such sites as are not already occupied. If a particular site of cultivation or oasis is left to de-

teriorate, it may be assumed to have been abandoned.

The first step in establishing an oasis is to identify the surface features that indicate water might be present. Then a well is dug, a laborious and sometimes risky task, followed by perhaps more wells, all to be enclosed by a stone wall indicating that it is being developed. The final steps are to level the surface, bring in topsoil from the mountain slopes to mix with clay, and erect a counterbalanced water hoist (*shaduf*).

For many families the oasis so created is something of a summer home, to be visited for a few months, and the fruit and vegetables raised are a welcome but secondary element in the household economy. Some 300 or more people may gather in a large oasis, but relatively few reside there throughout the year. The largest palm oases have been built or expanded in recent years using the proceeds of smuggling or tourism to employ mechanized well-diggers and pumps.

---

egalitarian—is slowly giving way to a more complex, stratified pattern with a variety of strategies feeding into one another and reinforcing economic differences.

### Future Prospects

In many respects, the Yörük are prospering in the rapidly developing domestic economy of modern Turkey, since animal production is a profitable endeavor. Few families still live in the traditional tent—at least not throughout the year. They now live in town, and the children are attending schools. However, many of the young among the Yörük are abandoning the pastoral lifestyle and moving to Ankara, the capital, or to Istanbul, which is now

swollen to more than 13 million people. Some have migrated, legally or not, to Europe or the United States to secure a better future.

The reasons the Yörük would leave a region in which their main subsistence strategy seems to be working very well are quite simple. With over two thirds of the population below the age of twenty, the local economy cannot absorb all of them into the work force. Education and access to information about the rest of the world give rise to demands for a standard of living and consumer items that cannot be met through local wage employment. Finally, pastoralism is now a highly specialized and capitalized mode of production and is engaged in by fewer and fewer households, each managing larger and larger herds.

## *Summary*

PASTORALISTS ENGAGE IN ANIMAL HUSBANDRY: THE breeding, care, and use of herd animals such as sheep, goats, camels, cattle, horses, reindeer, or yaks. Most pastoralists in nonindustrial societies are nomadic. Both the mobility of pastoralists and the degree to which they rely on animal husbandry vary with environmental, social, and economic conditions. Few pastoralist groups rely exclusively on their herds; they tend to pursue a more generalized subsistence strategy.

Nomads follow two basic patterns: horizontal migration, characterized by regular movement over a large area in search of fodder, and transhumance, or seasonal movement between upland and lowland pastures.

Specialized pastoralism, or exclusive reliance on animal husbandry, may have developed from a farming/herding pattern. Changes in agricultural practices, such as the use of canal irrigation, may have pushed grazing lands farther from settlements. The consequent increased demands of both herding and agriculture may have led some families to specialize in agriculture and others to choose herding exclusively. The divergence of strategies may have been encouraged by the failure of irrigation for some groups. Extensive irrigation may cause the water table (the level of water under the earth) to fall, or it may increase the salinity of the soil until crops no longer thrive.

Although pastoralism is a relatively efficient means of extracting energy from a harsh environment, it produces less energy per acre of land than agriculture, and population densities are correspondingly low. Pastoralism is an alternative to agriculture, but it is almost never independent of it. If pastoralists don't raise vegetable foods, they acquire them through trade.

In nonindustrial societies, sedentary pastoralism, or animal husbandry that does not involve mobility, is generally rare. The usual pattern is nomadic pastoralism—the practice of moving one's herds from pasture to pasture as the seasons and circumstances require. The main reason that pastoralists migrate is to secure adequate grazing land in a marginal environment. However, migration may also be a means to maintain political autonomy or even to control settled groups. The composition of local groupings in pastoral societies often shifts as nomadic camping units move, break apart, and come together with other units.

Virtually all pastoral populations are organized in tribes, communities of people who claim kinship, usually by descent from one or more common ancestors. Tribal organization provides for positions of leadership and allows for coordination of social and economic activities.

The basic economic unit is the household. Households may move frequently one year and be largely sedentary the next. One household may herd alone, while others may temporarily combine forces. Families may shift between agriculture and herding, or they may give up herding for other pursuits such as shopkeeping.

The Ariaal of Kenya maintain a subsistence economy through a balanced and diversified strategy of keeping cattle, camels, and small stock (sheep and goats). The Ariaal display many aspects of the East African cattle complex, a socioeconomic system in which cattle represent social status as well as wealth. The cattle play a significant symbolic role in social ties, obligations, and rituals. The traditional bridewealth is eight head of cattle given to the father of the bride-to-be.

The basic unit of social organization is the household. A household consists of one or more houses belonging to the wife or wives of the male head of household. Households are located in settlements usually belonging to one patrilineal clan, a large group whose common descent is traced through the paternal line. The Ariaal marry out of their natal clans and, to some extent, intermarry with the neighboring Rendille and Samburu. The groom's family gives bridewealth to the bride's family to compensate them for the loss of their daughter's services. The labor of women and girls is crucial to the functioning of households. Men tend the camels, as well as manage the family's livestock on distant grazing and browse lands.

The Ariaal are organized in age grades, each grade consisting of people of the same sex and approximately the same age, who share a set of duties, prohibitions, symbols, and privileges. Most important, age grades structure the organization of labor. Young men of the warrior grade, for example, will spend approximately fourteen years as herdsmen caring for the animals in the stock camps, which are distant from the households' main settlement residence. After completing their duties, the same named set of men will all become elders.

Although the Ariaal have survived drought and famine because of their ability to simultaneously exploit a number of species of livestock and different microenvironments in their 10,000 square kilometer range, they may not be able to withstand development. Northern Kenya has seen a great deal of missionary and governmental activity aimed at settling the pastoralists and, for rather different reasons, changing the Ariaal way of life. The pastoralists (as with other such populations in East Africa) are becoming dependent on food subsidies and handouts; their traditional grazing areas are restricted and their herds are limited in size.

The Yörük of southeastern Turkey traditionally have been nomadic pastoralists who move their sheep between summer and winter pastures. The Yörük are dependent on a market economy to sell their animal products, buy their food, and rent the lands on which they graze their sheep. The activities of the Yörük are shaped not only by climate and topography but also by political and social factors; the strategy of their migrations is determined by the availability of grass, village planting or harvest schedules, and the restrictions on migration set by the government.

Yörük social organization is flexible. The composition of a camp group may be determined by kinship, sentiment, or economic strategy. Each family within the camp group is a self-sufficient producing unit, although the camp group does rent pastureland jointly.

In recent years, the nature of animal husbandry has changed. The rents charged for pastureland have risen, but new opportunities have also opened up. Now many Yörük avail themselves of truck transport and sell animals in Arab countries. As a result, they now practice diverse and complementary strategies: sedentary agriculture, trade, brokerage, and shopkeeping, as well as pastoralism. Until recently, wealth determined whether a household herded or settled down. The rich herders tended to diversify into trading or farming, while the poor struggled to keep their herds. Although some of the poorest herders of earlier years have become rich in today's market, this economic system has created increasingly fixed classes of rich and poor for the first time in Yörük society.

## Key Terms

| | |
|---|---|
| age grade | nomadic pastoralism |
| age set | oasis |
| animal husbandry | sedentary pastoralism |
| cattle complex | segmentary lineage |
| clan | specialized pastoralism |
| economic stratification | transhumance |
| horizontal migration | |

## Suggested Readings

Abu-Lughod, L. (1988). *Veiled sentiments: Honor and poetry in a Bedouin society.* Berkeley and Los Angeles: University of California Press. A person-centered ethnography of a community of Bedouins in the western desert of Egypt that focuses on the oral lyric poetry that is used by women and young men in this once nomadic but still pastoral society.

Beck, L. (1992). *Nomad: A year in the life of a Qashqa'i tribesman in Iran.* New Haven, CT: Yale University Press. This political ethnography of elites is a historical and anthropological account of the Turkic-speaking Qashqa'i. The Qashqa'i are a predominantly pastoral nomadic people, but they have highly developed sociopolitical institutions, including a ruling elite that has participated in national and international politics.

Bishop, N. H. (1998). *Himalayan herders: Case studies in cultural anthropology.* New York: Harcourt Brace. In studies that span over twenty-five years in Nepal, the author documents daily life as it unfolds in an ever-changing social and economic milieu. She describes not only economic adaptations to mountain herding but also demographic and human biological adaptations to high-altitude life.

Bradburd, D. (1990). *Ambiguous relations.* Washington D.C. and London: Smithsonian Institution Press. This ethnography of the Komanchi, nomadic pastoralists of south-central Iran, views their society within the larger spheres of the nation-state, the Islamic world, and the global economy.

Fratkin, E. (1991). *Surviving drought and development: Ariaal pastoralists of Northern Kenya.* Boulder, CO: Westview Press. Focusing on drought and famine, this ethnography gives us a lucid narrative of the Ariaal and their ability to persist in being pastoralists despite environmental and political pressures to settle.

Galaty, J. G., & Bonte, P. (Eds.). (1991). *Herders, warriors and traders: Pastoralism in Africa.* Boulder, CO: Westview Press. A collection of articles on pastoralism in East and West Africa.

Goldstein, M. C., & Beall, C. M. (1994). *World of Mongolia's nomads.* Berkeley: University of California Press. This study looks at a community of Mongolian herders and their adaptation to a market economy since the Soviet bloc breakup.

Meir, A. (1997). *As nomadism ends: The Israeli Bedouin of the Negev.* Boulder, CO: Westview Press. An account of the social, spatial, and ecological changes faced by the Bedouin of the Negev.

Salzman, P. C. (1998). *The anthropology of real life: Events in human experience.* Prospect Hill, IL: Waveland Press. Short case studies focus on how people handled specific problems based on the author's research among pastoralists in Iran and on a Mediterranean island.

Williams, D. M. (2002). *Beyond great walls: Environment, identity, and development on the Chinese grasslands of Inner Mongolia.* Stanford, CA: Stanford University Press. The author has produced an outstanding book that brings into focus complex global and local interactions which shape the Mongolian grasslands. It is a delight to read.

# Chapter 6

# Intensive Agriculture: Feeding the Cities

Agricultural **intensification** is simply the elaboration of the use of domesticated crops and animals to produce more food, usable products, and energy for transport and other purposes. There are many ways for this to happen: Land can be sloped in terraces, soils enhanced, nutrients added, water and temperature controlled, seeds improved, and pests and competitors controlled, to mention a few. Ultimately, intensification rests on increasing yields by whatever means, the most common being irrigation, fertilizers, animal traction, storage, and efficient transportation and distribution.

In the final analysis, it is energy that distinguishes intensive agriculture—both energy invested in crop production and energy extracted from the land. The exact point at which horticulture becomes intensive farming is not always clear, but one can recognize the consequences of the shift even without employing economic criteria. Rarely can large numbers of people maintain themselves in stable year-round communities without intensive food production, and nowhere do we see urban centers without a hinterland containing highly productive farms. The vast energy surpluses that flow from  the countryside to the city result from the investment of energy in agriculture. The increase in the energy invested can come from many sources: from animals yoked to plows, from human labor spent in terracing land or digging wells, or from farm machinery powered by fossil fuels.

The impact of intensive land use is very evident in Egypt. For example, in 2003, more than 98% of Egypt's population was concentrated on less than 4% of its territory. Today, Egypt has to import large quantities of foodstuffs from other regions of the world. The irony is that both great productivity and accelerating social and economic hardship all too often march hand in hand. In Roman times, Egypt was a major source of grain for the Mediterranean world; an ancient historian, Ibn Batuta, said, "when famine strikes Egypt [whose lands have been irrigated longer than those of any other area], the world itself cannot feed her people."

Similar patterns of recurring famine and rural hardship are found in other regions where civilizations arose with the development of intensive farming. China, for example, where 1.2 billion people are supported by the production from 11% of its land area, has a long history of chronic famine and mass starvation—particularly among the people who themselves produce the food that sustains the country. As China's population continues to grow, the country has not only more people to feed but less land with which to do it. Urban centers are spreading and the fertility of the soil is diminishing. Land is being lost at a faster rate than it can be reclaimed. Per capita farmland availability was reduced by 10% in the 1990s, and a further 15% will be lost by the year 2035 (Smil, 1994). Even as the country strains to produce ever more food, the very fact of intensification has caused worsening erosion and soil degradation.

India and Bangladesh experience similar pressure on their land; Indonesia, once the most productive region of Southeast Asia, is seeing its people's well-being decline. To arrest such a decline, governments often encourage even greater efforts in agriculture, including the destruction of tropical rain forests, to support people forced out of other areas. In sub-Saharan Africa, where population-driven land-use intensification (along with long periods of drought) have often led to devastating environmental problems such as spreading desertification, the specter of mass starvation looms (Stevens, 1994, p. 10). Nevertheless, within each of these areas, we find numerous striking instances of human resourcefulness in the face of environmental problems. This chapter deals with the rise of intensive agriculture and its social corollaries: urbanism, social stratification, and the emergence of a class of peasant farmers who increasingly must cope with the demands of the global economy.

# The Development of Intensive Agriculture

The interrelated processes of agricultural intensification and ever-rising requirements for food in combination with declining resources are seen throughout the world. Anthropologists and scientists in other fields have long been concerned with the origins of intensive farming and early civilization, with the social and economic structure of rural society, and with the strategies that have enabled diverse populations to adapt to environmental and other problems. Most intensification involved increasing the yields from labor or land; this implies that there are at least two routes to intensification, and actually many more, due to the complex ways in which land and labor are interrelated. Usually, the perspective of most American or European economists is to concentrate on the former: Agricultural history is usually described in terms of progress in labor-saving technology—the plow, seed drills, cultivators, threshers, and the like—because the economies of the Western World experienced labor shortages over much of their histories. In the great rice-based agricultural systems of southern Asia, it is land not labor that is the limiting factor (Bray, 1994, p. 3).

Ester Boserup, a well-known Swiss agronomist, postulates that virtually all efforts to increase agricultural productivity have to be forced or induced by extreme circumstances since people naturally resist working harder than they have to (1970). People may be pressured by sheer numbers if there is growth in population, or they may be induced by market or political forces. These factors can be seen in the cases presented later. Increasing labor productivity, of course, not only may increase food production by allowing the same labor force to cultivate more land, but also may free up labor for other endeavors. Thus, Australia, Canada, and the United States produce massive amounts of food with a relatively small rural labor force.

But production can also be intensified by increasing the productivity of land without reducing the labor requirements—that is, expanding production using an existing labor force or even a larger one. This can be important, for example, where there are few alternative sources for employment, as is often the case in densely populated developing countries. Irrigation and the introduction of new crop strains are well-known examples of this form of intensification. Water control may allow for multiple harvests of a particular crop; new plant strains may also increase productivity without new capital inputs needed to reduce labor requirements. At least one anthropologist, Francesca Bray, argues that from this perspective traditional Asian rice-based farming using high labor inputs is not a case of "arrested development" when compared with Western agriculture, but is a solution to the problem of sustaining large populations with adequate nutrition (1994). Intensification and its consequences are discussed later.

One of the most ancient (and still important) ways land productivity can be increased is through water management. Water, whether from rainfall, rivers, or subterranean aquifers, is the primary limiting factor governing human habitation. Beyond the frontiers of cultivation often lies desolation, and the towns and villages of the world closely hug the rain-swept coasts, plains, and mountain valleys, the courses of major streams, and scattered oases. As archaeologist Robert Adams writes with respect to the ancient heartland of Mesopotamia, the prevailing uncertainties about water underlie all the human adaptations, whether farming, pastoral, or urban (1981). So diverse are the ways in which moisture can be

*Egyptian tomb fresco dating from about 3500 B.C. showing a man and his wife plowing and sowing; in the lower panel are various types of fruit trees. Egyptian farmers in a very early period developed plow technology and sophisticated systems of water control that transformed subsistence farming into the basis for sustaining large urban populations.*

(Robert Frerck/Odyssey Productions)

controlled that it is somewhat misleading to refer to them all as "irrigation." Simply adding pebbles to fields, as did the ancient Pueblo dwellers of North America, can enhance the field's ability to retain moisture (Lightfoot, 1993). In this sense, irrigation, or at least "moisture control," is as early as agriculture itself. Archaeological evidence in the Middle East indicates that simple systems of water control predate the rise of large agrarian states with their concomitantly dense populations. Populations near rivers or marshes would capture or divert annual floodwaters or runoff from rains. Irrigation refers to transporting the water to the field and then managing its direct application and subsequent drainage (drainage is important to maintain a salt-free soil base).

The earliest known large-scale system of irrigation in Egypt appears with the emergence of one government throughout that land in 5100 B.C. (Price & Feinman, 1997). We know that even fairly complicated irrigation systems can be managed by local farmers, although the potential for interfamilial or intercommunity conflict is substantial. People who share a common water resource may have very different interests in its use. As a consequence, we see a widespread pattern of large-scale irrigation systems coming to be run by special managers, with a corresponding reduction of control by households or even by local communities. Centralized decision making facilitates mobilizing large work forces, allocating water, conflict resolution, and the storage of surpluses.

In the emerging prehistoric states of Mesopotamia, this managerial role was first assumed by

religious leaders and only later by secular rulers (Fagan, 1992). It is interesting to note that the earliest large-scale irrigation systems in the southwest United States were managed by the Mormon Church (Abruzzi, 1993), as described in Chapter 2. To make water control feasible required the centralized control of a committed bureaucracy willing to use resources to sustain building and rebuilding dams and canals beyond the ability of local communities.

The main impetus for irrigation in most places is the need to have water available in areas where rainfall is unpredictable, not necessarily a wish to increase the average yield of a unit of land. But with the advent of irrigation, slight differences in the productivity of different pieces of land became greatly magnified. Those fields that lent themselves to irrigation—fields that were close to the water source or that drained well—produced far more than those less suited to irrigation.

Other routes to intensification include learning to breed strains of grains or other crops that mature more rapidly and bear more edible products. Rice, for example, was transformed into a substantially more productive grain staple through selective breeding by farmers in ancient China (Bray, 1994; see also Box 4.1, Red Rice out of Africa). Animal traction used to plow and cultivate fields developed very early in the Middle East and Far East (but not in the New World); a pair of oxen, it is calculated, produces over ten times the horsepower of a human being and, when relative costs are considered, is half as expensive as human power when used in tilling a field. Crop rotation and fertilizers, too, are means of

## Box 6.1

# A Philippine Frontier Community: Agricultural Intensification

W. Thomas Conelly, in field-work carried out in the Philippines on Palawan Island, where James Eder studied the Batak foragers, looked specifically at the point where extensive and intensive cultivation intersect, when farmers decide or are forced to change techniques to maximize outputs through greater investment of human labor (1996). Conelly went to the west coast of Palawan Island to investigate the transition underway from traditional swidden agriculture to irrigated rice production, which requires much more work than traditional swiddening. Through the 1960s, horticultural farmers, who were mostly settlers from elsewhere, together with indigenous farmers used land along the coast to grow rice in long swidden fields that they had cleared of both primary and secondary forest growth.

By the 1980s, land scarcity and population growth had led to a sharp shortening of the fallow period during which the soil would be replenished with nutrients, and rice yields plummeted. To make up the shortfall, some farmers turned to the sea to collect ocean products, and others turned to the remaining forests. Still others turned to irrigated farming to increase yields.

On the basis of Boserup's widely accepted theory, Conelly assumed that such a change would be resisted because the farmers would have to invest much more labor. With permanent irrigated production, the soil is no longer left fallow, forcing cultivators to adopt labor-intensive methods of cultivation to maintain yields. Another widely accepted parallel argument is that because extended agriculture involves a very diverse range of crops through interplanting a number of species in each plot, the quality and reliability of the food supply will decline with intensification.

However, what Conelly found was that whereas the long-term consequences of intensification may conform to these theories, in the short-term, which is what people take most seriously, standards of living improve. The reasons for this have to do with population pressure leading to a shortage of land for swiddening; as a consequence of this, swidden farmers had moved to a short-fallow form of horticulture in which fields were allowed only a year in which to recover—which they did poorly. Thus, farmers were not reaping the benefits associated with traditional, highly diversified cropping. At this point, irrigation, even with its high labor requirements, looks attractive. Rice yields on irrigated land were more than twice those of swidden but did not actually entail twice the labor, although there were other inputs to consider. What tipped the balance was not only higher yields but greater reliability.

Of course, not all families were affected by land pressures in the same way. Larger households having access to slightly larger holdings led the way to irrigation; one has not only to own the proper sort of land but also must have the labor available to convert it to irrigation, as well as the means to acquire a water buffalo with which to plow.

Once established, the efficiency of irrigation in terms of yields per hour of work begins to compare very favorably with those of swidden once the latter system is pushed into shortened fallow and weak soils. Thus, direct coercion may not be needed to induce people to change. Their own farming abilities may lead them to the choice.

intensifying yields. Arboriculture, as practiced in the Pacific, can be the basis for intensive production, as early travelers found when they first encountered the densely populated islands of Polynesia (Kirch, 1994). Here, carefully tended breadfruit trees provided a high yield in a form that could be stored in large, underground stone-lined pits.

## Social Complexity

Where and when there was agricultural intensification, human societies tended to increase in numbers and in social and technological complexity. When farming produced more food than the farmers themselves could eat, segments of the population came to specialize in crafts such as making tools and pots, which they then traded for food they had not produced themselves. The division of labor within society thus became more complex, with even spatially distant groups becoming mutually dependent.

Simple horticultural societies, such as the Yanomamö of Chapter 4, have remained politically autonomous until now and can be studied as distinct societies with distinct cultures. Intensive farming communities, on the other hand, are closely interdependent and must be studied as part of a larger

*A hill farmer steers a plow, pulled by cattle, in Jancapampa, Peru. The use of animal traction greatly enhanced agricultural production prior to the industrial era.*

(Galen Rowell/CORBIS)

agrarian society. Given the fact that much of their organization is tied to distant cities and national administrative offices, they cannot be understood outside the context of the larger political and economic system of which they are a part. Thus, as intensive agriculture developed, the land fed not only the farming households and the craft workers but other emerging classes of nonproducers: religious leaders, politicians, administrators. Increasingly, the economic demands of urban populations and the political power of their elites came to exercise a profound influence on the life of rural peoples, although the country folk often sought means to avoid the power of the state.

Town and country came to be part of an integrated system, although the results of increased productivity were not shared equally by all sectors of the economy. As agrarian societies evolved into large-scale states, as in the ancient Middle East, some communities inevitably prospered and grew; those far from the major markets, religious institutions, and other developments of the urban centers languished. In Mesoamerica, for example, regional or "core" centers such as the Valley of Oaxaca developed great urban complexes while peripheral zones, linked to the centers by trade or tribute, were relatively underdeveloped (Feinman & Nicholas, 1992). Such regional differentiation may be the basis for significant social and cultural variability within a society and is reflected in the subsequent development of industrialized societies.

The first Middle Eastern cities (and until recently, many African, European, and Asian cities) were little more than administrative and trading centers, established to control the surrounding countryside that provided them with food. Only after about the fifteenth century (with a few exceptions) do we see a change: the rise of cities not as agricultural trade centers and administrative centers but as manufacturing centers. The production of goods in great volume went hand in hand with the spread of trade and invention. Improved armaments and navigational equipment on sailing ships gave Europeans access to all the world's seas. European cities grew, fueled at first by the power of water, wind, and human and animal muscle, and later by fossil fuel.

Jared Diamond (1999) has reopened an old but somewhat neglected question: Why did great states arise very early in Eurasia, and why did a select subset, the Europeans, spread their influence globally, as witnessed by their colonization of the Americas, the Pacific, and much of Africa, together with their domination of the ancient heartlands of civilization in the Middle East, China, and India? Diamond avoids the Eurocentric or racial stereotyping that had tended to accompany discussions of this topic. Although his argument occupies a large and closely reasoned book, the gist of it is about the different ways in which humans, plants, animals, and technology intersected in different regions of the world. While humans have had their longest history in Africa, and obviously were biologically and culturally extremely successful there, sub-Saharan Africa was not particularly prominent in the development of early empires and great cities. Several factors facilitated the early spread of intensive agriculture and the parallel rise in early states and empires: topography, the availability of suitable wild variants of plants and animals to domesticate, and disease. The Eurasian land mass seems to offer advantages in these areas. The Middle East, Europe, and Asia form a huge contiguous land mass oriented east to west. Although the climate varies regionally, a large number of very similar plants and animals thrive across this huge expanse. Moreover, many of the wild animal variants were suited for domestication—unlike the New World and African fauna. Thus, while early states based on intensive farming first arose in the Middle East, the Indus Valley, and China, techniques established in one region quickly diffused throughout the area so that while Europe lagged initially in terms of population growth and urbanization, it quickly "caught up." The extensive use of animal power, together with the availability of iron, copper, and tin ore, gave these early empires a military might not rivaled on other continents. While states developed early in Africa and the New World, they lacked the agricultural potential of Eurasia and, in particular, lacked the ability to make the same use of animal power. The north–south orientation of these continents presented significant climatic and geographic obstacles to the easy spread of domesticates and even technology from one new center of development to another. Plants and animals adapted to one region did not thrive elsewhere—unlike in Eurasia, where much of its land mass is roughly on the same latitude. Importantly, too, humans throughout this vast region shared much the same disease history because many diseases, as we have noted, have animal vectors—and thus acquired resistance.

So why, Diamond asks, was it the Spanish, not the Chinese or the Ottoman Turks, who spread their domains throughout most of the New World, while the British and the French held sway over much of Africa, the Pacific, and Asia? Quite apart from specific technological developments in the form of weaponry, transport, and food storage, Diamond turns to an interesting, but somewhat contentious, sociopolitical explanation for European expansion, reminiscent of earlier thinking in anthropology: namely, that the Asian continent came into the early modern era dominated by large regional, highly centralized political systems—what used to be referred to as "Oriental despotism" in the literature of the nineteenth century. China, for example, had the world's biggest navy and trading fleeting in the fifteenth century, but in a single administrative stroke totally abandoned it; Japan similarly closed its doors to the outside world, but also to new military technology. Europe, on the other hand, had numerous competing centers of power with few natural frontiers, and this military and commercial competition stimulated invention and innovation just as it drove expansion into distant regions.

### An Archaeological Example: The Shang Dynasty of China.

The Shang Dynasty (1766–1122 B.C.) emerged after the rise of the great civilizations of Mesopotamia (ca. 3200 B.C.), Egypt (ca. 3000 B.C.), and the Indus Valley (ca. 2500 B.C.), and has been described as among the "civilized giants of the ancient world" (Chang, 1984). At its height, it controlled vast areas of northern China and boasted many walled cities. The complexity of Shang society has been reconstructed from archaeological evidence found at excavations including the late Shang capital of Yin, near the modern city of Angang in the Huang He (Yellow River) region. These excavations revealed numerous royal palaces, a ceremonial center surrounded by commoners' houses, and nonresidential buildings that probably served as public meeting places. Shang society seems to have been highly stratified, and the contents of the royal tombs indicate that the king and his family received tributes of food and luxury items such as jade, jewelry, and the pottery and bronze work (including vessels, weapons, chariots, and musical instruments) for which Shang craftsmen were famous. The late Shang period also saw the emergence of the first Chinese script, consisting of approximately 3,000 phonetic, pictographic, and ideographic symbols, the oldest form of writing system in Southeast Asia. Such a complex society rested on a successful economy and effective political administration.

The Shang economy was based on agriculture, primarily the cultivation of millet, wheat, and rice, and fishing and hunting. Domesticated animals such as cattle, sheep, pigs, and water buffalo were kept for their products and meat, and the cattle and water buffalo were probably also used to pull primitive plows. Excavations have revealed hoes, spades, and sickles to cultivate the land. There is evidence of irrigation canals, and it seems possible that two crops of millet and rice could have been harvested each year.

The observable increase of production per unit of land during the Shang period was probably due to a rapid increase in population coupled with an increasingly centralized administration as the ruling elite controlled the distribution of the economic surplus being generated. The population increase led to more people being employed in farming, and there was a consequent increase in land under cultivation. There is evidence that the ruling classes even conscripted prisoners of war as farmworkers on their lands. Local lords, loyal to the king, were responsible for collecting tributes, for drafting men for war or public works, and for disseminating edicts and laws from the central government. This spectacular flowering of culture preceded the emergence of the Roman Empire by more than a millennium.

## *The Organization of Energy*

Howard Odum (1971, 1992) was one of the first ecologists to observe that the structure and function of animal, plant, and human social systems are understood at least to some extent by the way they acquire, channel, and expend the energy necessary for their maintenance. Anthropologist Leslie White was one of the first to recognize the importance of the role of energy in cultural evolution. What is often called the Industrial Age, White (1949) has called the Fuel Age.

Societies vary greatly in their energy budgets and in how energy is organized. Mechanized use of nonhuman energy sources—fossil fuel or hydroelectric power, for example—distinguishes the technologically advanced societies. In the United States, about 230,000 kilocalories of energy are expended per capita per day; in Burundi, central Africa, 24,000 are expended (Giampietro et al., 1993, p. 239). Moreover, in the United States, only 10% of the country's "total time" (the population × 24 × 365) is allocated to work. In Burundi, 25% of the nation's total time is needed; in short, they work twice as hard to extract a fraction of the usable energy that the U.S. worker does (p. 239). Where human labor constitutes the main power supply, there is little spare energy to devote to anything other than maintaining current infrastructure, reproduction, and food procurement. Thus, intensification, which we have defined earlier as the process of increasing yields through an increase in energy expenditure, is best achieved when that increase is accomplished with nonhuman energy sources.

***Human Labor as Energy.*** Economists define human labor productivity as the monetary value of

**Figure 6.1.** *The advanced agrarian system often makes greater use of animal traction to create orderly fields with crop rotations that allow for near continuous cultivation. What is not depicted in this sketch is the regular appearance in the village of the urban-based tax collector, the military conscription officer, and itinerant traders. Often, too, the land itself may be owned by urban dwellers.*

Intensive Agrarian System

what is produced (dollar value added per hour of work) by a unit of human labor. This definition, however, does not work well in thinking of labor in nonmonetary societies or in developing societies with a significant subsistence economy. Also, it is hard to compare a monetary economy with a partially monetary one. Energy is an alternative measure of productivity that offers new insights into the changing role of human labor in relation to technological development. Giampietro et al. (1993) have created a sophisticated model based on this principle, which is described next in a simplified manner.

Assessing the productivity of labor requires two measurements: what has been achieved energetically and what energy has been expended to gain it. A simple model illustrates this. If we compare the horsepower (hp) efficiency of human power (0.1 hp), a pair of oxen (1.2 hp), a 6-hp tractor, and a 50-hp tractor in tilling a one-hectare field, applied human power is twice as effective as that of the pair of oxen and over four times as effective as the tractors (that is, effective in the amount of work performed per horsepower). However, if we calculate the gross energy requirements (metabolic and fuel inputs, shelter, construction costs, or—for living components—reproductive costs, etc.), this is reversed: Human power is 3.45 times more expensive than the tractors and twice as expensive as the oxen.

The indirect costs of human power are very high: People must have food, clothing, and shelter whether or not they are actually working. Furthermore, it takes time and energy inputs to "produce" a worker.

Eighty percent of the metabolic expenditure for a human worker is outside the workplace. A related issue is time constraints. Productivity has to consider how the power level affects the time to complete a task. While one person may be able to harvest a crop that requires 700 labor days, this is clearly not feasible; more reasonable would be seven farmers working 100 days or 100 workers working one week. Thus, human power, while very efficient in terms of the work that can be accomplished by a unit of horsepower, is both low in absolute levels and costly.

Any system can be seen as having energy *sources* and energy *converters* that generate power or useful work. In preindustrial or partially industrialized societies, energy sources are largely in standing biomass: the trees, plants, and animals available to support humans and that can be converted into useful work to support the population and its material culture through human labor. This may be supplemented by animal traction, but even so, the available power is limited. In the United States in the 1850s, 91% of energy expended came from standing biomass; today, only 4% does. The balance largely comes from fossil fuels, converted into useful work by machinery. Industrial societies are more limited by energy sources; nonindustrial societies are limited by the low rate at which energy can be converted through human labor only partially amplified by animals and machinery.

The implications for development are serious. The addition of one bullock for every ten villagers in

*Chinese farmers are masters at the science of intensive agriculture, combining skilled labor, water control, and fertilizers to reap rich harvests.*

(Reuters News Getty Images)

India would have the effect of doubling the power level per capita in that country, but it would still remain more than a thousand times less than the per capita power level in the United States. Preindustrial societies respond to the energy limitation by scheduling agricultural activities to be as constant as possible throughout the year—avoiding periods of peak demand. Thus, traditional farmers often make use of a mix of crops and livestock, each with different labor demands. In industrial agriculture, this is not necessary because labor is not the main means of converting energy—machines are.

## Agricultural Intensification, Fallowing, and Land Degradation

Investment of energy to gain an even greater return in energy is characteristic of intensive agriculture and is expressed in the management of fields and paddies. A crucial factor in the evolution of intensive agriculture was the advent of plow cultivation and fertilization, which allowed farmers to reduce the length of **fallow time**—the time that must be allowed between crops for the soil to rest and regenerate its organic and chemical content. The fallow period is critical to a high level of food production over the long term. When other factors—availability of water, type of soil, and the like—are equal, sustained agricultural yields vary with the length of the fallow period. The shifting agriculture practiced by the Yanomamö is a long-fallow system requiring as many as ten to twenty years of fallow time for each field.

In intensive agriculture, the fallow period can be reduced to the point where the land can undergo nearly continuous cultivation and, in some areas, can produce multiple crops each year. This approach requires developed technology, large inputs of human labor, and an investment in other forms of energy. Fields have to be prepared (often specially laid out for irrigation); plow animals must be cared for; tractors fueled and maintained; water collected, distributed, and controlled; fertilizers or other nutrients spread on the fields; and crops carefully tended throughout the growing period. The result is a vastly increased amount of food per unit of land.

Both land and farmers work harder under intensive agriculture, and the result is a great increase in the production not only of food but of such crops as cotton and flax. It may sometimes appear that the possibilities of intensification seem almost limitless. Even with modern techniques, however, only 11% of earth's land area is suited to intensive farming and the potential for intensification is limited. A point is always reached at which increased investment of la-

*Women planting rice seedlings in Bali, Indonesia. Human labor, as well as ingenuity, is the key to intensive agriculture.*
(© Jack Fields/CORBIS)

bor or capital is not matched by productive gains; we return to this point later. Further, intensification may lead to soil loss if nutrients are not maintained; erosion may accompany mechanized cultivation, and irrigation may result in waterlogged or salinized soils, which occurs when too much water is applied or where drainage is inadequate to prevent salts from building up in the soil. Worldwatch reports that 60 million hectares (150 million acres) of cropland worldwide have been damaged by salinization and waterlogging. India, which has the most irrigated land of any country, has damaged about one third of its croplands and abandoned 7 million hectares because of salinization. Paradoxically, the United States, which pioneered industrialized farming, also leads the world in soil loss due to erosion; 69 million acres are eroding at rates that diminish productivity (Cunningham & Saigo, 1995, p. 229).

### Environmental Resilience, Stability, and Change.
Intensive agriculture is accompanied by a massive re-

shaping of the landscape—a process that is ever accelerating. In swidden horticulture, the forest is partially cut or burned and allowed to grow back. Intensive agriculture entails laboriously clearing fields, building terraces, and excavating drainage ditches, ponds, and canals. These tasks completed, the work has just begun. The new agricultural environment must be maintained through constant effort. Although intensive agriculture allows humans more control over their environment, it can be as much a problem as a solution. By creating elaborate waterworks or clearing hillsides for terraces, a farming population may indeed protect its yields or even increase food production. But as agriculture becomes more complex and specialized, it becomes more vulnerable to disruption. Irrigation canals may silt up, fields may become unproductive as natural salts become concentrated in the soil, topsoil may erode—the list is long. These calamities accompany intensification as surely as the increased yields. A farmer who plants the same crop year after year to obtain the maximum yield is increasing the risk of total crop failure from soil depletion or disease.

The problem is not a lack of planning or a tendency of individual farmers to take this year's yield more seriously than environmental consequences a decade or a generation from now. In response to market demands or government inducements to produce more food, entire regions may be threatened by depletion or erosion of the soil or by its contamination by chemical residues. These problems arise in all major agricultural nations. Stability and continuity require investments in the infrastructure that are not immediately reflected in crop yields: soils protected from erosion, drainage maintained, crops rotated, and soils allowed to regenerate. If such investments are not made, the stability of the productive system is threatened.

So even as intensive agriculture solves some problems, it creates new ones. Irrigation has left such concentrations of minerals in the soil of California's Imperial Valley that productivity is leveling off and threatens to decline, and there is virtually no way to divert the contaminated water from the fields away from the downstream communities. Irrigation is often associated with environmental problems of this sort. Paradoxically, one response is to intensify production further by expanding the area under irrigation, building larger dams, digging deeper wells, using expensive chemicals to remove the salt, and using more water. Again, such efforts may solve the problem in the short run only to create more serious problems in the long run, such as causing the water table in the area to drop or further increasing the

salinity of the soil. Consequently, cultivators have to work harder just to maintain the same level of productivity.

With the development of intensive agriculture, the difference in productivity between richer and poorer lands was multiplied, creating and amplifying regional disparities. Similar processes of regional or national differentiation continued as societies industrialized, with more extensive effects. Today, we can still see this in economic disparities occurring on a global level, as regions with access to cheap energy and sources of capital, labor, and appropriate raw materials develop rapidly while adjacent areas suddenly appear underdeveloped by comparison. Within countries, the people who control land and capital can reap far greater rewards than those who have only their labor to sell; hence, great social and economic disparities are apparent.

# The Social Consequences of Intensive Agriculture: Peasant Farmers

The social consequences of intensive agriculture have been at least as far-reaching as its ecological consequences. In pre- or less-industrialized nations, the relationship of the intensive farming community to the general society is most striking. In such societies, smallholding farmers or farm laborers historically tended to have little voice in the urban dominated national social and economic system. They lacked control over the means of their production—the land, the capital, and other resources they need to grow their crops—and even the labor they contribute to the process is undervalued. These farmers are traditionally termed **peasants**. Although they may participate in national institutions, these institutions are controlled largely by the town-dwelling literate classes. Peasants or poor farmers trade and market, but they are often exploited by merchants and intermediaries. Peasants' fields may be owned by distant landlords, but even possession of land does not always serve as a basis for self-sufficiency or community autonomy. Money and energy left over from their labors are regularly siphoned off in the form of land rents, taxes, and even forced labor **corvée**—unpaid labor in lieu of taxes, usually in road construction and maintenance. Many of the great monuments of antiquity, such as the pyramids of Egypt and the Valley of Mexico, were built with the labor of a conscripted rural work force.

*The great temple of Abu Simbel in southern Egypt was erected by King Ramses II (1279–1213 B.C.) to demonstrate his power over the Nubians. Using corvée labor largely taken from the rural population, this Pharaoh built over half of the still-extant temples of ancient Egypt.*

(Daniel Bates)

## Varieties of Peasant Society

Peasants have been described as farmers, usually intensive agriculturalists, who produce primarily for family subsistence rather than for profits to be reinvested (Wolf, 1966). Much of their produce may be sold, but the profits accrue to intermediaries and urban elites, not to the peasants. For them, farming is a way of life and a means of sustaining a household within a community. It is, then, much more than simply a strategy for making money. Such farmers, often materially poor, closely identify with their villages and way of life. The terms *peasant* and *farmer* subsume great diversity in standards of living and agricultural technology, even within one country. The common element shared by those called peasants is a farming household whose efforts are directed to maintenance and subsistence—not reinvestment of capital for profits. In most cases, peasant families are dominated by holders of power outside the local community. In tsarist Russia before 1889, for instance, a peasant household was bound to a landed estate, and to leave without permission was to risk death or imprisonment. The peasants of Western Europe acquired full civil liberties by the nineteenth century, and often their standard of living, however simple in comparison with that of the well-to-do, set them apart from the poor people of the cities. Still, their form of farming permitted little accumulation of capital or material wealth. Today, there are few farmers in Western Europe, North America, and

Japan whom one would term peasants, but the category has considerable salience in Africa, Latin America, the Middle East, parts of Eastern Europe, and many parts of Asia.

In Latin America, India, and the Middle East, many peasants gain access to land through some form of **sharecropping**—that is, they work land owned by others in exchange for a share of the yield. In fact, as we will see, the sharecroppers of the American South, traditionally but not exclusively Black families, are a domestic example of peasant farming in all but name, as are many Chicano farmworkers of California today. Sharecropping is one means of getting land to farm; there are others. The way people control the lands they farm is a major determinant of the degree of political freedom they enjoy and usually of their material well-being.

Horticulturists who control their own land and tools, such as the Yanomamö and the Ariaal herders, decide for themselves how hard they will work and dispose of their produce as they choose. Peasants do not have this freedom. Their access to land, equipment, and capital—even the allocation of their own labor—is regulated by people more powerful than they. Even the local agriculturists who own their own small land holdings, elect their own leaders, and control their own labor are heavily dependent on an administrative and commercial network. In one way or another, the intermediaries who link the farm with distant markets, the rulers, governors, tax collectors, and even the merchants in faraway cities or on local estates determine how and what the peasants produce and what they get for it (Wolf, 1966). One corollary of this is the development of distinctive rural lifestyles and cultural practices that set them apart from the populations of urban centers.

## Peasants, Small Farmers, and Change

When tractors and other equipment are introduced, the richer farmer is usually the one to benefit. New technology always entails risks. Large farms offer their owners the security that enables them to assume the risks entailed by the adoption of innovations, such as new high-yield seeds. As we saw in earlier chapters, rural people have responded in diverse ways but rarely have avoided being drawn into new markets and a near total dependence on distant sources of energy.

Drawing on the experiences of a number of countries, it has been commonplace to assume that the effects of industrialization on rural farming communities follow a fairly predictable course: Peasant handicraft production will be replaced by factory goods, peasants will purchase in the marketplace much of what they used to produce at home (thus becoming dependent on money), farm production will focus on cash crops rather than on food for consumption, and wage labor will largely replace reciprocity and family-organized farming. The social consequences are often negative: Poor farmers are unable to compete in a fully monetarized economy and lose their lands; small farms and plots are consolidated into larger units that are run as businesses using hired laborers (usually those who have lost their own lands); and as the scale of agriculture increases, more and more work is provided by migrant farmworkers—the poorest of the poor. This in fact has occurred in many places, but it is not an inevitable scenario.

The loss of distinction between rural and urban households is another consequence of the transition to market dependence. This homogenizing effect is particularly evident when market dependence is coupled with industrial forms of transport and communication. Widely separated households end up eating, dressing, entertaining, and in general, living very much the same way. Farm families in the United States, for example, come to share most of the expectations and values of urbanites of the same cultural backgrounds. Even their daily diets are very similar. We can see this same process at work on a global level as cultural and ethnic distinctions fade,

with resultant worldwide similarities within class lines. Eskimos use jeeps and snowmobiles and watch the same TV shows as people in Florida and Brazil. Across continents, people are drawn into one global system; styles of life reflect this convergence.

## Access to Land

One way to understand the factors common to the structures of intensive farming is to determine how people gain access to land. Very often, the material circumstances of peasant households and the degree of exploitation depend on the way the land is controlled, which in turn depends on the political configuration of the larger society. The private property form of landholding most prevalent today is associated with profound societal changes stemming from the rise of capitalism and industrialism in eighteenth-century Europe and the beginning of colonial empires. Land came to be viewed not as the hereditary privilege and responsibility of a local lord or ruler but as a commodity like any other—the private property of individual owners. Land became another form of capital, with rents or the sale of crops providing the return to the owner. Wherever European colonialism reached, this form of land tenure was encouraged (Wolf, 1982). When land became a commodity, it was relatively easy to encourage increased production and the settlement of Europeans in the new colonies such as those in Africa and the Americas; this system of ownership encouraged landowners to reinvest rents in their lands and to modernize their farm technology.

## Sharecropping

Traditionally, *sharecropping* is a farming arrangement in which workers farm land owned by others for a share of the yield. Not infrequently, it is also very exploitative. Sharecropping reached its peak in the United States during the Great Depression of the 1930s, when more than 25% of American farms were operated on this basis. The arrangement had advantages and disadvantages. It did ensure the landless of access to farmland, even when market conditions left them so poor that they were unable to rent land for cash. At the same time, it yielded far greater profits to landowners than they could realize from rents. Sharecroppers were invariably among the poorest of the poor. These days, however, with the price of land high and rising, many family and corporate farms have returned to sharecropping of a sort: They invest in equipment rather than in more land, use it to farm land belonging to someone else,

## Box 6.2

# The Political Ecology
# of a Peasant Revolt

ON NEW YEAR'S EVE 1994, 800 members of the Zapatista National Liberation Party blocked the Pan American highway in the southern Mexican state of Chiapas, seized two gas stations belonging to the Mexican government, and declared war on the ruling party—all only hours after the ratification of the North American Free Trade Agreement (NAFTA). This was the first major demonstration against the growing integration of the world through modern trade agreements. The most recent ones were the Seattle demonstrations against the World Trade Organization (WTO) and the demonstrations in Bangkok in February 2000 against the International Monetary Fund (IMF). The often very diverse forces behind these responses still have one thing in common. Local people rightly or wrongly see their fates unfairly affected by distant forces. In the Chiapas case, the fact that Mexico and its powerful northern neighbors were now linked in trade gave the local people a platform from which to air grievances that the ruling party had long suppressed. The armed phase of rebellion subsided after twelve days, but an armed standoff involving over 70,000 Mexican

Army troops and over 5,000 rebel militia backed by perhaps half a million sympathizers continues, with little sign of abating.

Who are the participants? If you ask the government, they are outside agitators, either from foreign revolutionary groups or radical elements within the Roman Catholic Church. However, observers, including anthropologists, report that they are from indigenous groups, speaking the Mayan languages of the region. The rebellion, after centuries of rule by non-Mayans, is a powerful testimony to the extraordinary retention of distinctive ethnic cultures in Chiapas.

What has stimulated these people to express themselves so forcibly at this juncture in Mexican history? Anthropologist James Nations suggests that this is an "ecological revolution" (1994, pp. 31–33). It is about who controls the land and for what purpose. Since the colonial era, the Mayan highlands have been a source of products extracted for the benefit of outsiders: Its dams supply 30% of Mexico's surface waters and a third of its hydroelectric power; it has much of the nation's petroleum reserves. But the state is last in terms of households

with electricity, and its once-massive forest cover is being rapidly cut and the land converted to pasture for beef cattle. The Zapatista revolt took place in a region where three zones come together: the Tzotzil Mayan highland forests, an area of foothills now cleared for cattle, and a lowland tropical forest, which is itself rapidly being cleared.

In the colonial era, as the forest was cut back, much land was converted to hacienda production for the benefit of Spanish landlords. Mayan peasants were relocated to work on the haciendas. In the 1950s and 1960s, with agrarian reform, thousands of Mayan families were released from debt peonage and moved into forested lands to establish homesteads on state-owned forest land where timber had been cleared. Soon these were followed by wealthier outsiders who bought up or otherwise acquired their plots and consolidated them into cattle ranches, forcing the farmers out. By 1981, 80% of the cleared lands had been turned into privately owned cattle ranches, many of them fenced and patrolled. Not only were indigenous farmers increasingly desperate for cropland, turning to forest lands of the

---

and pay the landowner with a share of the crop. These sharecroppers are among the more successful farmers in their communities.

In some cases, Miriam Wells (1987) reports, migrant workers become sharecroppers. When crops require a great deal of skill and much labor to raise, it can make sense for the landowner to give the farmworkers a share in the proceeds. California is once more a case in point. Strawberry production has shifted to sharecropping in recent years, with much of the work being done by the same Chicanos who were formerly migrant laborers. By and large, the workers have benefited from this arrangement,

as they are their own bosses and share in the profits produced by their labor. Though few have yet moved from sharecropper to farm owner, many are hopeful.

## Rural Responses to Oppression and Change

Although the lot of peasant cultivators varies widely, it is rarely enviable; "peasants of all times and all places are structured inferiors" (Dalton, 1972, p. 406). Wherever a peasantry exists, it represents a politically dependent and often oppressed segment

*For the last decade, the Zapatista Movement has been able to mobilize a significant threat to the federal government of Mexico, using tactics that make sophisticated use of the Internet, media, and international press.*

(©Dan Groshong, CORBIS Sygma)

Montes Azules Biosphere Reserve, but ethnically different local Mayan populations were forced into competition.

In 1989, the government dismantled its coffee price control system, which meant that many coffee bean growers were forced into bankruptcy; the 1994 North America Free Trade Agreement was seen as the last straw by many. The remaining cash crop was corn, and with NAFTA, cheap American corn would destroy this market. The indigenous people came to feel that they would soon be without a market for their crops and without land to grow them on. Chiapas farmers faced some hard choices. They could move to the already crowded urban centers, they could perhaps work as hired hands on cattle ranches, or they could rebel. As Nations writes, it is not surprising they have chosen rebellion. Their goal is to reclaim land for farming by getting it back from the cattle ranchers.

Although the Mexican government says it is willing to negotiate with the rebels to redress long-standing social and economic problems in Chiapas, in the fall of 1996, peace negotiations broke down. In December 1997, forty-five indigenous villagers were killed by a pro-government paramilitary group, forcing the resignation of the minister of the department of the interior. The standoff continues with, in effect, two Chiapases emerging; of the 111 communities, the Zapatistas control 32 and the government controls the remainder. While all of the region can be fairly described as poor and backward relative to other parts of Mexico, the Zapatistas have virtually isolated themselves from the national economy—but not from the international media.

of the society. Some observers say that peasants have been beaten down too long to be able to change their circumstances; generations of oppression have turned them into passive drudges, resigned to the injustices of their position and indifferent to political events outside the confines of their villages. Others argue that peasants' passivity is a rational, conservative response: Poor farmers or peasants simply cannot afford to take risks.

Anthropologists report that most peasant farmers are far from passive and are quick to seize an opportunity. We see that all over the world peasants have effected drastic changes in the way they live. In communities throughout southern Asia, for example, small tractors are used to till the paddies, entrepreneurs start up rice mills, and people almost everywhere are raising crops and animals they never raised before. Rural change is highly visible in China, where peasant farmers are now encouraged to reap the benefits of agricultural entrepreneurship. The Russian Republic is at last taking the same approach, but very slowly. One problem faced by Russia is that after several generations of collective farming, people have become accustomed to having agricultural decisions made for them and to the security of salaries rather than uncertain profits.

Not all farming families can solve their immediate economic problems by adopting new agricultural techniques. Often, the prosperity of one village household depletes the resources of a less fortunate one. One very common response is to pack up and move, just as thousands of Oklahoma farmers did during the great Dust Bowl era of the 1930s. Tens of thousands of Brazilian farm families are attempting to settle in the Amazon region, and even more turn to the cities in the hope of betterment. We may deplore the social and environmental consequences of pioneer settlements in the rain forest and of the proliferation of urban slums, but we must recognize the tenacity of people who are doing their best in a world that does not always serve them well.

Peasants do periodically mobilize themselves into armed opposition. Indeed, history has witnessed a series of exceedingly bloody peasant revolts, in which centuries of accumulated resentment, masked by apparent docility, burst forth in massive waves of violence. England in the fourteenth century and Germany in the fifteenth and sixteenth centuries were shaken by peasant uprisings. In more recent times, the Algerian, Mexican, Russian, Chinese, and Cuban revolutionaries owed much of their success to peasant uprisings that furthered their aims. The irony is that today, these aging regimes are facing their own internal crises, including rural rebellions. In Algeria, Islamic fundamentalists are waging a battle rooted in part in the poverty-stricken countryside; in 1995, Indians in Chiapas, Mexico rose in rebellion against the government and demanded land (see Box 6.2, pp. 156–157).

As Eric Wolf (1966) points out, peasant uprisings are usually motivated by a drive not just for practical social change but for utopian justice and equality. Such hopes may serve to unite the peasants but not to organize them. The organization and leadership are usually provided by politically sophisticated outsiders. When a government is strong, the usual outcome of a peasant revolt is the death of many peasants and the return of the others to their fields. (An awareness of this likelihood has no doubt served to limit the number of peasant uprisings.) When, on the other hand, the government is already weakened, especially by war, then it may in fact fall if a strong leader manages to rally the peasants to his cause. This was the case in China, where Mao Zedong's revolution was furthered by the devastation of China's long war with Japan. Even when peasant revolts succeed, their success rarely brings complete equality because urban elites often replace the earlier or traditional elite. In China, as we have seen, even the newly installed Communist government continued policies that disadvantaged people in the countryside, particularly peasants. While the system of land control is usually changed and poverty may be alleviated, a sizable class of rural producers remains in a subordinate social and political position, so there is still a peasant class.

The following sections present four cases illustrating both shared and distinctive aspects of intensive farming. The Tamang of Nepal are just now emerging as intensive farmers in a market and commercialized environment. Historically, they were subsistence farmers with virtually no market involvement; more recently, they have begun to travel abroad for wage labor and to send their goods to market. Today, the countryside of Nepal is the scene of a violent, largely rural, revolt involving the so-called Maoists, and thousands have been killed. One of their demands is for the extension of urban services, such as education, to the villages. But the case study here comes from an earlier, less violent period. The second case, from northern Mexico, looks closely at how a village administers and secures its lands where peasants, large-scale farmers, and ranchers compete. The third case from central Nigeria shows how, without political coercion or direction from development experts, a resourceful population has successfully turned to intensive farming. Finally, there is a general picture of how Egypt, one of the world's first regions to develop intensive agriculture based on water control, now is coping with global change and the recent move to a fully market-driven economy.

# The Tamang

In June 1981, Thomas Fricke, armed with a Fulbright grant, an ability to speak Nepali, and a set of questionnaires, arrived in the Himalayan village of Timling after a week's walk through Tamang country.[1] While fully aware of the larger nation of which they were a part, few men in Timling (and even fewer women) had been to the capital of the nation, Kathmandu. They were relatively poor and isolated, but the people of Timling were warmly receptive to Fricke's presence. He quickly settled into the top floor of a rented house, made it known that people were welcome to drop in for tea and a cigarette, and more important, established an informal clinic from which he dispensed aspirin and treated minor wounds. Soon people came to take his presence for

---

[1]The following discussion, unless otherwise noted, is based on Thomas Fricke's *Himalayan Households: Tamang Demography and Domestic Processes*, originally published in 1986, but significantly revised in 1994.

granted, and he could turn to his main objectives: the study of population dynamics and the domestic economy in a small farming community (1994; Fricke et al., 1998).

Within weeks of his arrival, he began making a careful map of the village, giving each house a number for use later to ensure that his data did not exclude the poorer ones. Soon thereafter, he began the arduous task of visiting each of the 132 households and collecting detailed data on marriages, kinship, age, and gender of all members, as well as economic data. In the final stages of research, again using his list of households, he selected some thirty households as a special sample in which more detailed questioning would occur. Even though much of his research, like that of Chagnon among the Yanomamö, was highly structured and quantitative, the personal was never far removed:

> The anthropologist, crouching near a peasant's cooking fire and sharing corn beer, lives in a world of imposing immediacy. In a village of a hundred or so households, those events that are swallowed up by the grand scale of an urban or national context take on an enlarged, often passionate significance. One night there is laughter and joking with a father-to-be about the paternity of his child. Another day there is the intrusion of sudden death when a hunter loses his footing on a rain-soaked trail. The anthropologist observes, or hears about, these happenings as they occur and gives them a kind of permanency by writing them down. (p. 7)

The Tamang people, including the inhabitants of Timling, are a widely dispersed population of Tibetan origin living in Nepal. Their numerous villages stretch in a broad arc north and east from Kathmandu. Those who live near the capital are more integrated into Nepal's national life and culture than are those to the east and north, such as the people of Timling. The Tamang practice a form of Buddhism that closely resembles that of their more famous neighbors, the Sherpa, who are well-known internationally as mountaineers and guides. The village of Timling is only fifty miles from Kathmandu, but to reach it, the traveler has to take a five-hour bus ride, followed by a four- or five-day trek, depending on the season. Until the eighteenth century, the region of Timling was a small, independent chiefdom, one among many. Even though now, administratively, it holds a marginal and dependent status within the kingdom, it is somewhat misleading to characterize Timling as a typical peasant society. Unlike many peasants, the people maintain control over their own lands, and variation in wealth among households is not great.

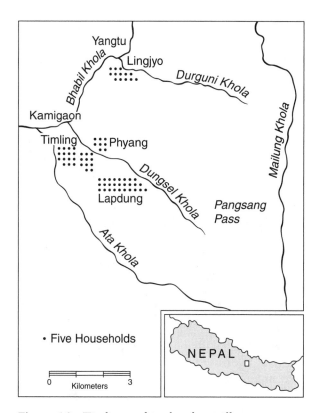

**Figure 6.2.** *Timling and its daughter villages.*

The Tamang as a whole are organized into patrilineal clans or lineages called *rui*. As is the case with the Yanomamö, the Tamang practice exogamy; that is, marriage must be outside the clan. In some parts of the country, the clans of the Tamang are ranked hierarchically so that wealth, social standing, and political influence are distributed unequally. This is not true in Timling, whose people are, writes Fricke, "an extraordinarily egalitarian group, with no institutionalized basis for distinguishing among the status of clans" (p. 32).

## The Village

The 132 households are laid out in four neighborhoods, or *tol,* each associated with a dominant clan (although others will be present as well) and each with its open-air meeting place. Sons build their homes on land they inherit from their fathers; thus, they may add to the size of a neighborhood. Most houses are of two-story construction and built with stone and timber, with wood or slate roofs. In one neighborhood, the homes of clan members display under the eaves large stone phalluses that are supposed to ward off ghosts and other malevolent beings. The upper stories are used primarily for storage, with the family living quarters downstairs

*A Tamang man and his cow. The man is wearing typical highland clothing except for his shirt, which was purchased at a bazaar five days' walk from Timling.*
(Courtesy of Tom Fricke, The University of Michigan)

where the symbolically important cooking hearth is located. The hearth is emblematic of the household as an independent unit. The fire from the open hearth fills the houses with smoke, but the overall effect is a warm, dry haven in the colder months or during the monsoon rains.

Timling is a fairly dangerous and dirty place. During the monsoon rains, the central paths of the village turn into running streams. Since these paths are also the repository of human waste, the drinking water frequently becomes contaminated during monsoons. On the often treacherous trails, the risk of accidents is high given the slippery rocks and sheer drops of hundreds of feet. On the positive side, the village is too high to be afflicted with malaria-bearing mosquitos, and leeches, fleas, and lice are limited seasonally by the winter cold and summer dry seasons (p. 114).

Religious practices incorporate both Buddhist beliefs and shamanistic practices. The two sorts of religious specialists reflect this mix; about half are *lamas* trained in the Buddhist tradition and capable of conducting elaborate rituals on a calendar that is coordinated with the agricultural cycle, and the others are *bompos* (shamans) who appease forest deities that bring illness to villagers and their herds. A shaman is an individual who has unique skills in curing, divination, or witchcraft, usually involving the ability to communicate with the world of spirits. Parents regularly bring in *bompos* to heal their sick children with all-night rituals involving spirit possession and the sacrifice of chickens and goats. The *lamas* carry out death rituals or funerals, cleanse the village periodically by casting out evil spirits (a task that involves the entire community working together for three days), and annually bless the fields.

Political organization is focused on the clans and neighborhoods. Technically, the village is part of a national system of administration; in practice, most decisions of communal interest are made within the clans through meetings and a council of elders. Disputes are resolved locally, usually by informal sanctions and fines, and violent conflict is rare.

## Field, Forest, and Pasture

Timling's agropastoral economy is directed toward the subsistence needs of its people and, until recently, has been largely (but never entirely) self-sufficient. Until 1956, they traded locally mined salt with Tibet; today, they trade for small amounts of grain and manufactured commodities in a market town some four days' walk to the south—part of a gradual but steady shift to a cash economy. As with any population, we have to think of their present adaptation as part of a long historical process that is ongoing. In previous periods, the ancestors of the present population had exploited the lowlands, using classic horticultural techniques. Gradually, as a result of pressure on resources and declining lowland forest area suited to swiddening, they increased their reliance on animal husbandry. Today, plow farming is the principal strategy of food production, supplemented by pastoralism, or animal husbandry.

The main characteristic of mountainous regions is that relatively short distances involve great changes in altitude, thus offering a wide variety of ecological zones for potential exploitation. Timling's territory contains three large vertical zones based on how people use the altitude-related climate differences: cultivated areas, forests, and pasture lands. The best cultivable land is the lowest (to which they have access), from 5,300 to about 6,000 feet. This lies below the critical snowline (the village itself is frozen hard through much of the winter) and is intercropped with millet and maize. Somewhat higher fields, from 6,000 to 7,000 feet, are planted in maize, potatoes, millet, and barley in an alternating cycle. The poorest arable land, 7,000 up to 8,500 feet, is used for potatoes and wheat in a three-year cycle, including a one-year fallow period. All in all, the 132 households farm approximately 418 acres (or 0.65 acre per person). This modest amount of land, when combined with animal production, supplies enough food to sustain a household. The typical breakdown of crops in terms of land is 26% planted in maize, 16% in millet, 15% in wheat, 29% in barley, and 15% in potatoes (p. 68).

Communal grazing is available to some degree in all three zones, but most grazing land lies in the high pastures above 12,000 feet. The seven square miles are grazed by herds of sheep and goats, including some from other villages, from May until mid-September (p. 65). To save labor, all of the village's sheep and goats (about five or six per household) are combined into three herds. In addition to sheep and goats, most families maintain cattle or oxen for plowing and, in a few cases, water buffalo for milk. Over half of what a family has invested in animals (in the sense of capital) is devoted to cattle, which are used primarily for traction; sheep and goats are used for food and wool. Most families produce their own sturdy clothing from wool—essential in this harsh environment.

Work in Timling is a matter of survival. Each household can be thought of as an independent economic unit defined by the need to provide food for the hearth (p. 73). All households are involved in agricultural, pastoral, and maintenance efforts in a cycle determined by the requirements of the different crops and animals. The principal sources of food are the crops, even though men regard herding, which they do almost exclusively, as preferable to the arduous tasks of plowing, seeding, weeding, harvesting—and even guarding the plots from monkeys and bears that would forage on them.

It appears that the people of Timling have to work almost twice as hard during the year as do the Yanomamö; even household maintenance requires great effort. The mountain environment requires substantial structures for housing. To build a house, the Tamang must go to the forest, cut logs, float them downstream, and then laboriously drag them up the hillside and fashion them into boards. The Tamang must also work hard to gather firewood, since a single family will burn about 154 personloads of firewood each year. Water has to be fetched. The family makes its own tools, storage baskets, and clothing. In this cold environment, each person requires two outfits of heavy clothes. In all, a typical home requires 185 ten-hour person-days

per year of hard work just to perform general maintenance, even though cooking itself is a fairly simple procedure. Daily meals usually consist simply of flour and water cooked as a thick gruel, perhaps accompanied by boiled nettles or potatoes. Meat is eaten only occasionally, when sacrificed in rituals or when an animal falls to its death, as they sometimes do on the steep trails.

## The Domestic Cycle

Given the nature of agriculture and private ownership of fields and cattle, the **domestic cycle,** or how households are formed and organized and how they develop, is very important. If one simply looks at Timling's households at a point in time, as Thomas Fricke did in his initial study, almost 70% were nuclear in composition—that is, a married couple and their unmarried children.[2] But as he notes, this is misleading because each family unit is transformed over time. Children are born, grow up and marry, and deaths occur. The rule is that daughters, when they marry, leave their natal home and move to their husband's, where they reside with his parents, single siblings, and possibly married brothers. Anthropologists call this **patrilocal residence.** A more mature household will often contain at least two married couples of two generations and their children—referred to as an **extended family household.** Even though most households go through this phase in their development, only a few (about 5%) are extended at any given time. The reason is that soon after the oldest son marries, the next son begins thinking along similar lines. Once the second son does marry, the eldest son, his wife, and children are likely to move out to build their own house, set up their own hearth, and tend their own plots—thus beginning their own domestic cycle within a new nuclear household.

A son inherits his share of lands and animals at this point, usually prior to his father's death. The rule is for the youngest son to marry and continue to live in his parents' house until their deaths, when he will inherit the remaining property. This mother/father/youngest son unit is termed a **stem family;** about 25% of Timling's households were of this sort. The composition of the household is of vital importance to its members' quality of life; the sudden death of a young adult can dramatically affect the ability of the family to adequately provision itself. Generally, mature households have a more

---

[2]The people of Timling accept polygyny, but it is now rare. The most common cases occur when men from the village move to India to work, often establishing second marriages there.

favorable ratio of workers to consumers, which reduces the effort devoted to sustaining daily consumption and which may allow for the purchase of additional land or the opening of new fields—all of which can be used to support new households when married sons leave.

*Sexuality and Marriage.*  Marriage is a vital transition event, far surpassing such earlier celebrations as those marking the maturation of the child: a girl's first menses and a boy's *chewar* (first hair cutting). Marriage marks the move to adulthood and ties households together in a web of mutually supportive relationships. Marriages can be arranged by parents or simply entered into by a couple choosing to live together without ritual or money changing hands. When money or wealth is exchanged, it is given by the husband's family and relatives to the girl's father and then passed on to the bride as a form of inheritance: She will have no further claim on her parents' property. Sexual activity begins at puberty and is not viewed with disapproval. Unmarried couples find their ways into the forest and young girls bring their lovers home at night, although trying to keep their amorous activities secret in a crowded communal room is a virtual impossibility.

Clearly, attitudes in Timling toward sex, and especially female sexuality, are drastically different from those of the Yanomamö, where men regularly fight over women and adultery is considered a serious offense. In Timling, if an unmarried woman has a child, she simply names the father. If he is a single man, he may or may not marry her, and if he is already married, he is asked to help support the child. A male child will inherit from his father even if his father and mother never marry, and he is reared in his mother's household. In any event, by age twenty, most women are married and either beginning their own households or residing patrilocally as part of their husband's natal household. Children of unwed parents are not stigmatized. The main concern is to establish paternity for reasons of clan membership and inheritance. Clan membership is socially crucial, since one is the member of one's father's clan and to marry within the clan is forbidden.

The people of Timling do not practice any form of contraception; on the contrary, they promote fertility. While the birth rate is not among the world's highest, probably for reasons of health and because of spousal separation when men go to work abroad, a woman can typically expect to have five or six children. For the time being, at least, children are seen as a source of future household wealth and security, not as dependents who must be supported and among whom land must be divided.

## Prospects for Timling's Future

When Thomas Fricke came to the end of his first fieldwork, he was mildly pessimistic regarding Timling's future. Judging from the experience of other Himalayan communities, he feared that as they continued to be drawn into Nepal's national economy and as the population continued to grow, standards of living would decline and an increasingly uneven distribution of wealth would ensue. Children would no longer be a source of family security but simply mouths to feed from a declining resource base. The villagers themselves were optimistic, thinking that the then-approaching road that would link them to markets would enable them to sell fruit and find better employment.

In his most recent visits, Fricke found both views to be true. The village has changed greatly: in some ways for the better but in other respects not. Now there is an active government-run school, and children are receiving a formal education; a clinic has opened, and health and hygiene have improved. By 1992, most of the villagers had converted, at least nominally, to Christianity; the effects of this transition on traditional attitudes and values are yet to be seen. Now many people are living and working outside the village; some have second homes in the capital. Younger men are finding employment as trekkers—working with parties of tourists who come to hike in the spectacular mountains. The economy has become monetary at the expense of the previous era's system of reciprocity, and some villagers have clearly improved their standards of living. Others, particularly older people, feel that they are being neglected in their old age as their sons and daughters go abroad to work or settle elsewhere where resources are more abundant. Willingly or not, they are becoming active players in an increasingly interconnected world with perhaps the first harbinger of change being the sudden visit by an anthropologist.

# Where the Dove Calls: The Mexican Village of Cucurpe

There is little of greater importance to farmers than access to land and water. What follows is a description of the complex ways in which land can be held in even a small community and the logic that underlies what seems to be a strange combination of private and public or communal resources. Cucurpe, whose name, according to the Opata Indians, means "where the dove calls," is a farming community in northwestern Mexico studied by Thomas Sheridan. He writes:

To those of us who have grown up in the modern cities of Mexico or the United States, a place like Cucurpe seems idyllic, offering us a vision of a distant agrarian past. But if we go beyond that vision, we see that life in Cucurpe is predicated on struggle, not pastoral harmony: struggle to raise crops when the rains won't come or when floods wash away the topsoil; struggle to keep cattle from turning into emaciated ghosts; struggle to prevent neighbors from diverting your irrigation water or fencing your pasture or stealing your land. (1988, p. xv)

The modern community of Cucurpe is, as it has been since the arrival of the Spanish, caught up in conflict between corporate and private land tenure. It is one of the more than 22,000 corporate farming communities in Mexico where 70% of the farm population live (Sheridan, 1988, p. 198). "Corporate" here means that some village resources are legally owned by the community as a whole—in this case, about half the land and most water rights. This conflict over access to land is complicated: It involves fending off the private ranchers, who are ever ready to intrude on the grazing lands of Cucurpe. The conflict is also internal: between those who have land and communal rights, those with some land and no communal rights, and those without land at all but who seek it.

Even though the community is described as corporate, this does not mean that there is economic equality or even that all have equal access to resources. Communal lands are interspersed with private holdings, the owners of which also can claim rights to corporate lands. Wealth distinctions are extreme. People view these distinctions of wealth in terms of three groupings. *Los ricos,* the rich, produce entirely for the market, not for domestic consumption, employ labor, use mechanized technology such as pumps and tractors, and own considerable land and cattle. The wealthiest ten households own over half of all private land in the community and have little interest in preserving any communal rights; generally, they would prefer to privatize all resources. *La gente ordenada,* or middle class, about 60% of the households, are generally self-sufficient peasant-farmers utilizing both some private land (*milpa*) and running cattle on the commons, or corporate lands. They work their own fields and do not employ labor. Their interests in the corporate resources are very strong because they rely on free grazing for their cattle and free water for their fields. *Los pobres,* or the poor, about 18% of the families, own no more than five or six cattle, little or no land, and must work for others to make ends meet. Many of los pobres feel that they should be given

community-owned land to develop and farm and thus find themselves in competition with the others who view these claims as threatening to their own interests. However extreme these differences may appear, within the community care is taken to minimize them socially. The wealthy do not flaunt their wealth, and all take pains to avoid conspicuous consumption within Cucurpe itself.

This is an extremely arid region where water is a critical resource. There are three major forms of land use, largely distinguished by the availability of water. Milpa are fields created laboriously by clearing stones and brush, leveling them by hand, and then bringing in water via canals from one of the drainage systems. They are usually privately owned or treated as though they were private even if technically the title is with community. *Temporales* are fields carved out of the margins of water courses. They are not irrigated, but absorb sufficient runoff water in good years to raise squash and vegetables;

*Milpa farmers in northern Mexico tilling their garden plot of squash and corn.*
(©Phil Schermeister/CORBIS)

they are also treated as though they were private. *Agostadero,* or grazing land, is communal and members can use it at will if they are not restrained by some community decision. These three forms of land use allow people to pursue a diversity of strategies depending on whether they emphasize raising cattle for market, cash crops, subsistence crops, or some mix of these and wage labor. For those who would specialize in ranching, something to which most aspire, a privately owned spread of less than 1,000 hectares would be an unreliable economic base. Any family without outside sources of income—as some have from jobs on ranches or remittances from relatives in America—will require access to at least two of the three major zones of land use; no one can make a living by committing to only one. Here lies the root of both conflict and cooperation.

Politics are heated and unrelenting, reflecting the inequitable division of resources. Ranchers cut fences and are confronted by armed youths from the village. Delegations of the poor petition for land. Others complain about inequitable use of pastures. Those with milpas come together to resist the claims of those without. But usually, these conflicts are played out in nonviolent ways: in the courts, town meetings, and ever-changing coalitions.

As this suggests, the community is not an expression of peasant communal solidarity (Sheridan, 1988, p. 189). Households plot, compete, and only sometimes cooperate. Sheridan's analysis indicates a predictable order underlying the ever-present disputing and alliance making—what he terms the political ecology of land use. Agostadero, or rangeland, is a resource that individuals cannot own and defend alone, unless they happen to be extremely wealthy. Members of the community can best get access to this by working together in defending their rights, keeping outsiders off, and convincing the government of their rights. The land itself is not very valuable in small aggregates, but when taken as a whole, it is worth maintaining as a corporate or common grazing area. Thus, while the rich try to use their influence to gain control of common grazing, or even to steal it, most of the others in the community will respond cooperatively to defend it, even when it is necessary to suppress old antagonisms.

Another resource held corporately is surface water: Whereas rich families can drill wells and run pumps, most must use surface water diverted to the fields by canals and dams. This cannot be done by families acting alone; they must cooperate or not gain access. Here the "middle class" of peasantry gets little support from either the rich or the poor: Both, one way or another, would like to get access to milpas and temporales. All small landowning

families assist in building and maintaining these canals, and each has a right to a specific amount of water for the household's milpa. They guard this right jealously and pass their fields onto their sons and daughters, even though technically some of the land is really corporate property. Families invest great effort in building their fields and planting them and resist any attempt by the landless to have them redistributed. For middle-class peasants, the milpa is the key to survival; even though they make more money from cattle, they can rely on the milpa for food.

Thus, the ranchers and the wealthy continually spar with those who defend the corporate rights of the community; those with fields contend with those without, while those without strive to get the community to grant them land on which to farm. Both the landless and the smallholders unite (or partially unite) to defend the grazing areas from the rich, but even in this, there are bitter divisions: Some of the farmers own many cattle, but others only a few. Everyone knows that the grazing is being damaged by overstocking, but since it is common land, there is little regulation. Thus, the owners of only a few cattle feel that they are victimized by those who own many. Still, "Cucurpe is not a battle ground between collectivism and free enterprise. On the contrary, most Cucurpeños want to be as independent as possible—to run their own cattle, farm their own fields" (Sheridan, 1988, p. 146). Most peasant villages, upon close examination, are likely to show similar sentiments and similar divisions.

## The Kofyar of Central Nigeria

The experience of the Kofyar farmers of Plateau State in central Nigeria offers an interesting example of uncoerced, self-generated change in land use and technology. The Kofyar lived as subsistence farmers on the southern edge of the Jos Plateau when Robert McC. Netting first studied them in 1968. However, over the next thirty years, thousands of farm families voluntarily migrated southward, down from the plateau to the bushlands of the Benue Valley. While continuing to produce their own subsistence crops with traditional hoe technology, they began producing yams on a commercial scale for the Nigerian domestic market. To do this, they have adopted new techniques and systems of land use but have mobilized the increased labor input necessary for this undertaking by manipulating traditional social networks. They have also "used their cash earnings enthusiastically to purchase a variety of manufactured goods and modern educational, medical, and transportation services" (Netting et al., 1996, p. 329). This major agricultural expansion has taken place with almost no direct government or development agency intervention to provide planned extension services or credit. In fact, Netting et al. argue that the success of the Kofyar in managing this transformation lay in the very fact that outside agencies were generally unaware of their existence and the government made no attempt to direct their cultivation methods or control their economy (1996, p. 345).

In 1968, Netting was interested in why Kofyar households in their homeland on the Jos Plateau were uniformly small, stable, and nuclear, and lived in permanent compounds on farms where they held permanent rights. The Kofyar occupied villages clustered on the rugged hilltops separated by steep gorges, where much of the terrain was difficult or impossible to cultivate, and hundreds of contiguous farmsteads on the plain at the base of the southern escarpment. The high ratio of population to productive land meant that the Kofyar engaged in intensive agriculture, producing staples of millet, sorghum, maize, cowpea, and other minor crops in an "infield" surrounding the household compound; the hill slopes were extensively terraced to cultivate further produce. Such small-scale but intensive farming was manageable by a small number of people, and Netting was able to show that the Kofyar household was closely fitted to the conditions of production.

Beginning in the 1930s, since the British had by then put a stop to the raiding that kept the Kofyar on their inaccessible plateau, a few Kofyar had begun a minor expansion of subsistence farming to seasonal swidden plots outside the homeland around Namu and in the Benue lowlands. By 1960, this had become an agricultural frontier, with over 100 compounds growing cash crops of rice and yams. To start with, the migrants continued to maintain their homeland farms, moving household members from homestead to bush farm as labor was needed. However, as the profitability of their cash crops increased, and in response to the need to protect the frontier farms from animal predators, and later from human competitors, households moved permanently to their frontier farms, building houses with kitchens, brewing huts, yam barns, pigsties, goat shelters, and granaries. As the population density increased on the frontier, the Kofyar abandoned swidden cultivation and brought their fields into permanent cultivation by crop rotation, frequent weeding, intercropping, manuring, and chemical fertilization (Netting et al., 1996, p. 333). By 1984, a survey of 979 households showed that 74% had migrated to the frontier, and over half the sample had abandoned their homeland farms to reside there.

This pattern of settlement and agricultural intensification obviously required increased labor inputs. Netting et al. note that "[N]either Kofyar migration nor greater output was contingent on the adoption of a new technology" (1996, p. 333). As on the homestead farms, the bulk of labor on the migrants' farms came from the household, and to meet the increasing need for labor, migrant households grew. Large households could not only provide for the seasonal demands of cash crops but could also allocate some labor to the maintenance of homestead farms. Whereas in the 1960s homeland households had averaged 4.17 members, migrant households averaged 6.44; by 1984, the average migrant household had 8.38 members. Growth in household size reflected in part an increased frequency of polygyny facilitated by using cash from crop sales for bride wealth and in part a tendency to form multiple family households by, for example, keeping married sons on their fathers' farms. However, as the frontier bushlands filled up, and as homestead farms were finally abandoned, households have become less complex and smaller, averaging only 5.70 members.

While the household is the principal source of labor, cooperative groups of friends and neighbors also provide an important input. Netting et al. note that although the Kofyar traditionally exchanged some agricultural labor, ". . . we had predicted that the major emphasis on cash-cropping and the end of the free land for frontier expansion would lead to more wage labor and less interhousehold collaboration" (1996, p. 335). In the event they were wrong, for although labor is occasionally hired, its role is minor compared with the cooperative work groups, which have increased in frequency and variety from traditional groups of thirty to eighty neighbors who "farm for beer" or smaller groups of eight to twenty who regularly exchange work, to new forms of collective labor groups centered on churches, schools, and social clubs. One reason the Kofyar say they prefer beer party or exchange labor is that in their intensively interplanted fields they can rely on the skill and experience of their neighbors in weeding and ridging not to damage maturing crops. And the fact that, although farms are getting smaller, there is still land available means that the Kofyar themselves are not forced by lack of resources to participate in wage labor. "As long as population density on the frontier remains below the level at which small holdings are economically viable, intensification maintains adequate returns on labor, and out-migration reduces pressure on land, the role of wage labor may not appreciably increase" (Netting et al., 1996, p. 338).

The Kofyar have voluntarily and enthusiastically become incorporated into the market economy. They have done so gradually, and because no one has told them what to do or when to do it, they have had the time and opportunity to learn from their mistakes. Although they could have continued to maintain themselves from their homestead farms, they chose to invest their time and effort in producing for the market, and they eagerly invest the cash they earn in buying manufactured goods, medical services, and education. Nevertheless, despite severe depopulation, the Kofyar still strongly identify with their ancestral homelands on the plateau, and they have devised deliberate strategies to maintain homeland settlement in the face of the continuing economic pull of the frontier. Stone (1998) identifies five basic strategies.

**Enhancing homeland infrastructure:** The inaccessibility of the homelands was a key reason for original Kofyar settlement, but by the 1970s, it had become a factor in the abandonment of homestead farms. However, Kofyar who have left for careers in the city frequently want to build vacation houses in the homeland, and they have used their influence to arrange for the building of roads to facilitate access. The building of these vacation homes in itself has served to keep the homeland communities alive, and in Bong, the Protestant community of nineteen adults has built a large church. The increasing influence of Kofyar in local and regional government has also attracted state investment in the form of a borehole well with a pump providing a year-round water supply.

**Maintenance of home farms:** Many migrants kept their homestead farms to use for lodging during social events and festivals; others kept them as secondary farms, which the male head of household would visit a few times during the growing season.

**Public events:** Traditional and modern ceremonies and events are frequently held in the homelands, including "launchings" inaugurating civic programs, installations of chiefs, and funeral rituals. These events attract large crowds, sometimes in the thousands, from the frontier and the city. In 1994, Stone attended an enormous gathering that celebrated the appointment of a Kofyar to administrative head of Plateau State.

**Schools:** Stone describes the use of schools as the most important strategy to preserve homeland settlements. From the 1940s through the 1960s, the British built a total of ten primary schools in the hills. When in the 1970s the military government of Nigeria began a program of school building in the region, Kofyar leaders argued for their location in the homelands, an argument helped by the fact that many frontier households continued to pay tax through their home communities. Five more schools were built. The presence of the schools entails the presence of an adult population to look after the children, and the children can work on agricul-

*Kofyar family tilling their homeland fields. Older or retired relatives look after children attending school in the homelands, while parents live on frontier farms.*

(©Glenn Stone with permission)

tural tasks when school is not in session. Even for families living full time on the frontier, sending children to homeland schools is considered a civic duty. This, and the fact that most of the adult population is aging or "retired," has led to a bimodal age distribution in the current homeland population.

**Retirement:** Some migrants "retire" to the homelands because they have always regarded their frontier farms as temporary, even after twenty-five years; others return to set an example of commitment to their ancestral lands; still others return for medical treatment because traditional medicine is felt to be more effective in the homeland. Furthermore, the homeland is the preferred place to die.

Stone argues that their homeland is more than a symbol of their ancestry for the Kofyar: "it serves as a facility for reaffirming . . . traditions, for celebrating and publicizing accomplishments, establishing and renewing political and economic connections" (1998, p. 261). He also notes that political districting in Nigeria is usually closely tied to ethnic identification, and since government resources are generally allocated to local administrations, the Kofyar have very practical incentives to maintain their homeland identification to attract political and economic investment from the state.

# Directions of Change in Rural Egypt

Egypt, where the first steps toward intensive land use occurred and where early civilization thrived, is presently in the midst of an economic and social transition that is having a great impact on its millions of *fellahin,* or smallholder farmers and farm laborers. Rural Egypt is a land full of life, dynamic and changing, but treading a fine line between progress and impoverishment. In 1997, a group of Egyptian and foreign researchers, close observers of rural Egyptian society, met in Aswan to compare their findings. This conference resulted in the volume edited by Nicholas Hopkins and Kirsten Westergaard from which the following report is largely drawn. This is not a study paralleling the others in this chapter, but is more of a brief snapshot of one nation's efforts to reconcile a long tradition of peasant farming with the demands of the global economy.

*The Transition to a Market Economy.* One of the big changes affecting Egyptian society, and of course many other countries as well, as the next chapter

shows, is the effort to move from a planned or heavily socialized economy to a market-driven economy. Other changes affecting rural society include the spread in importance of mass education and television. Also, urban and even foreign wage labor migration has opened up new options and opportunities for rural people. As elsewhere in the world, people are on the move; Cairo is one of the world's megacities along with Mexico City, Istanbul, Calcutta, New Delhi, and many other centers bursting with new arrivals from the countryside—mostly poor peasants whose presence gives many urban places a distinctly rural hue. Although people have new choices and opportunities, they still cope within a framework set by the ruling classes in Egypt, by institutions inherited from the past, and by the global economic system.

In 1997, 57% of the 61 million population of Egypt were rural dwelling and predominantly engaged in agriculture (Hopkins & Westergaard, 1998, p. 2). But one should not confuse the countryside with farming because in Egypt, as elsewhere, the urban and rural domains are merging. In Egypt, one can speak of the urbanization of the countryside just as one can speak of the ruralization of the city; factories abound and offer employment, universities and schools have been opened, rural housing is rapidly being transformed, rural people share in the recreational activities of urbanites, and many people move back and forth between village and city. Most farmers, or fellahin, live in villages in the Nile Valley and delta, which range in size from hamlets of several hundred people to agro-towns, with the average village size of about 7,000. Comparatively speaking, these are extremely large villages, reflecting Egypt's dense population concentrated on limited agricultural lands. Farming is rooted, for the most part, in smallholdings with the individual farmer having access to an average of only 2.5 acres, or about 1 hectare.

Of all the recent changes, the most important developments, which became effective in 1997, are the abolition of state control over the rents that landowners can charge and the abolition of tenants' rights to renew leases and to pass their leases on to their children. It is estimated that 800,000 farmers lost their access to land for these reasons (Müller-Mahn, 1998, p. 256). This legal change, which so greatly affected smallholders in Egypt, is part of what economists call **structural adjustment**—a somewhat obscure way to describe the extension of the free market and privatization of the productive infrastructure. In Egypt, this included an end to most crop subsidies and supports and price controls of food, land, and other commodities. This is part of a global movement pushed strongly by U.S. and European economic policies, primarily implemented by the World Bank and the International Monetary Fund through conditions attached to vital loans these organizations make available to developing countries. "The dominant theme in the description of the rural Third World at the close of the twentieth century remains the story of its capitalist transformation. The theme is exemplified in rural Egypt, where the reform and removal of state controls through the program known as structural adjustment is intended to turn the land and its produce into market commodities and remake the countryside for the twenty-first century as a fully capitalist economy" (Mitchell, 1998, p. 19).

***Responding to Structural Adjustment.*** It is hard to predict the long-term effects of these changes, which are meant to stimulate market production, innovation in agriculture, and extend prosperity to the countryside. In the past, farmers had virtual hereditary title to the lands they rented, often at a nominal price. The observers participating in the Aswan conference generally felt that these economic changes risk impoverishing many fellahin families and will push them out of rural areas (Hopkins & Westergaard, 1998, p. 7). But at the same time, looking at data from the 1990s, conditions of rural life in general are gradually improving, as measured by increased consumption, longer life expectancy, and rising rates of literacy (1998).

However, one has to go from the general to the specific instances of villages and even individual men and women. Timothy Mitchell, in his analysis of market relations in a sugarcane-producing village six kilometers north of Luxor on the Nile, revealed some interesting and paradoxical results. Until the introduction of free market prices for food crops, especially for wheat, which is the main food staple for fellahin smallholders, almost all wheat flour was purchased in sacks as needed to prepare large loaves of *'aysh shamsi*, bread leavened in the sun and baked in earthen ovens at home (p. 21). Of the 2,000 farm families in the village, only a dozen households grew their own wheat, and all these owned 100 or more acres of land. For the average household, bread is the main source of food. With the end of price control, wheat flour became prohibitively expensive for most families, and smallholders rapidly took to raising their own wheat at the expense of sugarcane, their cash crop. Some families with access to only very small amounts of land put all their fields into domestic food production. The paradox from a developmental point of view is that the free market has led to a decline in the participation in the market because many peasants are forced to move ". . . toward increased self-provisioning and protection from the market" (p. 23).

A similar response is witnessed in the area of farm mechanization since the 1990s. In the village studied by Mitchell, by 1987 almost all tillage was by tractor. Once fuel subsidies were withdrawn, people turned again to camels to transport sugarcane and to buffalo with which to plow. As one villager put it, a cow uses homegrown fodder and trains its own calf as it plows to eventually replace it (p. 24). At a more general level, discussed by François Ireton (1998), Egypt is witnessing the end of an era in which farm size disparities were being reduced and seeing the beginning of a period of reconcentrating landholdings.

Just as with changing land access and land use, domestic relations within the family household are also in flux. As more and more men migrate to the city or abroad in search of wage labor, women come to play a more important role in the rural work force, and many manage what are in effect female-headed households. Women have always played an important role in social networking (Bach, 1998, p. 196). In traditional village society, Bach reports, women and girls would meet regularly on the canal to wash clothing together, bathe children, and socialize—each representing a familial grouping much as their men would in their meetings at the mosque or teashops. Their homes, too, built of mud brick, had a broad entranceway in which family members would invite other villagers to sit and exchange conversation and small snacks. Now, according to Bach, there is a significant change in interpersonal relationships in that the village in the course of modernization has piped water and washing is done at home. And since communications have improved, most villagers shop in nearby market towns where their children now attend school. Thus, socialization is more individualized and less family to family as in the past, in particular as far as women are concerned (p. 196).

Another change among fellahin due to education and wage labor migration is in patterns of consumption. Prior to the mid-1980s, villagers had little access to or even desire for expensive consumer goods. Now two "social fields" are emerging: the fellahin who are left behind in the new economy and those who now have education and access to urban or foreign employment. This latter grouping is suddenly visible with the building of red brick houses with modern kitchens, indoor bathrooms, new furniture, and appliances. Patterns of consumption and income are reflected in sociocultural cleavages. Fellahin who have money are buying land, as they

*Village on the Nile south of Luxor, Egypt. While mechanization is evident in pumps and waterworks, much tillage is still done by hand or with animals, particularly among poorer farmers after "structural readjustment."*
(Daniel Bates)

might have before, but now this new class views land purchase as an investment strategy, not as a means to achieve household sufficiency (p. 199).

*Religion and Change.* A final dimension of the transformation of rural and urban society is religion. Religion, both for the rural Coptic Christian minority and the Muslim majority, has always been very important. Historically, for Muslims, religious experience has focused on the local "saint" cults and mystical brotherhoods. The saints offered a spiritual analogy to the secular patron–client hierarchy in that saints could be asked to help as intermediaries with God; the brotherhoods taught ways to achieve mystical union with God (Hopkins & Westergaard, 1988, pp. 8ff). With the urbanization of the countryside and the movement of millions to urban centers in search of work, a third religious style has emerged that some would call "scriptualist" or "Islamist." In the approach to the Islamic faith, there is a strong emphasis on the strict observation of rules and codes of behavior. In some respects, this reflects the adoption by hitherto illiterate classes of society

of some of the normative aspects of clerical Islam. According to James Toth (1998), working in the south in communities where militant Islamic groups are prominent, farm laborers and smallholders, when displaced from their villages, responded to the problems they encountered in trying to survive in the city by embracing a politically active Islamism of this sort. While such Islamic groups originally recruited members from the educated population, following the economic crises of the 1980s they attracted large numbers of urban-dwelling fellahin. Increasingly, the government was unwilling or unsuccessful in providing neighborhood or community social services in poor districts, a role which has come to be filled by religious organizations. This is a phenomenon found not only in other Muslim countries, but elsewhere where rural people are displaced by large-scale economic and social change.

While it is impossible to predict the future, and despite the problems noted, in the long term, Egypt's rural society may be transformed for the better. There still is no question that the transition is a deeply wrenching experience for those caught up in it.

## Summary

INTENSIVE AGRICULTURE IS DISTINGUISHED FROM horticulture by both an increased investment in energy and increased productivity per unit of land. The additional energy may come from a variety of sources, including animals yoked to plows, fossil fuels for farm machinery, fertilizers, and human muscles. Methods of intensification include irrigation canals, terracing, crop rotation, and selective breeding of crops and livestock. Through these techniques, the output of cultivated fields is increased, more fields can be cultivated, and fallow periods can be decreased or eliminated. While both the land and the farmer work harder under intensive agriculture, the result is much higher production.

Intensive agriculture substantially reshapes the environment. By constructing irrigation systems to overcome the problem of insufficient rainfall, for instance, farmers may create new, complex problems that become increasingly difficult to solve. The more people alter their ecosystems, the more labor and organizational effort are required to maintain their bases of production.

The social consequences of intensification are far-reaching. The development of irrigation is associated with the emergence of cities and territorial states, with accompanying social changes: higher population densities, economic stratification, increased trade, the appearance of craft specialists, and the development of hierarchical civil and religious organizations. The need for centralized authority to make decisions, variations in the productivity of land in the region, and a surplus of food all contributed to the rise of cities and states. Farming communities that were at one time autonomous were absorbed by the states, and the farmers (or peasants) lost control over the social and economic system and the means of production. Peasants are agriculturists (usually villagers) who do not control the land, capital, and labor on which they depend; further, they are often subject to corvée, unpaid labor to build and maintain roads and bridges. In some parts of the world, peasants gain access to land by sharecropping, or working land owned by others in exchange for a share of the yield.

Under exceptional circumstances, peasant farmers may find their situation intolerable and rise in revolt. In the twentieth century, they supported revolutions in Algeria, Mexico, Russia, China, and Cuba. Even when such uprisings are successful, the farmers often remain disadvantaged in relation to the urban population.

The Tamang of Timling village in Nepal live in a mountainous environment in which they exploit a variety of vertical climate zones. Some they plow and plant in wheat, corn, potatoes, and millet; others they use for animal production and foraging for firewood and building supplies. Unlike many peasants, the people of Timling maintain control over their own lands, and variation in wealth among households is not great. In contrast to the Yanomamö discussed in Chapter 4, they have a relatively relaxed attitude toward sex, prize peaceful relations with others, and engage in no warfare. As they are drawn into the national culture and its market economy, the Tamang risk losing their independence and self-sufficiency.

Like the Tamang, the villagers of Cucurpe in northwestern Mexico value their independence. However, their complicated systems of land tenure and the inequitable distribution of resources lead to constant conflicts and shifting alliances among the three groups of farmers that make up the community: los ricos (the rich), who produce entirely for the market; la gente ordenada (the middle class), who are generally self-sufficient peasant farmers with access to both private and communal lands; and los pobres (the poor), who own little or no land and must work for others.

The Kofyar of central Nigeria offer an illustration of subsistence farmers moving on their own initiative, and with no government or development agency intervention, into intensive agriculture and active and enthusiastic participation in the market economy. They have adopted new techniques and systems of land use, but mobilized the increased labor input necessary by manipulating traditional social networks. Their success seems in large part due to the very fact that outside agencies were generally unaware of their existence. Thus, they were able to make the change gradually, and because no one has told them what to do or when to do it, they have had the time and opportunity to learn from their mistakes.

Recent reforms in Egypt abolishing state control over land rents and tenants' rights to renew leases or pass leases on to their children have led to wrenching changes in rural society as the fellahin adapt to the "structural adjustment" of the extension of the free market. Women's roles in particular have changed as men migrate in search of wage labor, and there has also developed a division between two "social fields" of fellahin: those who have some education and have been successful in the market economy and those who have been unable to take advantage of new opportunities. Nevertheless, despite the many problems economic reform entails, in the long term Egypt's rural society may be transformed for the better.

## Key Terms

| | |
|---|---|
| administrative system | intensification |
| corvée | patrilocal residence |
| domestic cycle | peasants |
| extended family | sharecropping |
| household | stem family |
| fallow time | structural adjustment |

## Suggested Readings

Bray, F. (1994). *The rice economies: Technology and development in Asian societies.* Berkeley: University of California Press. This book extensively describes the history and techniques of rice cultivation.

Cole, J. W., & Wolf, E. R. (2000). *The hidden frontier: Ecology and ethnicity in an alpine valley.* Berkeley: University of California Press. This is a reprint of a now classic comparative study of ethnicity, identity, and the political ecology of two farming communities. While faced with very similar environmental conditions, the two villages developed very different family structures and work organization.

Durrenberger, E. P., & Tannenbaum, N. (1990). *Analytical perspectives on Shan agriculture and village economics,* Monograph Series, 37. New Haven, CT: Yale University Southeast Asia Studies. This volume discusses and analyzes the economics of Shan agriculture and farmer decision making.

Hopkins, N. S., Mehanna, S. R., & el-Haggar, S. (2001). *People and pollution: Cultural constructions and social action in Egypt.* Cairo and New York: American University in Cairo Press. This book provides a unique look at how the Egyptian people understand their environment and how they cope with massive problems of pollution, including dirty streets, poor air quality, pesticide use, and noise pollution.

Hopkins, N. S., & Westergaard, K. (Eds.) (1998). *Directions of change in rural Egypt.* Cairo: American University in Cairo Press. A collection of original essays on various dimensions of rural change in Egypt. It is particularly insightful in terms of how people must cope with a new political environment in which peasant farmers must survive in a free market and one in which they no longer have guaranteed access to rented fields.

Kirch, V. P. (1994). *The wet and the dry: Irrigation and agricultural intensification in Polynesia.* Chicago: University of Chicago Press. A fine-grained review of intensive agriculture in a region that is often overlooked.

Loker, W. M. (Ed.) (1999). *Globalization and the rural poor in Latin America.* Boulder, CO: Lynne Rienner. A collection of essays dealing with important development issues whose significance goes beyond Latin America. People everywhere have to contend with some of the same problems as they attempt to secure a livelihood from the land.

Schroeder, R. A. (1999). *Shady practices: Agroforestry and gender politics in the Gambia.* Berkeley: University of California Press. A cultural geographer looks at the political ecology of development and land use in a West African village. In particular, he documents the conflicting interests of women who farm profitable market gardens and male-dominated irrigated farming where men would prefer their wives to work.

## Chapter 7

# Industrial Society and Beyond: Feeding the World

### From Intensive Agriculture to Industrialized Farming

In Europe, particularly in England, France, and Germany in the early nineteenth century, steam and internal combustion engines were harnessed to machines both for manufacturing and for transport. Just as with the rest of society, industrialism has transformed farming and farm society, but it can still be seen as a series of adaptive responses much like those already examined in other subsistence systems. It is a way of coping with challenges and resolving specific problems. As in all other instances of behavioral adaptation, the very act of coping creates the potential for negative as well as positive effects. The success or failure of industrial adaptations to human problems can be evaluated only in terms of long-range survival. It can be understood only in terms of specific people solving specific problems. Industrialism is a major societal commitment that has been underway for some 250 years. Not all the consequences are clearly understood even now. Further complicating the picture is the fact that industrialism is not an adaptation to a single local set of constraints or problems,

and so the costs and benefits vary widely. Can one truly say that urban youths employed in the service sector are benefiting from the system to the same degree as computer specialists in California's Silicon Valley? Are the unemployed young farmers of eastern Turkey, where the soils and rugged terrain limit mechanized farming, benefiting to the same extent that their western counterparts are when they use tractors and combines or export fruit and vegetables raised in heated greenhouses? Unfortunately, one of the consequences of intensive agriculture and industrial development is an increase in disparities among individuals occupying different positions within the economy. This also has profound and ongoing effects on the world's population.

### Intensification through Science and Industry

Increasing population demands an increase in food production through intensification, and during the Industrial Revolution, this

*With industrial inputs, economic development is often very uneven within countries. Here the disparities are evident between a poor Kurdish village in eastern Turkey with limited potential for intensification and the well-watered lands of a west central community.*

(Daniel Bates)

process proceeded at an incredibly rapid pace. In fact, one of the first areas in which factory production made itself felt was the farm. Steel plows, threshers, combines, reapers, and mowers developed in the nineteenth century were followed by the gasoline tractor early in the twentieth.

*Mechanization.* Much of the energy involved in industrialism is channeled through machines rather than through animals and humans. However, **mechanization**—the replacement of human and animal labor by mechanical devices, enabling humans to vastly increase the amount of product derived from one unit of land and labor—began long before the Industrial Age. Sails have been used to power ships for millennia. Mechanical devices of increasing size and complexity have been developed over the centuries for a variety of purposes: waging war, forging metals, constructing monumental buildings, grind-

ing grain, making cloth. It is quite astonishing to note how far mechanization had proceeded even during what are sometimes called the Dark Ages. Outside Paris in the sixteenth century, an ingenious system of hydraulic pumps drew water from the Seine for manufacturing purposes. However, it was only with the invention of the steam engine (and later the diesel and internal combustion engines) that populations were able to harness the concentrated solar energy stored in the fossil remains of organic matter (coal, oil, and gas). With these sources of energy, people throughout the world have vastly increased the scale of intensive agriculture, enabling humans to harness more energy per capita, as explained earlier.

Despite the ingenuity of these machines, it was not until the relatively recent development of sophisticated metallurgical techniques and power transmission systems that a breakthrough was achieved in the amount of power that could effectively be delivered. Such machinery has transformed our idea of work. Labor is increasingly devoted to the management and maintenance of machinery rather than to the products the machines make. The whole field of robotics is a case in point. Specialists in programming and maintaining industrial robots are now key personnel in heavy, light, and service industries.

New sources of energy and the technology to harness them laid the groundwork for expansion of agricultural production on a scale never witnessed before. However, farmers in industrial societies often invest more energy in fertilizer and gasoline for their tractors than they harvest in calories of food energy, even with high-yield grains. Moreover, large quantities of energy are diverted to non–food-producing activities. Thus, an industrial society is significantly less efficient than a nonindustrial society in the sense that it requires more energy to support a unit of population—but it is this pattern of high consumption that produces high standards of living.

*Nonmechanized Approaches to Intensification.* Another means of intensifying yields is by developing new crops and new strains of established ones. Francesca Bray documents how, over the centuries, Asian farmers developed new varieties of rice, increasing productivity and shortening the growing season (1994). The UN's Food and Agriculture Organization (FAO) predicts that sixty-four countries will be unable to feed their peoples by the year 2025 (Cunningham & Saigo, 1995, p. 204). The main hope is that new crops and strains will produce ever more food, since croplands are limited.

Following World War II, research began on ways to increase yields of cereal crops, mainly rice, corn, and wheat. The results have ushered in what is called the **Green Revolution;** new strains have tripled or quadrupled yields per hectare. Without these new varieties, there would be even more widespread hunger in the world, but the so-called "miracle crops" are really "high responders" rather than high yielders (Cunningham & Saigo, 1995, p. 105). They respond more efficiently to increases in fertilizers and water and have higher yields in optimum conditions; they often do poorly in bad years. Thus, the benefits of the Green Revolution tend to accrue to the richer farmers who can afford to buy the seeds, fertilizers, and water.

Scientists in the Philippines are rapidly closing on yet a third generation "super rice" that will help to feed Asia's growing population. "The challenge now is that every day 2.5 billion people eat rice—by 2025 . . . that number will be four billion, and that means we have to produce 70 percent more rice from less land with less water and less labor." The prototype of a promising strain has already been developed that will go some way to meeting that challenge; so-called "super rice" will allow farmers to increase crop yields 20 to 25% (Mydans, 1997, p. 9).

In recent years, the use of **genetically modified (GM) crops** has grown rapidly in the United States and Canada. But GM crops have turned out to be highly controversial, especially in Europe and the developed countries of Asia. In the strictest sense, all domesticated crops are genetically "modified"; that is what natural selection is all about. What is special

*Large combine-harvester working in a field of genetically modified soybeans in Ohio, USA, where much of the farming is industrialized. Virtually all soybeans grown in the US are genetically modified to enhance their resistance to pests and to increase their tolerance for insecticides and weed killers.*

(© CORBIS)

*Fish farming has spread to virtually every coast on most continents. Here small skiffs shuttle 80 meter circumference salmon pens around the harbor in Dover, Tasmania.*
(© Paul A. Souders/CORBIS)

in the current group of GM crops is that the gene that is modified is taken directly from another species, often entirely unrelated. *BT* corn takes its name from a soil bacterium, *Bacillus thuringiensis*, a gene from which makes the entire corn plant toxic to the corn-borer parasite, enabling the farmer to achieve greater yields and to use less pesticide (*The Economist*, 2000, p. 54). Most soybeans grown in the United States are now from GM seeds. Consumers who have very recently sparked intense interest in organic foods are leading the protest against GM crop imports in Japan and Europe. While there is no evidence that there are any health hazards to GM foods, consumers are wary and this is causing a problem for farmers. Even big food producers or processors such as fast-food chains, supermarkets, and poultry producers may increasingly avoid purchases of GM crops or animals raised on them. Europe and the United States have been locked in a trade dispute that is just now being resolved by the United States agreeing to label all GM exports—which will hurt sales. There is also one important environmental issue that may force this technology off of the market. Although only theoretically possible, some fear that with time GM organisms may spread into wild variants, changing their resistance to disease, need for nutrients, or climatic tolerances, which could result in serious but as yet unmeasurable negative impacts.

## The Blue Revolution

It has often been said that if agriculture were invented today, it would never have passed environmental scrutiny: It threatens wildlife, pollutes waterways, reshapes habitats, and produces animals pumped up with hormones and antibiotics. Since the mid-1970s, a new form of farming has developed that supplies a significant portion of the nutrients used by the world's peoples. This is aquaculture, often referred to as the **Blue Revolution**. And while agriculture developed over the centuries, commercial aquaculture was developed by scientists in the full light of environmental knowledge and awareness. As a consequence, like genetic engineering, it is extremely controversial. Although heralded initially as a solution to declining fisheries worldwide and a source of high-quality low-cost protein, it soon came into disrepute once it became a major industry. The main charge is that it is extremely polluting, as a typical fish farm raising salmon has about 75,000 fish, which produce the waste equivalent of a town of 20,000 people. In South America and Southeast Asia, millions of hectares of mangrove swamps have been cleared for shrimp farming, thus threatening many species of wildlife (Cunningham & Saigo, 1995, p. 209). Also, many domesticated fish escape each year and compete with their wild cousins. Up to 90% of the fish in some of Norway's fiords are domesticates. In the United States, farmed fish including Asian carp have escaped into rivers such as the Mississippi, where they are a threat to native species; should they make it into the Great Lakes, they might endanger a very large number of native fish.

Although commercial aquaculture is a recent phenomenon, raising fish in ponds has been practiced in Asia for several thousand years. But this form of aquaculture was usually seasonal when paddies were flooded and generally aimed at domestic consumption. The fish raised are usually herbivorous. Modern fish farming is as industrialized as the battery raising of chickens, pigs, or beef and, often, as with trout, salmon, cod, and bream, requires that the fish be fed other fish in the form of fishmeal. Each kilo of most farmed fish requires several kilos of wild fish to feed them (*The Economist*, Aug. 9, 2003, pp. 20–21), and this results in a greater buildup of harmful PCBs in the farmed fish. The fish caught to produce the 30 million tons of fishmeal needed each year are the so-called "industrial" fish: anchovies, sardines, menhaden, and eel. Nevertheless, since 1990, the industry has been growing at a rate of 10% a year and is the world's fastest growing form of food production. About one half of all seafood consumed by Americans is farmed. Similar patterns of consumption are found throughout the industrialized world because farming allows fish to be sold in supermarkets alongside beef and poultry.

The question is: Can this mode of food production be sustained? Certainly, it would be very difficult to do without this new source of protein. While the environmental problems are real, there are some positive signs. One is that the tilapia, a fresh water fish now much favored in the United States, is herbivorous and is an efficient converter of grain meals into flesh. Most shellfish do not cause pollution. There are ways of reducing the amount of fishmeal that has to be fed carnivorous fish by some 50%. One environmental advantage that fish farming has over the wild fisheries is that it is more easily regulated by governments. Even inland shrimp farming can be made less polluting by raising them together with tilapia, which "mop up" the waste. What wildlife experts argue for is a process of regulation and certification of domesticated fish and shellfish much as we see with dolphin-friendly tuna.

## Specialization

Some key components of the Industrial Era are as important for their cognitive as for their technological effects. The development of precise instruments for measuring time was critical to most sophisticated technologies and processes. At the same time, the gears that drove elaborate mechanical clocks were pivotal elements in directing human attention to a mechanical view of the world, which in turn became a key to the physical knowledge on which industry is based. The view of the world as a machine underlies the concept of the assembly line, which depends on quality (or more accurately, precision). Specialization in high-volume production depends on the availability of interchangeable parts, which requires a level of precision that did not develop in a significant way until the early nineteenth century (initially in the weapons industry). Centralization is also required because industry standards must be developed to facilitate the use of interchangeable parts. Even on the assembly line, tasks are broken down into simple components. This division of labor permits the employment of unskilled labor, and the worker becomes one more component in the productive process.

Workers often come to see little of themselves in their product. Their labor is used impersonally, and they respond in kind. Perhaps belatedly, industrial employers are realizing that this is not necessarily the most efficient way to organize production in a high-technology society. General Motors now operates facilities at which teams of workers have the responsibility for producing entire cars. Increasing amounts of knitwear are being manufactured in New England homes, reviving a cottage industry that had almost died out by the end of the nineteenth century.

Along with the specialization of tasks, spatial specialization continues to intensify in industrial as well as postindustrial societies. Regions, cities, and even neighborhoods become associated with particular products, while agricultural districts come to depend on a limited array of crops. In fact, the bulk of the world's population is sustained by three crops: rice, wheat, and maize (corn) (Cunningham & Saigo, 1995, p. 215). This is in sharp contrast to the self-sufficiency that marked local adaptations in earlier eras where local populations relied on local and very diverse food sources. The city's workplaces or factories come to be highly specialized. Each produces only a limited range of products, but often, they are of exceptionally high volume and quality.

Today, we can see this specialization on a global scale. The increasing congruence of the world's cultures is a direct product of industrialization. Advanced transportation and communication systems, along with international migration, have brought peoples once isolated into contact with other societies. Above all, geographical barriers have been broken down by the economic forces of an international market system. Products are manufactured on one continent from the raw materials of another and sold on still another. The decisions made by Iowa wheat farmers affect the price of bread in India; the cost of oil in the Persian Gulf helps determine the cost of corn in the United States. In essence, the world's people are coming to live and produce under increasingly similar economic conditions.

When agriculture becomes specialized, farmers tend to view their work as a business, emphasizing cash flow and yield per unit of capital invested. Contemporary farmers in the United States, Europe, and the Third World concentrate on producing cash crops while buying food for themselves in the marketplace. In most countries, it is the exception rather than the norm for a rural household to rely directly on what it produces for food, shelter, and clothing. As mentioned in the discussion of Turkey, nomadic herders now sell their milk and wool and use the cash to buy margarine, flour, and factory-made clothing. Agricultural specialization allows for broader participation in a market economy. This generally provides access to a wider range of goods and services, but it also has some negative consequences. Reliance on cash crops increases the risk of

**Industrialized system**

**Figure 7.1.** *Oil or other exogenous fuel sources drive industrial food production: They are used to manufacture and power equipment, to produce fertilizers and insecticides, to process livestock fodder, and to transport food over long distances. While massive food surpluses can be readily produced in favored regions, it is a system that, as currently structured, can produce great regional disparities in wealth.*

failure. Moreover, this risk increases as intensified agriculture moves toward industrialism. Now many of the world's most important cash crops are not only volatile in price, but inedible. A farm family cannot eat the cotton it cannot sell.

Agriculture has become specialized in another fashion that some feel can be dangerous over the long term. As the Green Revolution has succeeded, the number of crop varieties has dramatically decreased. A few so-called "miracle varieties" have replaced several hundred types of wheat in the Middle East; the same is true of corn in the Americas. A hint of what might happen is the U.S. corn leaf blight of 1970, in which nearly all the hybrid (bioengineered, high-yield) corn was threatened (Cunningham & Saigo, 1995). The lack of genetic diversity makes crop failure on a massive scale possible.

Social relations also change with increasing specialization because households no longer operate as integrated, self-sufficient units. When agribusiness supplants traditional farming, the farm family is increasingly removed from the family network on which it once relied not only for social interaction but for labor and loans. In places of urban employment, kin groups become removed from production or redistribution: People rely less on family members than on fellow employees or associates. Social class, professional affiliation, ethnicity, and union membership take on functions of mutual responsibility and support formerly restricted to relatives. This is not to say that kinship is unimportant, but its functions do change.

## Population Growth

The industrial age ushered in a host of social changes. First, and perhaps most obvious, population increased rapidly. Europe's population grew from 100 to 187 million between 1650 and 1800; it then leaped to 400 million in the nineteenth-century coal age—an increase of 260% (White, 1949, p. 384). Today, the world's population is doubling every thirty-five years (Cowell, 1994, p. 10). Birthrates are significantly higher in the Third World than in industrial nations today, while death rates are declining; the result is explosive population growth. The Central American nation of El Salvador, the most densely populated country in the Western Hemisphere, has more than 670 people per square mile, or 5.6 million people packed into an area smaller than New Hampshire. The world's highest fertility rate is found in one of its poorest countries, Rwanda, with eight children per woman. India's population is growing at a rate of 18 million a year (Cowell, 1994, p. 10). In the industrialized nations, on the other hand, the rate of population growth has leveled off and even declined in a number of cases.

The changes that are occurring in human populations around the world are part of what demographers call the great **demographic transition:** a rapid increase in a society's population with the onset of industrialization, followed by a leveling off of the growth rate. Until approximately 200 years ago, the world's population stayed remarkably constant. Then, with urbanism and industrialization, it started to grow rapidly and continues to grow as more and more countries become industrialized (see Figure 7.2). The point at which it will again stabilize is still distant. Every country appears to follow roughly the same trajectory as it develops: a spurt of rapid growth followed by a slowing of the rate of increase. The economically advanced nations may have zero growth rates, as the existing population simply maintains itself. The reasons for rapid explosion followed by a declining rate of population growth are exceedingly complex. The initial spurt of growth may be caused by a declining death rate attributable to improved health care in combination with high fertility.

One factor that encourages high fertility is the value of child labor. Peasants in largely rural El Salvador say that "every child is born with his bread under his arm"; not surprisingly, the birthrate in that country is over forty-five per thousand of population—more than double that of the United States. More and more families come to depend on the sale of labor to meet their needs, and very often, the income they derive in this way buys less food than they could produce directly. The mechanization and commercialization of agriculture preclude that option for most families. Rural people who have migrated to the cities do not earn enough to get by unless their children work as well. Children can help in the fields, work in the factories, peddle or produce crafts, scavenge, and otherwise bring in needed income. Given high rates of infant and childhood mortality, the more children a couple has, the more likely some will survive to take care of them when they are too old to support themselves. In countries that have no publicly supported health or welfare programs, these are vital considerations.

The reasons for a decline in the rate of growth following economic development are equally complex. It appears that the decline in the usefulness of child labor together with a rise in the costs of education are often important factors in the decision to limit family size. Changes in the work force are important, too, as women who work outside the home find it difficult to care for many children.

Europe's population has in fact moved beyond the "demographic transition" in one important sense: It is becoming older and it is decreasing. In 1999, there were only 266,000 more births than deaths, which is lowest figure since World War II. While Ireland has a baby boom, and the United States continues to grow largely due to immigration, Germany, Italy, and Spain have so few births that their populations will decline sharply unless replaced with migrants. The population of Russia is expected to decline from 57 million today to 41 million by 2050 due to low birth rates combined with high death rates. The implications are quite serious: Governments ultimately will either have to raise taxes on fewer and fewer active workers, raise retirement ages, or cut benefits. As it is, they face a major pension crisis (*The Economist*, Aug. 2, 2003, p. 63). Alternatively, they will have to allow more migrants and thereby increase their tax base. None of these

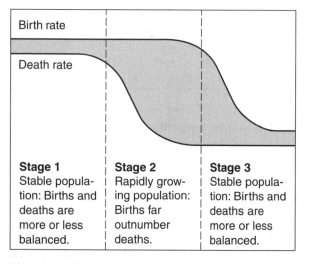

**Figure 7.2.** *Demographic transition*

will be easy decisions. The situation in Central and Eastern Europe is even more striking than in Western Europe. In most countries, the collapse of communism in 1989 produced a sharp drop in the fertility rate that could reduce the region's population by nearly 20% by 2050 according to a UN report cited in the *New York Times* (Erlanger, 2000, p. 13). The decline in most of these countries is far sharper than in Western Europe but for very different reasons. Fundamentally, people in the so-called "transition" countries such as Bulgaria, Estonia, Latvia, Hungary, and elsewhere are having fewer children because of poverty and unemployment, not because of an aging population. Russia is the most dramatic case. Its population has declined by more than 2 million since 1989, and male life expectancy is now lower than the age of retirement, dropping from sixty-four to fifty-nine. The threat here to the country's ability to pay pensioners is that the decline in population strikes at middle-aged workers, where alcoholism and poor health, including growing numbers infected with the AIDS virus, already take a big toll. Within twenty years, there will be one worker for every retired person—a major calamity waiting to happen unless steps are taken to reverse this trend (*The Economist,* Aug. 2, 2003). But ultimately, all Europeans will have to face a future in which there are few workers available to support an aging population. And tough decisions will have to be made regarding immigration and benefits policy.

Conversely, many developing countries in which fertility remains very high for a considerable time after mortality has dropped find that their population levels are so high that the standard of living cannot be raised. All that can be said for certain is that present rates of growth cannot long continue: If they did, in 700 years, there would be one person for every square foot of earth! One of the important decisions taken by the 1994 United Nations Conference on Population in Cairo was to emphasize the role of education and, in particular, education for women in encouraging decisions for smaller families.

Finally, the postindustrial world is a world on the move: from farms to cities and from one country to the next, always searching for a way to escape the poverty that only seems to grow more pervasive throughout the world. The surge of people seeking entry into Europe and North America is tremendous. In China, a country with 900 million peasants, people are abandoning the land; over 200 new cities have sprouted up since the 1980s, and people are flocking to them to find jobs that pay better than farming (Tyler, 1995, p. A4). Not only does this exacerbate China's loss of farmlands to urbanization, but even the diminishing farmlands are increasingly underused. A Chinese farmer working a one-acre plot, larger than average, explained to an American, "Look, I work on four *mou* of land year in and year out, from dawn to dusk, but after taxes and providing for our own needs, I make $20 a year. You can make that much in a day. No matter how much its costs to get there, or how hard the work is, America is still better than this" (Kwong, 1994, p. 425). This simple statement expresses the motivation that underlies the decision of millions to move each year— the knowledge of better conditions elsewhere.

# Centralization, Collectivization, and Communism

Cultural evolution generally involves centralization, as growing populations and social complexity require that central authorities coordinate diverse activities and interests. This process, which had been going on for centuries in Europe and elsewhere, continued during the Industrial Revolution as intensification and industrialism took hold around the world. One of the early signs of political centralization is the emergence of state institutions. More recently, centralization has moved beyond state boundaries and is now evident in the formation of large regional confederations, in the United Nations, and other global organizations. Economic centralization occurs as economies become closely interdependent, and a small number of institutions such as major stock, bond, and commodity markets determine the prices of items produced and consumed around the world. Centralization is also at work when key regions emerge as highly developed economic cores and create (or at least dominate) distant, less developed peripheries. Within countries, centralizing tendencies can be seen in the agricultural sector.

The twentieth century produced an extreme form of centralization, what Wolf calls the **administrative system** or **commune**, in which land is owned and managed by the state (1966). In most Communist countries such as China (until 1980) and the former Soviet Union, collective and state farms were the basis of most agricultural production. Peasants on a state-owned farm work under the direction of government agricultural experts, who set production quotas and determine how labor will be allocated. Collective farmers may escape the extreme poverty and social degradation that often characterize peasant life under the other forms of land control, but as their labor and income are at the disposal of a bureaucratic ruling class, they are still peasants in the economic and political sense of the term. Variants of this arrangement are seen in the large state-run farm projects in some parts of Africa and Latin America.

Collectivization has seemed attractive to many governments for several reasons, not all of them laudatory. The main argument in favor of collectivization is that large agricultural enterprises gain from economies of scale; that is, expensive equipment can be shared, large fields tilled and irrigated efficiently, and labor pooled. In developing countries, particularly, it often seems easier to provide schools, clinics, and marketing facilities to large concentrations of people than to dispersed hamlets and villages. Also, collectivization may be seen as a way of consolidating dispersed, small holdings. Another reason for collectivization is one not often openly argued: It is one means of controlling rural people and ensuring a level of agricultural production adequate to meet the objectives of the ruling elite. Box 7.1 illustrates some of the positive and negative aspects of modern collective farms.

## *Expanding Cities and Migrant Workers*

The process of devaluing agricultural products and labor in relation to other commodities, along with the mechanization of agriculture, serves to push people off the land and set up population movements both within and between nations. The migration of Europeans to North America, closely paralleling the spread of industrialization through Europe, reached a peak at the beginning of the twentieth century. More than 52 million people, or a fifth of Europe's population, migrated overseas between 1840 and 1930. By and large, the immigrants were displaced from farming by mechanization, monoculture, and other changes. They came to America believing that U.S. factories offered limitless opportunities for wage labor.

Today, small-scale agriculturists displaced by large-scale industrialized agriculture are leaving the land at an alarming rate. This is the case with Egyptian farming (Chapter 6). Some settle in towns, where they work as unskilled laborers when there is work to be had. Some settle in large urban centers. Still others become migrant laborers. Northern Europe is dotted with temporary settlements of Turkish, Greek, and Spanish laborers who travel north every year for a few months of labor in the factories or fields and then return home. Many more migrants establish long-term residence in large cities. The organization of this mobile labor force varies considerably, as does the profitability of the arrangement for the laborers.

The Turks—nearly a million and a half of them—who labor as "guest workers" in the factories of northern Europe generally receive the same wages as native workers and are able to return to Turkey with substantial savings. But at the same time, they are the first to be fired in times of recession, and they suffer considerable social isolation and discrimination. Migrant workers in the United States, most of them Mexicans or Central Americans, are seldom able to earn a living that is considered adequate by North American standards or to save enough to allow them to upgrade their salable skills. Throughout the year, they move from harvest to harvest, staying

*A family of migrant workers in Denizli, Turkey. Rural poverty and landlessness are problems that farmers face in countries throughout the world.*

(Waugh/Peter Arnold)

## Box 7.1

# Feeding a Fifth of the World: From Chinese Communes to Farms

CHINA RADICALLY TRANSFORMED its land tenure and rural society in the twentieth century—not just once, but several times. Following the success of the Communist Revolution in 1949, the traditional patrimonial estates were abolished and private family holdings were restricted in size, with much property redistributed to the landless. Very rapidly, this arrangement gave way to collectivization on the Soviet model, and by the early 1950s, all farming was organized around collective farms or communes.

At first, these communes were relatively small and often consisted of closely related families, but soon the government ordered them consolidated into far larger entities, with all planning and administration carried out centrally. In 1956, for example, the government forced cooperatives to purchase over a million double-wheel, double-blade plows, even though they were virtually worthless in paddy cultivation. Authorities even dictated a specific planting density for rice regardless of local conditions (Cunningham & Saigo, 1995, p. 203; Lardy, 1985, p. 38). By 1960, the government eliminated almost all aspects of rural entrepreneurship and private trading, closely controlled the prices of all produce, and set rigid quotas for grain production. The most consistent aspect of agricultural policy was the underpricing of rural products so as to support a large urban population.

Because central planning was unresponsive to local conditions and prices were low, production of critical food crops dropped drasti-cally while the authorities continued to set high production quotas in an effort to feed the teeming cities. It has been estimated that between 1959 and 1961, food shortages and rural economic dislocations resulted in the deaths of 10 to 60 million Chinese, possibly the worst famine in the history of the world (Cunningham & Saigo, 1995, p. 203)! Most of these deaths occurred in the countryside, where 80% of China's people still live. Agriculture improved somewhat after 1961 but then stagnated until 1978, when the post-Mao government decided to return to decentralized family-run farming. In the subsequent four years, the proportion of people earning less than 100 yuan a year (the rural poverty line) fell from 30 to 3%—an achievement hailed around the world. China is now number one in both rice and wheat production (p. 203). Production is 50% higher than in the best of the commune years; China now has less than 3% of its population underfed (p. 203). Yet some Chinese communes had prospered during the years of collectivization, particularly those that were small, that enlisted members who trusted one another, and that offered greater rewards for shared labor than members could reap alone. When farming was returned to the private sector, many, but not all, profited (Parish, 1985). But since private farming requires less labor than the inefficient communes, this has led to unemployment on a scale not seen since World War II (Kwong, 1994).

*Collectivization in China initially produced positive results but ended in near collapse when the government created oversized farming collectives managed centrally. Now almost all agriculture has returned to private ownership.*

(H. Topping/Photo Researchers Inc.)

in crowded and often squalid migrant camps. Most of these camps are under the direction of crew leaders, who make the arrangements between the farmers and the laborers and provide the trucks to transport the laborers from place to place. Laborers are heavily dependent on their crew leader. When work is delayed, as it often is, they must borrow from him to buy their food. And often, it is the leader who sells them their food—at an inflated price. Of course, migration is not limited to rural populations. The true nomads of industrial society are middle-class, white-collar workers who move from job to job or from city to city in the same job.

The rural landless have options other than settling in industrial farming communities or joining the migrant labor force. The overwhelming majority have chosen to try their luck in the cities. Since the Industrial Revolution, population movement has been a steady stream from the countryside to the city. In many nations now becoming industrialized, this stream has become a flood as unskilled rural people pour into cities. In most countries, one or two cities become the targets for the majority of the migrants, and these cities swell beyond their capacity to provide employment or social services. In the Arabic-speaking countries of the Middle East, only 30% of the population was urban in 1962, but as of 2000, more than 50% is. The population of Cairo, for example, increased from 3 million in 1947 to more than 13 million in 2000. Mexico City, now the world's largest city with more than 20 million inhabitants, is experiencing massive problems: the world's worst air pollution, frequent breakdowns in public transportation and other services, and high rates of infant mortality. Like similar cities around the world, much of Mexico City's growth is due to an influx of rural dwellers. As elsewhere, these recent migrants form an extremely disadvantaged and socially distinct segment of the population, with high rates of unemployment, high rates of crime, and substandard housing. In some respects, these poor city dwellers are fortunate. A UN study indicates that more than 12 million people around the world live in refugee camps, and many more live on the brink of starvation—displaced not just by a changing global economy but by the brutal facts of war, famine, and political oppression. The FAO estimates that 15 to 20 million people (mostly children) die of malnutrition each year (Cunningham & Saigo, 1995, p. 212).

The European Community sees this migration from the land as a threat to its future ability to feed itself, not to mention maintaining its traditional rural/urban settlement patterns. Consequently, countries in the European Community provide massive subsidies to farms, which allow them to continue to compete with North American agribusiness.

The remainder of this chapter looks at the social and ecological impacts of a number of major dam projects around the world. Then it turns to the United States to observe how the American family farm has changed and see the effects of the farmerless farm in the San Joaquin Valley in California. Finally, there is the case of a village in Bulgaria that has undergone two major transformations.

*In the Philippines, a family living in a slum on Manila's Smokey Mountain. The "mountain" is a garbage dump.*

(Michael Macintyre/The Hutchison Library)

# Dams and Their Consequences

Since water control is so critical to agricultural intensification, it is not surprising that attempts to control the flow of rivers and streams are almost as old as agriculture itself and in fact may predate agriculture in some places. The Australian aborigines controlled water flows in places without actually planting domesticates to increase the usable wild products they obtained. At the dawn of great urban-based polities in China, Egypt, Mesopotamia, the Indus Valley, and the Valley of Mexico, major waterworks were undertaken to extend cultivation and minimize the risk of droughts or floods. But it was only with the advent of the advanced Industrial Era that truly massive impoundments of water emerged, and these usually had electrical power production in mind as well as agricultural intensification. In fact, by the late twentieth century, giant dams became emblematic of economic development and were, and still are, heavily charged with political significance beyond even their economic potential. India's leader Nehru famously said, "Dams are the temples of modern India" (Roy, 1999, p. 13). Dam building was equated with nation building, and now India has 3,600 large dams and plans 1,000 more.

What has changed in the last few years is the wider realization that large water projects are very risky for environmental and social reasons in addition to the fact that they do not always pay off economically. They are rarely built in the prosperous so-called "first world," and existing large dams are in fact regularly being decommissioned and dismantled. The World Bank was a major sponsor of dam projects in China, the Middle East, South America, and Africa but has recently all but ceased any support. A recent project, the Bujagali dam on the headwaters of the Nile in Uganda, was halted prior to construction in August 2003.[1] The private corporation that was building the dam with World Bank support finally concluded it would not be profitable. But given that dams are still being built and massive resources are allocated to their construction and maintenance, it is worthwhile looking at a few cases and at the pros and cons of these undertakings.

For an articulate, intelligent, but implacable foe of large dams, one need go no farther than the writings of the Indian social critic and best-selling author Arundhati Roy. In her 1999 book *The Cost of Living,* she likens dams to nuclear bombs: Both are weapons of mass destruction! The object of her de-

rision is the massive dam complex under construction in the Narmada Valley in the state of Gujarat—then just beginning and now half completed. As she puts it, "Big dams are obsolete. They are undemocratic. They're a government's way of accumulating authority (deciding who will get how much water and who will get to grow what where). . . . They are a brazen means of taking water, land and irrigation from the poor and gifting it to the rich. Their reservoirs displace huge populations of people, leaving them homeless and destitute" (Roy, 1999, p. 14). Ecologically, she and others say they cause floods, waterlogging of soils, and salinity and massive waste of water. In India alone, Roy asserts, 30 to 50 million people have been displaced by large dams (p. 17). As for the dam which captured her attention in 1999, the official name of which is the Sardar Sarovar Project (SSP), it has been on the planning boards since the late 1970s, and each year estimates of the number of people to be displaced have shifted wildly—from 6,000 families to 80,000 families. The number of villages that would receive drinking water rose from 0 to 8,219, but when pressed, the government admitted that many of the benefiting villages were uninhabited (p. 32). Although feasibility studies were carried out in 1998, no money was budgeted for drinking water because this was not the dam's purpose to begin with but merely a "selling point" (Whopays, 2003). At the moment, what will happen is unclear. The World Bank has withdrawn support for the project. It is half completed and has already displaced many thousands of people. The local state government said that in spite of promises to the contrary it is unable to resettle those displaced (some 200,000) because there is no suitable land available (the people are being absorbed in urban slums for the most part); the water flow is now seen to be below projections; the only obvious benefits are to provide more water to already well-endowed and politically connected commercial users, to sugar mills, water parks, and golf courses, which are already being sited on the upper reaches of the main canals (Whopays, 2003).[2]

The Indian case, in broad outline, can be replicated in many other countries. Of international political significance because of its potential for conflict is Turkey's ongoing Southeastern Anatolia Project, or GAP as it is known by its Turkish acronym. This involves twenty-two dams on the upper Euphrates-Tigris Basin and aims to provide irrigation for 1.7 million hectares of land by 2017. The social and

---

[1]The author was involved in this project as consultant to the World Bank's Inspection Panel.

[2]www.narmada.org/sardar-sarovar/faq/whopays.html is an admittedly partisan Web site, which purports to cite government and official SSP sources and World Bank sources.

*Turkey has invested massively in one of the world's largest systems of waterworks, in which numerous dams, such as this one on the Tigris, now control most of the upland flow of the Euphrates and Tigris Rivers. The water is allowing for great expansion of irrigated agriculture, but it is yet unclear how the average farmer will benefit or what are the long-term environmental implications.*

(Daniel Bates)

ecological consequences are as yet unknown as the projects have not been carried out under World Bank auspices, which would require public disclosure of detailed impact statements. The reclaimed land is mostly devoted to cotton production, a commodity that is yielding quite low profit margins due to oversupply. The main political issue is that the GAP, as of 2001, controls the headwaters of these two major rivers that flow through Syria and Iraq, providing these countries with vital irrigation and drinking water (see Bates & Rassam, 2001). In Turkey, more than 2,000 villages were relocated, and many culturally significant sites inundated. Although the construction of the dams has certainly stimulated the economy of the impoverished southeast of Turkey, the long-term consequences are difficult to predict. If other such projects are an indication, salinity will have to be monitored very closely and mitigation will eat into the waterworks' efficiency and profitability.

Another huge water management project is the Three Gorges Dam Project in China. In 2003, the first stage of the dam was completed on the Chang Jiang (Yangtze) River and the first generators were started up. The shipping locks opened in 2004. The project, at an estimated cost of up to $100 billion, is one of the world's largest, entailing the displacement of 1.13 million people. Most of the expected benefits are seen to lie in flood control and electrical production, which supports Arundhati Roy's comment to the effect that big dam projects largely benefit people at far remove from the water rather than those who traditionally rely on it. Again the consequences await the passage of time for their evaluation. What is clear now is that the massive disruption of settlements has not been handled to the benefit of the majority of displaced persons. Also, just as in India, China's small dams and reservoirs, which supply most of the nation's irrigation, get the least money for repair and maintenance.

Ensuring long-term proper drainage is extremely costly, and the benefits of such investment are not immediately visible to users until damage has been done. Vast areas of Iraq, Pakistan, and India have seen declines in productivity due to soil salinity. And this is not a so-called Third World problem. Currently, the most fertile region of Australia, southeastern New South Wales, is experiencing salinization on a massive scale. It is so serious that salt pans form on roadsides and on the walls of abandoned buildings (*The Economist*, Feb. 5, 2000, p. 62). In a major engineering feat some fifty years ago, the flow of the Snowy River was reversed so that its discharge, instead of flowing into the Pacific Ocean, could be diverted into tunnels and canals to generate hydroelectric power and irrigate much of Australia's best farmland in the Murray-Darling basin. This region produces three fourths of Australia's irrigated crops. Now salt levels are rising at a rate that might mean the end of production altogether within twenty years.

There is no reason for North Americans to feel complacent. The Imperial Valley of California has been irrigated since 1901 and today requires massive investments to ensure that salinity does not overwhelm the area, which contributes one seventh of U.S. agricultural production, or approximately $1 billion a year. The vast drainage area, which is several hundred feet below sea level, includes the Salton Sea, itself created in the early 1900s by the diversion of rivers and later enhanced by the Hoover Dam flow. This body of water is highly saline but is kept more or less in balance by massive inputs of fresh river water each year. The soil salinity of irrigated fields is limited by a massive system of drainage tiles laid at approximately six feet beneath the surface. The quandary facing water managers here is that there are many competing claims or needs for water. Farmers, who now regard the water as theirs, pay $15 for the equivalent of one acre flooded with fresh water to a depth of one foot; in 2003, San Diego offered to pay $268 an acre/foot but was unable to secure an agreement. While the current system is an artificial habitat created by the scheme, it nevertheless supports rich wildlife in addition to farming and thus requires continued flows to prevent a collapse of both wildlife habitat and agriculture.

The issue is a complex one. It is safe to say no expert can calculate the long-term effect of huge projects. The Aswan Dam of Egypt is a good example. Built in the early 1960s, it was much excoriated by social and natural scientists. Originally, it was to be built by the U.S. government as an aid project, but support was withdrawn in 1956 to punish President Nasser for his program of nationalization and pro-Soviet leanings. Within weeks, the U.S.S.R. stepped in to build what Egyptians called the "new pyramid." It was completed in 1971. Critics were concerned that changes in the flow of the Nile could cause downstream salinity problems, a large-scale decline in the Mediterranean fisheries due to nutrients being trapped behind the dam, and problems in maintaining soil fertility due to silt no longer being deposited on fields in the annual floods. Now more than thirty years later, there are a number of economists and social scientists who feel that on balance the dam has been beneficial. It has prevented what would have been a catastrophic flood in 1988 (which hit the Sudan very hard), it alleviated droughts in several years, the fish now being caught in the impounded Lake Nasser more than compensate for the decline in downstream fisheries, and the abundant electricity is used to produce large amounts of nitrate fertilizers. Still it is an inescapable fact that the entire country is now held hostage to the well-being and security of this dam, that the reservoir is fast filling with silt, and that due to high rates of evapo-transpiration, much water from the Nile is lost each year. Executive Director of the UN Environmental Programme, Dr. Mostafa Tolba, concluded, "The real question can no longer be whether the dam should have been built, since without it the Egyptians would have been facing a continuing economic and social catastrophe over the past three decades, but rather what steps should have been taken to maximize further the positive socio-environmental benefits and reduce the negative ones so that the net benefit to the Egyptian people could have been even higher" (cited in Biswas, 2002, pp. 25–26).

# Urbanized Rural Society: Farming in the United States

Over 90% of American farms are family operated (contrary to the perception of many), although there are far greater differences among them than there were a generation or two ago. Farms of 3,000 acres that gross more than $500,000 a year account for only 2% of the total but produce 35% of the output; the top 5% account for more than 50% of the output (Feder, 1994, p. 1). The majority of American farmers have significant off-farm income; it is the larger ones that adopt new technology, often working directly under contract with food processors such as Frito-Lay or McDonalds. The modern American farmer has to be as much a financial and marketing expert as anything else. This section examines the development of American farming with material from California and the Midwest.

## The Development of Agribusiness in California

American anthropologists were somewhat slow to recognize the importance of studying farming communities in their own society. In the early 1940s, however, Walter Goldschmidt (1947, 1971) undertook a now classic study of Wasco, California, a town of 7,000 to 8,000 people, most of them involved in various aspects of industrialized commercial agriculture. By living in the town, participating in local organizations, conducting interviews, and examining official records and historical documents, Goldschmidt was able to trace the radical transformation that the town had undergone in the previous few decades.

Until the first decade of the twentieth century, the land on which Wasco's farms are now situated was desert, and the main activity in the area was sheepherding. Wasco itself consisted of one store, one hotel, and a handful of saloons frequented by ranch hands and an occasional homesteader. Then in 1907, a developer persuaded the corporation that owned the entire Wasco area to sell him part of its holdings, and he began to advertise for homesteaders, promising to provide the necessary irrigation. The sales pitch worked (the land was bought quickly), but the irrigation system did not. In all probability, the farmers would have abandoned Wasco to the sheep if a power company had not brought in a line enabling the settlers to install electric pumps. This was the beginning of the industrialization of Wasco.

For small farmers, as most of the original settlers were, an electric pump is a major investment. To recoup that investment, the farmers turned to cash crops, specializing in potatoes, cotton, sugar beets, lemons, or grapes. Both the profits and the settlement grew. In some years, the payoff for commercial farming was spectacular. In 1936—a Depression

*Agricultural land is disappearing in most parts of the world as urban and industrial centers spread, such as this one north of Los Angeles.*

(David Parker/Photo Researchers Inc.)

year—one farmer was rumored to have made over $1 million from his potato crop.

Such booms encouraged Wasco's farmers to expand. Some of them rented land on which to grow profitable but soil-depleting crops for a year or two. (Once the soil was exhausted, the owner would revitalize it by planting alfalfa and then rent it again.) This strategy of expansion required the planter to hire large numbers of workers and to make substantial investments in tractors and other motorized equipment. Other Wasco farmers used their profits to expand in other areas. Having made a large investment, a farmer would look for ways to maintain a steady flow of produce and income. He might, for example, buy the fruits of another landowner's trees and hire his own laborers to pick them. Or better still, he might purchase more land. In this way, the average size of landholding increased from about 20 acres when the homesteaders first moved in to about 100 acres at the time of Goldschmidt's study—a 500% increase in about thirty years.

In no time, Wasco was attracting outside corporations—first the utility companies and then a national bank, oil companies, and chain supermarkets. These developments changed the social landscape. The representatives of the state and national government agencies and of corporations (whose loyal-

ties lay outside Wasco) tended to become leaders within the town. Even farmers with relatively small holdings began to see themselves as entrepreneurs rather than as tillers of the soil. One informant told Goldschmidt, "There is one thing I want you to put in your book. Farming in this country is a business, it's not a way of life" (1978, p. 22).

Wasco began to attract large numbers of unskilled laborers who could find work in the town and dream of buying a place of their own one day. First Mexicans (Chicanos), then (after World War I) African Americans, and in the 1930s, refugees from Oklahoma, Arkansas, and other drought-stricken states poured into the town. They were markedly poorer than the Wasco farmers, who did not consider them their racial, cultural, or social equals. The social contact between the two groups was very limited. At the time of the study, the Mexicans, the African Americans, and to a lesser extent the Oklahomans lived in their own separate communities with their own stores and churches. They were outsiders in every sense, and that was just what Wasco's commercial farmers needed: "a large number of laborers, unused to achieving the social values of the dominant group, and satisfied with a few of the luxuries of modern society" (1978, p. 62). In its urban orientation, its commercial production and consumption, and its economic gap between owners and laborers, Wasco might as well have been an industrial center. Above all, in its social structure—the impersonal, purely economic relationship between the landowners and the laborers—the town showed its urban-industrial face. To see how Wasco continues to change, we turn to a more recent California study.

Mark Kramer describes the subsequent phase in the transformation of California agriculture: the farmerless farm (1987, pp. 197–278). It is tomato harvest time in the San Joaquin Valley, 3 A.M., and 105,708,000 ripe tomatoes lie ready for picking on some 766 absolutely flat acres of irrigated cropland. Out of the darkness rumble giant tractor-drawn machines resembling moon landers—two stories high, with ladders, catwalks, and conveyors fastened all over and carrying fourteen workers each. As they lumber down the long rows, they continually ingest whole tomato plants while spewing out the rear a steady stream of stems and rejects. Fourteen workers sit facing a conveyor belt in the harvester, sorting the marketable tomatoes from the discards.

It is a giant harvest carried out almost without people; only a few years ago, more than 600 workers were needed to harvest a crop that 100 manage today. There are no farmers involved in this operation: only corporation executives, managers, foremen, and laborers. The word "farmer" has virtually disappeared; in this operation, one refers to "growers" and "pickers." Managers take courses in psychology to help them determine appropriate incentives to offer tractor drivers for covering the most ground (if speed is too great, they may damage equipment; if it is too slow, productivity falls). Managers similarly calculate pickers' productivity very precisely and regulate it by varying the speed of the conveyor belts and by minimizing the time spent turning the machines around at the ends of rows, when the workers are prone to get off for a smoke. Right now, Kramer reports one manager as saying, the industry is moving to a new-model harvester that will do the job of fourteen men with only two. The other twelve can move on to other employment if they can find it.

Tomato consumption closely reflects the changing eating habits of American society; these days, each of us eats 50.5 pounds of tomatoes every year, whereas in 1920, consumption was 18.1 pounds. This change is accounted for by the fact that far more of our food is prepared somewhere other than in the home kitchen. This development has produced a demand for prepared sauces and flavorings, such as ketchup and tomato paste. The increased productivity required to meet demand has resulted in dramatic genetic changes in the tomatoes we eat.

Processors of tomatoes demanded a product that is firmer; growers needed standardization of sizes and an oblong shape to counter the tomatoes' tendency to roll off the conveyors; engineers required tomatoes with thick skins to withstand handling; and large corporate growers needed more tonnage per acre and better resistance to disease. The result is the modern American tomato: everything but flavor. "As geneticists selectively bred for these characteristics, they lost control of others. They bred for thick skins, less acidity, more uniform ripening, oblongness, leafiness, and high yield—and they could not also select for flavor" (Kramer, 1987, p. 213). Even the chemists made their contribution: A substance called ethylene (which is also produced naturally by the plants) is sprayed on fields of almost ripe tomatoes to induce redness. Quite like the transformation of the tomato itself, the ownership of the farms that grow them has been altered. As one might expect in view of the massive inputs of capital needed to raise the new breed of tomatoes, most are raised on corporate spreads. The one Kramer describes consisted of more than 27,000 acres and was owned by several general partners, including a major insurance corporation, an oil company, a newspaper, and thousands of limited partners, most of them doctors and lawyers, who invested in the operation for its tax benefits. There is little room un-

der these conditions for the small farmer—or so it would seem.

## Family Farmers in the Midwest: The Immigrant Legacy

Even in food production, there are limits to the efficiency of large farms: They require middle-level managers and get less out of individual workers than do smaller family-managed operations. Large corporately managed farms can make large-scale mistakes. Kramer reported that one worker in California sprayed a huge area with the wrong insecticide, and some managers' heavy investment in unsuitable crops resulted in big losses. In fact, the large farm Kramer describes subsequently sold off half its holdings as unprofitable. Under some conditions, a smaller farm can be more efficient than a huge one, but it still will be highly capitalized and employ modern equipment, up-to-date accounting methods, and trained management. Most successful farmers in the United States are college graduates.

Many observers report a revival of the family farm in North America, but one with a new face (Gladwin & Butler, 1982; Salamon, 1992). The family-run farm now often involves a new division of labor, with the wife assuming primary responsibility for farming operations, often of a specialized nature, while the husband holds down a salaried job and helps out when he can. This is clearly the pattern in the Midwest on smaller farms, but on large spreads of over 500 acres, the family manages today much as before: with its own labor and skills.

Sonya Salamon has spent many years studying midwestern farming communities and families (1992). Most of her research concerns seven farming communities in Illinois where she has been carrying out research for over a decade. Land and family are her main interests, since families cannot farm without land. Yet this resource has to be acquired and passed on for the community (if, indeed, it is one) to have continuity. Family land, then, is a cultural patrimony, and land tenure and farm management and inheritance shape the personalities of rural communities. About half of the communities she studied were of German descent, coming from both the Protestant and Catholic regions of Germany; the other half, which she calls "Yankees," were of largely Protestant backgrounds and came to the Midwest from New England and the British Isles. One unexpected finding of her research is that far from being homogeneous after so many years, there is a definite mosaic effect in the rural American settlement pattern—and one that is changing with time.

*Mechanization of agriculture may cost far more in terms of energy invested in farm equipment and fertilizers than is yielded in food energy. Giant tractors are used throughout North America and other industrialized countries to prepare the fields and to harvest crops.*

(John Colwell/Grant Heilman Collection)

These two groups are only part of the ethnic diversity of region; Michigan, for example, has many farmers of Polish, Dutch, and Finnish descent, but the processes of community formation seem remarkably similar. In the mid-nineteenth century, with the coming of the railways, the Midwest saw development unparalleled in American history. Within fifty years, the Midwest was transformed from forests and prairies into densely settled and intensively farmed agricultural lands. Towns and villages shot up almost overnight, populated by immigrant Europeans. There were many reasons for them to emigrate, including inheritance rules in Europe that encouraged farm fragmentation and rural poverty. The newly established railroads provided easy access to the Midwest, and land grant acts by Congress made it easy, if not free, for settlers to acquire land. Even the railroads offered inducements for migrants to settle. This was not, of course, altruism—just good business. With farming came the need to transport produce to markets and industrial products to the farms.

All immigrants faced similar challenges, but different ethnic groups responded to these in different ways. Those Salamon calls Yankees came from predominately English backgrounds. Although unlikely to have been landowners at home, they tended to approach farming much as in the home country. Land was viewed as a commodity, which, if possible, should be worked for profit using hired help or ten-

ant farmers. Children of owners were not so much induced to stay at home but rather to strike out and find new farmsteads for themselves. This set the basis for settlement; successful farmers set their sons up with farms in distant regions, not necessarily next door. Absentee ownership was also common, and in general, these farmers were not known for their "stewardship of the soil"—looking instead to profit rather than sustainability. The Yankees had the advantage of being part of the linguistic and political majority and could move rather easily.

The German settlers came from different regions of Germany, spoke different dialects of German, and belonged to different churches. They shared, however, a common origin in tightly knit peasant communities that they intended to replicate in their new country. Some of the newcomers were able to acquire land; some simply worked for Yankee farmers as tenants. But even as tenants, their objective was to save enough to acquire land near other German-speaking members of their local church. Initially, the Midwest was predominantly Yankee, with much land in Illinois held in huge spreads of over 10,000 acres used mostly for livestock production. As settlement progressed, the absentee owners often took advantage of rising land prices to sell out. Usually, they sold to their German tenants or neighbors. Thus, with time, the German component in the settlement pattern grew until today it is the dominant one.

Salamon distinguished two divergent strategies that shaped settlement and community patterns and continue to do so. One strategy, which she terms the "yeoman" approach, is more characteristic of the German population. The other is the "entrepreneur" approach more characteristic of the Yankees.

The yeoman sees land as a sacred trust and farming as a means of membership in a community. There is a relative hierarchy in the family, since whoever owns land has power and seniority in management decisions. The yeoman's goals are to own as much land as feasible without undue debt or risk, maximize kin involvement, and avoid anything that would alienate the land from the family.

In contrast, the entrepreneur views land as a commodity and farming as a business. There is a weaker family hierarchy, as farming is not necessarily thought to be the logical thing for an heir to do. The entrepreneur does not always favor ownership over renting land; renting land allows the entrepreneur to expand and utilize capital better. For this reason, their farms are larger, more capital intensive, and more in debt.

In recent decades, the approaches have necessarily drawn closer together; almost all farms are heavily capitalized, few are free of debt, and all must be as skillful in marketing as in crop production. What is clear from Salamon's research is that the family is very much part of the family farm in America, perhaps even more than ever. Since farm sizes have increased so much in recent years, something of the older prairie feeling has returned to farm life in some areas. Houses are now farther apart and families rely on church and community get-togethers to see friends and neighbors. Of course, this is counterbalanced by increased sprawl of single-family housing and shopping malls, which devour much farmland every year.

# The Rise and Fall of Collective Agriculture in Bulgaria

Bulgaria, a Balkan nation of some 11 million, hardly comes to mind as a model of industrial agriculture. But few countries anywhere have so completely industrialized their farm sector as had Bulgaria under Communist rule. Gerald Creed was strategically placed to witness both the socialist system in full bloom, its collapse, and the transition that followed a return to a market economy. He arrived in Zamfirovo in northwest Bulgaria in 1987 to carry out an ethnographic study of socialist agriculture at work.

After difficult formalities had been taken care of (Bulgaria under the Communist regime was hardly an open society), he settled into a family's home to begin his project. Zamfirovo is a village set in the rolling foothills of the Balkan Mountains, renamed in the Communist era after an early village activist, Zamfir Popov. The village, like almost all in socialist Bulgaria, had been extensively rebuilt since World War II and was home to some 750 households, mostly dwelling in tidy two-story houses with running water and electricity, facing along paved streets with street lighting and, again like many Bulgarian villages, the setting for a number of small industries.

Creed pursued a twenty-month-long study followed by repeated return visits through the 1990s. His work, unlike that of Richard Lee, Napoleon Chagnon, Elliot Fratkin, and others reported in earlier chapters, made much use of statistical and archival data because the village is part of a paper-focused bureaucratic culture. But still, most of all, he relied on his increasingly close relationship to his hosts, neighbors, and network of village friends. One experience was a turning point in his fieldwork, he writes. A neighbor's elderly mother died suddenly while her son was managing a large herd of goats, belonging to numerous families, in the village pastures. Creed, perhaps rashly, volunteered to take charge of the flock, which he did with difficulty but without loss, and thus became even closer to the community (1998, pp. 26–27). From then on, he combined observation and interviews with participating in the work of the harvest or planting as the seasons indicated.

Because of his close ties to his informants, he gained a fine-grained perspective on how socialist agriculture came to the village, transformed it, and how socialism itself was transformed in turn by the villagers—a process he calls "domesticating the revolution." Domesticating the revolution involves taking sometimes alien and oppressive institutions and procedures imposed by the state and adapting them to local needs or at least arriving at a locally viable accommodation. Zamfirovo cannot, he writes, be seen as a typical Bulgarian village because no village can really be typical, but it is illustrative of how people generally coped with the socialist version of industrialized agriculture.

Bulgaria, ruled by the Ottoman Empire from the late fourteenth century until the late nineteenth century, when Turkish rule was broken by the Russians, was long known as a country whose dense networks of agricultural villages were extremely productive—largely due to the skills and knowledge of the inhabitants. Most farmers worked their own small

*Zamfirovo villagers after decollectivization working their newly privatized fields. While productivity is slowly picking up, farming is much less mechanized than before.*
(©Gerald Creed, with permission)

tracts of land with great care and hard labor. The Bulgarian proverb cited by a friend of Creed's captures the spirit and pragmatism of the countryside: "The soil wants a hoe not a prayer." This smallholder tradition is in contrast to most of Russia, Hungary, Poland, and eastern Germany, where much farming was carried out on large estates prior to World War II. The deeply held and much commented upon Bulgarian values of egalitarianism are undoubtedly rooted in this tradition. The pragmatism of villagers and their sense of egalitarianism are important factors in both the initial acceptance of socialist farming and how the transition to free-market farming was handled. Even prior to World War II, the Communist Party and a rival socialist Agrarian Party tapped into these values for substantial rural support.

Even so, after the Communists succeeded in coming to power in 1944, collectivization came as a shock. While Creed disputes the common view that collectivization was simply imposed by the policies of the USSR, he does note that the Soviet influence was important as a model and that the Communists clearly desired to control the countryside. But there were economic reasons for collectivization as well. Prior to 1944, 88% of the population was engaged in farming, and all foreign exchange was generated by agriculture. But when examined on the village level, agriculture was inefficient. Even smallholdings were in fact divided up into tiny parcels, often only a strip a few meters wide and distributed among the different zones of the village, lowlands, highlands, forest, orchards, and so forth, making mechanization next to impossible. In Zamfirovo alone, where average landholdings were under three hectares,

there were 12,300 separate parcels of worked land for 763 households, or about seventeen parcels per farming family. Families often spent as much time walking between fields as working on them. There was an excess of population relative to the land, and the result was further fragmentation and the extension of cultivation into forest and commons. Collectivization, regardless of its ideological or political merits, was a response to a real problem, and it further conformed to a national need to free up farm labor for new factories.

During World War II, the government, under German direction, imposed a system of taxation by requisition of quotas of most crops and animals raised in the village. The post-War Communist regime continued the requisition system but quickly put it to work in the effort to encourage the proliferation of farm cooperatives, which paid a proportionately smaller levy. The first cooperatives were voluntary albeit induced; by 1947, few villagers in Zamfirovo had signed up because cooperatives in neighboring villages had not prospered (p. 53). In 1948, local party leaders were strongly promoting what was called the "Labor Cooperative Agricultural Economy," commonly referred to by its acronym TKZS. These cooperatives were still voluntary and generally lacked machinery and thus achieved little economy of scale. Poor farmers joined and some better off did as well. Some households, Creed writes, signed up for what seems like a strange reason: trouble with relatives, especially in-laws. Some men joined so as to avoid being subjected to direction by their wife's father or their older brother. In 1951, party-trained leaders took over the Zamfirovo TKZS and sharply increased the level of produce requisitioned from non-TKZS villagers, putting pressure on holdouts to join. One person told Creed "of course, you did not *have* to join the cooperative unless you wanted shoes on your feet and a shirt on your back" (p. 61). Even alternative ways of making a living through craft production were no longer allowed. As requisitions increased, villagers became increasingly adept in finding ways of avoiding or minimizing them, by hiding animals in the forest, surreptitious harvesting, underreporting, and the like. Thus, Creed says, they honed important skills at coping, which they came to perfect during the subsequent height of collectivization when participation was no longer voluntary in any sense.

In 1956, collectivization was mandated by law, making Bulgaria the second country in the world to fully collectivize its agriculture. In Zamfirovo, this was met with little physical resistance, although there was conflict in other villages. All land thus came fully under state control, although the term *cooperative* was still officially used, and officially, one still "owned" the land that one had "contributed" to the cooperative. In fact, boundary markers were removed, and land was converted to other uses—for example, for factories or reservoirs—with no compensation to putative owners.

The first ten years or so of collectivization were very difficult, even for ardent supporters of the cooperative system. Most felt that they were worse off than before. With limited mechanization, villagers worked long hours in the fields, pay was low, and those who could sought urban jobs and urban resi-

*This collective farm in Bulgaria collapsed along with the Communist regime in 1990. It has proved very difficult for collectivized farmers to take up private farming; they lack most equipment formerly supplied by the state.*

(Daniel Bates)

dence. But ultimately, as mechanization progressed and small local factories and places of employment opened, such as a fruit cannery, life became easier. Each household was allowed a garden plot on which they lavished time and attention. Store-bought food and apparel were heavily subsidized, and most rural households had several incomes: those of the husband and wife often in addition to the pensions of grandparents. The household, Creed observes, as have others working in socialist societies, was the key to survival—an island of autonomy in a system completely dominated by party and state institutions. Even urban dwellers relied on rural kinfolk for access to the garden plots.

From the onset of collectivization, planners and party leaders were convinced that socialist agricultural production required large units; thus, the Zamfirovo TKZS was soon consolidated with one of a neighboring village. Later, because of poor results, it was disaggregated only to be consolidated into a yet larger multivillage collective. The high point of collectivization in Bulgaria was achieved through the Agro-Industrial Complex, or AKZ. By 1982, all of the collectives in Bulgaria were organized under 296 AKZ schemes. Nevertheless, Zamfirovo villagers resisted losing local control, and in the end, a paradox emerged in which the village came to identify and defend its cooperative against the AKZ. The AKZ would, for example, demand that unprofitable crops and animals be raised or would pay trivial amounts for produce that later would appear in the market at high prices. Villagers, utilizing the networks and special relations that were ubiquitous in the socialist world, would strike their own barter arrangements with other villages and firms. By the late 1980s, considerable decision making in effect occurred at the local level.

By the end of the socialist era, agriculture came to be a full-time occupation for only a very few. In Zamfirovo, only thirty or so administrators and workers were full-time employees in the cooperative, including some who were retirees and on pensions. Of course, every household remained committed to its own subsistence gardening. Those who did work in the cooperative did not identify themselves as farmers but by whatever job title they happened to hold: tractor driver, combine operator, accountant, and so on. The system as it existed on the eve of the collapse of Communist rule was the product of countless changes in party and government policy, usually taken without consultation, but each decision was adapted to and even exploited by the ever-resourceful Zamfirovans. While wages were still low, most families could provision themselves, make use of cheap apparel, housing, and heat, and thereby save even low wages to buy televisions, refrigerators, and even automobiles. While by no means a consumer economy, Bulgarian socialism had transformed the rural landscape much as had capitalism in the West. Farming, apart from gardens, was entirely mechanized. Agriculture labor and, to a considerable extent, village culture and identity took on a new meaning largely disassociated from farming per se.

The collapse of socialism in 1989 was the result of many of the contradictions that had sustained it or at least ameliorated its effects on people. Massive inefficiency in production, management, and distribution allowed (perhaps forced) individuals to syphon off time and goods for their own survival. Once a new center-right democratic government was elected in 1991, yet another era began in earnest for the villagers, usually referred to as "the transition." The irony of this term is not lost on the villagers who have endured one reform after another as long as they can remember, and who, as Creed relates, say that Bulgaria is always in transition, neither capitalist nor socialist. The present transition, which is still underway, began with the return of land confiscated by the Communists to its original owners. This was complicated not only by the passing of time and the number of heirs but also by the loss of documents and a dramatically changed landscape; the entire pattern of field use had been altered, new houses and structures built on farmland, land put into vineyards and orchards, and so on. Once again, the villagers were faced with the problem of fragmented fields compounded by the fact that the rural population no longer considered themselves farmers in the old sense.

But this was not the main problem they faced. Once again, as with the Communists in the 1950s,

they now had to contend with policies and laws over which they had little control emanating from the capital. Most villagers had incorporated the village cooperative with all its inefficiencies into their everyday lives. They had not only physically built the stables and barns but had also domesticated the cooperative system so that its resources served their individual needs. They not only derived an income from cooperative salaries but also made use of machinery, transport, and other facilities for private ends. The new government had a different perspective altogether. It viewed the old collective system as a relic of communism and contrary to principles of a free-market economy. As part of the transition, it not only abolished the old TKZSs, ignoring village sentiments in the matter, but also mandated that assets be sold off. Thus, very rapidly, the old structures, including the physical structures, were dismantled in the absence of new ones. Village opinion in Zamfirovo, as in many other parts of the country, was in favor of continuing the cooperative under democratic administration. Not only did this not happen, but the newly emerging cooperative efforts faced many obstacles because of government policy, not to mention a lack of equipment and infrastructure. Even now Bulgarian agriculture has not recovered, so the transition can be said to continue—subsistence plots supporting an industrialized economy. One elderly woman, looking back on both the coming of socialism and its collapse, described it as like receiving two slaps on either side of her face. Another villager said in 1995, "We have no system in Bulgaria, no capitalism, and no socialism. We are without a system" (p. 178). Now the economic situation is better, but many younger people have migrated abroad in search of employment.

## Summary

NO POPULATION IS UNTOUCHED BY THE PRODUCTS OF industrial society. Even without venturing beyond our own society, we can see immediate costs and benefits of life in the postindustrial world. Among the benefits we can count advances in the medical sciences, and among the costs is the pollution of our skies and seas. Genetically modified crops are a concern to many environmentalists who fear they might spread deleterious genes to wild variates. The ways the world is economically and socially integrated seem to be increasing inequities between the developed and developing world,

with the rural poor especially hard hit. Since processes of globalization are not likely to be reversed, the question is how to manage the changes they bring so that everyone can reap the benefits.

Industrialism is characterized by a highly developed factory system of production based on the harnessing of vastly increased amounts of energy, on specialization, and on mechanization—the replacement of human and animal labor by mechanical devices. The rise of industrial society has provoked dramatic changes in our physical and social environments. The more energy industrial societies extract, the more they require for their survival.

Industrialism has numerous social consequences. Human populations are increasing more rapidly than ever before, with consequent pressures on natural resources. Industrialization brings a demographic transition: The population increases rapidly and persistently before the growth rate finally levels off. Massive migrations both between and within nations have occurred as people have left rural communities for the cities in the hope of industrial jobs. Increasing specialization of labor and concentration of wealth have resulted in new kinds of social relations and organizations. Differentiation between classes has increased, whereas differentiation based on cultural and ethnic distinctions within classes has declined. The economy brought about by industrialism has transcended geographical barriers.

In the early twentieth century, a new form of land tenure arose and became widespread. Under the administrative system, formerly prevalent in all Communist countries, the state owns the land and can control much of the peasant's labor and income. The administrative form of land control has had a mixed record. Collective farming led to the near collapse of food production in China and was largely abandoned there as public policy. Some collective enterprises do prosper, particularly those that are small, which offer participants some advantage and produce items that farmers could not produce by their individual efforts.

This chapter focused on the industrialization of agriculture, the adaptations that people have made to this phenomenon, and the impact of technology and multinational corporations. It paid special attention to three cases: the social and ecological impacts of major dam projects; California's industrialized farming system; and a village in Bulgaria that has undergone a major transition to collectivized farming and an equally major transition back to a free-market economy.

With the advent of the advanced Industrial Era, truly massive impoundments of water emerged, and these usually had electrical power production in mind as well as agricultural intensification. In fact, by the late twentieth century, giant dams became emblematic of economic development and were, and still are, heavily charged with political significance beyond their economic potential. Ensuring long-term proper drainage is extremely costly, and the benefits of such investment are not immediately visible to users until damage has been done. Vast areas of Iraq, Pakistan, and India, in addition to China and Egypt, have seen declines in productivity due to soil salinity. And this is not a so-called Third World problem. Currently, the most fertile region of Australia, southeastern New South Wales, as well as the Imperial Valley in California are experiencing salinization on a massive scale.

The experience of Wasco, California, illustrates the urbanization of a rural community by mechanization—the transformation of farming as a livelihood to farming for profit, the change in social reference from the local community to that of the wider world, and the breakdown in social relations from close personal ties to relatively impersonal ones. In the San Joaquin Valley, large corporations run giant farms without farmers, relying on managers and foremen to supervise crews of migrant laborers. The family farm is still the dominant form of farming in the United States, even though a commercially successful operation now involves more than 1,000 acres of land. In the Midwest, there is still a definite ethnic texture to the settlement pattern, with families of German descent now predominant in Illinois.

Collectivization came as a shock to the villagers of Zamfirovo, Bulgaria, when the Communists came to power in 1944. For the first ten years, people felt they were much worse off than they had been before, but gradually, they learned to "domesticate the revolution"; that is, they took the oppressive institutions and procedures imposed by the state and adapted them to their local needs. They found ways to avoid, or minimize, government requisitions by hiding animals in the forest, harvesting at night, underreporting harvests, and the like. As mechanization progressed and small local factories opened, life became easier. Each household had its own garden plot, food and clothing were heavily subsidized, and most households had several incomes, including pensions. And cooperative equipment was regularly put to private use. By the late 1980s, only about thirty administrators and workers were full-time employees in the cooperative, and farming, apart from the gardens, had become entirely mechanized. By the time the Communist regime collapsed in 1989, the resourceful villagers had domesticated the cooperative system, with all its inefficiencies, so that its resources served their individual needs. In 1991, the new center-right government made the abolition of the cooperatives a priority, even though villagers in Zamfirovo, and many other parts of the country, were in favor of continuing them under democratic administration. So the villagers were faced with another "transition" as old structures were dismantled in the absence of new ones and with policies and laws over which they have no control formulated in the capital. Bulgarian agriculture has still not recovered, so the transition can be said to continue.

## Key Terms

administrative system
Blue Revolution
commune
demographic transition
genetically modified crops
Green Revolution
mechanization

## Suggested Readings

Creed, G. W. (1998). *Domesticating revolution: From socialist reform to ambivalent transition in a Bulgarian village.* University Park: Pennsylvania State University Press.

This is one of the best works available describing how the collapse of state socialism in 1989 in Eastern Europe affected average people in the rural sector. Creed achieves this by taking a long-term perspective beginning with the initial move to collective farming, its development into highly centralized and industrialized agribusiness, and into the 1990s, when decollectivization was imposed and land reprivatized.

Davis, D. S. (Ed.) (2000). *The consumer revolution in urban China.* Berkeley: University of California Press. One of the first group of studies to examine changing consumer practices in China, a transformation that, because of the numbers alone, has great implications for the rest of the world. Almost all of the studies are based on participant observation.

Diamond, J. (1999). *Guns, germs, and steel: The fates of human societies.* New York: W. W. Norton. An ambitious and readable Pulitzer Prize winning treatment of how the modern world was formed. Ranging over some 13,000 years, Diamond traces theories of human origins and dispersion, the development of agriculture and its diffusion, the rise of cities and early empires, and the ultimate early modern predominance of those based in Eurasia.

Fiege, M., & Cronon, W. (1999). *Irrigated Eden: The making of an environmental landscape in the American West.* Seattle and London: University of Washington Press, Weyerhauser Environmental Books. This book describes the coming of irrigation to Idaho's Snake River Valley, where human actions inadvertently create a strange new ecology.

Roy, A. (1999). *The cost of living.* New York: Modern Library Paperbacks. A very readable polemic against the building of large dams—and indirectly a critique of large-scale development projects in general. Roy likens dams to nuclear bombs: Both are weapons of mass destruction! The object of her fierce criticism is the massive dam complex under construction in the Narmada Valley in the Indian state of Gujarat, at the time of her writing just beginning and now half completed.

Salamon, S. (1992). *Prairie patrimony: Family, farming and community in the Midwest.* Chapel Hill: University of North Carolina Press. An excellent account of family farming in the Midwest.

Wolf, E. R. (1998). *Envisioning history: Ideologies of dominance and crisis.* Berkeley: University of California Press. Wolf examines three cases of political power applied in excess and the cultural and ideational systems in which they occur.

Wong, B. (1998). *Ethnicity and entrepreneurship: The new Chinese immigrants in the San Francisco Bay Area.* Boston: Allyn & Bacon. A good description of how people adapt existing institutions and traditions to new circumstances; here extremely versatile and successful immigrants to the United States from China thrive as they establish international trading networks and global business strategies.

## *Chapter 8*

# Change and Development: The Challenges of Globalism

### The Emerging Fourth World in the New Millennium

Starting early in 2000, a series of international conferences was convened more or less specifically to address issues of globalization and equity, with topics ranging from free trade, the regulation of multinational corporations, biogenetic engineering, or the proper place, if any, of genetically modified organisms, to a host of environmental issues. But underscoring all of these is the awareness that following an unparalleled period of economic and demographic growth through the 1990s, a very significant percentage of the world's people are not sharing in the apparent prosperity. Manuel Castells (1998), the eminent Spanish-born sociologist of global transformations, sums up how serious this problem is. We have long been accustomed to refer to a basic distinction, coined by a French demographer just after World War II, between the so-called First World and Third World, or between populations of the highly developed West and the less developed populations of the poorer countries of Africa, Asia, and the Americas. (The Second World

referred to the socialist states of Europe prior to the 1989 break up of the USSR and is today little used.) Castells suggests that now economic disparities are such that the socially and economically excluded, be they underfed or seriously overexploited, form a distinct category on a global scale—the new face of poverty, extreme poverty, or the Fourth World. "In a global approach, there has been, over the last three decades, increasing inequality and polarization in the distribution of wealth." Of the world's gross domestic product (GDP), only about 20% was generated in the developing countries even though they are home to over 80% of the world's population; more than 20% of the world's population has seen their share of the global GDP decline, whereas the share of the richest 20% has risen from 70% to 85%.

By the late 1990s, 1.3 billion people lived below the extreme poverty line of a consumption equivalent of $1 a day. Oddly enough, income disparities even in the wealthiest countries also increased, making polarization a global phenomenon. Part of the global problem is infrastructural, argues Castells; for example, there are more telephones in New York City or Tokyo than in all of sub-Saharan Africa, seriously disadvantaging this vast region in the new age of information. Moreover, considering Africa as an example, weak infrastructure in the form of poor or no education and health facilities, unsanitary living conditions, rapid urbanization, and widespread and rising unemployment further reinforce marginalization. Even in terms of specific diseases, such as the HIV or AIDS epidemic, the poorest of the poor are most seriously affected. HIV infections in Africa were first reported in the early 1980s; in sub-Saharan Africa, there are now 4.7 million people infected—one in nine. In South Africa alone, as many as 1,000 people die of AIDS every day. This has created a huge population of orphaned children, who will themselves be disadvantaged as well as a drain on the national economy.

Closely related to global polarization, in Castells's view, is the increase in the social exclusion and overexploitation of children, exacerbated by the AIDS epidemic. By social exclusion, he refers to individuals so seriously marginalized that they cannot participate in the legal or mainstream social or economic activities of their nations. Overexploited children sacrifice their social and economic future because they cannot work and receive proper education; in addition, many literally sacrifice their health, even their lives. He finds that child labor rates have virtually exploded in recent years. At the end of the twentieth century, the International Labor Organization estimated that 250 million children between the ages of five and fourteen were working in industry, with 153 million children employed in Asia, 80 million in Africa, and 17.5 million in Latin America. In Africa, some 40% of all children in this age range work. Beyond the reach of statistics is the visible growth in numbers of "street children" in the developing world. The reasons for both child labor and the increasing numbers of bands of homeless children living in the streets are deepening poverty and the crises in subsistence economies worldwide. Families desperate to generate income either send their children to work or to fend for themselves on the streets. Those who employ children are themselves usually relatively poor small producers. It is a global phenomenon because of the ". . . network between small producers and larger firms exporting to affluent markets, often through intermediation of wholesale merchants and large department stores in these markets" (p. 154). In short, Castells describes the emerging Fourth

*Two readily recognizable global symbols confront one another in Istanbul, Turkey.*
(Daniel Bates)

World as a global string of "black holes" of social exclusion, people devalued or populations made, in his words, "worthless" in the new information-based global economy.

While individuals from all points of the political spectrum see growing inequity as a potential threat to world order, the problem remains of how to mitigate it. Here too most would agree that globalization is a process that is not likely to be reversed. Virtually all agree that globalization has to be "properly managed—but how to do so is the big question." Although International Monetary Fund (IMF) policies are often vilified because of their impacts on the poor when strict monetary controls and high interest rates are insisted upon as a basis for loans, the IMF remains adamant that international trade is the mechanism that offers the best hope for the world's poor, but this also depends on affluent countries directly assisting poorer ones. There can be no return to either the statist systems of the now collapsed Second World nor to unfettered capitalism.

Peggy Barlett (1999) notes that the nineteenth century, in the guise of colonialism, was very much a global century both politically and economically. The fact that English is spoken in North America, Australia, India, New Zealand, South Africa, and the Caribbean, and Spanish in much of Central and South America is evidence of the deep roots of global processes. Today, the United States Committee for Refugees (2003) estimates there are 13 million refugees worldwide, displaced by famines, wars, and natural disasters, in addition to the many millions of people who migrate in search of work and better living conditions. According to Barlett, ". . . This massive dislocation fractures the unique connections of people and the land and destroys cultural traditions adapted over centuries to a particular locale. But are these traditions broken, or merely stretched?" This question is as good a starting point as any in exploring contemporary society, especially rural society. It is not change but the *rapidity* of potential change that presents a challenge unique to our age.

The late Douglas Adams, British author of the bestselling *Hitchhiker's Guide to the Galaxy,* has an insightful view of change that is both global and personal. The personal nature of perception is critical; after all, it is against the measure of our individual experience that change becomes meaningful. He writes:

> . . . (a) everything that's already in the world when you're born is just normal; (b) anything that gets invented between then and before you turn 30 is incredibly exciting and with any luck you can make a career out of it; (c) anything that gets invented after you're 30 is the end of civilization as we know it until it's been around for 10 years, when it gradually turns out to be all right really. Apply this list to movies, rock music, word processors and mobile phones to work out how old you are. (1999)

We are still in the first generation of many technologies whose future is unknown but whose impacts are tremendous—in fact, as Adams notes, we haven't even assimilated the language of some of these as, for example, with the Internet. So we have to struggle with such cumbersome words as "interactivity" to speak of many connected to many. Throughout much of the urban world, mobile phone use has skyrocketed in recent years and not just in the centers where one might expect new technology to thrive. In many neighborhoods in Istanbul, for example, it is a rare high school or university student who does not have his or her mobile phone; the first thing a teacher, lecturer, or even a concert conductor now says to the audience is, "Please turn off your phones!" Even telephone etiquette has shifted—the new greeting is "Where are you?" Text messaging has generated a slew of new language conventions, and the capacity to transmit video clips has raised ethical issues of privacy and veracity. This mania for constant contact is not really new behavior; people are simply keeping in touch with their peers, as young people do in any age.

But it is different in that their networks are larger and perhaps more closely integrated. This aspect of "interactivity" is discussed later.

People react to change in a variety of ways. Usually, the rate of change is so slow that people are hardly aware it is occurring. When women entered the U.S. work force in great numbers during World War II and later in the 1960s, few people observed, let alone anticipated, the social consequences. Only many years later did public policy come to recognize the changes taking place in the way we lived, married, and reared our children. Even today, little or no attempt has been made to shift public policy in ways that would cushion the social costs of this transformation that are borne by women and children.

Observations from many sources indicate some recurring long-term processes of systemic change that cumulatively have transformed human society and continue to do so. These patterns of general evolution—the patterns of behavior or organization that can be observed in a group or population—are the products of short-term adaptations, and none is universal. One way to see the long-term consequences of specific adaptations is to go back in time: Archaeological data offer an insight into the processes of long-term change. They also caution us not to predict long-term success or failure on the basis of short-term perspectives. By some criteria, bacteria may be considered better adapted than humans. They have remained virtually unchanged for over 2 billion years and thrive in an incredible range of habitats.

# Adaptation and Processes of Cultural Transformation

## Long-Term Change: The Vikings in the North Atlantic

The history of Viking exploration and settlements in the North Atlantic provides one example of an accumulation of short-term adaptations that result in an ultimately dramatic long-term change. Thomas McGovern and other archaeologists who specialize in Norse or Viking history have attempted to unravel the checkered history of Norse settlement in the North Atlantic (McGovern, 1980; McGovern et al., 1996). Numerous islands were settled between A.D. 790 and 1000, including the Shetland and Faeroe Islands, Iceland, Greenland, and very likely the east coast of North America as well. The colonies had rather different histories, and the westernmost ones, Iceland and Greenland, mark the outer limits of significant Viking settlement. The once thriving settlements of Greenland (which failed by 1500) and Iceland (which suffered a significant decline in population after several centuries) offer some insights into the processes of long-term adaptation.

The Viking settlers brought with them an established food procurement system: They raised cattle and sheep, fished, and where possible, cultivated wheat or barley. They also came equipped with a social and political hierarchy that separated the free from the slaves and encompassed quite rigid distinctions among servants, tenants, landowners, and chiefs. By law, every free landowning farmer or household had to be associated with a particular chief. Each tenant—a family that was contracted to run a farmstead for a specified period—was bound to a landowning householder. The entire colony was run by an elite comprising chiefs and, in the later periods, the Norwegian king's appointees and church dignitaries. The early colonial period was quite successful; most of the settlers were free, and they established independent holdings on which to raise sheep and cattle wherever they found sufficient pasturage. The settlers were quick to incorporate the rich marine life into their diets. The population of Greenland's settlements grew, as did that of Iceland; the two together reached some 60,000.

With success, however, came the gradual transformation of the Viking colonies. In the beginning, each settlement was relatively autonomous, and the predominant form of homestead was that of a free family working pastures and lands that they owned and on which they paid taxes. Though slaves were brought over initially, no more were imported and the labor that nonfamily members performed was provided by servants and tenants. As time passed and settlements grew, churches were erected and homesteads spread to the outer limits of pasturage in this severe environment.

Gradual social and political changes had profound effects. First, the number of tenant farmers increased in relation to freeholders as many freeholders had to sell their lands to pay the taxes levied. Thus, land became much more subject to indirect management. The people who worked the land were under pressure to produce as much hay or to raise as many sheep and cattle as possible, with little thought to possible long-term effects. Evidence of overgrazing and soil erosion is abundant. Second, what were formerly petty chiefs became powerful leaders, controlling considerable land and often warring with rivals. By the mid-thirteenth century, a few families had come to control most of the land. In short, land use became intensified. Socially, the society was more stratified; specialized priests, warriors, smiths, and urban craftworkers proliferated; and decision making became more centralized as power accrued to the chiefs and bishops.

In 1262–1264, Greenland and Iceland came under the direct control of the Norwegian state, and most land was now controlled by church and crown. The church sent bishops to rule and encouraged the building of monumental structures quite disproportionate to the size and resources of the colonies. Taxes and tithes were collected, administered, and forwarded to the state by foreign-born appointees. The colonies were closely integrated into a growing

*This reconstructed Viking chieftain's farmstead at Borg, in North Norway, is one of the largest known. This form of dwelling, which housed a chief, his retainers, and livestock, was commonly used in Viking colonies in Greenland, Iceland, and (most likely) Nova Scotia (Vinland).*

(Sophia Perdikaris)

North European economic system. But economic integration did not bring prosperity to most of the people of the colonies, and ultimately, it had dire consequences. Environmental degradation through soil erosion and depletion of marine resources caused hardship. Much of the pasturage became barren rock, and by 1500, the colony on Greenland had become extinct, unable to cope with the demands of its top-heavy administration, a depleted resource base, and the harsh climate. Greenland was once more left to its North American inhabitants—the Eskimos, whose time-proven adaptations the Vikings chose to ignore or dismiss. By 1600, 94% of Iceland's people were reduced to tenant farming, and the population declined sharply. This colony survived, but prosperity returned only in the twentieth century when Iceland reorganized itself as an independent and locally self-sufficient society (see also McGovern et al., 1996).

## Processes of Long-Term Cultural Change

This case study provides a backdrop to review some very general processes involved in long-term cultural change, most of which have been introduced earlier.

*Intensification.* The per capita energy requirements of the simplest human cultures are very small when compared with those needed by the most complex societies. As a society increases in complexity, more and more of its energy budget must go to maintaining institutions—churches (as in the Viking example), universities, banking systems, stock markets, and so forth. A key element in the increasing complexity of the infrastructure is the **intensification** of food production. This process of intensification involves increasing the product derived from a unit of land or labor.

Most societies that rely on hunting and gathering obtain less food from a unit of land than do populations that rely on intensive agriculture. In the latter, increasing numbers of people rely on a relatively constant amount of land to produce increasing amounts of food. Again, we have seen this dynamic at work in the Viking settlements. Quite apart from land-use intensification, ever more nonfood energy is harvested and consumed on a per capita basis.

Presently, the world's population stands at 6,500,000,000, more than double what it was thirty years ago, and thanks to agricultural intensification using fertilizers and new seeds, food production has roughly kept pace. Some economists feel that it will continue to do so, but at the 2000 Bangkok UN Conference on Trade and Development, this was a matter of considerable debate. However, one thing can be agreed upon: There are no reliable guides as to how long growth in food production can be sustained. Moreover, high levels of productivity entail high costs in energy use and waste removal.

*Specialization.* A process parallel to intensification involved in long-term change is **specialization,** the increasingly limited range of productive activities in which a single individual is likely to engage. As specialization increases, the average person is engaged in a smaller and smaller percentage of the entire set of activities carried out in a society. Industrial society (or postindustrial society) is simply the latest point reached in a process that is as old as human culture. As individuals have become increasingly specialized, societies have tended to be characterized by increasing **differentiation**—that is, organization in separate units for various activities and purposes. Hunter-gatherer societies contain no more than a few dozen distinct occupations, while industrial societies may have over a million. Overspecialization, however, is a problem of some concern. How, for example, can a region whose agriculture has been devoted to one or two cash commodity crops, such as coffee, cocoa, or tea, adapt to declining prices on the world market?

*Centralization.* A third evolutionary process has been **centralization,** the concentration of political and economic decisions in the hands of a few individuals or institutions. This process has been related to the growth of political, economic, and social differentiation. A strong centralized power is useful, even necessary, in efforts to orchestrate diverse activities and interests—not to mention efforts to defend extant resources and possibly to acquire those of neighboring populations.

The development of political centralization probably began not long after the Neolithic Revolution—the changeover from hunting and gathering wild food to domesticating plants and animals. With food production, populations became larger and denser and sustained themselves through increasing economic specialization. All of this required the growth of more centralized institutions to process information, manage more complex distributive and productive systems, and maintain public order in the face of conflicting interests. As a consequence, today almost all of the world's peoples live within the political structures of highly centralized states. However, as the history of the Viking settlements shows, centralization can have dire consequences when

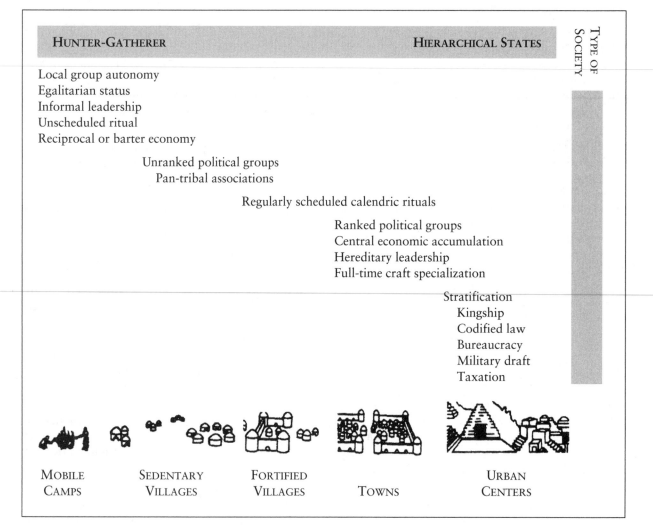

| HUNTER-GATHERER | HIERARCHICAL STATES | TYPE OF SOCIETY |
|---|---|---|

Local group autonomy
Egalitarian status
Informal leadership
Unscheduled ritual
Reciprocal or barter economy

Unranked political groups
Pan-tribal associations

Regularly scheduled calendric rituals

Ranked political groups
Central economic accumulation
Hereditary leadership
Full-time craft specialization

Stratification
Kingship
Codified law
Bureaucracy
Military draft
Taxation

| MOBILE CAMPS | SEDENTARY VILLAGES | FORTIFIED VILLAGES | TOWNS | URBAN CENTERS |

**Figure 8.1.** *Type of societies and the appearance of institutions and major features in the evolution of social complexity.*
(After Price & Feinman, 1997)

those making the decisions—levying taxes and tithes in this case—cannot perceive the long-term consequences of those decisions.

Another example is in Türkmenistan, formerly part of the Soviet Union, which is today facing an ecological disaster of almost unparalleled magnitude. The Aral Sea, in 1960 the fourth largest lake in the world, is drying up so rapidly that in 2003 it was one third its original size. Soon it will be nothing more than a vast briny swamp. Water that formerly fed the Aral has been diverted to complex and distant irrigation projects, some more than 1,300 kilometers away. The water that does flow into the Aral from surrounding agricultural areas is contaminated by chemical fertilizers and pesticides. Gone is the rich fishing industry, and communities once located on the lake's shores are being stranded as the shoreline recedes. The rapidly diminishing surface area of the lake is already resulting in hotter, drier summer

temperatures and lower winter temperatures in the surrounding regions. These temperature changes and the falling water table have disrupted oasis farming in the region and contributed to the desertification of the area.

A disaster happening within a disaster is due to the fact that for years the Soviet military had disposed of its most dangerous chemical weapons material on what was once a deserted island in the Aral; today, these extremely dangerous agents are no longer on an island at all, increasingly vulnerable to theft and potentially the cause of deadly pollution.

The main culprit in this case and in many others is an abstraction: a highly centralized system of planning and decision making with inadequate ability to anticipate long-term costs. Of course, we know that abstractions have no influence over environmental events: The decisions are made and carried out by myriad individuals united in a bureaucratic hierar-

*Rusting vessels far from what water remains in the Aral Sea—a victim of Soviet-era land- and water-use policies. Such disasters worldwide may be exacerbated by centralized planning and decision making.*

(©David Turnley/CORBIS)

chy, each concerned with such mundane matters as career advancement, job security, and day-to-day survival. Adhering to productivity goals, limiting one's liability and responsibility for mistakes, and demonstrating bureaucratic achievement in extending the scope of one's authority are critical to the success of individuals in bureaucracies. In this context, local information and early warning signs that might signal impending environmental or social problems are easily ignored.

*Stratification and Inequality.* Another trend in the long-term evolution of cultures is **stratification**—the division of a society into groups that have varying degrees of access to resources and power. In complex societies, entire groups may have very little or no access to decision-making processes and little access to the resources of the larger society. The Viking settlements in Greenland and Iceland eventually collapsed because the tenant farmers were excluded from the decision-making process and were forced by the church and the crown to overexploit the land.

In no society do all people enjoy equal prestige or equal ability to participate in all social and economic activities. Even within the simple foraging society of the San people of Africa, some men acquire the title of "headman" and are accorded great respect. Among the Tiwi, another foraging group located in Australia, inequality in terms of status may affect a male's chances of marrying. Older men use accumulated social credits and status to acquire a large number of wives, creating a shortage of mates for the younger men.

While inequality of this sort may entail great hardship for some members of a society, it is not the same as socioeconomic stratification, which can lead to a situation where entire segments of a population are disadvantaged in comparison with other members of the same society. This disadvantaged position, which is largely passed from generation to generation, engenders systematic constraint or exploitation by other segments of the population over a substantial period of time. In this sense, the groupings formed in stratified societies perpetuate inequality, and such

*The collapse of communism and state-dominated redistributive systems led to informal markets springing up, such as this one in Hungary. These markets have now been largely replaced by chains of supermarkets.*

(Daniel Bates)

inequality has little to do with the personal strengths or weaknesses of individuals.

*Settlement Nucleation.* In almost every part of the world, stratification and centralization have been associated with **nucleation,** the tendency of populations to cluster in settlements of increasing size and density. Cities are an exclusive characteristic of state-organized societies and arose comparatively recently in human history—at most, 7,000 years ago. Without question, the world's population is increasingly focused or dependent on cities, although we might see shifts away from this as some productive systems and communication networks come to depend less on concentrations of workers. Still, the overall trend is toward larger and larger urban "megaregions," always at the expense of agricultural land. Istanbul's population in 1964 was approximately 750,000; in 2003, it was over 13 million people—far outstripping the city's ability to provide basic services such as water and sanitation. Similar instances of hypergrowth can be found in cities on every continent: Cairo, Beijing, Lagos, New Delhi, and Mexico City, to name a few.

These trends are not, of course, inevitable. New developments in technology, especially in areas related to communication and production, may alter things dramatically. Nor are these general, long-term evolutionary trends independent in a causal sense. First, important systemic relationships link them. Second, changes in each may be responses to similar environmental changes. Intensification and specialization, for example, may both serve to extract more resources from a deteriorating environment through the reorganization of work. Centralization may accomplish the same end through increased efficiency in the flow of resources or information concerning their availability. Also, we have to make a clear distinction between trends or processes that can be seen in individual populations or social systems and those that appear to extend to societies around the globe. Any particular society may as easily be in the process of decentralizing or deintensifying land use as centralizing and intensifying it. The Viking settlements are again a case in point: After several centuries of political and economic centralization, the trend was reversed rather dramatically.

The case of Bulgarian agriculture discussed in the previous chapter is another instance of this. At one time, the country had perhaps the most centralized agricultural sector in the world and one of the most industrialized. Now farming is individualized, small plots predominate, much land is untended, and much less mechanization is evident.

Put in terms of the earlier discussion of stability and resilience, a complex society may reach a stage where it achieves stability at the expense of resilience. Though it is true that if one considers all societies over the course of human existence as a whole, cultural evolution has tended to proceed from the simple to the complex, it is a mistake to believe that all societies pass smoothly or uniformly in this direction. And it is also a mistake to equate increasing complexity with progress or with "improved" adaptation.

## The Individual Dimension of Adaptation and Short-Term Change

There are many ways to view cultural change, and all of the social sciences are involved in the quest to

*A major problem throughout the world is the increasing gulf between those with resources and those without, as seen here in Calcutta.*

(Jehangir Gazdar/Woodfin Camp & Associates)

understand the dynamics of societal change. But underlying the multiplicity of perspectives, most research has focused on the costs and benefits of change to the people involved. For example, which social grouping or class benefits from innovation and which pays the costs, who within a social setting is likely to introduce new techniques of production or marketing, or what are the environmental impacts of a new agricultural technique?

In all societies, certain individuals walk a fine line between conformance to social rules or customary practice and deviance: between doing the expected and striking new ground. Deviating from the norm, however negatively it may be viewed when certain moral codes are involved, is essential for innovation. When certain members of a society violate the rules of expected practice or dare to go beyond acceptable limits and their actions succeed in resolving some problem, they are called entrepreneurs or innovators. If they fail, they are simply "losers," "fools," or "deviants." Probably most innovations are as much a matter of serendipity as of cold, clear calculation; people, as noted earlier, cope with their problems opportunistically using whatever comes to hand.

## The Individual and Entrepreneurial Innovation

Like all aspects of adaptation, strategies of production and exchange are never static. By experimenting with new approaches or by being forced to alter traditional ones, people inevitably discover new methods that may eventually modify their economic organization. Frederick Barth's pioneering study (1963) of fishing villages in northern Norway reveals that conditions of ambiguity can prompt acceptance of innovation. Isolated geographically and culturally, the villagers (most of whom were Lapps) occupied a marginal position in Norwegian society. Many wanted the goods that industrialization promised but lacked the means to obtain them. Fishing for export and farming for home consumption made for a precarious existence. The villagers had neither the capital nor the financial know-how to make connections with the modern world. Such conditions create a niche for the people that Barth identifies as entrepreneurs—individuals who are willing to take risks and break with traditional practices to make a profit. Barth suggests that in marginal communities the entrepreneur acts as an agent of change by playing the role of mediator between local communities and outside institutions. By making use of existing possibilities in ways neither local people nor state bureaucrats perceive or plan, the entrepreneur is able to bring together a relatively self-conscious group of people who see the utility of change. Under other conditions, entrepreneurs may be considered and treated as deviant or even criminal, as are drug dealers.

## Acceptance of Innovation

The acceptance of innovations depends to a great extent on the fact that customary ways of acting are always subject to variation. Individuals in every society constantly make decisions, and decision making gives rise to behavioral variation. There are, nevertheless, limits to innovation. As noted in Chapter 2, the individual with the best chance of long-term success is not necessarily the one most perfectly adjusted to its environment at any particular point but rather the one that maintains the ability to respond to its environment in a flexible variety of ways—that is, with a high degree of resilience. Given that we have only limited means of responding to environmental challenges and that we have limited ways of predicting how our responses to these challenges will turn out, what is the best strategy? Generally speaking, it will be the cheapest possible response—the strategy that involves the least possible loss of future adaptive ability, the minimum sacrifice of flexibility. In other words, choices among alternatives should be made to minimize uncertainty, not simply to look to large possible gains. As noted, this seems to be the case with humans because people are generally conservative in their behavior and hesitant to change ways of doing things that appear to work.

The move toward organic farming is instructive in this regard. In the United States in the early 1970s, a few nontraditional farmers, mostly young urban-educated garden farmers, ventured into producing for the "organic food" trade, itself limited to a handful of specialty stores in the large cities. By the 1980s, the interest in such food items had vastly increased, and farmers more in the "mainstream" began very slowly to adopt organic methods—no chemical fertilizers, no hybrid seeds, no pesticides. The practice had moved from the fringe toward the center, but very cautiously and only after individual farmers were able to see their more risk-prone neighbors succeed—or at least not go broke. By the end of the 1990s, organic farming had become big business. In England, for example, the organic produce sections of supermarkets are the fastest growing in the food trade. Of course, not all such innovations catch on, even where one might suppose they would. Buffalo meat has many health advantages because it is naturally low in cholesterol and buffalo range well on pastures where cattle might not thrive. But low

*Box 8.1*

# No More Pigs: Changing Subsistence Strategies in Papua New Guinea[1]

ANTHROPOLOGIST DAVID BOYD has been visiting the Awa village of Irakia since 1970 and has described how, beginning in the late 1980s, the villagers started to deliberately change their basic subsistence patterns, including, most significantly, the elimination of pig husbandry. Pig husbandry has long been recognized as an important feature of human adaptations throughout Melanesia and especially in the New Guinea highlands. Explanations of why people devoted so much effort to the production of domesticated pigs have changed along with theoretical interests. However, whether pig husbandry was interpreted as an economically irrational use of human resources, as a protein storage mechanism, as a managed resource important for human well-

[1]This material is based on David J. Boyd (2001), Life without Pigs: Recent subsistence changes among the Irakia Awa, Papua New Guinea, *Human Ecology,* 29(3), pp. 259–282.

being, or as an indicator of social complexity, it was generally recognized that pigs were crucial for any transaction of social importance—from marriages, to dispute settlement, to compensation, to curing the sick, and to burying the dead.

Irakia is one of eight Awa-speaking communities living on both sides of the Lamari River in the southeastern part of the Eastern Highlands Province. Its total population is approximately 1,400 people. In 1996, Irakia itself had a population of 299, with a density of about 36 people per square mile. The Irakia Awa still depend mostly on their garden produce for subsistence, although they grow a small amount of coffee as a cash crop. Until recently, pigs were an important part of their adaptation, and pork (rather than live pigs) was the usual medium of exchange. Pigs would spend most of their time foraging away from the village but would return regularly to be fed small amounts by their caretakers.

So gardens had to be planted to provide fodder, but they also had to be sturdily fenced to keep the pigs out, a demanding and time-consuming task.

During the 1970s, Irakia had been disrupted by a number of deaths attributed to sorcery, and consequently, more than half of the community moved away. There was also a prolonged period of hostilities with a neighboring village, which finally culminated in 1986 with a truce. At this point, the Irakians began to assess village conditions and to formulate a plan for improvement. By this time, most adults and many of the children had lived at coastal and urban employment locations and had experience with basic health care, schooling, a range of consumer goods, and entertainment provided by movies, sports, and church activities. So younger Irakians especially found village life rather dull by contrast. In addition, many neighboring communities on or near the re-

consumer interest has yet to enable more than a handful of ranchers to make money, with most failing to do so in spite of considerable investment.

Whether or not the efforts of successful entrepreneurs reflect a conscious strategy, they can have important consequences. First, entrepreneurs most commonly engage in activities that take them over the boundary between traditional and modern economic organization. They may recognize the potential of market exchange, for example, and bring the products of new factories or imported goods into the countryside to compete with traditional handicrafts and to create new needs. Second, while an entrepreneurial effort may originate with an individual, it rarely succeeds unless others join and support the new enterprise. And finally, these entrepreneurial actions typically lead to fundamental changes in the systems of production and distribution. Farmers

may begin to produce more cash crops; they—or their children—may choose to work in the factory rather than the fields. These changes in turn will begin to transform gender relations, social and family structures, and eventually, the whole society.

## Gender, Inequality, and Change

As discussed in earlier chapters, gender is vital to any analysis of social change. Social and economic change affects the division of labor in society and, in particular, women. As Manuel Castells sees it, gender relations—the sexual and familial relationships among men, women, and children—is, in every society, a "contested domain" (1996a, p. 15). One aspect of this contest has to do with the gender structure of work and access to employment opportunities. Castells stresses the global nature of invest-

gional road system were in much more intensive contact with the outside world and had greater access to government services and to markets. They also attracted missionary groups, who brought with them many desirable modern amenities in addition to the word of God.

When Boyd visited in mid-1991, he reported that the villagers were uncertain of exactly what steps to take. Younger Irakians were keen to attract a mission and had just completed construction of a small church. While the village elders remained dubious of adopting a new religion, they nevertheless recognized that successful local improvement depended on the assistance of outsiders. However, with 52% of members living away from the village, the prospects for improvement were not encouraging. It was during this visit that two young men in their thirties told Boyd that they wanted to stop raising pigs. When he expressed dismay, they explained that the pigs needed daily attention, were always causing trouble among villagers, and the effort was no longer worth it. They indicated that they had support among their peers but that the elders refused to discuss the issue. But

within a few years, new support for the discontinuation of pig husbandry arrived in the form of a number of young people returning to the village after conversion to Seventh Day Adventism at the plantations where they had been working. Seventh Day Adventism prohibits the consumption of pork, and these young people refused to have anything to do with the pigs.

In mid-1995, following the deaths of several prominent elders, younger families began to slaughter their pigs so that by the end of the year the entire village herd was gone, with the exception of one sow belonging to a respected elder who said that she could be slaughtered only for his funeral feast—which is exactly what happened in August 1996. When Boyd returned to Irakia in mid-1996, not only did he notice the fence that had enclosed the village was totally dilapidated, but also that he ". . . did not have to calculate carefully every footfall along the path to avoid soiling my boots . . . Incidentally, the largely barefoot Awa consider stepping in pig manure a vile experience" (p. 271). The villagers eagerly explained the local improvement plan they had implemented, including

encouraging people to adopt Christianity, to build larger houses, to plant more coffee as a cash crop, and to organize competitive sports teams. Alcohol consumption and gambling with playing cards had been banned. People were learning to live without pigs and had reduced their reliance on the labor-intensive crops of true taro and yam in favor of the more easily cultivated sweet potato, manioc, and New World taro. The plan was intended to make the village a more attractive place to live, and this was beginning to happen. In 1996, only 22% of villagers were living away from Irakia. Boyd concludes, "Irakians believe that these attempts to disintensify subsistence effort, . . . and intensify cash-earning and religious and recreational activities will provide opportunities to local residents that previously had been missing. To date, most residents and returned migrants seem committed to the new ways and express confidence that Irakia has embarked on an effective, locally generated course of village improvement" (p. 280).

---

ment capital and managerial control, utilizing very recent developments in communication technology such as the Internet, or Web, but also including all facets of computer-assisted information flow and exchange (1996). The broader implications of this view are presented later, but with respect to gender in the workplace, the new industrial order has led to the feminization of wage labor globally. While this is a complex issue, one major trend has been labor market deregulation and the cheapening of wages due to the diminished power of organized labor.

Helen Safa has long studied this phenomenon in the Caribbean Basin. According to Safa, the idea of the male breadwinner is rapidly becoming a myth worldwide and most particularly in the Caribbean (1995). In the past three decades, the size of the female work force has more than tripled, with more women than men entering wage employment. But in

many instances, this is less advantageous for women than it might seem. As Safa (1995) and Castells (1996a, 1996b) emphasize, labor is becoming increasingly organized outside contractual agreements between a localized management and a collective labor entity—a union, for example. It is now common for an individual worker's agreement to be with a management entity that represents a multinational company. Not uncommonly, workers are hired part time, or on short-term contracts, with few fringe benefits such as health and retirement plans.

Women are favored recruits because they are less likely to complain about working conditions, less likely to organize, and are more willing to accept low wages for part-time opportunities to support their families (Safa, 1995, pp. 10–11). Safa has followed the processes of gender restructuring in the Dominican Republic, Puerto Rico, and Cuba. All three share a similar colonial and cultural heritage, and all three made strenuous efforts in the 1960s to break away from a sugarcane-based economy by launching export industries.

In Puerto Rico, Operation Bootstrap was part of an ambitious program to diversify the economy away from monocrop agriculture. As is often the case in efforts to industrialize, the first stage was to offer tax incentives designed to encourage the expansion of the apparel and food processing industries (Safa, 1995, p. 13). While intended to provide employment for men displaced from agricultural employment, in practice the program attracted women for the reasons mentioned earlier. Although manufacturing jobs increased rapidly through the 1980s, new jobs did not offset the decline in the agricultural sector. Later investment, focused on high-tech industries such as investment banking and insurance, offered white-collar opportunities to both men and women, but for the bulk of the working poor, the man's role as primary breadwinner was greatly diminished, leading to new patterns of authority and power within the household (p. 17). Since many of the new jobs taken by women were offset by jobs lost by men, net family income did not necessarily rise with female employment. Of course, since Puerto Rico is a U.S. territory, families could easily take advantage of employment opportunities on the mainland, and remittances from these migrants serve to maintain higher wage levels than would otherwise obtain (pp. 18–19).

The Dominican Republic's experience is similar in many respects, but without the same opportunities for migration to ease competition for low-paying jobs. Juana Santana, for example, works in a free trade zone and sustains her family of three children on a weekly salary of $20, which has to cover food, rent, child care, and transportation (Safa, 1995, p. 1). Her husband does not hold a steady job. According to Safa, this is the situation many women in the free trade zones face: low wages, poor working conditions, and partners who can provide only limited assistance (p. 1). In both Puerto Rico and the Dominican Republic, a decrease in marital stability can be attributed to male unemployment; however, the essential patriarchal nature of the household remains (p. 167).

Cuba, as one would expect, is rather different due to the social policies of the state and centralized production. Men were guaranteed full employment (until 1990, at least), and women were strongly encouraged to enter the work force (Safa, pp. 163ff). Women are further organized in various officially sanctioned groups that emphasize education as well as domestic issues such as child care and birth control. Nevertheless, women are underrepresented in managerial positions and, in general, continue to view their employment as secondary to their role as mothers. As a consequence, they are generally perceived as playing a secondary role in the workplace. While gender inequality persists in Cuba, in spite of a state ideology to the contrary, it is somewhat different from the other regions discussed. Young women are considerably more independent of male control than in earlier generations (p. 165). Marital instability also has increased in Cuba, but part of the cause may be the severe housing and food problem which puts a strain on marriages. The current economic depression, occasioned by the collapse of international communism that deprived Cuba of its

*Women working in one of many "enterprise zones." For many, it is welcome employment; for the companies, it is inexpensive labor—almost always female labor.*

(©Keith Dannemiller/Corbis Saba)

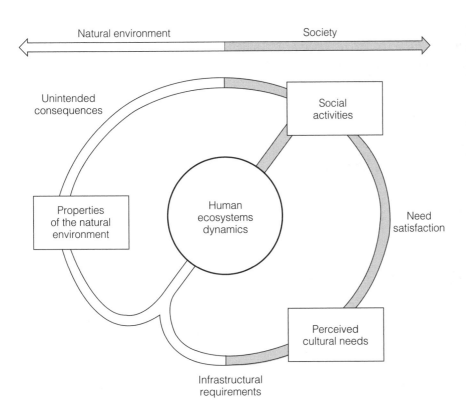

**Figure 8.2.** *The demands of a dynamic or growing human population frequently work at cross-purposes with the long-term sustainability of natural environmental systems. Thus what we think of as social and economic progress often occasions unexpected consequences for the local as well as the global human ecosystem.*

cheap oil and most of its trading partners, falls heavily on women, who have to wait in long lines to secure even basic commodities for their families (p. 166). Gender roles are profoundly affected by economic change—sometimes for the better, sometimes to the detriment of women.

## Beyond Industrialism

The technological and social transformation known as *industrialism* started on a small scale and was restricted to certain forms of production in a few countries, but it did not remain limited for long. In a relatively short period, peoples all over the world were affected by it. Today, we have moved into yet another era in the organization of production and integration of peoples. This has been termed variously the communications era, the age of the computer, and the high-tech age. The labels are not important. What is interesting from an anthropological perspective is that the processes of change appear to occur at an increasingly rapid rate.

The organization of commerce and industry is changing. Historian David Noble (1984) describes this transformation as the triumph of "numerical control" in industry. Following World War II, there was a great advance in the development of servomechanical and electronic controls capable of running complex precision tools. This development, Noble suggests, opened up the possibility of moving the ef-

fective control of manufacturing from the shop floor to the main office. The outcome is a reduction of blue-collar power in industry and further centralization of control in productive organizations. This thesis is interesting, though in some instances the same technology has broken up large industries into smaller components—another outcome of high-speed communications. Certainly, it is clear that job opportunities for production-line workers are rapidly decreasing while new ones open up for people who have skills appropriate to the new technologies. The long-term significance of these changes will be profound; not only are entire segments of the populations of already-industrialized nations marginalized, but the peoples of many countries lacking an educational infrastructure will not participate fully in the economies of the future.

### Theories of Development

A development paradigm called **modernization theory** emerged in the 1960s and became a blueprint for international development assistance designed by the World Bank and industrialized countries for the less developed countries of Africa, Asia, and Latin America. Proposed by economist Walt Rostow (1960), modernization theory sees development as a stage that all countries must pass through, much as England and the United States did in the nineteenth century when they transformed from agricultural to industrial societies. Rostow described economic transition or "take-off" to modern society as occurring through five stages (traditionalism, precondition for take-off, take-off, drive to maturity, and age of high mass consumption). Take-off occurs when obstacles to economic growth are removed by the existence of two conditions: individual entrepreneurship and access to capital to industrialize. The first condition, entrepreneurship, involves breaking from traditional values such as loyalty to family groups and blind submission to centralized authority and promoting individual achievement through Western education and the support of rising entrepreneurs. The second condition, capital accumulation, would be provided by loans and grants from the Western industrialized countries until a country is sufficiently industrialized to provide its people with goods they demand. Modernization theory continues to drive much of the Western development assistance effort, which encourages industrial development, large-scale agriculture, and increased integration of poorer countries into the world market, a point that will be taken up again shortly.

A major weakness of modernization theory is that forty years of development assistance and billions of dollars in aid have not reduced poverty in the world. Today, over 1 billion people (of the world's 6.5 billion) live in extreme poverty, and many more are not far above it (Wilson, 1993, p. 27). A competing interpretation of underdevelopment and poverty is **dependency theory,** associated most strongly with Andre Gunter Frank (1969) who analyzed Latin American economies in the context of larger global capitalism. Frank attacked modernization theory's explanation of inequality and poverty as due to a "lack of appropriate modernizing values." Frank argued that the massive poverty in Brazil, Argentina, and Peru was caused not by a lack of entrepreneurial spirit but by economic and political exploitation from the West (particularly, the United States). Western capitalism, Frank argued, forced a specialization of production on Third World (underdeveloped) countries that was primarily limited to the export of raw material materials, such as lumber, copper, coffee, and sugar to the First World's manufacturing centers. Third World elites, such as the repressive regime in Chile under the former dictator Pinochet, were *compradors* (compromisers) who helped repress local and national worker or peasant movements in the interests of Western capital. For Frank and other dependency theorists, the only way to break the chain of dependency was revolution from below to remove the comprador elite.

Dependency theory was enthusiastically embraced by revolutionary organizations and their supporters in the West. But the theory has been criticized as a circular argument—dependent economies

are not autonomous because they are dependent. Furthermore, there are many exceptions to the rigidity of the First World–Third World distinction. Both Mexico and Canada are dependent on United States's capital, for example, but have viable independent manufacturing centers. Furthermore, since the 1970s, there has been rapid growth in many areas of the developing world including Mexico, Argentina, Korea, Indonesia, India, Turkey, Taiwan, and Malaysia. Dependency theorists argue, however, that while there is some independent manufacturing, these countries are still dominated by multinational corporations and banks located in the West and Japan. Furthermore, many of these countries, such as Malaysia and Singapore, are characterized by strong autocratic governments, repression of labor unions, low wages, and lack of environmental or worker protections. They point out that the era of revolution from below is not over, as witnessed most recently in Mexico by the activities of the Zapatista National Liberation Front (see Chapter 6, Box 6.2).

It is not that some populations or nations are being left out; quite the contrary, the rural and urban poor of many agrarian countries are closely integrated into the world economic and political system, but at its peripheries. That is, they have little control over the resources to which they have access, profit little from what they sell in a market characterized by worldwide competition, and generally are without vote or voice in their own countries. This, in many respects, reflects a process of incorporation of peoples around the globe that began long before anthropology was a discipline: the expansion of European power and economic influence far beyond that continent (Wolf, 1982). Much of the present unequal distribution of the benefits of the postindustrial era, together with attendant environmental degradation as people desperately try to make a living, "is not a problem of the relationship of people with their habitats, but of relationships *among* peoples competing for access to productive resources" (Horowitz, 1994, p. 8). As the world's population grows, so will the competition for productive resources. "The awful truth remains that a large part of humanity will suffer no matter what is done" (Wilson, 1993, p. 27).

## The Integration of the Postindustrial World

Today, it is commonplace to refer to the "global economy," to the "new world order," or to the "world system." While in many ways accurate, the phenomenon of global integration or transcontinental linkages is not new. Since the mid-eighteenth

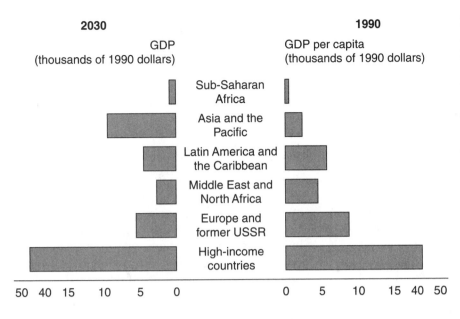

**Figure 8.3.** *The gross domestic product (GDP) per region and per capita in high-income and less developed regions of the world for 1990 and projected for 2030 shows that income distribution will remain extremely skewed in favor of the already-developed countries.*

century, the vast majority of tribal populations throughout the world have been in direct contact, usually to their detriment, with representatives of the industrial world. What is new is the qualitative change that occurred in such linkages in the mid-twentieth century.

In 1974, Richard J. Barnet and Ronald E. Muller wrote a book on a phenomenon closely related to the organization of production in the postindustrial era: the growth of multinational corporations. At the beginning of the twenty-first century, their ideas have increased in relevance. They suggest that the degree to which international corporations have taken over functions once performed by governments and succeeded where governments have failed in creating a "global organization for administering this planet" is difficult to comprehend. This is not to suggest that corporations have consciously evolved into multinationals to dominate the world. They simply make use of the communications and transport technology available to compete in the world marketplace. The sheer size and complexity of their operations, however, have made them a force unto themselves.

Even in 1974, the operating budgets of about 500 giant multinational corporations exceeded those of most nation-states. In the 1980s, the operating budgets of global corporations grew at over twice the rate of the GNP of the United States and other advanced industrial nations, and this continued through the 1990s. This fiscal expansion is based on what has been called the corporations' "global reach"—today, they know no boundaries. The European Union and the 1995 North American Free Trade Agreement (NAFTA) are regional arrangements that facilitate the global organization of production, exchange, and consumption.

Through expansion and diversification, global enterprises insulate themselves from many political and market pressures. High-speed communications permit a multinational corporation to control everything from raw materials to final distribution. It may, for example, buy raw materials from a subsidiary company at less than the actual market price to avoid taxes, or it may sell to another foreign division at inflated prices to transfer income out of a country. Price-fixing cannot really be controlled under such circumstances. Further, and of greater social consequence, a giant corporation can easily shift operations to areas of low labor cost. Such a move can be catastrophic for the workers the corporation leaves behind. The very fact that a corporation operates on a global scale places it beyond the reach of national governments. Regulatory agencies lack the information and in many cases the jurisdiction to investigate global enterprises. Corporations plan centrally and act globally, and nation-states do not.

A more subtle problem, which underlies Barnet and Muller's analysis, is the instability that such global interdependence implies. India's ability to feed its people depends on modern farming, which in turn requires reliance on chemical pesticides, fertilizers, fuel, and machinery. All of these inputs are globally interconnected. Local disasters can now have immediate global repercussions, be it the forest fires in Southeast Asia, arctic pollution, or acid rain in the United States and Canada. There is an obvious good side to interdependence in that global trade and communications even out some disparities—the goods of the industrial states are widely available, people can move great distances to seek a livelihood, the effects of famine and natural disasters can be mitigated. But it also puts all of us at the mercy of events in distant places. The 1995 Kobe earthquake was followed shortly by the bankruptcy of England's oldest investment bank, Baring and Sons, with branches all over the world. The bank's traders had invested heavily in Japanese stocks, betting on anticipated short-term rises, when they were hit by a sudden decline in share prices caused by the earthquake. The impacts of the acts of terrorism on September 11, 2001, were felt globally and helped fuel the incipient economic recession in both the United States and Europe.

Of course, the development of a global system of free trade and its domination by multinationals have not gone unchallenged. On the contrary, these developments have aroused considerable passion and outrage around the world—not always well focused, however. In December 1999, the World Trade Organization meeting in Seattle that was slated to pass agreements to further liberalize trade ended in a stalemate occasioned, in part, by the same global processes it was meeting to further. Thousands of protestors, of very different goals and backgrounds, gathered together in opposition making full use not only of their bodies to demonstrate but also coordinating their opposition to free trade using the most advanced global communications technology. Trade unionists came fearing loss of jobs in industrialized economies, environmentalists were concerned with resource depletion, Third World representatives gathered to complain that their voices were insufficiently heard. The protestors managed to ignore the fact that their objectives were often contradictory, even conflicting; and in the end, they succeeded in bringing the Seattle meeting to an inconclusive halt. The irony might lie in the fact that while there are serious deleterious aspects to global trade and multinational corporate behavior, whatever solutions there may be must also be through global trade agreements. Since 1999, annual WTO meetings have all seen violent protests.

## Globalism and Development

Although globalization affects people in cities as well as in the countryside, it is useful to concentrate here on its effects on rural communities. William Loker (1999, p. 38) notes with reference to Latin America, but with wider implications, that to the extent that solutions to the problems created by a globalized economy are not found in rural areas, then these problems will be transferred to urban areas, where they may be even harder to resolve as these cities receive the sometimes desperate rural poor.

To have access to the foreign capital needed for economic growth (the primary means of reducing poverty), poor countries are required to abide by the rules set by the lending countries. From the late 1970s, in Latin America and in other parts of the developing world as in the discussions of China, Egypt, and Bulgaria, this meant programs of **structural adjustment** aimed at privatizating the public sector and thereby "downsizing" government. Measures such as privatization of state monopolies, the reduction of the state's role in economic planning and policy, and frequently, massive cuts in government-supplied social services have highly disruptive social conse-

*Marchers in New York in a September 2003 march to protest the policies of the World Trade Organization (WTO). Hundreds of demonstrators from various anti-WTO and antiwar groups attended the rally, marching through Manhattan's Greenwich Village.*

(© Chris Hondros/Getty Images)

quences, which are typically felt before the benefits become apparent.

Loker argues that one of the most important consequences of these changes is that development can no longer be thought of as something happening only in the developing world. Rather, these changes affect everyone on our planet, albeit to different degrees and in different ways. Globalization even threatens the very idea of development, which is criticized by environmentalists as fostering an unsustainable relationship between the world's population and its resources; by right-wing thinkers as wasteful and primarily serving the interests on an entrenched elite; and by postmodern thinkers as reflecting ". . . a misplaced belief in progress . . . that promotes a vision of society that is imitative, culturally derivative, and politically oppressive" (p. 15). This last line of thinking, intentionally or not, lends support to those who hold that the richer countries are under no obligation to provide economic assistance to poorer ones.

The effects of globalization are, of course, different within different environmental and social contexts, but it is possible to identify a number of variables that will affect the way a community responds. Access to land, the agricultural potential of the land, and ease of access to markets are crucial in determining how well or otherwise a community can respond to pressures from the national economy. In addition, rates of population growth and the potential for intensification (dependent not only on the factors just mentioned but also on available technology and local knowledge and skills), linked to the availability of off-farm employment, are determining variables (Loker, 1999, p. 34).

## Emergence of the Information Revolution

Satellite communications, global television networks, fax machines, the Internet, and electronic mail have contributed to an information revolution. The 2003 launch of the war in Iraq was covered by thousands of journalists from all over the world. For several weeks, the world's television sets and radios were tuned to the events unfolding in this Gulf state. Reporters covered the war from every vantage point, calling in their stories on mobile phones and supplying real-time video clips of the action. It was truly a global media event. Or was it really global? Quite interestingly, all the interconnectedness contributed to many diverse interpretations of the same events, and in some respects, the news consumer was seemingly offered wider coverage than in any war in his-

tory. What we see is a paradox in that, while global culture comes to share more and more elements, individuals with access to media technology have more options than ever before in what information they communicate and the ways in which they do so.

For better or for worse, the twenty-first century is participating in a globally shaped media culture. The good aspects of this are obvious: Free communications are critical to maintaining shaky movements toward democracy and economic recovery in many countries. The negative aspects are visible not just in the extreme cases of mass distribution of pornography and myriad fraudulent investment schemes, but in a diminishment of regional cultural heterogeneity. Just as world material culture is becoming more homogeneous, so is expressive culture—the arts, dress, and even social conventions. But at the same time, individuals might have more sources of quite divergent opinions.

Closely linked to new developments in computer, information, and biological technology is what some have termed **cyberculture** (Escobar, 1994). The term comes from "cybernetics," or systems theory, and refers to the emerging importance of computer-mediated communication, including the Internet, linking a vast variety of electronic bulletin boards, conference systems, and data bases, which in turn bring together millions of users. This is fundamentally different from telephone or television communication: Entire groups of individuals can interact with one another in "on-line communities" or "virtual communities." Groups are formed to play team games; business executives on different continents plot strategy. What makes this a form of culture is that a learned, shared code of behavior with a specialized language has emerged that does not conform to existing national and cultural frontiers.

## The Global Informational Society

Manuel Castells, who was referred to earlier, characterizes the global economy as part of the "informational society" that arose in the 1980s from the restructuring of global flows of capital in conjunction with the development of computer-driven "informationalism" (1996a; 1996b, pp. 145ff). This restructuring of capital flows, critical to economic growth, was a result of massive investment in the communications/information infrastructures. This facilitated the twin developments of market deregulation and the globalization of capital (1996b, p. 85). The social consequences are, he argues, "informational," not just "information based"—as were earlier productive systems. The chemical industry, for example, has always been information- or science-based; the new socioeconomic world order is "informational" not just because particular industries are dependent on flows of information but because the "cultural-institutional attributes of the whole social system must be included in the diffusion of and implementation of the new technological paradigm" (1996b, p. 91). In short, individuals are now immersed in a new socioeconomic culture that comprises a continually expanding variety of ways to acquire and communicate information.

According to Castells, the structure of this emergent economy is characterized by the asymmetrically interdependent organization of the world's regions. At the moment, there are three major economic regions in which there are specific pivotal nodes (that is, cities or localities, such as Silicon Valley in California or New York City). These dominant regions are Western Europe, North America, and the Asian Pacific (1996b, p. 145). By asymmetrical, Castells means that each of these regions is integrated into networks that determine how their hinterlands are incorporated into the world economic order (1996b, p. 145). An example (not his, however) is the ancient city of Istanbul, located on the eastern edge of Europe but closely integrated economically with Western Europe. The city is today experiencing an economic renaissance as an informational center, with over 360 multinational corporations having established major offices there since 1992. Following the collapse of the Soviet Union in 1991, the huge markets of Central Asia and the Caucasus have opened up, and these multinationals find the informational infrastructure of Istanbul far superior to the faltering communications systems of Russia. Using advanced technology, these corporations affect the flow of goods and services, as well as the output of far-flung factories for a large hinterland and Istanbul's traditional hinterland in Eastern Europe and the Middle East.

This informational economy is not static, however. Currently, Asian Pacific nodes in the network are facing competition from new sites in India. What is important in considering future development is not that any particular country has a lock on the technology—none do—but that within each of these regions there are large numbers of people who are marginalized because they lack access to the technology. Moreover, outside these regions, considerable areas of the globe are becoming marginalized to an even greater extent than during the era of colonialism; they simply lack the resources that would allow them to invest in the educational and informational infrastructure needed to compete in the global marketplace.

# The Ecological Consequences of Postindustrialism

Not only is cultural diversity yielding to a global culture, but diverse habitats are also being brought into a measure of global conformity. Amazonian and Malaysian forests are converted to pastures or farms; African bush and Chinese forests are cleared for farming; farmlands in China, North America, Egypt, and elsewhere are paved over to accommodate urban expansion and industry. There are few stands of native European forest left; farmlands, highways, and planted or managed forests have replaced them. Tropical rain forests, containing about one half of the earth's species, have declined to about one half of their prehistoric area and continue to be cleared at the rate of 2% a year—an amount of land equal to the size of Florida. Thus, as technology spreads over the globe, humans increase their energy consumption with too little attention paid to the inevitable result: resource depletion.

## Energy Consumption and Resource Depletion

Since World War II, per capita energy consumption throughout the world has risen at an ever-increasing rate. However, while technology requires higher energy consumption, it also helps to make energy sources such as low-cost fossil fuel, nuclear energy, and solar energy widely available. A recurring political issue is the need for cheaper and more readily accessible energy sources. The 1990 Gulf War was fought to retain European and North American access to oil; energy prices in the United States are lower than almost anywhere else in the world. There are those who would argue that oil security underlay the decision to invade Iraq in 2003. On every continent, we see the material effects of abundant energy harnessed to advanced technology: Millions of people routinely commute long distances to work and move from country to country, homes are filled with appliances, items from around the world are available in neighborhood stores from Albania to Zambia. In the case of Albania, for example, since the collapse of communism in 1991, it is difficult to find anything but foreign products in shops; in most of Africa, this has long been the norm.

The availability of cheap energy and high rates of consumption stimulated the mass use of numerous items that only a few years ago would have been considered luxuries, if they were imagined at all. Forty years ago, few homes or workplaces in the United States were air-conditioned; today, most are.

## Box 8.2

## Imaging Resource Depletion

ANTHROPOLOGISTS AND HUMAN ecologists are increasingly using space-age technologies to extend their analyses of local ecologies to a regional scale. Satellites routinely collect basic data from a wide range of geographic areas. These data consist primarily of electronic records, in the form of analytical units called pixels, of the intensities of electromagnetic radiation reflected or emitted from the earth's surface. These data, over time, reflect changes in the average amount of radiation recorded and thus can be used to identify and monitor changes in land use patterns, loss of tropical forest cover, and even ecological stress on coral reefs. The technologies involved are primarily remote sensing (RS), geographic information systems (GIS), global positioning systems (GPS), and developments in computer hardware and software associated with these systems.

While these new technologies allow for a regional view of land use not easily obtainable from ethnographic or archaeological research on the ground, many of the patterns revealed by the analysis of these data are creations of human decision making and historical events. Satellites cannot interpret what is observed nor explain changes. Consequently, all researchers emphasize the importance of understanding land use from the perspective of the people who manage the land; this is known as "people truthing." In addition, sound ethnographic information on demographic trends and land-use practices is a safeguard against erroneous or exaggerated claims made on the basis of remotely sensed data; this is known as "ground truthing." (See Turner & Taylor, 2003, pp. 177–182).

Stoffle et al. (1994) conducted a study of the coastal waters and coral reefs on the north coast of the Dominican Republic, in the area around Buen Hombre. This is a community of approximately 900 residents, living much as did the indigenous people at the time Columbus first sighted the coast in the late fifteenth century. Stoffle et al. argue that were the pressures on this coastal marine ecosystem derived only from the people of Buen Hombre and similar villages along the coast, the human population could exist in sustainable balance with the ecosystem. However, this is not the case, and the future of the ecosystem is in doubt. Fishermen report lower fish catches and smaller fish sizes over the past generation. A dive shop operator from a nearby international resort hotel reports having to take tourists to new reefs because the ones close to the hotel have died during the past five years. Fishermen from distant towns are beginning to fish in the area's coastal waters with illegal large nets, and the local fishermen say that the manatee have disappeared from the areas where these nets are used. And similar coral reefs to both the west and east have been characterized as "dead."

Stoffle et al., an interdisciplinary team of cultural anthropologists, remote sensing scientists, and a marine ecologist, used satellite imagery to identify changes in small areas of the coastal marine ecosystem of Buen Hombre, including the coral reef. Even though their study showed that the coastal waters and coral reefs on the north coast are still in good condition, they did find ecologically significant changes associated with changes from dark to light, indicating losses of highly productive coral, seagrass, and mangrove. By comparing the satellite imagery with marine and ethnographic data, they found these changes were closely related to fishing, tourism, and land-use practices. They concluded that if global warming is affecting this ecosystem, its effects are still masked by the effects of these more predominant stresses. They further concluded that there are differences in the types of impacts on the ecosystem being made by the local people, who have a sense of ownership and an intergenerational commitment to its resources, and those being made by outsiders, such as urban fishermen and tourists. "Given the opportunity, local inhabitants seek to preserve the long-term productivity of the coastal environment, even at the expense of current harvest" (1994, p. 375).

While the satellite data provided a comprehensive technique for studying changes in this coastal marine ecosystem, Stoffle et al. were also able to use them to transfer information about these changes to policymakers at the village, regional, and national levels. Satellite images of the north coast reef system were shown to villagers and national government officials at two meetings in Buen Hombre, and the local fishermen were immediately able to identify familiar locations and point to named fishing spots. The images, supplemented with ethnographic and marine ecological data, were instrumental in persuading government officials that measures were needed to protect the coral reef and secure the rights and interests of the local community.

This is not an isolated case. Bernard Neitschmann (1995), a cultural geographer, has assisted the Miskito people of Nicaragua to map and inventory the extensive Miskito Reefs in the Caribbean in order to protect their traditional fishing grounds. A well-designed map can convey a great deal of information and can be sent to international organizations to document claims.

The studies cited here stress the interdisciplinary nature of research utilizing satellite data and the importance of "on the ground" research in the analysis and interpretation of the images.

Even the poorest individual in almost any country has access to vehicular transportation, uses facilities that run on electricity, and consumes imported goods. In short, the material culture of the world is rapidly becoming homogeneous.

The energy that pulses through human society affects where and how people live, the material goods available to them, and their relations with their physical environment. Cheap energy allows huge cities to emerge because they are sustained by foods grown in distant fields and by water from distant reservoirs. Because energy is cheap, people are consuming the world's resources at a phenomenal rate.

Although development planners, economists, and politicians usually see the supply of energy as a factor limiting growth and development, and hence favor huge hydroelectric and other projects, this is short-sighted. What is more important is **sustainable energy,** energy recovery that does not damage the environment, and manageable energy. Energy experts predict that Central Africa will run out of wood—a major energy source for cooking among the very poor—before it runs out of food, although the two are closely related. Fossil fuels are a nonrenewable resource and, although inexpensive relative to long-term abundance, are being depleted. Louisiana is losing vast amounts of wetlands each year, to the point that much of the state is sinking about one foot per annum. While partially due to natural shifts in the Mississippi River's course, this disaster is largely the result of industrial land-use practices that affect ground water levels. Hydroelectric projects that flood vast areas of cropland, or potential cropland,

as in China and Amazonia, are also counterproductive since, as discussed in Chapter 7, maintaining extant farms is extremely important. Finally, energy management—control over its downstream impact—is as important as simply securing it.

## Pollution and Toxic Waste

Quite apart from how people will cope with the depletion of their resources, there is the even more urgent problem of how to dispose of the toxic by-products of what has already been consumed. Unfortunately, this is not usually viewed as an energy-related issue except with regard to nuclear energy. The use of any energy source has consequences, whether they are higher population levels, consumption of nonrenewable resources, habitat destruction, or environmental impacts such as global warming, water shortages, deforestation, or waste disposal. All industrialized countries are faced with the unanswered question of what to do with nuclear and other radioactive wastes. With the breakup of the Soviet Union and the economic chaos in its successor states, there is great uncertainty as to the security and safety of vast quantities of spent nuclear material. The nuclear energy program of every country was developed for political reasons far in advance of any solution to the problem of disposing of highly toxic by-products. However serious, nuclear waste is probably less critical than chemical waste in general, generated by massive deployment of cheap energy sources to build the infrastructure of the postindustrial world. There is still no easy and safe

*The world's first commercial oil fields were established in Azerbaijan in the nineteenth century. In the 1970s, they were largely abandoned, but wells were never properly capped nor cleaned up. The once pristine Caspian Sea is now badly polluted.*

(Karen St. John)

way to dispose of highly toxic chemicals, such as PCBs and dioxin, which are necessary ingredients in constructing our telecommunications systems, plastics industries, and so on.

Less apparent but still very important to our future, the world's oceans are under siege. As a result of global warming, the temperature of the Pacific Ocean off the coast of California and Mexico has increased by 1°F over the mean recorded temperature since records were first kept. As a consequence, plankton, temperature-sensitive microorganisms, have declined approximately 40%. Since plankton are fundamental to the marine food chain, this is likely to be reflected very soon in declining fish catches in this once-rich fishing region.

In the Pacific and Atlantic, vast amounts of human waste, toxic and nontoxic, threaten marine life as never before. The same crisis threatens the Caribbean and Mediterranean: The fishing industries of these areas are experiencing severely declining catches. In 1987, the American National Academy of Sciences reported that each year the world's fishing fleets dump 350 million pounds of plastic debris in the world's oceans. It is thought that over 30% of the world's fish have ingested bits of plastic that can interfere with their digestion. Since 1995, much of the American North Atlantic fishing fleet has stayed in port. On the open seas, nations compete for a dwindling supply of wild fish, and politicians and fishermen alike routinely ignore scientific warnings and advice (*The Economist*, 2003, Aug. 9, p. 21).

The problem of pollution and waste disposal is not, of course, restricted to the oceans. Over half of the solid landfill areas available to American cities in 1980 are now full. Each year, the United States produces more than 20 million tons of plastics, most of which require more than 500 years to degrade fully. Every country has petrochemical plants churning out polyethylene and other plastics. Megacities in the Third World face enormous problems; Mexico City generates 10,000 tons of waste a day, most of which is left in giant piles exposed to wind and rain. Manila has at least ten huge open dumps (Cunningham & Saigo, 1995, p. 501). Thousands of people live and work on a dump called "Smokey Mountain" because of its constant smoldering fires; they make a living sorting out edible and reusable items. Archaeologists of the future may find this global accumulation a treasure trove, but meanwhile, the time is rapidly approaching when our wastes will overwhelm us. This is particularly imminent in ghettos around the world, where overcrowding and poverty exacerbate the problems of pollution and waste, seriously threatening the environmental rights of the individuals living there.

In December 1997, representatives from 150 countries met in Kyoto, Japan, to discuss and negotiate efforts to curb global warming. Global warming is an increase in the earth's atmospheric temperature and is occurring at an alarming rate. While the earth periodically goes through warming and cooling cycles, as with the global warming accompanying the end of the last ice age 12,000 years ago, the evidence is mounting that current global warming is caused mainly by human activities. Huge amounts of carbon dioxide have been emitted into the atmosphere by the burning of coal, oil, and natural gas in power plants and factories and gasoline in automobiles, leading to "greenhouse effect" where the heat from the sun is trapped in the atmosphere. Increased population growth has also led to increased burning of firewood for fuel, while increased cattle production has led to increases in methane gas, a greenhouse gas, emitted during digestion. A rise in global temperature, even 1°C, can lead to tremendous damage such as the melting of polar ice sheets, which would lead to a rise in sea levels that could flood coastal cities, including New York and Hong Kong. Global warming will also raise health risks from heat waves and increased pollutants. In 2003, an unparalleled heat wave in Western Europe killed an estimated 13,000 people in France alone, most of them elderly and infirm. Extreme weather fluctuations seem to have become the norm. While it is not clear to what extent the enormous El Niño event of 1997 is linked to human-induced climate change, it caused massive rainstorms in California and dessication in Indonesia. Also in 1997, a combination of drought and human mismanagement led to extensive forest fires in Borneo, producing smoke and pollution that could be felt hundreds of miles away in Malaysia and Singapore.

The Kyoto Conference followed the earlier Rio de Janeiro Conference of 1992, where the United States called for voluntary cuts to reduce emissions of greenhouse gases to 1990 levels by the year 2000. When it became apparent that the United States could not meet these voluntary targets, President Clinton agreed to participate in the creation of a treaty that would obligate cuts in greenhouse gases by all signatory countries. However, when delegates met in Kyoto, it was apparent that there was little agreement among and even within countries as to how much to limit production. Corporations in the United States, including gasoline giants such as Mobil Oil, argued that the treaty would be useless if major industrializing countries such as China and India refused to sign it. Countries in the developing world argued that the West had already industrialized, and now that it was their turn, they should not be penalized or inhibited by environmental restrictions. In the end, a compromise was reached, which included lesser and longer delayed cuts by all signatory countries, and the selling of "pollution coupons" from less developed to more developed countries. In 2001, President George W. Bush declared that the United States was withdrawing from the Kyoto Protocol.

## Toxic Accidents

We accept the fact that modern life demands that we continually submit to new risks; any day a major industrial accident might occur. We rely on technology that we do not understand, and we have little say in its deployment and regulation. Chronic technological disasters, as Eric Wolf has argued, are revealing events because "the arrangements of society become most visible when they are challenged by crisis" (1990).

Within one month in 1989, there were four oil spills causing significant environmental damage: the Exxon *Valdez,* in Alaska; off Rhode Island; in the Delaware River; and in the Houston shipping canal. The *Valdez* spill alone dumped over 11 million gallons of crude oil into a fragile marine environment. In 1993, there was a similar very costly oil spill in the Shetland Islands, UK, which has still to be fully assessed in terms of damage. This spill, like many others, created great uncertainty among the affected populations because of misleading and confused reports offered by the government agencies concerned (Button, 1995). Early in 2000, there were two very serious oil spills, again within a one month of each

other. A Russian tanker ran aground near Istanbul spilling its cargo of oil, and a Maltese-registered tanker broke up in a storm off the French Atlantic coast. Both caused massive environmental damage that will take considerable time and great expense to rectify even partially. But even more dangerous, as the long-term costs cannot yet be measured, is the January 30, 2000, spilling of 100,000 tons of cyanide-laced waters into the Tisza and Danube Rivers. The highly poisonous waters were residue from gold-mining operations carried out by an Australian corporation in Romania; the immediate impact was to render long stretches of both rivers entirely lifeless, with marine and terrestrial food chains adversely affected for many miles in four countries: Romania, Hungary, Yugoslavia, and Bulgaria.

Quite apart from toxic accidents, the unintended consequences of modern farming using massive environmental engineering can result in ecological devastation. It has long been known that irrigation, for example, carries with it the risk of soil salinization. Huge areas of Pakistan and Iraq, to name only two regions, have been lost to farming in earlier periods because of salinization. Poor drainage can easily result in salts naturally found in all soil being concentrated in surface layers. California is now experiencing this in places on a large scale, as discussed in Chapter 7.

What distinguishes such disasters from other environmental calamities such as the spread of the desert in the African Sahel or the burning of the

*Massive oil damage to a long stretch of France's coastline resulted from the sinking of this Maltese-registered tanker; within the week, a Russian oil tanker sank near Istanbul also causing serious environmental damage.*

(AP/Wide World Photos)

### Table 8.1  Major Oil Spills

| Name of Tanker & Place of Spillage | Tonnes '000 spilt | Year |
|---|---|---|
| Atlantic Empress, Tobago | 287 | 1979 |
| ABT Summer, Angola | 260 | 1991 |
| Castillo de Bellver, South Africa | 252 | 1983 |
| Amoco Cadiz, France | 223 | 1978 |
| Haven, Italy | 144 | 1991 |
| Odyssey, Canada | 132 | 1988 |
| Torrey Canyon, Britain | 119 | 1967 |
| Urquiola, Spain | 100 | 1976 |
| Hawaiian Patriot, Northern Pacific | 95 | 1977 |
| Independenta, Turkey | 95 | 1979 |
| Jacob Maersk, Portugal | 88 | 1975 |
| Braer, Britain | 85 | 1993 |
| Khark 5, Morocco | 80 | 1989 |
| Prestige, Spain | 77* | 2002 |
| Aegean Sea, Spain | 74 | 1992 |
| Sea Empress, Britain | 72 | 1996 |
| Exxon Valdez, United States | 37 | 1989 |
| Erika, France | 20 | 1999 |

*Load. Spillage not yet established.

Source: After The Economist (2002) from International Tanker Owners Pollution Federation.

Amazon, writes Lee Clarke, is that *organizations* have played primary roles both in causing the problems and in seeking solutions (1989, p. 2). These are tragedies over which the victims have no control and for protection must necessarily rely on organizations: state and federal governmental agencies, international agencies, and myriad private and public ones. These are a form of disaster for which our previous adaptations have not prepared us.

## Can We Survive Progress?

Chapter 2 discussed "resilience," or the amount of change or impact that an ecological system might be able to sustain before becoming unrecognizably altered. Biodiversity is thought to be the key to resilience. The exponential growth of human population and technology continually erodes the resilience of our biosphere. One source of this threat is through mass extinctions of species in every part of the world. As one noted naturalist and evolutionary biologist, E. O. Wilson, writes:

> With people everywhere seeking a better quality of life, the search for resources is expanding even faster than the population. The demand is being met by an increase in scientific knowledge, which doubles every 10 to 15 years. It is accelerated further by a parallel rise in environment-devouring technology. Because Earth is finite in many resources that determine the quality of life—including arable soil, nutrients, fresh water and space for natural ecosystems—doubling of consumption at constant time intervals can bring disaster with shocking suddenness. Even when a nonrenewable resource is only half used, it is still only one interval away from the end. (1993, pp. 26–27; see also 1998)

What is to be done? There is no easy solution; as Wilson notes, while scientists may have the ability and political will to control the nonliving components of the biosphere (the ozone layer and carbon cycles), they have no ability to micromanage natural ecosystems, which are simply too complex. The only real solutions are population limits and habitat preservation—both very difficult to achieve for political reasons.

Postindustrialism is a recent development, and it remains to be seen how humans will adapt to its consequences. As history has shown, an increase in energy sources creates as many problems as it solves. The impending advent of superconductors—materials that can transmit electricity with no loss to resistance—will make available even more usable energy. If we merely use this energy to support more people and to speed up consumption, the results are quite likely to be disastrous for the environment.

The problem is that change is coming so rapidly that it may outrun our ability to respond appropriately, especially with regard to natural resources. We must keep in mind that individual behavior is basic to adaptation; people generally alter their behavior to serve their self-interest as they see it. What is in the interest of elites and corporations may not be appropriate for long-range conservation of the world's resources and habitats. In earlier eras of human adaptation, people were severely constrained by their technology and by their limited access to sources of energy. By and large, people had to deal directly with the environmental consequences of their activities. Farmers who allowed their fields to erode might face hunger. Now, many decisions that affect the environment are made by people far removed from the consequences. The manager of the factory whose sulfuric wastes contaminate a water supply distant from the head office may receive a bonus for efficiency. Perhaps we shall have to devise ways to reward those who, in the words of the ecologist René Dubos, "act locally but think globally."

## Globalism and Global Terror

Without worrying about causality or even intent, one can still safely say that many breakthroughs in technology and social organization have their costs in terms of extending human capabilities for violent behavior. Alexander the Great could not have conquered Asia Minor, Persia, Egypt, and gone on to India without metallurgy, domesticated mounts, fast naval vessels, and methods of communicating over vast distances. His formidable logistical organization supported what was then the world's largest army far from its home bases. Two wars in the twentieth century were truly global conflagrations and could not have been waged on such a scale with the technology of even the late nineteenth century. The September 11, 2001, attacks on the World Trade Center in New York City and on the Pentagon in Washington, D.C., are a stark illustration of how the world has been transformed by the emergence of worldwide systems of communication and movements of population.

What has emerged, of course, is not entirely novel or even surprising, although at the time it may seem so. While politicians and media use the language of warfare, it is likely that social scientists and historians of warfare will quickly come to distinguish this occurrence from warfare as practiced by nation-states—and even tribes—in the past. As mentioned earlier, the 9/11 attack represents a new form of collective violence. Some are using the term "asymmetric warfare" to describe a phenomenon in which a small, relatively unstructured network of like-minded individuals collaborate to inflict huge damage on a perceived foe. Michael Klare of Hampshire College's Peace and World Studies program argues that terrorism is the weapon of the weak, while war is the weapon of the strong (Klare, 2001). As Scott Atran, a terrorism expert with long experience in the Middle East puts it: "Contemporary suicide terrorists from the Middle East are publicly deemed crazed cowards bent on senseless destruction who thrive in poverty and ignorance. Recent research indicates they have no appreciable psychopathology and are as educated and economically well-off as surrounding populations. A first line of defense is to get the communities from which suicide attackers stem to stop the attacks by learning how to minimize the receptivity of mostly ordinary people to recruiting organizations" (Atran, 2003, p. 1534).

Asymmetric warfare is not unprecedented in history. At various points in maritime history, piracy flourished, with groupings of culturally diverse individuals forming quite large, if ephemeral, coalitions that attacked coastal cities and shipping lanes—a problem that persists today, notably in the Caribbean and Moluccas Straits in the South China Sea. We base this analogy on the following similarities, keeping in mind differences as well: Cooperating terrorists often have different cultural, ethnic, religious, and national backgrounds; they may speak different languages; they do not have a defined territorial base; they need not have a secure financial base but may finance themselves as they go along. Further, because they are united for limited objectives, they may bring together individuals with vastly differing motivations. What occurred is, in retrospect, the inevitable conjoining of groupings similar to pirates, the Mafia, or drug cartels, with the global organizational potential of the World Wide Web. Unlike other criminal networks, these new terrorists avoided the e-mail capabilities of the Internet but relied on postings in chat rooms or virtual bulletin boards. It seems that the ideological gloss that best describes or rationalizes the actions of the September 2001 terrorists is Islamic extremism. Religious rhetoric and beliefs around the world have long been potent in mobilizing people to action—and certainly have not been restricted to any one faith. In fact, in this case, it would appear that the terrorists varied greatly in their knowledge of, training in, and actual practice of religion. One very interesting organization deemed "terrorists" by the U.S. Department of State is the People's Mujahedeen, sometimes called the Cult of Rajavi (Rubin, 2003). This group is largely comprised of women who use terror tactics against the Islamic government of Iran. They take vows of celibacy, deify their husband–wife team of leaders, the Rajavis, and practice self-immolation to further their cause. They were largely disarmed by 2004.

Global terrorism, while here sharing an Islamic rhetoric, knows no denomination in practice. Just weeks before the events of September, three members of the IRA were discovered training South American leftist guerilla forces, who themselves were heavily involved in the drug trade, in bomb making techniques. Looking at the Middle East, it is obvious that the motivations of those now venting anti-Western enmity go beyond simple religious belief: They may live under regimes that they perceive to be despotic that are supported by the United States, in countries ruled colonially by France or Britain, in areas now under Israeli occupation, or in countries whose oil wealth is being squandered by a small elite.

*The Iranian Mujahideen—labeled a terrorist organization by the US State Department—are unusual in the high percentage of female fighters. Here female soldiers with the Mujahideen Khalq Organization work on their armored vehicles at the MKO main base outside Baghdad shortly after the end of the 2003 Iraq war. After May 2003 the group was disbanded and largely dispersed.*

(© Lynsey Addario/CORBIS SABA)

Paradoxically, many of those shouting the strongest slogans are often themselves captivated by Western popular culture—be it fast food, entertainment, or dress. Much of this dissatisfaction can be summed up in the word "alienation"—not necessarily poverty-driven but in a sense of seeing values and ideals trampled by global forces, the most prominent symbols of which are in the United States. Thus, the participants need not be simply the disadvantaged but may include many with middle-class backgrounds and secular education—as has been witnessed in Egypt over the past several decades. As John Esposito, a leading scholar of political Islam, put it, "You see a minority of Moslems who wind up believing—and therefore being driven by—a perception that they have no way of responding within the system. You are talking about a small but very deadly minority" (quoted in Jehl, *New York Times,* September 22, 2001, p. B4). The Internet and ancillary communications technologies support networking of all sorts, criminal as well as benign. Perhaps one implication of "asymmetric warfare" is that we have globalism without global accountability.

## Development in Ecological Perspective

About forty years ago, a U.S. congressional mandate tied all foreign aid to a commitment to study its impacts on equity and the poor. Even though the dis-

cipline of anthropology had from its beginnings been concerned with the theoretical issues of cultural and economic change, from the 1970s onward it became engaged in the practical problems of alleviating poverty, environmental degradation, disease, malnutrition, gender inequity, and ethnic conflict.

Following Michael Horowitz (1994), who is himself a leading practitioner, some of the main contributions **development anthropologists** have made include:

1. Providing a critical understanding of the nature of development. This has included showing that indigenous expertise cannot be ignored, that forced resettlement of populations is costly and rarely results in improving standards of living, that "top-down" planning usually only benefits those at the top, and that local communities are rarely homogeneous and should be carefully studied to determine who really benefits and who does not.

2. Showing the importance of long-term research. Typical development projects bring experts through for extremely brief periods of time; "rapid rural appraisal" say some, "rural development tourism" say others. Anthropologists at the World Bank and elsewhere have successfully argued for long-term social research in a number of regions. This has led to important recommendations, as with a project in the Middle Senegal River Valley where the anthropologists demonstrated the need to augment the flood of a

## Box 8.3

# International Development and the Chiquitanos of Bolivia[1]

OVER THE PAST THREE DECADES, an increasing number of indigenous communities around the world have begun to organize themselves politically and have become active in influencing the direction of their own development as they interact more and more with the wider national and international communities. At the same time, there has been a significant increase in the number of nongovernmental organizations with unprecedented financial resources and political influence that are concerning themselves with the struggles of indigenous peoples. Josh McDaniel (2002) has examined the impact of nongovernmental organizations' policies and practices on the political organization of the Chiquitanos of the lowland region of southeastern Bolivia.

The Chiquitanos, descendants of indigenous people who lived in

Jesuit missions during the seventeenth and eighteenth centuries, make their living primarily from farming, raising cattle, and hunting and gathering in the forest. In 1982, a group of twenty-eight Chiquitano communities in Lomerio, a district in the center of the region, founded the Central Intercommunal Campesina del Oriente Lomerio (CICOL), one of a number of indigenous organizations then spreading across lowland Bolivia and indeed across many countries in Central and South America. The authority of the organization was bolstered at the beginning by a series of victories against the logging companies then encroaching into Chiquitano lands. However, over the years, CICOL (which changed its name to Central Indigena de los Communidades Originarios de Lomerio in 1998 to emphasize the traditionally perjorative "Indigena" over the nonethnic "Campesina") expanded its focus to include economic development and political participation as well as defense of territorial integrity. The organization, repre-

senting about 1,200 families, or 5,500 residents, has nine directors, most of whom are men, although three women have served as directors. The directors' duties require that they are literate, and most have graduated from high school, while a few have received some further professional training.

The ruling body of the organization is the general assembly, which meets once a year and when important decisions have to be made. The delegates to the assembly, five from each of the twenty-eight communities, set the goals and activities of CICOL as well as electing the directors, who are chosen for their ability to work with and communicate Chiquitano ideas and ideals to outside agencies, in addition to their skills in attracting projects that promote economic development in the region. Decision making in CICOL is generally open and participatory, and discussions usually continue until an agreed level of consensus is reached. The annual meeting, which lasts up to three days, is viewed as much as an expression of unity as it

[1]This box is based on Josh McDaniel (2002), Confronting the structure of international development: Political agency and the Chiquitanos of Bolivia, *Human Ecology*, 30(3), pp. 369–396.

---

hydropower dam for the benefit of downstream ecosystems and smallholder productivity.

3. Increased sensitivity to environmental issues and the need for an alliance between anthropologists, social scientists, and biophysical ecologists. Environmental sustainability requires a social component because both poverty and resource abuse are caused or exacerbated by similar policies seeking short-term returns on investments.

*Environmental and Ecological Factors in Development.* A development project may have a profound effect on the ecological system, as has just been noted. Large dams, for example, almost always have a legacy of large-scale environmental damage such

as destruction of habitat, downstream pollution, increased salinity of the soil as a result of a rise in the water table, increased risk of flooding and erosion, and even, many people argue, an increase in the risk of earthquakes. But innovations need not be so massive as a huge irrigation project or a giant dam to have significant effects on ecological systems. The introduction of shotguns, for example, has dramatically reduced the numbers of many game species used by the Yanomamö, not to mention the human toll (Chagnon, 1993). A new strain of rice introduced in Nepal increased yields as much as 200%, but because the rice grew on short, tough stalks that produced little fodder for cattle and required threshing machinery that was not available locally, the innovation was not without serious costs. More

is a mechanism for setting the next year's agenda.

Research is a highly politicized and contested activity in Lomerio, and an area where CICOL found political leverage in relations with outside organizations, so when Josh McDaniel undertook his fieldwork there (1997–1998), he was concerned that the fact he was funded by one such organization (the Bolivian Sustainable Forestry Project) would limit his ability to work with certain groups. However, when he went to the CICOL office with his project—an ethnographic study of the forest management project and the interactions between CICOL and the associated development organizations—they readily agreed on the condition that he worked as an assistant in their office, since they needed someone to organize their archives and train the directors to use the recently donated computers. "I gladly took the 'position' . . . and soon found myself in the middle of the daily workings of CICOL" (p. 375).

The Lomerio Project is the umbrella term for a range of forest management development projects launched under the auspices of the Apoyo para Campesina Indigena del Oriente Bolivia (APCOB), an or-ganization formed to work for the defense of indigenous rights of the communities of eastern Bolivia. APCOB was instrumental in convincing the people of Lomerio to start up forest management and sawmill operations and found funding through a constantly changing pool of donor agencies. Although APCOB works closely with CICOL on the Lomerio Project, there are conflicts over authority and decision making. APCOB controls the majority of the funds, which, as a consequence of current international interest in sustainable development, are earmarked for the logging and sawmill operations at the expense of the community-focussed aspects of the project favored by CICOL. Chiquitano leaders argue that the development organizations involved in the project are more concerned with catering to the agendas of their international donors than with the actual situation in Lomerio. As a consequence, negotiations between CICOL and APCOB and the other agencies have become characterized by "threats, counter-threats, and bluffs" (p. 390). APCOB controls the funding, the equipment, and the technical know-how; CICOL controls only the labor supply and access to Lomerio. So at times of conflict, CICOL plays the "access card" and APCOB plays the "cutting off funding card" (p. 390). While both groups are aware of the inherent limitations of the project as currently formulated, both are constrained by the requirements of donors and their funding cycles.

One of the founding directors of CICOL told McDaniel that, even in the early days of the organization, he had been concerned about the nature of its relationships with outside development organizations and donors. "They wanted the money, technical support, and political leverage that came with the alliances, but they did not want to create a dependency that would threaten their autonomy. They feel that those initial fears are proving to be well-grounded" (p. 393). Nevertheless, they are learning to maneuver within the wider economic, social, and political systems and are making headway in forcing governmental and nongovernmental organizations to take account of their legitimate local interests. McDaniel urges continued work to develop new approaches in mediating relations between indigenous groups and the national and international organizations concerned for their future.

intensive cultivation has led to the loss of topsoil from erosion, and an increased dependence on firewood instead of straw for fuel has resulted in deforestation and increased risk of downstream flooding. Everywhere, we see the effects of fertilizers, pesticides, and herbicides in contaminated water sources. Environmental costs must figure in any evaluation of the effectiveness of a proposed innovation.

The researcher concerned with development must always consider the strengths as well as the weaknesses of the local system of knowledge or practice. In Bali, Indonesia, according to J. Stephen Lansing (1991), an elaborate network of temples dedicated to water goddesses is controlled by priests who regulate and coordinate the irrigation of fields belonging to thousands of farmers. In the 1970s, in an effort to modernize farming, the government encouraged farmers to irrigate their fields according to whatever schedule they judged would increase their rice production. As a consequence, fields were irrigated according to individual farmer's timetables, and unexpectedly, this provoked an ecological crisis that resulted in a massive decline in overall yields. When farmers planted and irrigated on their own schedules, pests that were formerly controlled by the coordinated flooding dictated by the temples simply moved from field to field. Coordinated irrigation turned out to be a vital means of crop cycling and pest control. In this case, we see a traditional religious institution playing a critical role in resource management. Stephen Lansing, an anthropologist, was instrumental in making government planners

*Villagers in Chimalapas, Mexico, attend an NGO-sponsored workshop on ecological land use and planning.*
(Molly Doane)

aware of the value of this supposedly noneconomic and anachronistic cultural system.

***Social Ties.*** Development may have unintended consequences for social relations as well. If these consequences are negative, they must be included among the costs of planned change. Attempts to introduce improved clothes-washing facilities, for instance, may cause women to lose the opportunity to meet and exchange information with their neighbors at a community washing place. The building of modern high-rise apartment houses to replace slum housing may have negative social consequences by breaking down established social networks, patterns of social control, and even pride of residence. Of course, an innovation may have an even more significant impact on traditional social ties, as when a minority or a traditionally subordinate group is placed in an economically competitive position with the majority population.

***Managing Social Change.*** Any country faces problems when it sets out to manage social change and tries to anticipate the costs. The social scientist can help at the community level, where detailed knowledge can mean the difference between success and failure. Respect for indigenous solutions and ways of doing things can also make a difference. All too often, planners work from the top down, with little interest in or respect for traditional, time-proven methods. Indigenous solutions in the areas of land use and food production are almost always critical to the long-term success of a new strategy. As Della

McMillan (1995) found in her study of a land-use project in the Sahel, the effectiveness of any development plan is dependent on the involvement of the people who are the intended beneficiaries of the project.

Much of the present crisis in food production is attributable to the fact that the growth rates of the populations of many countries in the tropics have outstripped their ability to feed themselves. But most of the techniques that are being imported by such countries are based on farming methods first developed in temperate climates. In the Amazon region, large development projects involving the clearing of forests, introduction of new food crops, and mechanization have had very poor economic results. Most cleared land in the Brazilian Amazon is used for cattle ranching; 85% of recently cleared land is now altogether unproductive because of soil degradation. Tropical soils are generally thin and subject to rapid erosion and breakdown of nutrients once the protective cover of the rain forest is removed. As a consequence, intensification of agriculture or other uses of once-forested land often result in less rather than more food. Many people who have worked in tropical agricultural systems think the way out of this dilemma is to pay more attention to developing more productive farming based on plants and techniques that are already locally established.

George Appell, who has worked on development projects in Indonesia, offers a set of principles that, in somewhat abridged form, aptly summarize the sorts of negative impacts that planned change occasions and that have to be weighed against possible benefits (Appell, 1988, p. 272):

Every act of development necessarily involves an act of destruction.

Any new activity introduced is likely to displace an indigenous activity.

Each act of change has the potential to cause physiological, nutritional, psychological, and/or behavioral impairment among some segment of the subject population.

Modernization can erode indigenous mechanisms for coping with social stress, such as regulating conflict and solving family problems.

One more caution might be added to this list: The costs and benefits of any innovation or planned changed are not going to be distributed equally throughout the population; some people will benefit and some will lose. What must be kept in mind is whether the distribution of costs and benefits is fair or desirable.

The ultimate cost-benefit outcome of any development project or effort to effect some form of desired social change can be influenced by many factors. Some of the most important are environmental and ecological factors, traditional values and beliefs, and social ties.

# Development and Malnutrition in Northern Kenya

In the past twenty-five years, pastoralists in northern Kenya, including the Ariaal and camel-keeping Rendille, have lost large numbers of their animals to periodic drought and livestock raids. As a consequence, many individuals have moved to small towns seeking security and famine-relief food. When Elliot Fratkin first visited the Ariaal in the 1970s, they were living in relative isolation, and towns were few and small. When he returned in the 1980s, over half of the Ariaal and Rendille were living in or near the towns. International relief organizations, including Catholic Relief Services and World Vision, with strong support from the Kenyan government, were actively encouraging the pastoralists to settle down. As in many pastoral regions, international developers felt that town life was a healthier and safer existence than "wandering" and that pastoralism was "primitive, irrational, and wasteful," environmentally harmful and detrimental to the national economy (Fratkin, 1998; Fratkin et al., 1999).

It was not clear to what extent settling down did in fact benefit Ariaal pastoralists, and in 1990, medical doctor Martha Nathan, anthropologist Elliot Fratkin, and anthropological demographer Eric Abella Roth began a long-term study measuring differences in women's and children's health between nomadic and settled Rendille communities (Nathan et al., 1996).

Ariaal and Rendille pastoralists obtain over 70% of their calories and 85% of their protein from the milk (their daily staple), meat, and blood of their animals, supplementing their diet with grains (maize meal) during extensive dry periods. Like most rural African populations, pastoralists suffer from a variety of health risks, including malaria, pneumonia, measles, and accidents, most severely affecting small

*Dr. Marty Nathan examines the vaccination record of a Rendille child for maternal and child health research in northern Kenya.*

(Elliot Fratkin)

children and older people who face the highest risk of mortality. In addition, pastoralists are susceptible to livestock diseases, including anthrax, brucelloisis, and tick borne typhus. While children in towns are also at risk of disease, particularly malaria conveyed by mosquitoes during the short rainy seasons, they have better access to health care at local dispensaries. However, the families in towns did not have direct access to their animals, which were often herded great distances away, and many were dependent on famine-relief foods consisting mainly of maize meal and powdered milk. Nathan, Fratkin, and Roth wanted to determine if town life was indeed a safer and healthier life than nomadic pastoralism, as claimed by the relief organizations.

The three communities selected for their pilot study were the nomadic Lewogoso community (population 250), a mountain town where the Ariaal could keep animals (population 800), and a lowland town built around a Catholic mission where 1,000 Rendille lived, mainly dependent on famine-relief foods. In each community, an equal number of women (35) of childbearing age and their children under six years old were interviewed and measured in June 1990, a year of higher than normal rainfall, and again in July 1992, a severe drought year. Women were asked about their pregnancy and childbearing history and history of previous child mortality. Mothers were also asked how many days in the previous month they and each of their children in the study suffered respiratory, fever, and diarrheal diseases and to name the foods they and their children consumed the previous day. These questions were not difficult for the mothers to answer and provided important information about differences in the three communities.

In addition, immunization histories were recorded (dispensaries give each mother health cards marking immunization type and dates). After the interviews, each woman and child was weighed and measured for height, head circumference, midarm circumference, and triceps skin fold to locate seasonal and longitudinal growth patterns. Finally, blood samples were obtained and hemoglobin counts were recorded with a battery-powered hemoglobinometer to determine relative levels of anemia, a problem particularly high in pregnant and birthing mothers.

The results of this preliminary study were both expected and surprising. Immunization rates for tuberculosis, DPT (diphtheria, pertussis or whooping cough, tetanus), and polio were much higher for children living in town than in the nomadic community—children over twelve months of age often had 100% immunization protection in the towns,

while those in the nomadic community had less than 5% immunization rates. Despite differences in health care, however, there were no statistical differences in childhood diseases among the three communities, although town children had slightly higher respiratory and diarrheal diseases. Most significantly, town women and children had substantially higher rates of anemia than nomadic children, suggesting higher rates of malaria (which destroys red blood cells), intestinal parasites, or poorer sources of iron (which builds red blood cells).

The most important finding was the relative differences in child nutrition measured by weight-for-height measurements in the three communities. If a child's weight for height falls to more than two standard deviations below the World Health Organization (WHO) mean (or 80% of the WHO standard), that child is considered severely malnourished. The Rendille results showed that there was less malnutrition in all three communities in 1990 (the wet year) compared to 1992 (the drought year). But most surprising to the researchers, the nomadic children were three times less malnourished than the town children during the drought year of 1992 (Nathan et al., 1996).

Nathan, Fratkin, and Roth attribute this difference in children's sizes primarily to the nomadic children's access to camel's milk both in drought and normal years, while the town children had very low consumption of milk at all times. Furthermore, towns have higher anemia rates due to greater parasite loads, poorer nutrition, or both. These findings provide a strong argument that traditional nomadic pastoralism remains a more efficient system of supplying adequate childhood nutrition than does town life, despite pronouncements to the contrary by relief agencies. Nathan forwarded her report to the Kenyan Ministry of Health and appropriate development agencies to incorporate these findings in the health plans of the region. The government did incorporate some of the findings, particularly to expand immunizations to the rural nomadic communities.

## The Ethics of Development Work

The data from Kenya, and the Bolivian case discussed in Box 8.3, each exemplify how applied social science can make a difference. Michael Cernea is an anthropologist who, together with some fifty other colleagues from the social sciences, works for the World Bank in Washington, D.C. In his 1996

Malinowski Award Lecture, he argues forcefully for a close relationship between applied and "pure" research: "Social analysis is as necessary for inducing development as economic analysis is" (1996, p. 10). More than 1,800 Bank-assisted projects are underway worldwide, amounting to total investment costs of some $500 billion (p. 10). But as Cernea notes, each project is "a social process, not just a commercial investment, and brings in play an array of *social actors*" (p. 11). Those projects that have a serious social or cultural component in their planning and implementation yield significantly higher rates of return than those that do not. Where the social sciences can have the strongest impact, he argues, is through policy formulation. Anthropologists and other social scientists should involve themselves in designing guidelines for project design and implementation that put people first—not just as lip service, but in practice. Where such guidelines have been put in place by the World Bank, as with projects dealing with the resettlement of refugees or forcibly displaced peoples, the results have been dramatically effective.

Ethical issues are a major concern in anthropological development work, from the time anthropologists make their initial decisions as to where and how they will do fieldwork through their final evaluations of the effects of their projects. Some anthropologists consider it unethical to interfere directly in other people's lives. Arturo Escobar, for example, has argued that development projects increase the incorporation of indigenous peoples into the larger economy, hence marginalizing them, and that anthropological assistance on development projects adds legitimacy to this process (1991). The assumption seems to be that participating in national economies is "bad" and that individuals affected by development projects have numerous options. Neither seem valid points. Further, if anthropologists were not involved, would the same people be less marginalized, less dependent? As Horowitz reports, World Bank projects where anthropologists and other social scientists are involved show a 15% higher rate of return of investment than comparable projects where they are not (1994) because anthropologists not only accumulate factual data, but they also bring together experience from other areas.

## Summary

CHANGE IS CONSTANT IN ALL SOCIETIES, DESPITE A marked human tendency to maintain the status quo. Anthropologists focus on a variety of aspects of social change, but common to all approaches is some measure of costs and benefits, success and failure. The problems facing today's world—food shortages, rapid population growth, depletion of resources, pollution, and the difficulty of adapting to rapid and continuous change—are many and complex.

Over the long term, we see a number of interrelated trends in cultural change or evolution. As societies increase in population size and complexity, their energy budgets must allocate a larger share to maintain infrastructure; to maintain larger populations, food production is intensified; society becomes increasingly differentiated in terms of tasks performed and activities engaged in; production in general becomes more specialized; political and economic power becomes more centralized; settlements become larger and denser; and socially, populations show increased stratification (division into groups that have unequal access to resources and power). At the same time, as with the Vikings in the North Atlantic, complex societies may succumb to political and demographic collapse.

Today, we have moved into yet another era in the organization of production and integration of peoples. This has been termed variously the communications era, the age of the computer, and the high-tech age. The organization of commerce and industry is changing. Historian David Noble (1984) describes this transformation as the triumph of "numerical control" in industry. It has removed control from the factory to the central office; it also has allowed for decentralized production. The long-term significance of these changes will be profound; not only are entire segments of the populations of already-industrialized nations marginalized, but the peoples of many countries that lack an educational infrastructure will not participate fully in the economies of the future.

Much of the present unequal distribution of the benefits of the postindustrial era, together with the attendant environmental degradation as people desperately try to make a living, is not a problem of the relationship of people with their habitats but of relationships among peoples competing for access to productive resources.

Since the middle of the twentieth century, per capita energy consumption throughout the world has risen at an ever-increasing rate. New technology makes low-cost fossil fuel, nuclear energy, and solar energy widely available. The energy that pulses through human society affects where and how people live, the material goods available to them, and their relations with their physical environment. Cheap energy allows huge cities to emerge because they are sustained by foods grown in distant fields and by water from faraway reservoirs. Because energy is cheap, people are consuming the world's resources at a phenomenal rate.

Energy management, or control over its downstream impacts, is as important as simply securing it. Quite apart from how we will cope with the depletion of our resources, there is the even more urgent problem of how we will dispose of the toxic by-products of what we have already consumed. Global communications and the emergence of cyberculture have also transformed culture. Satellite communications, global television networks, fax machines, and cellular telephones have, within the last decade, become part of world culture. People of all countries are participating in a globally shaped media culture. The good aspects of this are obvious: Free communications are critical to maintaining democracy, human rights, and economic exchange. The negative aspects are visible not only in the extreme cases of pornography and the like, but in a diminishing of regional cultural heterogeneity. Just as world material culture is becoming more homogeneous, so is expressive culture—the arts, dress, and even social conventions.

Closely linked to new developments in computer, information, and biological technology is what some have termed an "information revolution." This refers to the emerging importance of computer-mediated communication, including global networks such as the Internet.

Social scientists have become increasingly interested in analyzing the relationship between general trends and innovations on the one hand and development on the other. In the process of assessing the impact of change on society, some of them become personally involved in efforts to bring about change.

Anthropologists have identified themselves as "development anthropologists" for only about thirty years but have made numerous contributions: providing a critical understanding of the nature of development, including showing that indigenous expertise cannot be ignored; showing the importance of long-term research; increased sensitivity to environmental issues; and the need for an alliance between anthropologists, social scientists, and biophysical ecologists.

Some principles regarding development work have emerged. Every act of development necessarily involves an act of destruction. Any new activity introduced is likely to displace an indigenous activity. Each act of change has the potential to cause physiological, nutritional, psychological, and/or behavioral impairment among some segment of the subject population. Modernization can erode indigenous mechanisms for coping with social stress, such as regulating conflict and

solving family problems. And finally, the costs and benefits of any innovation or planned changed are not going to be distributed equally throughout the population; some people will benefit and some will lose. What has to be kept in mind is whether the distribution of costs and benefits is fair or desirable.

Ethical issues are a major concern in development work as well as other areas of anthropology. Many feel that anthropologists should use their expertise to facilitate the planning and modification of development projects so that they will provide the most benefit to the people they are designed to help. Others attribute the marginalization of indigenous groups to development and believe that any participation in development projects legitimizes that process. In the end, though, the breadth and depth of the expertise that anthropologists can provide should equip them to play a significant role in shaping the world in the twenty-first century.

## Key Terms

| | |
|---|---|
| centralization | modernization theory |
| dependency theory | nucleation |
| development anthropology | specialization |
| differentiation | stratification |
| globalization | structural adjustment |
| impact assessment | sustainable energy |
| intensification | |

## Suggested Readings

Bales, K. (1999). *Disposable people: New slavery in the global economy*. Berkeley: University of California Press. Slavery is illegal throughout the world, but millions of people are still entrapped in this institution. The author looks at slavery in factories, brothels, and agriculture, and even at how multinational corporations indirectly contribute to its persistence.

Bodley, J. H. (2003). *Anthropology and contemporary human problems* (4th ed.). Palo Alto, CA: Mayfield. An examination of resource depletion, hunger and starvation, and other problems of our industrialized world. The author reexamines tribal cultures and compares their solutions with those of our society.

Castells, M. (1998). *End of millennium. Vol. 3. The information age: Economy, society and culture*. Oxford: Blackwell. A challenging analysis of the emerging "information age" and the growing dangers of a deeply polarized world, including a spreading global criminal economy.

Cernea, M. M. (1996). *Social organization and development anthropology*. The 1995 Malinowski Award Lecture. (Environmentally Sustainable Development Studies and Monograph Studies Series No. 6). Washington, DC: The World Bank. Explores the close relationship between social anthropological theory and anthropological contributions to development work. Cernea argues that anthropologists and other social scientists have a vital role in creating development policy.

Chambers, E. (1985). *Applied anthropology: A practical guide.* Englewood Cliffs, NJ: Prentice Hall. A synthesis of the field of applied anthropology that reviews the ways in which the profession has adapted to new career opportunities, the ethical concerns associated with applied work, and the training of applied anthropologists.

Cooper, F., & Packard, R. (Eds.) (1998). *International development and the social sciences: Essays on the history and politics of knowledge.* Berkeley: University of California Press. A major review of the policies and impacts of major development agencies as they relate to the social sciences, including Planned Parenthood, USAID, the Ford Foundation, the Rockefeller Foundation, IMF, World Bank, and others

Frank, A. G. (1998). *ReOrient: Global economy in the Asian age.* Berkeley: University of California Press. A major development theorist restates his thesis in the context of the emerging economies of Asia.

Fratkin, E. (1998). *Ariaal pastoralists of northern Kenya: Surviving drought and development in Africa's arid lands.* Boston: Allyn & Bacon. A fine account of how the Ariaal respond to both drought and the well-intentioned but sometimes threatening efforts of those who would assist them.

Johnston, B. R. (Ed.). (1994). *Who pays the price? The sociocultural context of environmental crisis.* Washington, DC: Island Press. This fine collection of articles focuses exclusively on the victims of environmental change. The issues examined include loss of land and contamination of air, water, and soil, to name a few.

McMillan, D. E. (1995). *Sahel visions: Planned settlement and river blindness control in Burkina Faso.* Tucson and London: University of Arizona Press. McMillan's study examines a period of fifteen years in which a development plan was implemented to relieve population pressure, increase food production, improve health conditions, and establish communities in areas afflicted with onchocerciasis (river blindness) in Burkina Faso in West Africa. An insightful study on land settlement and human development concerns.

Miller, M. S., Project Director (with the Cultural Survival staff). (1993). *State of the peoples: A global human rights report on societies in danger.* Boston: Beacon Press. This text provides contemporary and well-researched data on critical issues such as human rights, endangered societies, and resources for action. A valuable contribution that presents innovative solutions.

Nolan, R. (2002). *Development anthropology: Encounters in the real world.* Boulder, CO: Westview Press. A textbook on development anthropology providing an exceptionally useful framework for analyzing development projects. It is written from a practitioner's point of view and contains numerous examples and case studies.

Southwick, C. H. (1996). *Global ecology in human perspective.* New York: Oxford University Press. Written by a well-known ecologist, this book deals with the ecology of planet Earth, focusing on the condition of the global environment and the quality of human life.

Stiglitz, J. E. (2003). *Globalization and its discontents.* New York and London: W. W. Norton. A Nobel Prize winner in economics makes a compelling case that "one size fits all" economic doctrines such as the World Bank's emphasis on "structural adjustment" can do more harm than good.

# Glossary

**acculturation** Cultural change that occurs in response to extended firsthand contacts between two or more previously autonomous groups.

**adaptation** The process by which organisms or populations of organisms make biological or behavioral adjustments that facilitate their survival and reproductive success in their environment.

**administrative system** A twentieth-century system of ownership in which land is owned and managed by the state; found in China, the former Soviet Union, and some parts of Africa and Latin America.

**affinal kin** Persons related by marriage.

**age grade** A category of people (i.e., warrior, elder) of the same sex and approximately the same age who share a set of duties and privileges.

**age set** A named grouping of individuals of approximately the same age which persists for the lifetime of those individuals; as with age grades, predominantly found in East Africa.

**alienation** The fragmentation of individuals' relations to their work, the things they produce, and the resources with which they produce them.

**animal husbandry** The breeding, care, and use of herd animals such as sheep, goats, camels, cattle, and yaks.

**archaeology** The study of the relationship between material culture and behavior; investigations of the ways of life of earlier peoples and of the processes by which their ways of life changed.

**authority** The ability to exert influence because of one's personal prestige or the status of one's office.

**balanced reciprocity** Gift giving that clearly carries the obligation of an eventual and roughly equal return.

**band** A loosely integrated population sharing a sense of common identity but few specialized institutions.

**biological (physical) anthropology** The study of the human species, past and present, as a biological phenomenon.

**biological race** A genetically distinct population within a species.

**biological species** A group of interbreeding populations that is reproductively isolated from other such groups.

**Blue Revolution** Modern aquaculture, producing fish, shellfish, and other products.

**bride price** Payment made by a man or his kin group to the family from whom he takes a daughter in marriage.

**bride service** Service rendered by a man as payment to a family from whom he takes a daughter in marriage.

**bridewealth** Property given by the family of the groom to the family of the bride to compensate them for the loss of their daughter's service.

**bureaucracy** Institutionalized political administration, usually hierarchically organized.

**call system** A repertoire of sounds, each of which is produced in response to a particular situation.

**carrying capacity** The point at or below which a population tends to stabilize.

**caste** A social category in which membership is fixed at birth and usually unchangeable.

**cattle complex** An East African socioeconomic system in which cattle represent social status as well as wealth.

**centralization** Concentration of political and economic decisions in the hands of a few individuals or institutions.

**chiefdom** A society distinguished by the presence of a permanent central political agency to coordinate the activities of multicommunity political units.

**clan** A group that claims but cannot trace precisely their descent from a common ancestor.

**closed corporate community** A community that strongly emphasizes community identity and discourages outsiders from settling there by restricting land use to village members and prohibiting the sale or lease of property to outsiders.

**cognates** Words so similar from one language to the next as to suggest that both are variants of a single ancestral prototype.

**commune** Collective ownership of land or other factors in production, ostensibly for members to share proceeds and expenses.

**consanguineal kin** Persons related by birth.

**consensual decisions** Arriving at decisions that the entire group can accept.

**corporate ownership** Control of land and other productive resources by a group rather than by individuals.

**corporateness** The sharing of specific rights by group members.

**corvée** Unpaid labor in lieu of taxation, usually on road construction and maintenance.

**creole** A pidgin language that has evolved into a fully developed language, with a complete array of grammatical distinctions and a large vocabulary.

**cross cousins** Mother's brothers' children and father's sisters' children.

**cultural adaptation** All of the learned or socially acquired responses and behaviors that affect reproduction, provisioning, shelter—in short, survival.

**cultural anthropology** The study of specific contemporary human cultures (ethnography) and of the underlying patterns of human culture in general (ethnology).

**cultural ecology** An approach to the study of cultural diversity that requires the simultaneous investigation of technology, culture, and the physical environment.

**cultural evolution** The idea that human culture has been transformed by regular and cumulative changes in learned behavior.

**cultural materialism** The theory, espoused by Marvin Harris, that ideas, values, and religious beliefs are the means or products of adaptation to environmental conditions ("material constraints").

**cultural relativism** The ability to view the beliefs and customs of other peoples within the context of their culture rather than one's own.

**culture** A system of shared beliefs, values, customs, behaviors, and artifacts that the members of a society use to cope with one another and with their world and that are transmitted from generation to generation through learning.

**cyberculture** The emergent worldwide system of communication via computers.

**demographic transition** A rapid increase in a society's population with the onset of industrialization, followed by a leveling off of the growth rate due to reduced fertility.

**dependency theory** Associated with Andre Gunter Frank who argued that massive poverty in the underdeveloped world is caused by large, developed countries keeping poorer countries dependent through selling raw materials and labor while importing manufactured goods (contra modernization theory).

**descent group** A group of consanguineal kin united by presumed lineal descent from a common ancestor.

**descent ideology** The concept of kinship as a basis of unambiguous membership in a group and possibly of property rights and political obligations.

**descent relationship** The ties between mother and child and between father and child.

**development anthropology** Employment of anthropological theory and findings to have a practical and ameliorating effect on the lives of people.

**dialect** A distinctive speech community within a language.

**differentiation** Organization in separate units for various activities and purposes.

**diffusion** The spread of an aspect of culture from the society in which it originated by migration or imitation.

**domestic cycle** The changes in household organization that result from a series of demographic events.

**domestic herds** Animals maintained for domestic consumption.

**domestic mode of production** The organization of economic production and consumption primarily in the household.

**domestication** The process by which people try to control the reproductive rates of animals and plants by ordering the environment in such a way as to favor certain species.

**dowry** Payment made by the bride's family to the groom or to the groom's family.

**ecology** The study of the interplay between organisms (or the populations to which they belong) and their environment.

**economic class** A group that is defined by the economic position of its members in relation to the means of production in the society—the wealth and relative economic control they may command.

**economic stratification** The segmentation of society along lines of access to resources.

**economic system** The ideas and institutions that people draw upon and the behaviors in which they engage to secure resources to satisfy their needs and desires.

**ecosystem** The cycle of matter and energy that includes all living things and links them to the nonliving.

**ecosystem equilibrium** A balance among the components of an ecosystem.

**empiricism** Reliance on observable and quantifiable data.

**enculturation** Becoming proficient in the cultural codes of one's society.

**endogamy** Marriage within a particular group with which one is identified.

**entrepreneurship** Economic innovation and risk taking.

**environment** Every factor that impinges on the life chances of the individual, not merely the obvious constraints of predators, food, and shelter.

**ethnicity** A basis for social categories that are rooted in socially perceived differences in national origin, language, and/or religion.

**ethnocentrism** The tendency to judge the customs of other societies by the standards of one's own.

**ethnographic present** Describes the point in time at which a society or culture is frozen when ethnographic data collected in the field are published in a report.

**ethnography** Gathering information on contemporary cultures through fieldwork or firsthand study.

**ethnology** Uncovering general patterns and "rules" that govern social behavior.

**evolution** The process by which small but cumulative changes in a species can, over time, lead to its transformation; may be divided into two categories: physical evolution (adaptive changes in biological makeup) and cultural evolution (adaptive changes in thought and behavior).

**evolutionary ecology** The study of living organisms within the context of their total environment, with the aim of discovering how they have adapted.

**exchange** The distribution of goods and services among members of a society.

**exogamy** Marriage outside a particular group with which one is identified.

**extended family household** A multiple-family unit incorporating adults of two or more generations.

**extensive agriculture** Farming using limited sources of nonhuman energy.

**fallow time** The time required for soils to regain nutrients following planting; industrial farming has greatly shortened this time leading to increased production.

**family household** A household formed on the basis of kinship and marriage.

**fieldwork** The firsthand observation of human societies.

**foraging** A subsistence form in which food-getting is dependent on naturally occurring resources, especially wild plants, but also fishing and hunting wild game (see also hunting and gathering).

**fossils** The naturally mineralized remains of earlier forms of plant and animal life.

**fraternal polyandry** Marriage of one woman with a set of brothers.

**freehold** Private ownership of property.

**gender** A cultural construct consisting of the set of distinguishable characteristics associated with each sex.

**generalized reciprocity** Informal gift giving for which no accounts are kept and no immediate or specific return is expected.

**genes** Individual units of hereditary information passed from parent to offspring as discrete particles according to certain regular patterns.

**genetically modified crops** Crops in which the gene that is modified is taken directly from another species, often entirely unrelated.

**globalization** Due to recent developments in communication and transportation, people all over the world are coming to share similar aspirations, cultural codes, and patterns of consumption.

**grammar** The formal structure of a language, comprising phonology, morphology, and syntax.

**Green Revolution** Use of recently developed new genetic strains of major food crops, which has transformed agriculture since the 1970s.

**habitat** The specific area where a species lives.

**headmen** Leaders in tribal- or band-organized societies, usually informally selected with limited formal coercive power.

**holism** The philosophical view that no complex entity can be considered to be only the sum of its parts; as a principle of anthropology, the assumption that any given aspect of human life is to be studied with an eye to its relation to other aspects of human life.

*Homo sapiens* The human species.

**horizontal migration** A nomadic pattern characterized by regular movement over a large area in search of pasture.

**horticulture** A simple form of agriculture based on the working of small plots of land without draft animals, plows, or irrigation; also called *extensive agriculture*.

**household** A domestic residential group whose members live together in intimate contact, rear children, share the proceeds of labor and other resources held in common, and in general, cooperate on a day-to-day basis.

**hypothesis** A statement that can be falsified that stipulates a relationship between a phenomenon for which the researcher seeks to account and one or more other phenomena.

**impact assessment** Measuring the social, economic, or cultural impacts of development efforts.

**independent family household** A single-family unit that resides by itself, apart from relatives or adults of other generations.

**industrial agriculture** Farming using large inputs of fossil fuel and industrial technology.

**institutions** A society's recurrent patterns of activity, such as religion, art, a kinship system, law, and family life.

**intensification** An increase in the product derived from a unit of land or labor.

**intensive agriculture** A form of agriculture that involves the use of draft animals or tractors, plows, and often some form of irrigation.

**joint family household** A complex family unit formed through polygyny or polyandry or through the decision of married siblings to live together in the absence of their parents.

**kula ring** A unique system of exchange among the Trobriand Islanders linking dispersed island communities, in which two varieties of ceremonial shell ornaments and essential good are traded in separate spheres of exchange.

**language** Uniquely human means of communication in which the number of messages that can be conveyed is infinite and in which meaning emerges from the way sounds are combined into words and words arranged to make sentences in accordance with a complex set of rules (grammar).

**lineage** A unilineal descent group composed of people who trace their genealogies through specified links to a common ancestor.

**lingua franca** Any language used as a common tongue by people who do not speak one another's native language.

**low-energy budget** An adaptive strategy by which a minimum of energy is used to extract sufficient resources from the environment for survival.

**market exchange** Trading goods and services through a common medium of value.

**material culture** The technology and all material artifacts of a society; used primarily by archaeologists.

**matrilateral** Relatives on the mother's side in a genealogy or kinship system.

**matrilineage** A lineage whose members trace their genealogies through specified female links to a common female ancestor.

**matrilineal descent** Descent traced through the female line.

**matrilineal descent group** A unilineal descent group in which membership is inherited through the maternal line.

**matrilocal residence** Residence of a married couple with or near the wife's kin.

**mechanization** The replacement of human and animal labor by mechanical devices.

**mediation** Intervention by an outside party in a dispute.

**medical anthropology** Specialization within anthropology focusing on medical knowledge and practice; often related to practical efforts in health-care delivery.

**modernization theory** The theory (advocated by the World Bank among other major lending institutions) that societies modernize or develop through specific stages driven by entrepreneurial values and access to capital.

**moiety** One of the two subdivisions of a society with a dual organizational structure.

**monogamy** An exclusive union of one man and one woman.

**nationalism** The feeling or belief that a people and land are inherently linked, and using this belief to legitimize a particular state or nation.

**natural selection** The process whereby members of a species who have more surviving offspring than others pass their traits on to the next generation, whereas the less favored do not do so to the same degree.

**negative reciprocity** An exchange between enemies or strangers in which each side tries to get the better end of the bargain.

**Neolithic Revolution** The development of agriculture and consequent cultural changes that occurred at different times and places in the Old and New Worlds.

**neolocal residence** Residence of a married couple in a new household established apart from both the husband's and the wife's kin.

**niche** The environmental requirements and tolerances of a species; sometimes seen as a species' "profession" or what it does to survive.

**nomadic pastoralism** The strategy of moving the herds that are one's livelihood from pasture to pasture as the seasons and circumstances require.

**nuclear family household** An independent family unit formed by a monogamous union.

**nucleation** The tendency of populations to cluster in settlements of increasing size and density.

**oasis** A human-constructed fertile area in an arid region.

**paleontologists** Experts on animal life of the distant past.

**parallel cousins** Mother's sisters' children and father's brothers' children.

**participant observation** Actual participation in a culture by an investigator, who seeks to gain social acceptance in the society as a means to acquire understanding of her or his observations.

**pastoralism** An economy largely or wholly based on the use of domesticated animals, even though actual consumption may rely on foods etc. acquired through trade.

**patriclan** A group that claims but cannot trace their descent through the male line from a common male ancestor.

**patrilineage** A lineage whose members trace their genealogies through specified male links to a common male ancestor.

**patrilineal descent** Descent traced through the male line.

**patrilocal residence** Residence of a married couple with or near the husband's kin.

**patron–client relationship** A mutually obligatory arrangement between an individual who has authority, social status, wealth, or some other personal resource (the "patron") and another person who benefits from his or her support or influence (the "client").

**peasants** Farmers who lack control over the means of their production—the land, the other resources, the capital they need to grow their crops, and the labor they contribute to the process.

**pidgin** A language based on a simplified grammar and lexicon taken from one or more fully developed languages.

**political ecology** Focuses on the ecological consequences of the distribution of power.

**politics** The process by which a community's decisions are made, rules for group behavior are established, competition for positions of leadership is regulated, and the disruptive effects of disputes are minimized.

**polyandry** Marriage between one woman and two or more men simultaneously.

**polyculture** Closely associated with horticulture, the planting of many species or strains of plants in close proximity.

**polygamy** Plural marriage.

**polygyny** Marriage between one man and two or more women simultaneously.

**post partum taboo** Supernaturally justified prohibitions on certain activities following a birth.

**potlatch** Reciprocal feasting and gift giving that can involve the conspicuous display and even the destruction of wealth.

**power** The ability to exert influence because one's directives are backed by negative sanctions of some sort.

**primates** A grouping of mammals that includes humans, apes, and New and Old World monkeys.

**primatology** The study of living nonhuman primates.

**production** The conversion of natural resources to usable forms.

**productive life span** The period bounded by the culturally established ages at which a person ideally enters and retires from the work force.

**productivity** The amount of work a person accomplishes in a given period of time.

**racism** Acting upon the belief that different races have different capacities for culture.

**random sample** A sample in which each individual in a population has the same chance of being selected as any other.

**rational economic decisions** Weighing available alternatives and calculating which will provide the most benefit at the least cost.

**reciprocity** Mutual giving and taking between people who are often bound by social ties and obligations.

**redistribution** Reallocation of a society's wealth by means of obligatory payments or services.

**regulation of access to resources** Control over the use of land, water, and raw materials.

**resilience** The ability of an ecosystem to undergo change while still maintaining its basic elements or relationships.

**revitalization movements** Conscious efforts to build an ideology that will be relevant to changing cultural needs.

**sampling bias** The tendency of a sample to exclude some members of the sampling universe and overrepresent others.

**sampling universe** The largest entity to be described, of which the sample is a part.

**scarce resources** A central concept of Western economics that assumes that people have more wants than they have resources to satisfy them.

**scientific theory** A statement that postulates ordered relationships among natural phenomena.

**sedentary pastoralism** Animal husbandry that does not involve mobility.

**sedentism** The practice of establishing a permanent, year-round settlement.

**segmentary lineage** A descent group in which minimal lineages are encompassed as segments of minor lineages, minor lineages as segments of major lineages, and so on.

**shaman** A medium of the supernatural who acts as a person in possession of unique curing, divining, or witchcraft capabilities.

**sharecropping** Working land owned by others for a share of the yield.

**slash-and-burn agriculture** A method of farming, also called *swidden agriculture*, by which fields are cleared, trees and brush are burned, and the soil, fertilized by the ash, is then planted.

**social class** A category of people who have generally similar educational histories, job opportunities, and social standing and who are conscious of their membership in a social group that is ranked in relation to others and is replicated over generations.

**social control** A framework of rewards and sanctions that channel behavior.

**social division of labor** The process by which a society is formed by the integration of its smaller groups or subsets.

**socialization** The process by which a person acquires the technical skills of his or her society, the knowledge of the kinds of behavior that are understood and acceptable in that society, and the attitudes and values that make conformity with social rules personally meaningful, even gratifying; also termed *enculturation*.

**sociolinguistics** The study of the interrelationship of social variables and language.

**specialization** The limited range of activities in which a single individual is likely to be engaged.

**specialized pastoralism** The adaptive strategy of near exclusive reliance on animal husbandry.

**spheres of exchange** The modes of exchange—reciprocity, redistribution, and market exchange—that apply to particular goods or in particular situations.

**stability** The ability of an ecosystem to return to equilibrium after disturbances.

**state** A complex of institutions that transcend kinship in the organization of power.

**status** A position in a pattern of reciprocal behavior.

**stem family** The basic coresidential unit in an extended family. Among the Tamang of Nepal, the stem family is the mother, father, and younger son (the other children move out upon marriage).

**stratification** The division of a society into groups that have varying degrees of access to resources and power.

**stratified sample** A sample obtained by the process of dividing a population into categories representing distinctive characteristics and then selecting a random sample from each category.

**stratified society** A society in which extensive subpopulations are accorded differential treatment.

**structural adjustment** Economic reforms directed to eliminating subsidies and encouraging market forces, often involving privatization of previously state-owned enterprises.

**subsistence agriculture** Farming directed to domestic consumption with limited nonhuman energy sources.

**sustainable energy** Energy sources that can be sustained without long-term depletion, such as some forms of water power or solar power, as opposed to energy sources which once harvested are no longer available, such as coal or oil.

**swidden agriculture** See *slash-and-burn agriculture.*

**taboo** A supernaturally justified prohibition on certain activities.

**time allocation** A method of collecting data by making observations according to a systematic schedule.

**tontine** A group of people who agree to collect and pool funds, and then use the pot in an agreed-upon order.

**totem** A plant or animal whose name is adopted by a clan and that holds a special significance for its members, usually related to their mythical ancestry.

**transhumance** Seasonal movement of livestock between upland and lowland pastures.

**tribe** A descent- and kinship-based group in which subgroups are clearly linked to one another, with the potential of uniting a large number of local groups for common defense or warfare.

**unilineal descent** A way of reckoning kin in which membership is inherited only through either the paternal or the maternal line, as the society dictates.

**vengeance** A form of social control arising from shared responsibility and the idea that each offense will be met with comparable and automatic retaliation.

**water table** The level of water under the earth.

**witchcraft** Use of religious ritual to control, exploit, or injure unsuspecting, or at least uncooperating, other persons.

**workday** The culturally established number of hours that a person ideally spends at work each day.

# Bibliography

Abruzzi, W. (1987). Ecological stability and community diversity during Mormon colonization of the Little Colorado River Basin. *Human Ecology, 15,* 317–338.

———. (1993). *Dam that river! Ecology and Mormon settlement in the Little Colorado River Basin.* New York: Pennsylvania State University Press.

Abu Lughod, L. (1988). *Veiled sentiments.* Berkeley: University of California Press.

———. (1993). *Writing women's worlds: Bedouin stories.* Berkeley: University of California Press.

Adams, D. (1999, August 29). A hitchhiker's guide to the Internet. *The Sunday Times of London,* p. 4.7.

Adams, R. M. (1966). *The evolution of urban society: Early Mesopotamia and pre-Hispanic Mexico.* Chicago: Aldine.

Adams, R. M. (1981). *Heartland of cities: Surveys of ancient settlement and land use on the central floodplain of the Euphrates.* Chicago and London: University of Chicago Press.

Adovasio, J. M., with Page, J. (2003). *The first Americans: In pursuit of archaeology's greatest mystery.* New York: Random House.

Adra, N. (1985). The concept of tribes in rural Yemen. In Nicholas Hopkins & Saad Eddin Ibrahim (Eds.), *Arab society: Social science perspectives.* Cairo: The American University in Cairo Press.

Agrawal, A. (1994). Mobility and control among nomadic shepherds: The case of the Raikas II. *Human Ecology, 22,* 131–144.

Aldona, J. (1999). *The Yuquot Whalers' Shrine.* Seattle: University of Washington Press.

Anderson, B. (1991). *Imagined communities.* London: Verso.

Anderson, M. K. (1999). The fire, pruning, and coppice management of temperate ecosystems for basketry material by California Indian tribes. *Human Ecology, 27*(1), 7–113.

Angier, N. (1995, January 3). Heredity's more than genes, new theory proposes. *New York Times,* pp. B13, B22.

———. (1997, March 14). "Sexual identity not pliable after all." *New York Times,* pp. A1, A18.

———. (2002, July 2). Why childhood lasts, and lasts and lasts. *New York Times,* pp. D1, D4.

Appell, G. N. (1988). Casting social change. In M. R. Dove (Ed.), *The real and imagined role of culture in development: Case studies from Indonesia* (pp. 271–284). Boulder, CO: Westview Press.

Atkinson, J. M. (1992). Shamanism today. *Annual Review of Anthropology, 21,* 307–330.

Atran, S. (2003). Genesis of suicide terrorism. *Science, 299*(5612), 1534–1539.

Bach, K. (1998). The vision of a better life: New patterns of consumption and changed social relations. In N. S. Hopkins & K. Westergaard (Eds.), *Directions of change in rural Egypt.* Cairo: The American University in Cairo Press.

Bailey, R. C., & Peacock, N. R. (1990). Efe Pygmies of northeast Zaire: Subsistence strategies in the Ituri Forest. In I. DeGarine & G. A. Harrison (Eds.), *Uncertainty in the food supply.* New York: Cambridge University Press.

Balee, W. (1994). *Footprints of the forest: Ka'apor ethnobotany-historical ecology of plant utilization by an Amazonian people.* New York: Columbia University Press.

Bales, K. (1999). *Disposable people: New slavery in the global economy.* Berkeley: University of California Press.

Balikci, A. (1970). *The Netsilik Eskimo.* New York: Natural History Press.

———. (1989). *The Netsilik Eskimo* (Rev. ed.). Prospect Heights, IL: Waveland Press.

Barfield, T. J. (1993). *The nomadic alternative.* Englewood Cliffs, NJ: Prentice Hall.

Barlett, P. F. (1999). Introduction. In William M. Loker (Ed.), *Globalization and the rural poor in Latin America.* Boulder, London: L. Rienner Publishers.

Barnet, R. J., & Muller, R. E. (1974). *Global reach: The power of the multinational corporations.* New York: Simon & Schuster.

Barth, F. (1959). Political leadership among Swat Pathans. *Monographs on Social Anthropology, 19,* London School of Economics.

———. (1961). *The nomads of south Persia: The Basseri tribe of the Kamseh confederacy.* New York: Humanities Press.

———. (1963). *Role of the entrepreneur in social change in northern Norway.* Bergen: Norwegian Universities Press.

———. (1966). The problem of comparison. *Royal Anthropological Institute* (Occasional Paper No. 23), pp. 22–23.

———. (1969). *Ethnic groups and boundaries: The social organization of cultural difference.* Boston: Little, Brown.

———. (1981). *Process and form in social life*. London: Routledge & Kegan Paul.

———. (1994). Brief comment. *Anthropology Newsletter, 34*(4), 1.

Bates, D. G. (1973). *Nomads and farmers: The Yörük of southeastern Turkey* (University of Michigan Museum of Anthropology Monograph), p. 52. Ann Arbor: University of Michigan Press.

———. (1994). What's in a name? Minorities, identity and politics in Bulgaria. *Identities, 1*(2–3), 201–225.

Bates, D. G., & Fratkin, E. M. (1999). *Cultural anthropology*. (2nd ed.). Boston: Allyn & Bacon.

Bates, D. G., & Lees, S. H. (1977). The role of exchange in production specialization. *American Anthropologist, 79*, 824–841.

———. (1979). The myth of population regulation. In N. A. Chagnon & W. Irons (Eds.), *Evolutionary biology and human social behavior: An anthropological perspective* (pp. 273–289). North Scituate, MA: Duxbury Press.

Bates, D. G., & Lees, S. H. (Eds.). (1996). *Case studies in human ecology*. New York: Plenum Press.

Bates, D. G., & Plog, F. (1991). *Human adaptive strategies*. New York: McGraw-Hill.

Bates, D. G., & Rassam, A. (2000). *Peoples and cultures of the middle east* (2nd ed.). Englewood Cliffs, NJ: Prentice Hall.

Bearak, B. (2003, July 13). Why people still starve. *New York Times Magazine*, pp. 32–37, 52, 60–61.

Beck, L. (1986). *The Qashqa'i of Iran*. New Haven, CT: Yale University Press.

———. (1991). *Nomad: A year in the life of a Qashqa'i tribesman in Iran*. Berkeley and Los Angeles: University of California Press.

Beckerman, S. (1983). Does the swidden ape the forest? *Human Ecology, 11*, 1–12.

Benbrook, C. M. (2003, July 11). Sowing seeds of destruction. *New York Times*, p. A19.

Bernard, H. R. (1988). *Research methods in cultural anthropology*. Beverly Hills, CA: Sage.

———. (1994). *Research methods in anthropology: Qualitative and quantitative approaches* (2nd ed.). Thousand Oaks, CA: Sage.

Berreby, D. (1995, April 9). Unabsolute truths: Clifford Geertz. *New York Times Magazine*, pp. 44–47.

Bettinger, R. L. (1987). Archaeological approaches to hunter-gatherers. *Annual Review of Anthropology, 16*, 121–142.

Bickerton, D. (1995). *Language and human behavior*. Seattle: University of Washington Press.

———. (2003). Symbol and structure: A comprehensive framework for language evolution. In M. H. Christiansen & S. Kirby (Eds.), *Language evolution: The state of the art*. Oxford: Oxford University Press.

Binford, L. R. (1968). Post-Pleistocene adaptations. In S. R. Binford & L. R. Binford (Eds.), *New perspectives in archaeology*. Chicago: Aldine.

———. (1989). Ancestral lifeways: The faunal record. In A. Podolefski & P. J. Brown (Eds.), *Applying anthropology: An introductory reader*. Mountain View, CA: Mayfield Press.

Bishop, N. H. (1998). *Himalayan herders* (Case studies in cultural anthropology). New York: Harcourt Brace.

Biswas, A. K. (2002, November/December). Aswan Dam revisited: The benefits of a much-maligned dam. Deutsche Stiftung für internationale Entwicklung, *Development and Cooperation*, 6, pp. 25–27. www.dse.de/zeitschr/de602-11.htm.

Blackwood, E. (1984). Sexuality and gender in certain Native American tribes: The case of cross-gender females. *Signs, 10*, 27–42.

Blanton, R. E. (1994). *Houses and households: A comparative study*. New York: Plenum Press.

Board of Education of the City of New York, Division of Bilingual Education. (1994). *Facts and figures*.

Boas, F. (1940). *Race, language and culture*. New York: Macmillan.

———. (1966). *The limitations of the comparative method of anthropology*. New York: Free Press. (First published 1896.)

Boehm, C. (1984). *Blood revenge: The anthropology of feuding in Montenegro and other tribal societies*. Lawrence: University Press of Kansas.

Bohannan, P. (1960). Africa's land. *Centennial Review, 4*, 439–449.

Bongarts, J. (1988). Modeling the demographic impact of AIDS in Africa. In R. Kulstad (Ed.), *AIDS 1988: American Association for the Advancement of Science Symposia Papers* (pp. 85–94). Washington, DC: AAAS.

Boone, J. (1992). Competition, conflict and development of social hierarchies. In E. R. Smith & B. Winterhalder (Eds.), *Evolutionary ecology and human behavior* (pp. 301–338). Hawthorne, NY: Aldine de Gruyter.

Borlaug, N. E. (2003, July 11). How to help Africa grow. *New York Times*, p. A19.

Borofsky, R. (Ed.). (1994). *Assessing cultural anthropology*. New York: McGraw-Hill.

Boserup, E. (1970). *Women's role in economic development*. Chicago: Aldine.

Boster, J. (1983). A comparison of the diversity of Jivaroan gardens with that of the tropical forest. *Human Ecology, 11*, 47–68.

Bowe, J. (2003, April 21 & 28). Nobodies: Does slavery exist in America? *New Yorker*, pp. 106–133.

Boyd, D. J. (2001). Life without pigs: Recent subsistence changes among the Irakia Awa, Papua New Guinea. *Human Ecology, 29*(3), 259–282.

Boyd, R., & Richerson, P. J. (1985). *Culture and the evolutionary process*. Chicago: University of Chicago Press.

———. (1991). Punishment allows the evolution of cooperation (or anything else) in sizable groups. *Ethology and Sociobiology, 13*, 171–196.

Boyer, P. (1998). Cognitive tracks of cultural inheritance: How evolved intuitive ontology governs cultural transmission. *American Anthropologist, 100*(4), 876–889.

Brace, C., Brace, M. L., & Leonard, W. R. (1989). Reflections on the face of Japan: A multivariate craniofacial and odontometric perspective. *American Journal of Physical Anthropology, 78*, 93–114.

Bradburd, D. (1980). Never give a shepherd an even break: Class and labor among the Komanchi of Kerman, Iran. *American Ethnologist, 7*, 604–620.

———. (1984). The rules and the game: The practice of Komanchi marriage. *American Ethnologist, 11*, 738–754.

———. (1990). *Ambiguous relations: Kin, class and conflict among Komanchi pastoralists.* Washington, DC: Smithsonian Institution Press.

———. (1996). Size and success: Komanchi adaptation to a changing Iran. In M. Bonine & N. Keddi (Eds.), *Modern Iran: The dialectics of continuity and change.* Albany: State University of New York Press.

Bray, F. (1994). *The rice economies: Technology and development in Asian societies.* Berkeley and Los Angeles: University of California Press.

Briggs, J. L. (1970). *Never in anger: Portrait of an Eskimo family.* Cambridge, MA: Harvard University Press.

Brondizio, E., Moran, E., Mausel, P., & Wu, Y. (1994). Land use change in the Amazon estuary: Patterns of Caboclo settlement and landscape management. *Human Ecology, 22*(3), 243–248.

Brosius, J. P. (1986). River, forest and mountain: The Penan Gang landscape. *Sarawak Museum Journal, 36*(57, New Series), 173–184.

———. (1988). A separate reality: Comments on Hoffman's *The Punan: Hunters and gatherers of Borneo. Borneo Research Bulletin, 20*(2), 81–106.

———. (1990). Penan hunter-gatherers of Sarawak, East Malaysia. *AnthroQuest, 42,* 1–7.

———. (1997). Endangered forest, endangered people: Environmentalist representations of indigenous knowledge. *Human Ecology, 25*(1), 47–69.

Brown, D. (1991). *Human universals.* New York: McGraw-Hill.

Browne, M. W. (1994, October 16). What is intelligence? And who has it? *New York Times Book Review,* pp. 3ff.

Buckmaster, M. (1999, October). *Evidence of prehistoric gardening in Michigan's Upper Peninsula.* Paper presented at the Midwest Archaeological Conference. East Lansing, MI.

Burbank, V. K. (1994). *Fighting women: Anger and aggression in aboriginal Australia.* Berkeley and Los Angeles: University of California Press.

Burch, E. S., Jr. (1994a). North Alaskan Eskimos: A changing way of life. In M. Ember, C. Ember, & D. Levinson (Eds.), *Portraits of culture* (pp. 1–36). Englewood Cliffs, NJ: Prentice Hall.

———. (1994b). The future of hunter-gatherer research. In E. S. Burch, Jr., & L. J. Ellanna (Eds.), *Key issues in hunter-gatherer research* (pp. 441–455). Providence, RI: Berg Publishers.

Burch, E. S., Jr., & Ellanna, L. J. (Eds.) (1994). *Key issues in hunter-gatherer research.* Providence, RI: Berg Publishers.

Button, G. (1995). What you don't know can't hurt you: The right to know and the Shetland oil spill. *Human Ecology, 23,* 31.

Byrne, R. (1999). *The thinking ape: Evolutionary origins of intelligence.* Oxford: Oxford University Press.

Cairo Population Conference. (1994, September 11). *New York Times,* p. 10.

Calhoun, C., Light, D., & Keller, S. (1994). *Sociology* (6th ed.). New York: McGraw-Hill.

Calvin, W. H. (1996). *How brains think: Evolving intelligence, then and now.* Basic Books.

Campbell, B. K. (1995). *Human ecology* (2nd ed.). Hawthorne, NY: Aldine de Gruyter.

Cane, S. (1996). Australian aboriginal subsistence in the western desert. In D. G. Bates & S. H. Lees (Eds.), *Case studies in human ecology* (pp. 17–54). New York: Plenum Press.

Cann, R. L. (1988). DNA and human origins. In *Annual Review of Anthropology* (Vol. 17, pp. 127–143). Palo Alto, CA: Annual Reviews.

Carney, J. A. (1993). From hands to tutors: African expertise in the South Carolina economy. *Agricultural History, 67*(3), 1–30.

———. (1996). Landscapes of technology transfer: Rice cultivation and African continuities. *Technology and Culture, 37*(1), 5–35.

———. (1998). The role of African rice and slaves in the history of rice cultivation in the Americas. *Human Ecology, 26*(4), 525–545.

Cashdan, E. (1992). Spatial organization and habitat use. In E. A. Smith & B. Winterhalter (Eds.), *Evolutionary ecology and human behavior.* New York: Walter de Gruyter.

Castells, M. (1996a). The net and the self: Working note for a critical theory of the informational society. *Critique of Anthropology, 16*(1), 11–39.

Castells, M. (1996b). *The rise of the network society. Vol 1: The informational age.* Oxford: Blackwell.

———. (1998). *End of millennium. Vol 3: The information age: Economy, society and culture.* Oxford: Blackwell.

Cavalli-Sforza, P., & Piazza, A. (1994). *The history and geography of human genes.* Princeton, NJ: Princeton University Press.

Cernea, M. M. (1996). *Social organization and development anthropology* (The 1995 Malinowski Award Lecture. Environmentally Sustainable Development Studies and Monograph Studies Series No. 6). Washington, DC: The World Bank.

Chagnon, N. A. (1967). Yanomamö social organization and warfare. In M. Fried, M. Harris, & R. Murphy (Eds.), *War: The anthropology of armed conflict and aggression.* New York: Natural History Press.

———. (1983) *Yanomamö: The fierce people* (3rd ed.). New York: Holt, Rinehart & Winston.

———. (1992). *Yanomamö: The last days of Eden.* San Diego: Harcourt Brace Jovanovich.

———. (1993, October 23). Covering up the Yanomamö massacre. *New York Times,* Op. Ed.

———. (1995). L'Ethnologie du déshonneur: Brief response to Lizot. *American Ethnologist, 22*(1), 187–189.

———. (1997). *Yanomamö: The last days of Eden* (5th ed.). San Diego: Harcourt Brace Jovanovich.

———. (2000). Manipulating kinship rules: A form of male Yanomamö reproductive competition. In L. Cronk, N. Chagnon, & W. Irons (Eds.), *Adaptation and human behavior: An anthropological perspective* (pp. 115–131). New York: Aldine de Gruyter.

Chagnon, N. A., & Hames, R. (1979). Protein deficiency and tribal warfare in Amazonia: New data. *Science, 203*(4383), 10–15.

Chagnon, N. A., & Irons, W. (Eds.). (1979). *Evolutionary biology and human social behavior: An anthropological perspective.* North Scituate, MA: Duxbury Press.

Chagnon, N. A., & Melancon, T. (1983). Epidemics in a tribal population. In *The impact of contact: Two Yanomamö cases,*

Report No. 11 (pp. 53–75). Cambridge, MA: Cultural Survival International.

Chance, N. A. (1990). *The Inupiat and Arctic Alaska: An ethnography of development.* Fort Worth, TX: Harcourt Brace College.

Chauvet, J-M., Deschamps, E. B., & Hillaire, C. (1996). *Dawn of cave art: The Chauvet Cave.* New York: Harry Abrams.

Cheal, D. (1993). Changing household financial strategies: Canadian couples today. *Human Ecology, 21*(2), 197–213.

Chew, S. C. (2001). *World ecological degradation: Accumulation, urbanization, and deforestation 3000 B.C.–A.D. 2000.* Walnut Creek, CA: Altamira Press.

Chibnik, M. (Ed.). (1987). *Farm work and fieldwork: American agriculture in anthropological perspective.* Ithaca, NY: Cornell University Press.

Chomsky, N. (1972). *Language and mind.* New York: Harcourt Brace Jovanovich.

Clark, J. D., Beyene, Y., WoldeGabriel, G., Hart, W. K., Renne, P. R., Gilbert, H., Defleur, A., Suwa, G., Katoh, S., Ludwig, K. R., Boisserie, J-R., Asfaw, B., & White, T. D. (2003). Stratigraphic, chronological and behavioral contexts of Pleistocene *Homo sapiens* from Middle Awash, Ethiopia. *Nature, 423,* 747–752.

Clark, K., & Uhl, C. (1987). Farming, fishing, and fire in the history of the upper Rio Negro region of Venezuela. *Human Ecology, 15,* 1–26.

Clarke, K. B. (1993). Racial progress and retreat: A personal memoir. In H. Hill & J. E. Jones (Eds.), *Race in America: The struggle for equality* (pp. 3–18). Madison: University of Wisconsin Press.

Clarke, L. (1989). *Acceptable risk? Making decisions in a toxic environment.* Berkeley and Los Angeles: University of California Press.

Coimbra, C. E. A., Jr., Flowers, N. M., Salzano, F. M., & Santos, R. V. (2002). *The Xavánte in transition: Health, ecology, and bioanthropology in Central Brazil.* Ann Arbor: University of Michigan Press.

Colchester, M. (1985). *The health and survival of the Venezuelan Yanomamö* (IGWA Document No. 53). Cambridge, MA: Cultural Survival International.

Cole, J. W., & Wolf, E. R. (2000). *The hidden frontier: Ecology and ethnicity in an alpine valley.* Berkeley: University of California Press.

Conant, F. P. (1982). Thorns paired sharply recurved: Cultural controls and rangeland quality in East Africa. In B. Spooner & H. Mann (Eds.), *Anthropology and desertification: Dryland ecology in social perspective* (pp. 111–122). London: Academic Press.

———. (1984). Remote sensing, discovery, and generalizations in human ecology. In E. Moran (Ed.), *The ecosystem concept in anthropology.* Boulder, CO: Westview Press.

———. (1988). Social consequences of AIDS: Implications for East Africa and the eastern United States. In R. Kulstad (Ed.), *AIDS 1988: American Association for the Advancement of Science Symposia Papers* (pp. 147–156). Washington, DC: AAAS.

———. (1994). Human ecology and space age technology: Some predictions. *Human Ecology, 22*(3), 405–413.

Condon, R., with Oguia, J., & Holman elders. (1996). *The Northern Copper Inuit: A History* (The Civilization of American Indian Series, V. 220). Norman, OK, and London: University of Oklahoma Press.

Conelly, W. T. (1996). Agricultural intensification in a Philippine frontier community: Impact on labor efficiency and farm diversity. In D. G. Bates & S. H. Lees (Eds.), *Case studies in human ecology.* New York: Plenum Press.

Conklin, B. A., & Graham, L. R. (1995). The shifting middle ground: Amazonian Indians and eco-politics. *American Anthropologist, 97*(4), 695–710.

Cooper, F., & Packard, R. (Eds.). (1998). *International development and the social sciences: Essays on the history and politics of knowledge.* Berkeley: University of California Press.

Coughenour, M. B., Ellis, J. E., Swift, D. M., Coppock, D. L., Galvin, K., McCabe, J. T., & Hart, T. C. (1985). Energy extraction and use in a nomadic pastoral ecosystem. *Science, 230,* 619–625.

Cowell, A. (1994, September 11). Cairo parley hits anew on migrants. *New York Times,* p. 10.

Creed, G. W. (1994). Bulgaria: Anthropological corrections to cold war stereotypes. In M. Ember, C. Ember, & D. Levinson (Eds.), *Portraits of culture.* Englewood Cliffs, NJ: Prentice Hall.

———. (1998). *Domesticating revolution: From socialist reform to ambivalent transition in a Bulgarian village.* University Park: Pennsylvania State University Press.

Cronk, L. (1991). Human behavioral ecology. *Annual Review of Anthropology, 20,* 25–53.

———. (1999). *That complex whole: Culture and the evolution of human behavior.* Boulder, CO: Westview Press.

Cronk, L., Chagnon, N., & Irons, W. (Eds.). (2000). *Adaptation and human behavior: An anthropological perspective.* New York: Aldine de Gruyter.

Cunningham, W. P., & Saigo, B. W. (1995). *Environmental science, a global concern.* Dubuque, IA: William C Brown.

Curran, J. W., Jaffe, H. W., Hardy, A. M., Morgan, W. M., Selik, R. M., & Dondero, T. J. (1988). Epidemiology of AIDS and HIV infection in the United States. In R. Kulstad (Ed.), *AIDS 1988: American Association for the Advancement of Science Symposia Papers* (pp. 19–34). Washington, DC: AAAS.

Cyriax, R. J. (1939). *Sir John Franklin's last Arctic expedition.* London: Methuen.

Daley, S. (1996). Botswana is pressing Bushmen to leave reserve. *New York Times,* July 14.

Dalton, G. (1972). Peasantries in anthropology and history. *Current Anthropology, 13,* 385–415.

Dao, J. (2003, July 14). A family get-together of historic proportions. *New York Times,* p. A9.

Davis, D. S. (Ed.). (2000). *The consumer revolution in urban China.* Berkeley: University of California Press.

Davis, W., & Henley, T. (Eds.). (1990). *Penan: Voice for the Borneo rainforest.* Vancouver: Western Canada Wilderness Committee.

Dawkins, R. (1995). *River out of Eden: A Darwinian view of life.* New York: Basic Books.

Deb, D. (1996). Of cast net and caste identity: Memetic differentiation between two fishing communities of Karnataka. *Human Ecology 24*(1), 109–124.

Denevan, W., Treacy, J., Alcorn, J., Paddoch, C., Denslow, J., & Paitan, S. (1984). Indigenous agroforestry in the Peruvian Amazon: Bora Indian management of swidden fallows. *Interciencia, 9,* 346–357.

Denham, T. P., Haberle, S. G., Lentfer, C., Fullagar, R., Field, J., Therin, M., Porch, N., & Winsborough, B. (2003). Origins of agriculture at Kuk Swamp in the highlands of New Guinea. *Science, 301*(5630), 189–193.

Denich, B. (1994). Dismembering Yugoslavia: Nationalist ideologies and the symbolic revival of genocide. *American Ethnologist, 21*(2), 367–390.

Dennett, D. C. (1994). *Darwin's dangerous idea: Evolution and the meaning of life.* New York: Simon & Schuster.

Dennett, D. (1996). *Kinds of minds: Toward an understanding of consciousness.* New York: Basic Books (HarperCollins).

DePalme, A. (1998, February 9). Canadian Indians win a ruling vindicating their oral history. *New York Times,* pp. 1, 8.

Diamond, J. (1994). Race without color. *Discover, 15*(11), 82–91.

———. (1999). *Guns, germs, and steel: The fates of human societies.* New York, London: W. W. Norton.

Dillehay, T. D. (2000). *The settlement of the Americas. A new prehistory.* New York: Basic Books.

Divale, W., & Harris, M. (1978). The male supremacist complex: Discovery of a cultural invention. *American Anthropologist, 80,* 668–671.

Dore, R. P. (1994). *Shinohata: A portrait of a Japanese village.* Berkeley and Los Angeles: University of California Press.

Dove, M. R. (1984). The Chayanov slope in a swidden society: Household demography and extensive agriculture in western Kalimantan. In P. Durrenburger (Ed.), *Chayanov, peasants, and economic anthropology* (pp. 97–132). Orlando, FL: Academic Press.

———. (1988). Introduction. In M. R. Dove (Ed.), *The real and imagined role of culture in development: Case studies from Indonesia* (pp. 1–37). Honolulu: University of Hawaii Press.

Downs, J. F. (1965). The social consequences of a dry well. *American Anthropologist, 67,* 1387–1417.

Dozier, E. P. (1970). *The Pueblo Indians of North America.* New York: Holt, Rinehart & Winston.

Draper, P. (1976). Social and economic constraints on child life among the !Kung. In R. B. Lee & I. DeVore (Eds.), *Kalahari hunter-gatherers* (pp. 199–217). Cambridge, MA: Harvard University Press.

Duarte, C., Mauricio, J., Pettitt, P. B., Souto, P., Trinkaus, E., van der Plicht, H., & Zilhão, J. (1999). The early Upper Paleolithic human skeleton from the Abrigo do Lagar Velho (Portugal) and modern human emergence in Iberia. *Proceedings of the National Academy of Science (USA), 96,* 7604–7609.

Dunbar, R. (1997). *Grooming, gossip, and the evolution of language.* Cambridge, MA: Harvard University Press.

Duranti, A. (1994). *From grammar to politics: Linguistic anthropology in a western Samoan village.* Berkeley and Los Angeles: University of California Press.

Durham, E. (1987). *High Albania.* Boston: Beacon.

Durham, W. H. (1991). *Coevolution: Genes, culture, and human diversity.* Stanford, CA: Stanford University Press.

Durkheim, E. (1964). *The division of labor in society.* New York: Free Press.

Durrenberger, P. (Ed.). (1984). *Chayanov, peasants, and economic anthropology.* Orlando, FL: Academic Press.

Dyson-Hudson, N., & Dyson-Hudson, R. (1982). The structure of East African herds and the future of East African herders. *Development and Change, 13,* 213–238.

Dyson-Hudson, R. (1988). Ecology of nomadic Turkana pastoralists: A discussion. In E. Whitehead, C. Hutchinson, B. Timmerman, & R. Varady (Eds.), *Arid lands: Today and tomorrow* (pp. 701–703). Boulder, CO: Westview Press.

Dyson-Hudson, R., & Smith, E. A. (1978). Human territoriality. *American Anthropologist, 80,* 21–42.

Eakin, E. (2002, May 18). Before the word, perhaps the wink? *New York Times,* pp. A13, B8.

Earle, T. (Ed.). (1991). *Chiefdoms: Power, economy and ideology.* Cambridge: Cambridge University Press.

Eder, J. F. (1996). Batak foraging camps today: A window to the history of a hunting-gathering economy. In D. G. Bates & S. H. Lees (Eds.), *Case studies in human ecology* (pp. 85–102). New York: Plenum Press.

Eggan, F. (1950). *Social organization of the Western Pueblo.* Chicago: University of Chicago Press.

Ember, C. R. (1978). Myths about hunter-gatherers. *Ethnology, 17*(4), 439–448.

Ember, M., Ember, C., & Levinson, D. (Eds.). (1994). *Portraits of culture.* Englewood Cliffs, NJ: Prentice Hall.

Erlanger, S. (2000, May 5). In East and Central Europe, "family downsizing" to shrink populations. *International Herald Tribune,* p. 13.

Escobar, A. (1991). Anthropology and the development encounter: The making and marketing of development anthropology. *American Ethnologist, 18*(4), 658–682.

———. (1994). Welcome to "Cyberia." *Current Anthropology 18*(3), 38–45.

Eshleman J. R. (2003). *The family* (10th ed.). Boston: Allyn & Bacon.

Estioko-Griffin, A., & Griffin, P. B. (1981). Woman the hunter: The Agta. In F. Dahlberg (Ed.), *Woman the gatherer* (pp. 121–151). New Haven, CT: Yale University Press.

Etienne, M., & Leacock, E. (Eds.). (1988). *Women and colonization: Anthropological perspectives.* South Hadley, MA: Bergin & Garvey.

Evans-Pritchard, E. E. (1940). *The Nuer: A description of the modes of livelihood and political institutions of a Nilotic people.* Oxford: Clarendon Press.

Fagan, B. M. (1992). *People of the Earth: An introduction to world prehistory* (7th ed.). New York: HarperCollins College.

Fagan, B. (2004). *Ancient lives. An introduction to archaeology and prehistory* (2nd ed.). Upper Saddle River, NJ: Pearson, Prentice Hall.

Farley, R. (1993). The common destiny of blacks and whites: Observations about social and economic status of the race. In H. Hill & J. E. Jones (Eds.), *Race in America: The struggle for equality* (pp. 197–233). Madison: University of Wisconsin Press.

Feder, B. J. (1994, March 7). Big decisions before spring planting. *New York Times,* p. D1.

Feinberg, R. (1988). Margaret Mead and Samoa: Coming of age in fact and fiction. *American Anthropologist, 90,* 656–663.

Feinman, G., & Nicholas, P. (1992). Prehispanic interregional interaction in southern Mexico: The Valley of Oaxaca and the Ejutla Valley. In E. M. Schortman & P. A. Urban (Eds.), *Resources, power, and interregional interaction* (pp. 77–114). New York: Plenum Press.

Feit, H. A. (1994). The enduring pursuit: Land, time and social relationships in anthropological models of hunter-gatherers and in subarctic hunters' images. In E. S. Burch, Jr., & L. J. Ellanna (Eds.), *Key issues in hunter-gatherer research* (pp. 421–439). Providence, RI: Berg Publishers.

Ferguson, B. R. (Ed.). (1984). *Warfare, culture, and environment.* New York: Academic Press.

———. (1992). Tribal warfare. *Scientific American, 256*(1), 108–113.

———. (1995a). A reputation for war. *Natural History, 104*(4).

———. (1995b). *Yanomamö warfare: A political history.* Santa Fe, NM: SAR Press.

Fiege, M., & Cronon, W. (1999). *Irrigated Eden: The making of an environmental landscape in the American West.* Seattle: Weyerhaeuser Environmental Books.

Fisher, H. E. (1987). The four-year itch: Do divorce patterns reflect our evolutionary heritage? *Natural History, 10,* 22–33.

Flannery, T. (2001). *The eternal frontier: An ecological history of North America.* Boston: Atlantic Monthly Press.

Flowers, N. M. (1988). The Spread of AIDS in rural Brazil. In R. Kulstad (Ed.), *AIDS 1988: American Association for the Advancement of Science Symposia Papers* (pp. 159–168). Washington, DC: AAAS.

Flowers, N., Gross, D., Ritter, M., & Werner, D. (1975). Protein capture and cultural development in the Amazon. *American Anthropologist, 3,* 526–549.

———. (1982). Variation in swidden practices in four central Brazilian Indian societies. *Human Ecology, 10,* 203–217.

Fondahl, G. (1998). Gaining ground? Evenkis, land, and reform in southeastern Siberia. In *Cultural survival studies in ethnicity and change.* Boston: Allyn & Bacon.

Ford, R. I. (1972). An ecological perspective on the Eastern Pueblos. In A. Ortiz (Ed.), *New perspectives on the Pueblos.* Albuquerque: University of New Mexico Press.

Fowler, B. (2002, January 15). Expert says he discerns "hardwired" grammar rules. *New York Times,* p. F5.

Fox, R. (1994a, March). Evil wrought in the name of good. *Anthropology Newsletter,* p. 2.

———. (1994b). *The challenge of anthropology: Old encounters and new excursions.* New Brunswick, NJ: Transaction Publishers.

Frank, A. G. (1969). *Capitalism and underdevelopment in Latin America.* New York: Monthly Review Press.

———. (1998). *ReOrient: Global economy in the Asian age.* Berkeley: University of California Press.

Fratkin, E. (1991a). *Surviving drought and development: Ariaal pastoralists of northern Kenya.* Boulder, CO: Westview Press.

———. (1991b). Surviving drought and development. Ariaal pastoralists of Kenya. *Human Ecology, 23*(3).

———. (1997). Pastoralism—governance and development issues. *Annual Review of Anthropology, 26,* 235–261.

———. (1998). *Ariaal pastoralists of northern Kenya: Surviving drought and development in Africa's arid lands.* Boston: Allyn & Bacon.

Fratkin, E., Galvin, K., & Roth, E. A. (1994). *African pastoralist systems: An integrated approach.* Boulder, CO: L. Reinner Publishers.

Fratkin, E., & Roth, E. A. (1996). Who survives drought? Measuring winners and losers among the Ariaal Rendille pastoralists of Kenya. In D. G. Bates & S. H. Lees (Eds.), *Case studies in human ecology* (pp. 159–174). New York: Plenum Press.

Fratkin, E. M., Roth, E. A., & Nathan, M. A. (1999). When nomads settle: The effects of commoditization, nutritional change, and formal education on Ariaal and Rendille pastoralists. *Current Anthropology, 40*(5), 729–735.

Frayer, D. W., Wolpoff, M. H., Thorne, A. G., & Pope, G. G. (1994). Getting it straight. *American Anthropologist, 96*(2), 424–438.

Freeman, D. (1983). *Margaret Mead and Samoa: The making and unmaking of an anthropological myth.* Cambridge, MA: Harvard University Press.

Freeman, J. D. (1961). On the concept of the kindred. *Journal of the Royal Anthropological Institute, 91,* 192–220.

Freeman, M. M. R. (1971). A social and ecological analysis of systematic female infanticide among the Netsilik Eskimo. *American Anthropologist, 73,* 1011–1019.

Freeman, M. M. R., Bogoslovskaya, L., & Caulfield, R. A. (1998). *Inuit, whaling, and sustainability* (Contemporary Native American Communities Series). Thousand Oaks, CA: Sage Publications.

French, H. W. (2003, July 26). Insular Japan needs, but resists, immigration. *New York Times,* pp. 1, 3.

Fricke, T. (1994). *Himalayan households.* New York: Columbia University Press.

Fricke, T., Thornton, A., & Dahal, D. R. (1998). Netting in Nepal: Social change, the life course, and brideservice in Sangila. *Human Ecology, 26*(2), 213–237.

Fromkin, V., & Rodman, R. (1988). *An introduction to linguistics* (4th ed.). New York: Holt, Rinehart & Winston.

Fromkin, V., Rodman, R., & Hyams, N. (2002). *An introduction to language* (7th ed.). Boston: Heinle.

Galaty, J. G. (1994). Rangeland tenure and pastoralism in Africa. In E. Fratkin, K. Galvin, & E. A. Roth (Eds.), *African pastoralist systems: An integrated approach* (pp. 185–204). Boulder, CO: L. Rienner Publishers.

Gardner, A., & Gardner, B. (1969). Teaching sign language to a chimpanzee. *Science, 165,* 664–672.

Geertz, C. (1969). Two types of ecosystems. In A. P. Vayda (Ed.), *Environment and cultural behavior.* New York: Natural History Press.

Giampietro, M., Bukkens, S. F., & Pimientel, D. (1993). Labor productivity: A biophysical definition and assessment. *Human Ecology, 21,* 229–260.

Gibbons, A. (2003). Oldest members of *Homo sapiens* discovered in Africa. *Science, 300*(5626), p. 1641.

Gilmore, D. D. (1987). *Aggression and community: Paradoxes of Andalusian culture.* New Haven, CT: Yale University Press.

———. (1990). *Manhood in the making: The cultural construction of masculinity.* New Haven, CT: Yale University Press.

———. (1991). Subjectivity and subjugation: Fieldwork in the stratified community. *Human Organization, 50,* 215–224.

———. (1994). The "mayete" as object and stereotype in Andalusian proletarian poetry. *Ethnology, 33*(4), 353–365.

———. (1998). *Carnival and culture: Sex, symbol and status in Spain.* New Haven, CT: Yale University Press.

———. (2001). *Misogyny.* Philadelphia: University of Pennsylvania Press.

———. (2003). *Monsters: Evil beings, mythical beasts, and all manner of imaginary terrors*. Philadelphia: University of Pennsylvania Press.

Ginguld, M., Perevolotsky, A., & Ungar, E. D. (1997). Living on the margins: Livelihood strategies of Bedouin herd-owners in the northern Negev, Israel. *Human Ecology, 25*(4), 567–591.

Gladwin, C., & Butler, J. (1982). Gardening: A survival strategy for the small, part-time Florida farm. *Proceedings Florida State Horticultural Society, 95,* 264–268.

Glantz, M. H. (1994a). Creeping environmental phenomena: Are societies equipped to deal with them? In M. H. Glantz (Ed.), *Workshop report on creeping environmental phenomena and societal responses to them* (pp. 1–10). Boulder, CO: National Center for Atmospheric Research.

Goebel, T., Waters, M. R., & Dikova, M. (2003). The archaeology of Ushki Lake, Kamchatka, and the Pleistocene peopling of the Americas. *Science, 301*(5632), 501–505.

Goldschmidt, W. (1947). *As you saw.* New York: Harcourt, Brace.

———. (1971). *Exploring the ways of mankind.* New York: Holt, Rinehart & Winston.

Good, K. (1995). The Yanomamö keep on trekking. *Natural History, 104*(4).

Gorkin, M. (1993). *Days of honey, days of onion: The story of a Palestinian family in Israel.* Berkeley and Los Angeles: University of California Press.

Gorman, P. (1994). A people at risk. In E. Angeloni (Ed.), *Annual editions: Anthropology.* Guilford, CT: Dushkin Publishers.

Gottesfeld Johnson, L. M. (1994). Aboriginal burning for vegetation management in northwest British Columbia. *Human Ecology, 22,* 171–188.

Gould, J. L., & Marler, P. (1987). Learning by instinct. *Scientific American, 256,* 74–85.

Gould, S. J. (1986). Cardboard Darwinism: This view of life. *Natural History, 95,* 14–21.

———. (1989). Tires to sandals: This view of life. *Natural History 98,* 8–16.

———. (1994, October 20). So near and yet so far. *New York Review of Books,* pp. 229–260.

———. (1996a, December). The Diet of Worms and the defenestration of Prague. *Natural History,* pp. 18–65.

———. (1996b, October). Creating the creature. *Discover,* pp. 43–54.

Greenberg, J. (1993). *Language in America.* Palo Alto, CA: Stanford University Press.

Grigg, D. B. (1974). *The agricultural systems of the world: An evolutionary approach.* Cambridge: Cambridge University Press.

Gross, D. R. (1983). Village movement in relation to resources in Amazonia. In R. B. Hames & W. T. Vickers (Eds.), *Adaptive responses of Native Amazonians* (pp. 429–499). New York: Academic Press.

———. (1984). Time allocation: A tool for the study of cultural behavior. *Annual Review of Anthropology, 13,* 519–558.

Gross, D. R., & Underwood, B. A. (1971). Technological change and caloric costs: Sisal agriculture in northeastern Brazil. *American Anthropologist, 73,* 725–740.

Hammel, H. A. (1994). Meeting the Minotaur. *Anthropology Newsletter, 36*(4).

Harlan, J. (1967). A wild wheat harvest in Turkey. *Archaeology, 20*(3), 197–201.

Harris, M. (1984). A cultural materialist theory of band and village warfare: The Yanomamö test. In B. R. Ferguson (Ed.), *Warfare, culture, and environment* (pp. 111–140). New York: Academic Press.

———. (1987). Comment on Vayda's review of good to eat: Riddles of food and culture. *Human Ecology, 15,* 511–518.

Hart, T. B., & Hart, J. A. (1996). The ecological basis of hunter-gatherer subsistence in African rain forests: The Mbuti of eastern Zaire. In D. G. Bates & S. H. Lees (Eds.), *Case studies in human ecology* (pp. 55–83). New York: Plenum Press.

Hayden, B. (1994). Competition, labor and complex hunter-gatherers. In E. S. Burch, Jr., & L. J. Ellanna (Eds.), *Key issues in hunter-gatherer research* (pp. 223–239). Providence, RI: Berg Publishers.

Headland, T. (1987). The wild yam question: How well could independent hunter-gatherers live in a tropical forest ecosystem? *Human Ecology, 15,* 463–492.

Hemley, R. (2003). *Invented Eden: The elusive, disputed history of the Tasaday.* New York: Farrar, Straus, Giroux.

Hernstein, R. J., & Murray, C. (1994). *The bell curve: Intelligence and class structure in American life.* New York: Free Press.

Herskovits, M. (1924). A preliminary consideration of the cultural areas of Africa. *American Anthropologist, 26,* 50–63.

Hertzberg, H. T. E. (1989). Engineering anthropology: Past, present, and potential. In A. Podolefsky & P. J. Brown (Eds.), *Applying anthropology: An introductory reader.* Mountain View, CA: Mayfield Press.

Hessel, I. (2003). *Inuit art: An introduction.* Vancouver: Douglas & McIntyre.

Hill, K., Hawkes, K., Hurtado, M., & Kaplan, H. (1984). Seasonal variance in the diet of the Ache hunter-gatherers in eastern Paraguay. *Human Ecology, 12,* 101–136.

Hill, K., & Hurtado, A. M. (1996). *Ache life history: The ecology and demography of a foraging people* (Foundations of Human Behavior). New York: Aldine de Gruyter.

Hill, R., & Baird, A. (2003). Kuku-Yalanji rainforest aboriginal people and carbohydrate resource management in the wet tropics of Queensland, Australia. *Human Ecology, 31*(1), 27–52.

Hoebel, E. A. (1954). *The law of primitive man.* Cambridge, MA: Harvard University Press.

Holden, C. (2003). Dates boost conventional wisdom about Solomon's splendor. *Science, 300*(5617), 229–230.

Hole, F., Flannery, K. V., & Neely, J. A. (1969). *Prehistory and human ecology of the Deh Luran Plain* (Memoirs of the Museum of Anthropology, University of Michigan, Anthropological Papers No. 1). Ann Arbor: University of Michigan.

Holling, C. S. (1973). Resilience and stability of ecological systems. *Annual Review of Ecology and Systematics, 4,* 1–23.

Hopkins, N. (1983). The social impact of mechanization. In A. Richards & P. L. Martin (Eds.), *Migration, mechanization, and agricultural labor markets in Egypt* (pp. 181–197). Boulder, CO: Westview Press.

Hopkins, N. S., Mehanna, S. R., & el-Haggar, S. (2001). *People and pollution: Cultural constructions and social action in Egypt.* Cairo and New York: The American University in Cairo Press.

Hopkins, N. S., & Westergaard, K. (Eds.). (1998). *Directions of change in rural Egypt.* Cairo: The American University in Cairo Press.

Horgan, J. (1988). The violent Yanomamö: Science and citizen. *Scientific American, 255,* 17–18.

Horowitz, D. (1985). *Ethnic groups in conflict.* Berkeley and Los Angeles: University of California Press.

Horowitz, M. (1994). Development anthropology in the mid-1990s. *Development Anthropology Newsletter, 12*(1, 2), 1–14.

Howell, N. (1976). *Normal selection rates of the demographic patterns of the !Kung San.* Paper presented at the meeting of the American Anthropological Association, Washington, DC.

———. (1979). *Demography of the Dobe !Kung.* New York: Academic Press.

———. (1990). *Surviving fieldwork: A report of the Advisory Panel on Health and Safety in Fieldwork.* Washington, DC: American Anthropological Association.

Hrdy, S. B. (2000). *Mother Nature: A history of mothers, infants, and natural selection.* New York: Museum of Natural History.

Hua, C. (2001). *A society without fathers or husbands: The Na of China.* (Translated from the French by Asti Hustvedt.) Sydney: Zone Books.

Hudak, A. T. (1999). Rangeland mismanagement in South Africa: Failure to apply ecological knowledge. *Human Ecology, 27*(1), 55–78.

Hultkrantz, A. (1994). Religion and ecology of northern Eurasian/Siberian peoples. In T. Irimoto & T. Yamada (Eds.), *Circumpolar religion and ecology* (pp. 347–374). Tokyo: University of Tokyo Press.

Humphries, S. (1993). The intensification of traditional agriculture among Yucatec Maya farmers: Facing up to the dilemma of livelihood sustainability. *Human Ecology, 21,* 87–102.

Hurd, J. P. (Ed.). (1999). *The significance of evolutionary biology for research on human altruism.* Lewiston, NY: Edwin Mellen Press.

Ingold, T. (1980). *Hunters, pastoralists, and ranchers.* Cambridge: Cambridge University Press.

International Energy Agency. (2001). *Toward a sustainable energy future.* Vienna.

Ireton, F. (1998). The evolution of agrarian structures in Egypt: Regional patterns of change in farm size. In N. S. Hopkins & K. Westergaard (Eds.), *Directions of change in rural Egypt.* Cairo: The American University in Cairo Press.

Irons, W. (1975). *The Yomut Turkmen: A study of social organization among a Central Asian Turkic-speaking population* (Anthropological Papers No. 58). Ann Arbor: University of Michigan, Museum of Anthropology.

———. (1979). Natural selection, adaptation and human social behavior. N. A. Chagnon & W. G. Irons (Eds.), *Evolution, biology and human social behavior.* North Scituate, MA: Duxbury Press.

———. (1991). How did morality evolve? *Zygon: Journal of Religion and Science, 26,* 49–89.

———. (1995). Morality as an evolved adaptation. In J. P. Hurd (Ed.), *The biology of morality.* Lewiston, NY: Edwin Mellen Press.

Jablonka, E., & Avital, E. (1995, January 3). Heredity's more than genes, new theory proposes. *New York Times,* pp. B13ff.

Johnson, G. A. (1983). Decision-making organization and pastoral nomad camp size. *Human Ecology, 11,* 175–200.

Johnson, P. L. (1988). Women and development: A highland New Guinea example. *Human Ecology, 16,* 105–122.

———. (1996). Changing household composition, labor patterns, and fertility of a highland New Guinea population. In D. G. Bates, & S. H. Lees (Eds.), *Case studies in human ecology* (pp. 237–250). New York: Plenum Press.

Johnston, B. R. (1994). *Who pays the price: The sociocultural context of environmental crisis.* Washington, DC: Island Press.

Jolly, C. J., & White, R. (1995). *Physical anthropology* (5th ed.). New York: McGraw-Hill.

Kehoe, A. B. (2003). *America before the European Invasions.* Boston: Longman/Pearson Education.

Kemp, W. B. (1971). The flow of energy in a hunting society. *Scientific American, 225,* 104–115.

Khaldun, I. (1958). *The Muqaddimah: An introduction to history* (Vol. 1) (F. Rosenthal, Trans.). London: Kegan Paul. (First published A.D. 1377)

Kili, S. (1991). *Modernity and tradition: Dilemmas concerning women's rights in Turkey.* Paper presented at the annual meeting of the International Society of Political Psychology, Helsinki.

Kirch, P. V. (1994). *The wet and the dry: Irrigation and agricultural intensification.* Chicago: University of Chicago Press.

Klare, M. (2001, September 20). The next move: War is neither the best, nor the only way to bring down Osama bin Laden. *Valley Advocate* (Springfield, MA).

Klein, R. G. (2003). Whither the Neanderthals? *Science, 299*(5612), 1525–1527.

Kolata, G. (2001, May 27). Putting your faith in science? *New York Times,* Section 4, p. 2.

Konner, M. (1983). *The tangled web.* New York: Harper & Row.

———. (1988, August 14). Body and mind: The aggressors. *New York Times Magazine,* pp. 33–34.

Kramer, M. (1987). *Three farms: Making milk, meat, and money from the American soil.* Cambridge, MA: Harvard University Press.

Kroeber, A. L., & Kluckhohn, C. (1952). *Culture: A critical review of concepts and definitions.* New York: Knopf.

Kwong, P. (1994, October 17). China's human traffickers. *The Nation,* pp. 422–425.

Laderman, C. (1983). *Wives and midwives: Childbirth and nutrition in rural Malaysia.* Berkeley and Los Angeles: University of California Press.

Lancaster, W. (1997). *The Rwala Bedouin today* (2nd ed.). Prospect Heights, IL: Waveland Press.

Lansing, S. J. (1991). *Priests and programmers: Technologies of power in the engineered landscape of Bali.* Princeton, NJ: Princeton University Press.

———. (1995). The Balinese. In G. Spindler & L. Spindler (Eds.), *Case studies in cultural anthropology*. Fort Worth, TX: Harcourt Brace College.

Lardy, N. R. (1985). State intervention and peasant opportunities. In W. L. Parish (Ed.), *Chinese rural development: The great transformation* (pp. 33–56). Armonk, NY: M. E. Sharpe.

Lee, R. B. (1968). What hunters do for a living, or, how to make out on scarce resources. In R. B. Lee & I. DeVore (Eds.), *Man the hunter*. Chicago: Aldine.

———. (1969). !Kung Bushmen subsistence: An input–output analysis. In A. P. Vayda (Ed.), *Environment and cultural behavior*. New York: Natural History Press.

———. (1979). *The !Kung San*. Cambridge: Cambridge University Press.

———. (1993). *The Dobe Ju/'hoansi*. Fort Worth, TX: Harcourt Brace College.

Lee, R. B., & Daly, R. (Eds.). (2000). *The Cambridge encyclopedia of hunters and gatherers*. Cambridge: Cambridge University Press.

Lee, R. B., & DeVore, I. (Eds.). (1968). *Man the hunter*. Chicago: Aldine.

———. (1976). *Kalahari hunter-gatherers: Studies of the !Kung-San and their neighbors*. Cambridge, MA: Harvard University Press.

Lees, S. H. (1994). Irrigation and society. *Journal of Archeological Research, 2*(4), 361–378.

Leslie, P. W., & Fry, P. H. (1989). Extreme seasonality of births among nomadic Turkana pastoralists. *American Journal of Physical Anthropology 16*(2), 126–135.

Leslie, P. W., Fry, P. H., Galvin, K., & McCabe, J. T. (1988). Biological, behavioral, and ecological influences on fertility in Turkana pastoralists. In E. Whitehead & C. Hutchinson (Eds.), *Arid lands: Today and tomorrow* (pp. 705–726). Boulder, CO: Westview Press.

Lewicki, T. (1974). *West African food in the Middle Ages*. Cambridge: Cambridge University Press.

Lewellen, T. C. (1992). *Political anthropology: An introduction* (2nd ed.). Westport, CT: Bergin & Garvey.

Lewis, P. (1993, November 10). Stoked by ethnic conflict: Refugee numbers swell. *New York Times*, p. A6.

Lewis, R. L. (1987). *Black coal miners in America: Race, class, and community conflict, 1790–1980*. Lexington: University Press of Kentucky.

Lewis-Williams, D. (2002). *The mind in the cave*. London: Thames and Hudson.

Lightfoot, D. (1993). The cultural ecology of Puebloan pebble-mulch gardens. *Human Ecology, 21*(2), 115–144.

Little, M. A. (1988). Introduction to the symposium: The ecology of the nomadic Turkana pastoralists. In E. E. Whitehead, C. F. Hutchinson, B. N. Timmerman, & R. G. Vardy (Eds.), *Arid lands today and tomorrow: Proceedings of an international research and development conference* (pp. 696–734). Boulder, CO: Westview Press.

Little, M. A., Dyson-Hudson, R., Ellis, J. E., Galvin, K. A., Leslie, P. W., & Swift, D. M. (1990). Ecosystem approaches in human biology: Their history and a case study of the South Turkana Ecosystem project. In E. F. Moran (Ed.), *The ecosystem approach in anthropology: From concept to practice* (pp. 389–434). Ann Arbor: University of Michigan Press.

Little, M. A., Galvin, K., & Leslie, P. W. (1988). Health and energy requirements of nomadic Turkana pastoralists. In I. de-Garine & G. A. Harrison (Eds.), *Coping with uncertainty in food supply* (pp. 288–315). Oxford: Oxford University Press.

Litvin, D. (2003). *Empires of profit: Commerce, conquest and corporate responsibility*. Houston: Texere.

Lizot, J. (1994). On warfare: An answer to N. A. Chagnon. *American Ethnologist, 21*, 841–858.

Loker, W. M. (1999) Grit in the prosperity machine. In W. M. Loker (Ed.), *Globalization and the rural poor in Latin America*. Boulder, CO: L. Rienner Publishers.

Lorenz, K. (1965). *Evolution and modification of behavior*. Chicago: University of Chicago Press.

Lowie, R. H. (1954). *Indians of the Plains*. New York: McGraw-Hill.

MacDonald, K. I. (1998). Rationality, representation, and the risk mediating characteristics of a Karakoram Mountain farming system. *Human Ecology, 26*(2), 287–321.

Madikwe Development Task Team. (1994). *Madikwe Game Reserve Management*. Rustenburg, South Africa.

Mahdi, M. (1971). *Ibn Khaldun's philosophy of history*. Chicago: University of Chicago Press.

Malinowski, B. (1927). *Sex and repression in savage society*. London: Routledge & Kegan Paul.

———. (1931). Culture. In *Encyclopedia of the social sciences* (Vol. 4). New York: Macmillan.

———. (1954). *Magic, science, and religion and other essays*. Garden City, NY: Anchor/Doubleday.

———. (1961). *Argonauts of the Western Pacific*. New York: Dutton. (First published 1922.)

Marks, J. (1994). Black, white, other. *Natural History, 103*, 32–35.

———. (1995). *Human biodiversity: Genes, race and history*. Hawthorne, NY: Aldine de Gruyter.

Marshall, L. (1960). !Kung Bushmen bands. *Africa, 30*, 325–354.

———. (1961). Sharing, talking, and giving: Relief of social tensions among !Kung Bushmen. *Africa, 31*, 233–249.

———. (1965). The !Kung Bushmen of the Kalahari Desert. In J. L. Gibbs, Jr. (Ed.), *Peoples of Africa*. New York: Holt, Rinehart & Winston.

Marx, E. (1999). Oases in south Sinai. *Human Ecology, 27*(2), 341–357.

Maybury-Lewis, D. (1992). *Millennium: Tribal wisdom and the modern world*. New York: Viking Penguin.

———. (1997). Indigenous peoples, ethnic groups, and the state. *Cultural Survival studies in ethnicity and change*. Boston: Allyn & Bacon.

McCabe, J. T., Perkin, S., & Schofield, C. (1992). Can conservation and development be coupled among pastoral people? An examination of the Maasai of the Ngorongoro Conservation Area, Tanzania. *Human Organization, 51*(4), 353–366.

McCorriston, J., & Hole, F. (1991). The ecology of seasonal stress and the origins of agriculture in the Near East. *American Anthropologist, 93*, 46–69.

McDaniel, J. (2002). Confronting the structure of international development: Political agency and the Chiquitanos of Bolivia. *Human Ecology, 30*(3), 369–396.

McGovern, T., Bigelow, G., Amorosi, T., & Russell, D. (1996). Northern islands, human error, and environmental degradation. In D. G. Bates & S. H. Lees (Eds.), *Case studies in human ecology* (pp. 103–152). New York: Plenum Press.

McGovern, T. H. (1980). Cows, harp seals, and churchbells: Adaptation and extinction on Norse Greenland. *Human Ecology, 8,* 245–276.

McGovern, T. H., Bigelow, G., Amorosi, T., & Russell, D. (1988). Northern islands, human error, and environmental degradation. *Human Ecology, 8,* 225–270.

McMillan, D. E. (1995). *Sahel visions: Planned settlement and river blindness control in Burkina Faso.* Tucson: University of Arizona Press.

McNeil, D. G., Jr. (1997, November 13). In Bushmanland, hunters' tradition turns to dust. *New York Times,* A1, B4.

Mead, M. (1935). *Sex and temperament in three primitive societies.* New York: William Morrow.

———. (1949). *Male and female.* New York: William Morrow.

———. (1956). *New lives for old: Cultural transformation—Manus, 1928–1953.* New York: Morrow.

———. (1971). *Coming of age in Samoa.* New York: Morrow. (First published 1928.)

———. (1975). *Blackberry winter.* New York: Random House.

Mearns, R. (1996). Community, collective action and common grazing: The case of post-socialist Mongolia. *Journal of Development Studies, 32*(3), 297–339.

Meir, A. (1997). *As nomadism ends: The Israeli Bedouin of the Negev.* Boulder, CO: Westview Press.

Micklin, P. P. (1988). Desiccation of the Aral Sea: A water management disaster in the Soviet Union. *Science, 241*(1), 170–171, 175.

Milan, F. (1970). The demography of an Alaskan Eskimo village. *Arctic Anthropology, 71,* 26–43.

Milliken, W., & Albert, B., with Gomez, G. G. (1999). *Yanomami: A forest people.* Kew, UK.: The Royal Botanic Gardens.

Milton, K. (1985). Ecological foundations for subsistence strategies among the Mbuti Pygmies. *Human Ecology, 13,* 71–78.

Mitchell, T. (1998). The market's place. In N. S. Hopkins & K. Westergaard (Eds.), *Directions of change in rural Egypt.* Cairo: The American University in Cairo Press.

Moorehead, A. (1963). *Cooper's Creek.* New York: Harper & Row.

Moran, E. F. (1990). Ecosystem ecology in biology and anthropology: A critical assessment. In E. F. Moran (Ed.), *The ecosystem approach in anthropology: From concept to practice* (pp. 3–40). Ann Arbor: University of Michigan Press.

———. (1990). Levels of analysis and analytical level shifting: Examples from Amazonian ecosystem research. In E. F. Moran (Ed.), *The ecosystem approach in anthropology: From concept to practice* (pp. 279–308). Ann Arbor: University of Michigan Press.

———. (1993). Deforestation and land use in the Brazilian Amazon. *Human Ecology, 21,* 1–21.

Morren, G. E. B., & Hyndam, D. C. (1987). The taro monoculture of central New Guinea. *Human Ecology, 15,* 301–315.

Moses, Y. (1997). An idea whose time has come again: Anthropology reclaims race. *Anthropology Newsletter, 38,* 1, 4.

Moynihan, D. P. (1993). *Pandaemonium: Ethnicity in international politics.* New York: Oxford University Press.

Müller-Mahn, D. (1998). Spaces of poverty: The geography of social change in rural Egypt. In N. S. Hopkins & K. Westergaard (Eds.), *Directions of change in rural Egypt.* Cairo: The American University in Cairo Press.

Murphy, Y., & Murphy, R. F. (1985). *Women of the forest* (2nd ed). New York: Columbia University Press.

Mydans, S. (1997, April 6). Scientists developing "super rice" to feed Asia. *New York Times* International edition, p. 9.

Nash. J. (n.d.). *The revindication of indigenous identity: Mayan responses to state intervention in Mexico.* Unpublished paper.

Nash, M. (1966). *Primitive and peasant economic systems.* San Francisco: Chandler.

Nathan, M. A., Fratkin, E. M., & Roth, E. A. (1996). Sedentism and child health among Rendille pastoralists of northern Kenya. *Social Science and Medicine, 43*(4), 503–515.

Nations, J. D. (1994). Zapatism and nationalism. *Cultural Survival Quarterly, 18*(1), 31–33.

Netting, R. M., Stone, P. M., & Stone, G. D. (1996). Kofyar cash-cropping: Choice and change in indigenous agricultural development. In D. G. Bates & S. H. Lees (Eds.), *Case studies in human ecology.* New York: Plenum Press.

Nietschmann, B. (1995). Defending the Miskito Reefs with maps and GPS. *Cultural Survival Quarterly* (Winter), 34–37.

Noble, D. (1984). *The forces of production.* New York: Knopf.

Nolan, R. (2002). *Development anthropology: Encounters in the real world.* Boulder, CO: Westview Press.

Nugent, D. (1994). Building the state, making the nation: The bases and limits of state centralization in "modern Peru." *American Ethnologist, 96,* 333–369.

Oates, J. F. (1999). *Myth and reality in the rain forest: How conservation strategies are failing in West Africa.* Berkeley: University of California Press.

Oboler, R. S. (1996). Whose cows are they anyway? Ideology and behavior in Nandi cattle ownership and control. *Human Ecology, 24*(2), 255–272.

Odum, H. T. (1971). *Environment, power, and society.* New York: Wiley-Interscience.

———. (1992). *Energy and public policy.* New York: Wiley-Interscience.

Özesmi, U. (2003). The ecological economics of harvesting sharp-pointed rush (*Juncus acutus*) in the Kizilirmak Delta, Turkey. *Human Ecology, 31*(4), 645–655.

Parish, W. L. (1985). Introduction: Historical background and current issues. In W. L. Parish (Ed.), *Chinese rural development: The great transformation* (pp. 3–32). Armonk, NY: M. E. Sharpe.

Parker, R. G. (1988). Sexual culture and AIDS education in urban Brazil. In R. Kulstad (Ed.), *AIDS 1988: American Association for the Advancement of Science Symposia Papers* (pp. 169–174). Washington, DC: AAAS.

Pasternak, B., Ember, C., & Ember, M. (1997). *Sex, gender, and kinship: A cross-cultural perspective.* Upper Saddle River, NJ: Prentice Hall.

Pasternak, B., & Salaff, J. (1993). *Cowboys and cultivators: The Chinese of Inner Mongolia.* Boulder, CO: Westview Press.

Peacock, J. (1995). Claiming common ground. *Anthropology Newsletter, 36*(4), 1, 3.

Peacock, N. (1984). The Mbuti of northeast Zaire: Women and subsistence exchange. *Cultural Survival Quarterly, 8,* 15–17.

Peet, R., & Watts, M. (1994). Introduction: Development theory and environmentalism in an age of market triumphalism. *Economic Geography, 69*(3), 227–253.

Pennish, E. (2003). Cannibalism and prion disease may have been rampant in ancient humans. *Science, 300*(5617), 227–228.

Peters, J. F. (1998). *Life among the Yanomami.* Ontario: Broadview Press.

Petkov, K., & Fotev, G. (1990). *Ethnic conflict in Bulgaria, 1989: Sociological archive.* (In Bulgarian with English summary.) Sofia: Profizdat.

Piaget, J. (1954). *The construction of reality in the child.* New York: Basic Books.

Pianka, E. R. (1974). *Evolutionary biology.* New York: Harper & Row.

Pinker, S. (1994). *The language instinct: How the mind creates language.* New York: HarperCollins.

———. (1999). *Words and rules: The ingredients of language.* New York: Basic Books.

———. (2002). *The blank slate: The modern denial of human nature.* New York: Viking Press.

Poggie, J. J., DeWalt, B. R., & Dressler, W. W. (1992). *Anthropological research: Process and application.* Albany: State University of New York Press.

Pojman, L. P. (1995). *Ethics: Discovering right and wrong.* Belmont, CA: Wadsworth.

Poole, P. (1995). Geomatics: Who needs it? *Cultural Survival Quarterly, 18*(4), 1.

Popkin, S. (1979). *The rational peasant.* Berkeley and Los Angeles: University of California Press.

Posey, D. (1983). Indigenous ecological knowledge and development. In E. Moran (Ed.), *The dilemma of Amazonian development* (pp. 225–257). Boulder, CO: Westview Press.

———. (1984). Ethnoecology as applied anthropology in Amazonian development. *Human Organization, 43,* 95–107.

Potkanski, T. (1993). Decollectivisation of the Mongolian pastoral economy (1991–92): Some economic and social consequences. *Nomadic Peoples, 33,* 123–135.

Price, D. (1981). Complexity in non-complex societies. In S. E. van der Leeuw (Ed.), *Archaeological approaches to the study of complex society* (pp. 57–97). Amsterdam: University of Amsterdam's Albert van Giffen Institute for Prehistory.

Price, T. D., & Feinman, G. (1997). *Images of the past.* Mountain View, CA: Mayfield Press.

Prince, A., & Smolensky, P. (1997, March 14). Optimality: From neural net to universal grammar. *Science, 275,* 1604–1610.

Pringle, H. (1997, February 14). Death in Norse Greenland. *Science, 175,* 924–926.

Rabben, L. (1993). Demarcation and then what? *Cultural Survival Quarterly, 17*(2), 12–14.

Rappaport, R. A. (1967). Ritual regulation of environmental relations among a New Guinea people. *Ethnology, 6,* 17–30.

———. (1968). *Pigs for the ancestors: Ritual in the ecology of a New Guinea people.* New Haven, CT: Yale University Press.

———. (1979). *Ecology, meaning, and religion.* Berkeley, CA: North Atlantic Books.

———. (1993). The anthropology of trouble. *American Anthropologist, 95,* 295–303.

Rasmussen, K. (1929). *Report of the fifth Thule expedition, 1921–1924. Vol. 7, No. 1: Intellectual culture of the Iglulik Eskimos.* Copenhagen: Glydendalske Boghandel.

Rensberger, B. (1989). Racial odyssey. In A. Podelefski & P. J. Brown (Eds.), *Applying anthropology: An introductory reader.* Mountain View, CA: Mayfield Press.

Reyna, S. P. (1994). Literary anthropology and the case against science. *Man, 29*(3), 555–581.

Reynolds, V., & Tanner, R. (1995). *The social ecology of religion.* Oxford: Oxford University Press.

Ridley, M. (2003). *Nature via nurture: Genes, experience, and what makes us human.* New York: HarperCollins.

Romaine, S. (1994). *Language in society: An introduction to sociolinguistics.* New York: Oxford University Press.

Romanucci-Ross, L., Moerman, D. E., & Tancredi, L. R. (Eds.). (1991). *The anthropology of medicine: From culture to method* (2nd ed.). Westport, CT: Bergin & Garvey.

Roosevelt, A. (1987). The evolution of human subsistence. In M. Harris & E. B. Ross (Eds.), *Food and evolution: Towards a theory of human food habits* (pp. 565–578). Philadelphia: Temple University Press.

Rosengarten, D. (1997). *Social origins of the African-American lowcountry basket.* Doctoral dissertation, Harvard University.

Ross, A., & Pickering, K. (2002). The politics of reintegrating Australian aboriginal and American Indian indigenous knowledge into resource management: The dynamics of resource appropriation and cultural revival. *Human Ecology, 30*(2), 187–214.

Rostow, W. (1960). *The stages of economic growth: A non-Communist manifesto.* Cambridge: Cambridge University Press.

Roy, A. (1999). *The cost of living.* New York: Random House Modern Library Paperbacks.

Rubin, E. (2003, July 13). The cult of Rajavi. *New York Times Magazine,* pp. 26–31.

Rubin, J., Flowers, N., & Gross, D. R. (1986). The adaptive dimensions of leisure time. *American Anthropologist, 13,* 524–536.

Rumbaugh, S. S., & Lewis, R. (1994). *The ape at the brink of the human mind.* New York: Wiley.

Rushforth, S., & Upham, S. (1993). *A Hopi social history.* Austin: University of Texas Press.

Rutz, H. J. (Ed.). (1992). The politics of time. *American Ethnographic Society Monograph Series,* No. 4.

Safa, H. I. (1995). *The myth of the male breadwinner.* Boulder, CO: Westview Press.

Saffirio, J., & Hammer, R. (1983). The forest and the highway. In *The impact of contact: Two Yanomamö case studies.* (Report No. 11), pp. 3–48. Cambridge, MA: Cultural Survival.

Sagan, C. (1996). *The demon-haunted world: Science as a candle in the dark*. New York: Ballantine Books.

Sahlins, M. D. (1961). The segmentary lineage: An organization of predatory expansion. *American Anthropologist, 63,* 332–345.

———. (1965). On the sociology of primitive exchange. In *The relevance of models for social anthropology* (Association of Social Anthropologist, Monograph No. 1). New York: Praeger.

———. (1968). *Tribesmen*. Englewood Cliffs, NJ: Prentice Hall.

———. (1972). *Stone Age economics*. Chicago: Aldine.

Salamon, S. (1992). *Prairie patrimony: Family, farming and community in the Midwest*. Chapel Hill: University of North Carolina Press.

Salzman, P. C. (1971). Movement and resource extraction among pastoral nomads: The case of the Shah Nawazi Baluch. *Anthropological Quarterly, 44,* 185–197.

———. (1980). *When nomads settle: Processes of adaptation and response*. New York: Praeger.

———. (1999). *The anthropology of real life: Events in human experience*. Prospect Heights, IL: Waveland Press.

Sargent, C., & Harris, M. (1992). Gender ideology, child rearing, and child health in Jamaica. *American Ethnologist, 19,* 523–537.

Saunders, L., & Mehenna, S. (1986). Village entrepreneurs: An Egyptian case. *Ethnology, 25,* 75–78.

Schick, K. D., & Toth, N. (1993). *Making silent stones speak: Human evolution and the dawn of technology*. New York: Simon & Schuster.

Schimmer, B. (1996). Anthropology on the Internet: A review and evaluation of networked resources. *Current Anthropology, 37*(3), 561.

Schneider, B. E. (1988). Gender and AIDS. In R. Kulstad (Ed.), *AIDS 1988: American Association for the Advancement of Science Symposia Papers* (pp. 97–106). Washington, DC: AAAS.

Schroeder, R. A. (1999). *Shady practices: Agroforestry and gender politics in the Gambia*. Berkeley: University of California Press.

Scott, J. C. (1976). *The moral economy of the peasant*. New Haven, CT: Yale University Press.

Sheets, P. (1989). Dawn of a new Stone Age. In A. Podolefsky & P. J. Brown (Eds.), *Applying anthropology: An introductory reader*. Mountain View, CA: Mayfield Press.

Sheridan, T. E. (1988). *Where the dove calls: The political ecology of a peasant corporate community in northwestern Mexico*. Tucson: University of Arizona Press.

Shostak, M. (2000). *Nisa: The life and words of a !Kung woman*. Cambridge, MA: MIT Press.

———. (2002). *Return to Nisa*. Cambridge, MA: MIT Press.

Sims, C. (1995, March 25). Argentina to issue new list of missing in "dirty war." *New York Times*, p. 4.

Skolnick, A., & Skolnick, J. H. (2003). *Family in transition*. (12th ed.). Boston: Allyn & Bacon.

Slobodkin, L. B. (1968). Toward a predictive theory of evolution. In R. C. Lewontin (Ed.), *Population biology and evolution*. Syracuse, NY: Syracuse University Press.

Small, M. F. (2003, April). How many fathers are best for a child? *Discover*, pp. 54–61.

Smil, V. (1984). *The bad earth*. Armonk, NY: M. E. Sharpe.

———. (1994, May 30). A land stretching to support its people. *International Herald Tribune*, p. 8.

Smith, A. (1994). For all those who were Indian in a former life. *Cultural Survival Quarterly* (Winter), 70–72.

Smith, A. (2000). *The Bushmen of southern Africa. A foraging society in transition*. Ohio University Press.

Smith, E. A. (2000). Three styles in evolutionary analysis of human behavior. In Cronk et al. (Eds.), *Adaptation and human behavior* (pp. 27–46). New York: Aldine de Gruyter.

Smith, E. A., & Winterhalder, B. (Eds.). (1992). *Evolutionary ecology and human behavior*. New York: Aldine de Gruyter.

Soffer, O. (1985). *The Upper Paleolithic of the central Russian Plain*. San Diego, CA: Academic Press.

Soffer, O., Vandiver, P., & Klima, B. (1995, May 4). *Paleolithic ceramics and clay objects from Pavlov I*. Paper presented to Society for American Anthropology, Minneapolis.

Sorensen, C. W. (1988). *Over the mountains are mountains: Korean peasant households and their adaptation to rapid industrialization*. Seattle: University of Washington Press.

Southwick, C. H. (1996). *Global ecology in human perspective*. New York: Oxford University Press.

Spear, T., & Waller, R. (Eds.). (1993). *Being Maasai: Ethnicity and identity in East Africa*. London: James Currey.

Stanford, D., & Bradley, B. (2002). Ocean trails and prairie paths. In N. G. Jablonski (Ed.), *The first Americans: The Pleistocene colonization of the New World* (Memoirs of the California Academy of Sciences, No. 27).

Stevens, W. K. (1994, January 18). Threat of encroaching deserts may be more myth than fact. *New York Times*, pp. C1–C10.

Steward, J. (1972). *Theory of culture change: The methodology of multilinear evolution*. Urbana: University of Illinois Press.

Stiglitz, J. E. (2003). *Globalization and its discontents*. New York and London: W. W. Norton.

Stoffle, R. W., Halmo, D. B., Wagner, T. W., & Luczkovich, J. L. (1994). Reefs from space: Satellite imagery, marine ecology, and ethnography in the Dominican Republic. *Human Ecology, 22*(3), 355–378.

Stoller, P. (1996). Spaces, places, and fields: The politics of West African trading in New York City's informal economy. *American Anthropologist, 88*(4), 777–788.

Stone, G. D. (1998). Keeping the home fires burning: The changed nature of householding in the Kofyar homeland. *Human Ecology, 26*(2), 239–265.

Stone, P. M., Stone G. D., & Netting, R. M. C. (1995). The sexual division of labor in Kofyar agriculture. *American Ethnologist, 22*(1), 165–186.

Stone, R. (2003). Late date for Siberian site challenges Bering pathway. *Science, 301*(5632), 450–451.

Stringer, C., & Bauer, G. (1994). Methods, misreading and bias. *American Anthropologist, 96*(2), 416–424.

Stringer, C., & Gamble, C. (1994). *In search of the Neanderthals: Solving the puzzle of human origins*. London: Thames & Hudson.

Stringer, C., & McKie, R. (1997). *African exodus: The origin of modern humanity*. New York: Henry Holt.

Strong, M. (2001). *Where on earth are we going?* Houston, TX: Texere.

Sturtevant, W. C., & Damas, D. (Eds.). *1984 Handbook of North American Indians, Vol. 5: Arctic*. Washington, DC: Smithsonian Institution.

Susser, I. (1986). Work and reproduction: Sociologic context. *Occupational Medicine: State of the Art Reviews, 1*, 517–530.

———. (1989). Gender in the anthropology of the United States. In S. Morgan (Ed.), *Gender and anthropology: Critical reviews for research and teaching* (pp. 343–358). Washington, DC: American Anthropological Association.

———. (1996). The construction of poverty and homelessness in U.S. cities. *Annual Review of Anthropology, 25*, pp. 411–435. Palo Alto: Annual Reviews, Inc.

Sussman, R. W., Green, G. M., & Sussman, L. K. (1994). Satellite imagery, human ecology, anthropology, and deforestation in Madagascar. *Human Ecology, 22*(3), 333–354.

Swardson, A. (2000, April 27). An aging Europe heads for a pension crisis. *International Herald Tribune*, pp. 1–4.

Sweet, L. E. (1965). Camel pastoralism in North Arabia and the minimal camping unit. In A. Leeds & A. P. Vayda (Eds.), *Man, culture, and animals: The role of animals in human ecological adjustment* (Publication No. 78). Washington, DC: American Association for the Advancement of Science.

Tapper, R. (1979). *Pasture and politics*. London: Academic Press.

Tattersall, I. (1995). *The fossil trail: How we know what we think we know about human evolution*. Oxford: Oxford University Press.

———. (1997, April). Out of Africa again . . . and again? *Scientific American*, pp. 60–67.

———. (1998). *Becoming human*. New York: Harcourt Brace.

———. (2000, January). Once we were not alone. *Scientific American*, pp. 39–44.

Tekeli, S. (Ed.). (1994). *Women in modern Turkish society*. London: Zed Books.

*The Economist*. (January 8, 2000). p. 54.

*The Economist*. (February 5, 2000). p. 62.

*The Economist*. (2001a, June 16). A survey of the new rich, pp. 3–10.

*The Economist*. (2001b, August 11). Putting it in its place, pp. 18–20.

*The Economist*. (2001c, September 1). A billion voices calling? Mobile phones in China, p. 54.

*The Economist*. (2002a, March 23). No swots, please, we're Masai. p. 45.

*The Economist*. (2002b, March 23). Deviations from the mean, p. 73.

*The Economist*. (2002c, November 23). A game of consequences, p. 75.

*The Economist*. (2002d, December 21). The last best place, pp. 58–60.

*The Economist*. (2003a, February 8). Please don't (all) go, p. 51.

*The Economist*. (2003b, April 12). The generation game, pp. 73–74.

*The Economist*. (2003c, August 2). Start saving. p. 63.

*The Economist*. (2003d, August 9). The promise of a Blue Revolution, pp. 19–24.

Thompson, L. (1950). *Culture in crisis: A study of the Hopi Indians*. New York: Harper & Row.

Thompson, L., & Joseph, A. (1947). *The Hopi way*. Chicago: University of Chicago Press.

Tierney, J., Wright, L., & Springen, K. (1988, January 11). The search for Adam and Eve. *Newsweek*.

Tierney, P. (2000). *Darkness in El Dorado: How scientists and journalists devastated the Amazon*. New York: HarperCollins.

Toth, J. (1998). Beating plowshares into swords: The relocation of rural Egyptian workers and their discontent. In N. S. Hopkins & K. Westergaard (Eds.), *Directions of change in rural Egypt*. Cairo: The American University in Cairo Press.

Turnbull, C. (1961). *The forest people*. New York: Simon & Schuster.

———. (1965). The Mbuti Pygmies of the Congo. In J. L. Gibbs, Jr. (Ed.), *Peoples of Africa*. New York: Holt, Rinehart & Winston.

Turner, M. D., & Taylor, P. J. (2003). Critical reflections on the use of remote sensing and GIS technologies in human ecological research. *Human Ecology, 31*(2), 177–182.

Turner, T. (1995). An indigenous people's struggle for socially equitable and ecologically sustainable production: The Kayapo revolt against extractivism. *Journal of Latin American Anthropology, 1*(1), 99–125.

Tutt, K. (2001). *The search for free energy*. New York: Simon & Schuster.

Tyler, P. E. (1994, March 27). Nature and economic boom devouring China's farmland. *New York Times*, pp. A1–A8.

———. (1995, April 10). On the farms, China could be sowing disaster. *New York Times*, p. A4.

Verburg, P., Hecky, R. E., & Kling, H. (2003). Ecological consequences of a century of warming in Lake Tanganyika. *Science, 301*(5632), 505–507.

Verdery, K. (1992). The etatization of time in Ceausescu's Romania. In H. J. Rutz (Ed.) *The politics of time* (pp. 37–61). (American Ethnological Society Monograph Series, No. 4). Washington, DC: American Anthropological Association.

Vondal, P. J. (1987). Intensification through diversified resource use: The human ecology of a successful agricultural industry in Indonesian Borneo. *Human Ecology, 15*, 27–52.

Wade, N. (2003a, February 11). A prolific Genghis Khan, it seems, helped people the world. *New York Times*, p. D3.

———. (2003b, August 24). Can it be? The end of evolution? *New York Times*, Section 4, pp. 1, 4.

Weiner, A. B. (1976). *Women of value, men of renown: New perspectives in Trobriand exchange*. Austin: University of Texas Press.

———. (1988). *The Trobrianders of Papua New Guinea*. New York: Holt, Rinehart & Winston.

———. (1992). *Inalienable possessions*. Berkeley and Los Angeles: University of California Press.

Wells, M. (1987). Sharecropping in the United States: A political economy perspective. In M. Chibnik (Ed.), *Farm work and fieldwork: American agriculture in anthropological perspective* (pp. 211–243). Ithaca, NY: Cornell University Press.

Welsch, R. L., & Endicott, K. M. (2003). *Taking sides: Clashing views on controversial issues in cultural anthropology.* New York: McGraw-Hill/Dushkin.

Wendorf, F., & Schild, R. (2001). *Holocene settlement of the Egyptian Sahara: Vol. I. The archaeology of Nabta Playa.* New York: Kluwer Academic/Plenum Publishers.

Werner, D., Flowers, N., Ritter, M., & Gross, G. (1979). Subsistence productivity and hunting effort in native South America. *Human Ecology, 7,* 303–315.

White, J. (1994). *Money makes us relatives: Women's labor in urban Turkey.* Austin: University of Texas Press.

White, L. (1949). *The science of culture.* New York: Farrar, Straus & Cudahy.

White, T. D., Asfaw, B., Dagusta, D., Gilbert, H., Richards, G. D., Suwa, G., & Howell, F. C. (2003). Pleistocene *Homo sapiens* from Middle Awash, Ethiopia. *Nature, 423,* 742–747.

Whiteley, P. M. (1985). Unpacking Hopi clans: Another vintage model out of Africa. *Journal of Anthropological Research, 41,* 359–374.

———. (1988). *Deliberate acts: Changing Hopi culture through the Oraibi Split.* Tucson: University of Arizona Press.

Wikan, U. (1992). Beyond the words: The power of resonance. *American Ethnologist, 19,* 460–482.

Wilcox, S., & Wilbers, S. (1987). The case for academic acceptance of American sign language. *Chronicle of Higher Education, 33,* 1.

Wilford, J. N. (1996, May 7). Mummies, textiles offer evidence of Europeans in Far East. *New York Times,* p. C1.

———. (2002, June 15). In ancient skulls from Ethiopia, familiar faces. *New York Times,* pp. A1, A8.

Wilk, R. R. (1991). *Household ecology: Economic change and domestic life among the Kekchi Maya of Belize.* Tucson: University of Arizona Press.

Wilkie, D., & Curran, B. (1993). Historical trends in forager and farmer exchange in the Ituri rain forest of northeastern Zaire. *Human Ecology, 21,* 389–417.

Williams, D. M. (1997). Patchwork, pastoralists, and perception: Dune sand as a valued resource among herders of Inner Mongolia. *Human Ecology, 25*(2), 297–317.

———. (2002). *Beyond great walls: Environment, identity, and development on the Chinese grasslands of Inner Mongolia.* Stanford, CA: Stanford University Press.

Wills, W. H. (2001). Pithouse architecture and the economics of household formation in the prehistoric American Southwest. *Human Ecology, 29*(4), 477–500.

Wilmsen, E. N. (1989a). *Land filled with flies: A political economy of the Kalahari.* Chicago: University of Chicago Press.

———. (1989b). *We are here: Politics of aboriginal land tenure.* Berkeley and Los Angeles: University of California Press.

Wilson, E. O. (1993, May 30). Is humanity suicidal? *New York Times Magazine,* pp. 24ff.

———. (1998). *Consilience: The unity of knowledge.* New York: Alfred A. Knopf.

Wilson, J. N. (2003, June 24). An early heartland of agriculture is found in New Guinea. *New York Times,* p. D2.

Wolf, E. R. (1966). *Peasants.* Englewood Cliffs, NJ: Prentice Hall.

———. (1982). *Europe and the people without history.* Berkeley and Los Angeles: University of California Press.

———. (1990). Facing power: Old insights, new questions. *American Anthropologist, 92,* 586–596.

———. (1994, March). Demonization of anthropologist in the Amazon. *Anthropology Newsletter,* p. 2.

———. (1998). *Envisioning history: Ideologies of dominance and crisis.* Berkeley: University of California Press.

Wolpoff, M. H., & Caspari, R. (1997). *Race and human evolution: A fatal attraction.* New York: Schocken Books.

Wong, B. (1998). *Ethnicity and entrepreneurship: The new Chinese immigrants in the San Francisco Bay Area.* Boston: Allyn & Bacon.

Worthman, C. M. (1995). Hormones, sex and gender. *Annual Review of Anthropology,* 593–618.

Wrangham, R., & Peterson, D. (1996). *Demonic males: Apes and the origins of human violence.* New York: Houghton Mifflin.

Wright, H. T., & Johnson, G. A. (1975). Population, exchange, and early state formation in southwestern Iran. *American Anthropologist, 77,* 267–289.

Wright, R. (1994). *The moral animal.* New York: Pantheon.

———. (1999, December 13). The accidental creationist. *The New Yorker,* pp. 56–65.

Yellen, J. E., & Lee, R. B. (1976). The Dobe-/Du/da environment: Background to a hunting and gathering way of life. In R. B. Lee (Ed.), *Kalahari hunter-gatherers.* Cambridge, MA: Harvard University Press.

Zilhão, J. (2000). The Ebro frontier: A model for the late extinction of Iberian Neanderthals. In C. B. Stringer, R. N. E. Barton, & J. C. Finlayson (Eds.), *Neanderthals on the edge* (pp. 111–121). Oxford: Oxbow Books.

# *Index*

Page numbers in italics indicate illustrations or boxed material.